PARKY'S
PEOPLE

PARKY'S PEOPLE

Michael Parkinson

HODDER

First published in Great Britain in 2010 by Hodder & Stoughton
An Hachette UK company

First published in paperback in 2011
1

A CIP catalogue record for this title
is available from the British Library

Paperback ISBN 978 1 444 70041 1
Ebook ISBN 978 1 848 94696 5

Design by Bob Vickers

Typeset in Nexus Serif by Palimpsest Book Production Limited,
Falkirk, Stirlingshire

Printed and bound in Great Britain by Clays Ltd, St Ives plc

Hodder & Stoughton policy is to use papers that are natural,
renewable and recyclable products and made from wood grown
in sustainable forests. The logging and manufacturing processes are
expected to conform to the environmental regulations
of the country of origin.

Hodder & Stoughton Ltd
338 Euston Road
London NW1 3BH

www.hodder.co.uk

This book is dedicated to all the producers, associate producers, researchers, directors, production managers, floor managers, studio crew, camera, lighting and sound crew, editors, make-up (particularly Chrissie Baker) and everyone who worked on the show at the BBC, ITV and Yorkshire Television in the UK, and ABC, Channel 10 and UKTV in Australia. They are the reason the show went to air, and why I enjoyed every moment.

In particular, this book is dedicated to Richard Drewett who designed the show, to John Fisher who nurtured it, to Bea Ballard who brought it back and to my son Michael who recharged the batteries. Quentin Mann was my floor manager for nearly every one, and indispensible, as were MDs Harry Stoneham and Laurie Holloway and the marvellous musicians they employed.

My publisher and friend Roddy Bloomfield was, as ever, both wise and encouraging, and Erin Reimer, whose essay at the end of this book is a comprehensive analysis of the talk show, was tireless, enthusiastic and meticulous in her research.

My thanks also to Camilla Coats-Carr and TV Transcriptions for their hard work in transcribing all the raw material.

Not forgetting my PA Teresa Rudge, who kept us all on the straight and narrow.

Finally, my love and thanks to Mary, who never missed a show; nor did my old friend Dabber Davis who can be heard laughing in just about every one – even the unfunny ones.

Photographic Acknowledgements

The author and publisher would like to thank the following for permission to reproduce photographs:

AFP/Getty Images, 64; Robin Anderson/Rex Features, 74; AP/Press Association Images, 6, 48; BBC Motion Gallery, 25; BBC Photo Library, 1, 30, 32, 42, 43, 73, 75; Bettman/Corbis, 66, 71; Paul Brown/Rex Features, 22; Nikki English/Rex Features, 28; Everett Collection/Rex Features, 4, 35, 53; FremantleMedia Ltd/Rex Features, 17, 18; Getty Images, 3, 7, 9, 11, 20, 31, 33, 36, 39, 51, 57, 58, 61, 65, 69, 70, 72; Diego Goldberg/Sygma/Corbis, 45; ITV/Rex Features, 13, 14, 19, 21, 34, 49, 54, 62; Keystone USA/Rex Features, 68; Kobal Collection, 40; Pier Luigi/Rex Features, 52; Ken McKay/Rex Features, 16, 24, 26, 27, 47, 56; Alastair Muir/Rex Features, 41, 63; NBCUPHOTOBANK/Rex Features, 2, 55; Michael Ochs Archives/Getty Images, 10, 12; Terry O'Neill/Getty Images, 44; PA Archive/Press Association Images, 67; J. Barry Peake/Rex Features, 59; Popperfoto/Getty Images, 50; Redferns, 46; Sten Rosenlund/Rex Features, 23; SNAP/Rex Features, 5, 38; Ronald Spencer/Associated Newspapers/Rex Features, 37; Sunset Boulevard/Corbis, 15; Tony Triolo/Sports Illustrated/Getty Images, 29; United Artists/Sunset Boulevard/Corbis, 60.

Contents

Introduction

I had always wondered what it might be like to be on *Parkinson* not as the host but as a guest. So I sat down and imagined an interview with myself, which seems an appropriate way to start a book of some of my favourite interviews during a span of thirty-seven years. First, the introduction:

Ladies and gentlemen, my guest tonight grew up in a Yorkshire mining community, believing that one day he would persuade Ingrid Bergman to give it all up and come and live with him in a terraced house near his beloved Barnsley Football Club, which he'd had his eye on for some time.

Tired of waiting for her reply to his letter of proposal, he became a journalist. The very first star he interviewed was the actor Sir Bernard Miles, who was so underwhelmed by the result he sent a telegram saying: 'After reading your article today I have come to the conclusion you should go far. Could I suggest Australia?'

Fame and fortune followed on television and radio. His first of many important awards came in the late sixties when he was called from a beach in Portugal to be informed he had been voted the second best-dressed man on Radio 2. The winner was Peter Wyngarde playing Jason King.

Dame Edna Everage once described her appearance on *Parkinson* as a 'monologue interrupted by strangers'.

Ladies and gentlemen, Michael Parkinson.

Q: Did you always want to host a talk show?
A: They hadn't been invented when I started my career as a journalist. I wanted to be Humphrey Bogart or Ernest Hemingway, and be seduced by women who looked like Ingrid Bergman and Lauren Bacall. As it was, I joined a local newspaper aged sixteen and started from there. Television came calling because, in the beginning, the TV companies had to raid Fleet Street (as it was then) for

people who knew how to interview and get the story. That's when I stepped on board.

Q: But during that time in television, did you have an ambition to host a talk show?

A: Never seemed likely. I was perceived as a current affairs journalist, so I covered wars and other events involving people being nasty to one another. I suppose the first inkling I had about making a living on the cushier side of journalism was when I was asked to write and present *Cinema* for Granada TV. It was while interviewing the director Sam Peckinpah that I was made aware of the joy to be had engaging celebrities in chat.

I said to Peckinpah: 'You made your film debut as a screen writer.' He said: 'No, as a director.'

I said: 'You made your film debut as a director.' He said: 'No, as a screen writer.'

I said to myself: 'This is more fun than I imagined.'

Q: So what was the breakthrough?

A: Bill Cotton at the BBC offered me eight shows during the summer lull to try out a talk show. No guarantees. I had a much more secure job at ITV at the time but I somehow knew we could make the talk show work. I sent my agent, a young shaver called Martin Sorrell, to talk to ITV. Mr Sorrell did as he was told but never settled to the idea of being a gofer. The suspicion he might be in the wrong job was substantiated when he went to negotiate a cricket bat contract for Geoffrey Boycott and managed to get his client less money than the amount on offer. He left the business sometime later and started the downhill slide to his present situation of a knighthood and riches beyond imagining.

Q: Did the BBC define what kind of talk show they wanted?

A: Bill Cotton loved the *Ed Sullivan Show* in America and I think he always saw me hosting a light entertainment show with a bit of chat. But I had other ideas and, fortunately, the producer Bill had selected to work with me shared them. Richard Drewett had worked on *Late Night Line-up*, so already had experience of booking shows where interviews were more than scripted set pieces, and where comedians sat cheek to jowl with actors and politicians. More than that, we shared the same interests. We both loved the movies, theatre, actors, music-hall turns, comedians, sportsmen, singers of the Great American Songbook and jazz.

We had a common list of heroes. We wanted Orson Welles, John Lennon, Shirley MacLaine and Benny Goodman on the show, and we got them. Those were the people we asked. We decided to try to break from the convention of three separate interviews and keep guests on together. The idea was to have a final section of conversation rather than a formal interview. In other words, we were taking the talk show away as much as possible from the American prototype, even down to getting rid of the desk, which, in my view, has always been the biggest obstacle to a proper interview. Why put furniture between you and your guest? It wasn't what Bill wanted but Richard fought him and the ratings, which had started well, got better. That gave us the independence we needed.

Q: When you looked back at the interviews, particularly those done in the 1970s, what were your thoughts?

A: There was so much I had forgotten, like how I used to open the show with a monologue, a few words crafted by comedy writers in the fond, and mainly forlorn, hope I might start the show with a laugh. There is also a sense of an uneasy blend of journalism and showbiz in my clumsy attempts at formality – 'Tell me, Mr Welles . . .' 'Why do you call me Mr Welles?' 'Out of deference to your talent.' 'Bullshit,' said Orson Welles – which took some getting rid of. It took a while to understand that if you walk down stairs on to a glittering set with a studio audience of five hundred and a band playing, you would be unwise to think you were still that bloke reporting a war or interviewing the Dalai Lama. On the other hand, any interview, whether it be with a red-nosed comedian or a po-faced politician, requires the same preparation. The difference was in approach, manner and style – the contrast between a conversation and an interrogation. It took some learning and I reckon that I was much better the second time around, when I returned to the talk show in 1998 after a long break.

Q: **But the critics, whenever they talk about the early** *Parkinson*, **always say it was a better time because the guests were more interesting and they weren't as intent on plugging a product as they are now.**

A: That could not be further from the truth. Distance leads to confusion, because I'm able to confirm there was just as much plugging in the seventies as at any time later. To suggest otherwise is to misunderstand the reason why people come on to talk shows. They walk down the stairs for the same reason they give interviews to the print media and radio, to publicise the product. What I learned was that the sooner you mentioned the product, the more relaxed the guest became and the easier it was for the real interview to proceed. Any delaying tactic, anything that might cause the guest to think there would be no mention of the book/film/play/album, meant disaster. It was best summed up by Miss Bette Davis when she told one interviewer, who was delaying mentioning the book she had written and was there to plug, that she had not come all the way from the States because she was his friend or a fan of his style; indeed, she had never heard of him. The reason she allowed him into her presence was to talk about her autobiography, which was available at all good bookshops etc., etc.

Q: So the critics don't know what they are talking about?

A: Let us say they have always been a little ambiguous about talk shows. They are no doubt as confused as the rest of us about what exactly constitutes a talk show nowadays. What started off in America as a comedy vehicle for Johnny Carson and others has transmogrified over the years into the present state where, as one critic observed, 'chat has been parodied into absurdity'. Erin Reimer – who helped me research and edit the book – mentions at the end of this book the talk-show hosts who have appeared on British television since *Parkinson* started in 1971, a compendium indicating that whatever producers were looking for in their choice of hosts, longevity was not uppermost in their thinking.

Q: You were sometimes accused of being too soft with your line of questioning. How do you answer?

A: It's an easy answer. I was not, so far as I knew, interviewing paedophiles or mass murderers, simply people who, in the main, had only to answer for entertaining and informing us in one way or another. So an aggressive tone would not simply have been inappropriate, it would also have been non-productive. That said, every interview must stand or fall by what the research indicates is the best story, and if that means getting into sensitive areas, then they must not be shirked, always providing the interviewer is doing it for the right reasons and not simply to discomfort or shock. Old-fashioned? Maybe, but that's the way I was taught.

Q: Which do you prefer, interviewing for print, radio or television?

A: Print interviewing is the easiest. You can relax your victim over a pleasant lunch, chat in a disconnected way for a couple of hours and then go and shape the interview as the whim dictates. Radio is the most informal medium, the most relaxing. The sooner you can convince the interviewee that there are only the two of you in the entire world for the next ten minutes or so, the more you believe it yourself and thereby share the illusion with your guest.

Television is much the most difficult medium for interviewing. In particular, the talk show is the toughest of the lot. Everything conspires to guarantee the guest arrives at the foot of the stairs and advances into the host's company feeling the exact opposite of relaxed and accommodating. The basic premise – that you walk down the stairs to the sound of a big band into a mixture of heat, music and applause with a microphone in every orifice, and having been told at the back of the set to 'enjoy yourself and have a good time' – is enough to discombobulate all but the most battle-scarred veterans. So the host's first job is to convince the guest that what they are about to undergo is much more pleasant than being boiled alive. Then the host has to shape the interview on air. He can't do what the print journalist does, which is to alter the shape and the form of the interview retrospectively. Whenever we edited, we did so for time and not shape. Then there are the signals from the floor manager, the chat in your earpiece (if you wore one, which I did only very occasionally), the lurking presence of the next guest and the anxiety about how you get him on with that funny intro you had written after saying farewell to the first guest when he has finished telling how he fell over a cliff and spent three years in traction. Then when the time does come to say goodbye you cannot remember his bloody name. But at the end of the show, if you have pulled it off – which is to say got away with it – you know a satisfaction like none other.

Q: How much of the show is yours, how much the producer's?

A: It's a collaboration, not just between interviewer and producer but everyone else concerned. Good researchers are a necessity. The best ones write well and entertainingly. Reading the best research – the notes that stick in the mind and inspire a question – should be a joy and not a chore. But you can get everything right and still the show goes wrong. The fascination of the talk show is that you cannot script it. Moreover, it is a consensual act. Therefore, if one party doesn't want to oblige by co-operating, there is nothing to be done except suffer one of those dreadful moments so beloved by people who spend their lives on the internet. My disasters have been caused by antipathy (sometimes mutual), drunkenness, drugs, marital breakup and, most spectacularly of all, by offending Rod Hull's right hand, which at the time was situated up an emu's backside.

Q: Is that what you will be remembered for, being attacked by an emu?
A: Most likely. But it wouldn't be a useless epitaph, defining as it does the meaning of humour, which is the disparity between man's ambition and his achievement. Moreover, it should stand as a lesson to all who follow in the talk-show conga line and seek fame for its own sake. They should remember we must all be careful of being granted what we wish for.

Q: How do you describe what follows in this book?
A: It's a retrospective of a time when the people who made television programmes were allowed to follow their instincts rather than be dictated to by focus groups and rating gurus. When *Parkinson* first started, shows such as *The South Bank Show* had not yet been imagined. So by bringing together Professor Jacob Bronowski, Peter Ustinov, Dame Edith Evans, Muhammad Ali as well as Lennon and McCartney, Arthur Rubinstein, Duke Ellington and Oscar Peterson, not to mention Jonathan Miller, Alistair Cooke, the Goons and most of the Pythons, we played a

significant part in breaking down the barricades that in those days separated various ghettos of culture. We were mixing *The Times*, the *Daily Mail* and the *Sun*, if you like.

What follows is also a tribute to my heroes, including Orson Welles, Fred Astaire, James Cagney, James Stewart, Bette Davis, Lauren Bacall, Ingrid Bergman and the rest who caused a youth in Yorkshire to dream a little. And then Richard Burton, Peter O'Toole, Judi Dench, Eric and Ernie, Billy Connolly, Tommy Cooper *et al.* And John Fisher, Richard Drewett and Michael T. Parkinson, who steered the ship for so many years with great skill and good humour.

So many memories, so vivid, so lasting.

Such a good time. Read on . . .

1 Golden Hollywood

Orson Welles

James Cagney

Kirk Douglas

John Wayne

James Stewart

David Niven

Jack Lemmon

Tony Curtis

Henry Fonda

Fred Astaire

Shirley Temple

Bette Davis

Bing Crosby

Memories of Marilyn Monroe

Orson Welles

When Orson Welles turned up, his reputation came through the door first and the man followed. The pleasant surprise was that he was even more charismatic, articulate and humorous than you'd imagined. One time he arrived at the studio in a black cloak carrying a staff as if about to part the Red Sea. The notion of being in a divine presence, of meeting a man who could (and did) achieve miracles – for what is *Kane* if not miraculous? – was apparent to even the most hard-bitten observers. Dorothy Parker said that meeting Welles was like meeting God without dying. And Herman Mankiewicz, who co-wrote *Citizen Kane* with Welles, said, 'There but for the grace of God, goes God.'

I was being investigated a lot during the time of the anti-American McCarthy period, and I never got to testify because I kept begging to be allowed to, and this was a line of argument that nobody else took. I said, 'Oh please let me go and explain why I'm not a communist.' They said, 'Well, we'll let you know.'

I was working a lot abroad, but I kept trying to come back and testify, and because I had written a daily political column for several years and I'd attacked the Soviet Union about Finland and all sorts of things, I was so clean that it was ridiculous from McCarthy's point of view, no matter what he wanted to say. So he wouldn't let me testify.

There was one congressional committee, which was run by a fellow called Dies, who ended up in jail for one of those minor crimes that seem to tempt our people in elected office, and he was a strong patriot. He wrapped himself in the American flag as fully as it was possible to do, and he had an un-American affairs committee, long before McCarthy started, and he sent a few louts over to see me in my office in Hollywood.

They were particularly uneducated and dumb and they fell into a marvellous trap, because they said to me, 'Are you a card-carrying communist?' First, I wasn't even faintly pro-communist but I am on the progressive side, as I imagine you've guessed, but I said, 'Will you define what a communist is?' and this is where they fell in the trap. They said, 'What do you mean?' I said, 'Well, I want to answer your question honestly. How can I answer your question if you don't tell me what you mean? What's communist?' 'Well, I guess it's where whatever you make goes to the government.' I said, 'Well, I'm 86 per cent communist, the rest capitalist, that's the income tax that one pays.'

Harry Cohn, the head of a movies studio, had me bugged in such an obvious way. I had a radio programme every week in those days and I used to come into my office in the morning and I'd say, 'Good morning everyone, this is Orson Welles's office welcoming you to another day of fun and laughter,' and then when the day would end, I'd say, 'This is Orson Welles signing off.' We'd play a little music and treated it like a radio show and Harry Cohn got rather angry about that because he thought the buggee ought to take it seriously.

When I ran the federal theatres, we were all bugged and it was so primitive then that you could hear buzzing and screeching on the phone when they were listening. As a result of one of those operations, I put on Christopher Marlowe's *Dr Faustus* and a congressman got up on the floor and said, 'It is a known fact that Orson Welles is producing and acting in a play by the notorious communist, Christopher Marlowe.' But it took a lot of electronic work to get that information.

What really made me sicker than McCarthy were my colleagues in the theatre and films who gave in – who were communists or communist sympathisers, and who, in order to maintain not their bread and butter but their swimming pools, handed in the names of fifty or sixty other people so they could get their hands clean. That sickened me as much as McCarthy himself, because I always deeply felt that he was a temporary aberration, and not the beginning of something in America. But he was an abhorrent creature.

I think that when important film directors, actors and playwrights and people like that turned in the names of little sound-effects men, people in the crew and so on so that they could keep their arse in Beverley Hills, I feel that they're worse than McCarthy, because he was simple, primitive – an opportunist. He didn't mean a word he said.

I like living on this side of the Atlantic very much, but I like living in America, too. I'm not a refugee, either politically or emotionally, from my country. I'm neither very nationalistically inclined, as I hate that in anybody. I do truly believe that patriotism is the last refuge of the scoundrel.

When I came to Hollywood, I was this terrible maverick. I was sort of forty or thirty years ahead of my time. Whatever it is, there was a ghost of a Christmas future, there was one beatnik, there was this guy with a beard who was going to do it all by himself. I represented the terrible future of what was going to happen to that talent, so I was hated and despised theoretically, but I had all kinds of friends among the real dinosaurs, who were awfully nice to me.

And I had a very good time, but I believe that I have looked back too optimistically on Hollywood, because my daughter has a group of books about Hollywood that she bought – I don't know why, probably vainly looking for references to her father – and I took to reading them lately and I realised how many great people that town has destroyed since its earliest beginnings. How almost everybody of merit was destroyed or diminished, and how few were the good people who survived, what a great minority they were, and I suddenly thought to myself, 'Why do I look so affectionately on that town?' It was because it was funny and it was gay and it was an old-fashioned circus and everything that we're nostalgic about made it funny and gay when it was really happening. But really, it was a brutal place. And when I take my own life out of it and see what they did to other people, I see that the story of that town is a dirty one, and its record is bad.

1973

James Cagney

Orson Welles told me James Cagney was the greatest film actor of them all. I said I'd love to interview him. Welles replied, 'You never will. He doesn't give interviews.' Ten years later the miracle happened. Aged eighty-two and in England making *Ragtime*, he agreed to come on the show in the company of his lifelong friend, Pat O'Brien. He told me he never said 'You dirty rat' but I didn't believe him. Fred Astaire said he was the greatest dancer of them all. Cagney once explained he learned how to dance when learning how to fight. We showed his phenomenal finale to *Yankee Doodle Dandy*. 'No sweat,' he said. If movies are about moments, he created more than most. James Cagney was more than a film star, he was the Statue of Liberty with a gun in his hand.

I was fairly handy with my fists – everybody was a street fighter in my neighbourhood. You have to know how to get on, you have to fight your way through. There was a beaut – three fights, one after the other, and the first one, the cops came and chased us. The second one, the cops came and chased us. The third one, the boy and I went in again and the result was interesting because I hit him on the bridge of the nose with my right hand, and broke my hand. He was just a very nice guy, but he was as tough as could be. The girls could do it, too. My girl, Maude, was a left-handed gal and she could punch her way through a brick wall. She was really something to cope with.

I wanted to pick up some small change, and I could get $10 down at an athletic club for fighting one fight, so what do you do? Get $10 worth of fighting done without any trouble, and my mother saw I was getting thinner. I was running in the morning and so on, and she said, 'What are you doing, son?' I said, 'Why, Mom?' She said, 'You're getting thinner.' I said, 'Oh well, I'll tell you what. I'm getting in shape, I've got a fight coming up at the so-and-so.' She said,

'You're what?' I said, 'Yeah.' She said, 'Mmm, can you lick me?' I said, 'No, Mom. I'm not going to try.' 'You better not, son, you're always with the fighting,' and that was true.

My first job – are you ready – was as a female impersonator. There was an act, it had five fellows and five girls, so I jumped into the act on a Monday and I was with them for about three months. Vaudeville taught me everything. Anything came along, you grabbed it, didn't matter what it was, whether it be a straight act, a sketch or a musical act, whatever. You did it all.

I went to Hollywood to get a job that paid living-room money, that was the sole idea involved. It wasn't terribly different really. Being involved in vaudeville, you were used to anything. Whatever came along, you grabbed it.

I used to write poetry – just little things that don't amount to anything. As the idea came along, I put it down in writing. Humphrey Bogart had a nervous habit of picking his nose. So I was driving north on Ventura Boulevard and he was driving south, and he came to a stop. So then I wrote this thing:

In this silly town of ours
One sees odd primps and poseurs.
Movie stars in fancy cars,
Shouldn't pick their famous noses.

Jack Warner described me as being the 'Professional Againster'. He would pay me $400 a week when they were paying other actors $125,000 – $150,000. So I just left the studio. I walked out. Six months I was out and stayed at home, on the farm – my second love. They tried to get somebody to fill the shoes and finally they came on me with an offer. And I went back.

When I'm asked for advice, it's hard to put your finger on it, but I do remember one little girl who asked me about it. We were doing a show and this girl is a delightful child, and I could see that she was self-conscious. She started to look all over the room, observing what was going on. I said to her, 'So honey, let's make a little talk.' I said, 'You wanna hear something?' She said, 'Go ahead.' Eighteen years old, mind you, no age at all, and I said, 'You walk in, plant yourself, look the other fellow in the eye and tell the truth.' She said, 'Walk in, plant yourself, look the other fellow in the eye and tell the truth.' And that was that. She never asked me again, but I walked by her and she was saying to herself, 'Walk in, plant yourself, look the other fellow in the eye and tell the truth, walk in . . .' and she was memorising it.

1981

Kirk Douglas

I always thought interviewing Kirk Douglas was surplus to require-ments. All you needed him to do was sit in the chair and let the camera focus on him and you would know the complete story of his life without him ever saying a word. It was all there, in the jutting chin, the unflinching, challenging stare, the cut of his jib. He shared with James Cagney the physiognomy of the all-American dream. He didn't need to tell you the journey had been a battle for survival, that he was an implacable competitor in pursuit of success and riches. But for all he conquered Hollywood, his greatest victory was refusing to concede to a stroke that robbed him of both looks and speech. Typically, his illness made him determined to become 'the most popular actor in the world with a stroke'.

My story is typical of so many people in the United States who come from immigrant parents. You work your way through college, you go to dramatic school and you are fortu-nate enough to go into the work you'd like to do, and it's what I call a corny American story.

My wife once said to me, 'You know, Kirk, one of these days you're going to be shattered because you might meet someone who was poorer than you.' I came from what you'd call abject poverty. It's not having enough to eat – days where you didn't have food. I guess that's poor. I not only had six sisters and my mother, but my parents separated at an early age and that left me with seven women, which was a very difficult upbringing, and I found going to college was really a form of escape. I found the environment really smothering.

My father, by the way, was quite a character. He was a very powerful man, a peasant. He also drank a lot, and I have often thought that one of the bravest moments in my life was one day, when I stood up to him. I was about ten years old, and we were all sitting around the table – my six sisters, my mother and I, and my father in one of the rare moments that he was with us. We were drinking tea out of Russian-style glasses. My father was breaking off a piece of sugar and sipping the tea and everybody was frightened of him. He was just overpowering and in a mean mood, and I don't know why, suddenly I took a spoon, filled it with the hot tea and flicked it right in his face. Well, I tell you – he grabbed and he threw me. I'm so restrained usually, but that moment is so vivid in my mind. It's almost like an act that I feel saved me, a moment that dared me to do something and I did it. When you're that young, you actually think you're risking your life.

Kids are the greatest actors of all. They're so natural, they pretend to be whatever they want to be, and I think you have to retain a childish quality within you. It's a childish profession to pretend to be a cowboy, shooting Burt Lancaster. You have to be childlike, and I think most actors and performers go into it as a form of escape. It's a continuation of your daydreams.

I was in several Broadway plays, none of them were successes. Then a very dear friend of mind, Betty Bacall, was talking to Hal Wallace and she said, 'Look, if you go to New York, you've got to look up this actor I went to school with called Kirk Douglas,' and he gave me my first offer, which I turned down, because I never thought of myself as a movie actor. So in a sense I'm a failure because I always thought I was going to be a Broadway star, which I never became. It was only months later, out of desperation, when my wife at the time was pregnant with my son, Michael, and I needed money, that I wondered if he still wanted me. I called him and the next day I was on a train to Hollywood and did my first picture.

I think that for most of us, it's very clear what's make-believe and what's reality, but I think very often audiences get carried away. I remember after *Champion*, I walked into a bar and people recognised me. I was sitting at the bar having a drink and I saw two tough fellows at a booth. I couldn't hear what they were saying, but it was like, 'He doesn't look so tough.' One guy put his glass down and I saw him walking over toward me and I thought, 'Oh boy, here it comes. Now what am I going to do? If I hit him, I'll get in trouble. If he hits me, I may get more trouble.' So as he came over, I slammed my fist down on the bar and everybody turned around, and I said, 'Anybody in this bar can lick me.' Everybody laughed and he stopped, turned around and went back to his seat.

So many funny things happen. I was once rushing to a luncheon date and suddenly heard a fellow across the street. 'Hey!' he said, 'Gee, my favourite movie star!' I said, 'Oh, thank you very much,' and I kept going. I said, 'I'm late.' 'Gosh,' he said, 'I'm so excited, you're my favourite movie star.' I said, 'Thank you, sir.' He said, 'You know, I'm so nervous, your name went right outta my head. Well, tell me, what is your name?' I said, 'Yeah, my name is Douglas.' 'Yeah,' he said, 'Douglas Fairbanks, you're my favourite . . .'

As a matter of fact, Burt Lancaster and I have a pact. If someone comes up to Burt and calls him Kirk, he acknowledges it. If someone comes up to me and calls me Burt, I acknowledge it, because I think it's a form of a compliment.

When I first came to Hollywood, everyone was under contract to a studio. Now, that's quite rare, but at that time everyone was. I had one contract with Warner Brothers that I got out of. Finally, I couldn't take it, and I did a picture for nothing to get out of the contract, so I've always been a loner in that sense. I didn't always like it because you really felt alone. Most people had their own group, they could complain about things, but they'd belong to a studio, and I never did.

I called my company 'Bryna', which is my mother's name. My mother, a Russian peasant, would always say, 'America's such a wonderful land. My son, he's a movie star, his name in lights.' I said, 'Mom, you think America's such a wonderful land, it can put your name in lights.' She started to laugh. A year later, I took her in a limousine to Times Square and I pointed out to her there was a big theatre opening and in lights it said 'Bryna presents *Spartacus*' and I said, 'You see, Mom, your name in lights,' and she said, 'America's such a wonderful land.'

1979

John Wayne

John Wayne was weary from ill-health and jet lag when he appeared at the top of the stairs, but he still looked like a star. When he ambled towards me I saw the sherriff about to make an arrest. No one represented the Wild West, the American frontier spirit, better than John Wayne. The director John Ford said of Wayne, 'He is a splendid actor who has very little chance to act.' The political side of Wayne was more controversial. He was president of the Motion Picture Alliance for the Preservation of American Ideals, an organisation aimed at defending Hollywood from communist infiltration. He didn't much like being questioned about the part he played in the blacklisting of Hollywood talent. One such, Carl Foreman, directed *High Noon*, a film that John

Wayne described as 'un-American'. I asked him why, and thirty-six years later I still find his reply both sad and baffling.

Michael: I was going to ask you first of all about this style that you have – the walk and the talk we've seen over the years. Was this an acquired thing?

John: Well, I don't know about any walk or talk. When they changed over from silent pictures, they brought a lot of people from New York to Hollywood, because they said the silent directors and silent actors would be out. Mr Walsh was going to do a picture, *The Big Trail*, and he'd been sitting in New York for about three hours, looking at these phoney beards and guys standing on phoney stilts walking around throwing bull whips not used to whip bulls. He was just sick and tired of it, so he came out and saw me walking across and he said, 'Who's that kid?' – I want to tell you that was a few years ago – 'Tell him not to cut his hair, I'm going to make a test of him.' And that's how I ended up in the acting end of this profession rather than directing.

Michael: Ever since then you've been top of the box-office charts for more years than anybody cares to remember. What's kept you there?

John: Luckily, I've been in a great number of pictures about folklore, which the whole world understands, and when you play a cowboy that's probably the most written about, in prose, poetry and song, of any folklore hero, it gives you a greater popularity. And therefore more people come to see it.

Michael: You don't resent the charge that in the majority of your films you've played yourself?

John: I want to play myself, if myself is what I've been playing. The only thing that I will not do is a mean or petty scene. I don't mind playing rough, tough, cruel, but not mean or petty.

Michael: What is it about the character you admire most of all? The man of the West I'm talking about, the frontiers man.

John: I think there's no nuance. They laugh lustily, hate heartily, drive ahead, fighting something bigger than a petty little argument with someone, fighting the elements.

Michael: What background did you come from? Was it a showbiz background?

John: No, my father was a druggist, and he was in poor health. We moved out to California, as a matter of fact *way* out into California, to the Mojave Desert. I used to ride a horse to school, and that gave me a little background for what I finally got into.

Michael: And when did you change your name from Michael Marion Morrison?

John: The studio figured that Marion was not exactly a proper name for an American hero. They forgot about Francis Marion, I guess. And Duke, they said, sounded a little too vulgar. It wouldn't be over here, but for some reason, it was over there. And so they came up with John Wayne.

Michael: Not a bad name for a film star, is it?

John: It's worked all right for me. Took me a long time to get used to it.

Michael: I suppose the thing that really changed your career was the relationship you developed with John Ford?

John: It was a pretty wonderful friendship. He had a great deal to do with my thinking. Every young fellow, I'm sure, when he goes into pictures, wants to play every part – you want to play the dashing hero, the heavy. I was spouting off one day, and John said, 'Duke, would you like to see Harry Carey any different than you see him?' Old Harry Carey was the top actor in those days. I said, 'No.' He said, 'Well then, what the hell's the matter with you? In pictures, it's like sitting in a room, you're looking at people. If you go overboard at a cocktail party, they can get up and walk away, but if you do that to them in a theatre, they're stuck, and they start looking at you. Be yourself.' Which was pretty good advice.

****

Michael: Can I talk to you now about another much-publicised aspect of your life, which is the political views you hold. I'd like to ask you about that period in Hollywood when you were to the forefront of people who were black-listing alleged communist members of the industry.

John: That's not a true statement, we were not blacklisting.

Michael: Well you were . . .

John: No, they were blacklisting, we didn't name anybody. We stayed completely out of it and said 'We are Americans'. Anybody who wanted to join us, it was fine. We gave no names out to anybody at any time, ever.

Michael: But when you look back at that now, John, are you proud of what happened in Hollywood at that time?

John: I think it was probably a necessary thing at the time because the radical liberals were going to take over our business and you wouldn't have had any pictures like that then.

Michael: But seriously, the people who got kicked out of Hollywood . . .

John: Who were kicked out?

Michael: The people . . .

John: Wait a minute, tell me who was kicked out?

Michael: Let's take for an example Carl Foreman.

John: Yeah, Carl Foreman.

Michael: There was Dalton Trumbo.

John: Carl Foreman, Dalton Trumbo.

Michael: Look what happened to Larry Parks.

John: About Larry Parks, he admitted he'd been a commie and he went on working.

Michael: He didn't work for some time, he'd had a very unpleasant . . .

John: He hadn't worked a hell of lot before that had he?

Michael: Well no, but these aren't people who you would expect to take over the industry?

John: At the time, it seemed serious. They were getting themselves into a position where they could control who would do the writing.

Michael: But isn't it right that people of all shades of opinion should be able to make movies, if they're from the extreme right wing or extreme left wing?

John: Definitely, anytime, if that's their opinion. But the trouble was that they were spouting by rote somebody else's way of life, and that's all right for those fellas over there, that's the way they want to live, but we don't have to have it in our country.

Michael: But you could say your point of view was reflecting the capitalist way of life.

John: Well, I don't think 'capitalist' is such an unpopular word. In two hundred years we've taken a wilderness and built a factory that feeds the world, a farm that feeds the world. And we've been doing our best to help everybody out that we can. I think it's a pretty good way of living.

Michael: What about Carl Foreman? I read an interview in which you said you objected to *High Noon*. You said it was un-American. I saw that film, and for the life of me I can't see what's un-American about it.

John: A whole city of people are afraid to help out a sheriff because three tough men are coming into town. He goes into the church and for some reason the women are sitting on one side and the men on the other. He pleads his case and the men say, 'No, no, no.' The women say, 'You're yellow, you're cowards.' I don't think that ever happens in the United States. Then at the end of the picture he took the United States Marshall badge, stepped on it and walked off. I think those things are just a little bit un-American.

Michael: It's amazing because I've seen that film, not once, but four or five times.

John: When you saw those things, do they strike you as being a true picture of the pioneer West? Or what Carl Foreman, or somebody, would like to give our children the impression it was like?

Michael: No, but I'm sure a lot of the movies that you would approve of were similarly not a true picture of the West, nor of American society. I took it to be a dramatic exposition of something or other, certainly not a knock at the American way of life. And when I read about this, I thought, 'My God, it's an extraordinary ultra-reaction.'

John: You must realise what was going on at that time in our business. A lot of fine writers weren't being used and it was rough on them. That's why I took up for that side. Morrie Ryskind, who was a Pulitzer Prize winner, couldn't get a job because he didn't think exactly like these fellas. That's what started it, not us trying to throw them out.

1974

James Stewart

James Stewart was the agreeable face of Hollywood. The place Orson Welles described as 'brutal and dirty' was airbrushed whenever he appeared. Of all the Hollywood stars I interviewed, he had the easiest, most attractive manner. Frank Capra, the great director with whom Stewart made some of his best films, said, 'Jimmy Stewart's appeal lay in being so unusually usual.' More pertinently, the actor Anthony Quayle observed, 'Jimmy Stewart is everything the British audience wants an American to be, but so rarely is.' Stewart achieved the almost impossible task of managing to live up to the awesome challenge of being regarded as a hero while also behaving like one. He was one of the first American film stars to join up in World War II and became a combat pilot, leading bombing missions to Germany. He remained in the Air Force Reserve after the war and retired as a Brigadier General in 1959. Not simply a great star, also a convivial man.

My father had a hardware store in Western Pennsylvania, that's in the soft coal area of our country, near the big industrial city of Pittsburgh. His father established the hardware store, and he was able to celebrate the one hundredth anniversary of the hardware store before he died. I think the reason he kept the hardware store for so long was because he was sure that people were going to catch up with me out in Hollywood and I would have something to go back to.

He wasn't too happy about the acting profession as a way to make a living. When I came back and announced that I wasn't going to go to graduate school and learn to be an architect, I was going to Broadway and have a small part in a play, he just reached for a chair and sat down, but bless their hearts, both my mother and my father said, 'OK.' My father's brother had the final say. When I was leaving to seek my fortune on the stage, he said, 'Well, I expect this is fine.' He said, 'There haven't been any Stewarts in show business except one, a third cousin of yours, Ezra, and he ran away and joined the circus, and he's the only Stewart that I know of that's ever been to jail, but good luck to you.'

I remember I was in a play in New York, I played an Austrian nobleman. That'll give you a little idea that I needed the work, and it was a very sad, terrible, tragic play, and I somehow felt that I should give some suggestion of an Austrian accent. There was a woman in New York in those days by the name of Frances Robinson Duff, who people would go to when they got a part and she would coach them mostly in voice and projection. I went to Miss Duff and this was tough going. It was five bucks a throw for lessons but I thought that it was important. She said, 'Yes, I think that we can work out some kind of a suggestion,' but after three lessons, she said, 'I'm going to have to let you go.' She said, 'There's no way I can teach you an Austrian accent, but any time in the future that you feel that you'd like to learn to speak English properly . . .'

All the big studios had scouts and offices in New York and a man from MGM saw a play I was in. I was given just a photographic test first. I was put on a stool and the man said, 'Now, I want you to imagine that a white horse runs over to the wall and then runs up the wall and across the ceiling and down the other wall, and I want you to follow the white horse.' Why did it have to be a white horse? Of course, this was my first experience with movies, so I followed the white horse all the way round, that was the first test.

The casting director of MGM, Billy Grady, who was really responsible for getting me into the movies, said, 'This fellow Stewart, maybe he'd be good for the part of Shorty in *Motor Men*.' The producer said, 'But the fellow's twelve feet tall!' Billy said, 'I thought maybe we might change the name, you wanna rewrite the script too?' I got the part, but I was still Shorty.

When you were under contract to one of the big studios in those days, you worked all the time. You had little parts in big pictures, and every once in a while you would get a big part in a little picture. You did tests of all kinds. I was called in to test for the part of a Chinaman in *The Good Earth*. Jack Donovan, a very famous make-up artist, had designed eyes that made Oriental features. I was stripped to the waist and darkened down. I was to do the test with Paul Muni – a walking shot of maybe fifty feet – and the first thing Paul Muni said was, 'This is a helluva tall Chinaman.' So what they did, they dug a trench. Muni walked there and I walked in the trench. I didn't get the part. They gave it to a Chinese person.

I had the same horse for twenty-one years. Stevie Meyers, who was a daughter of an old wrangler for W.S. Hart, had the horse and the horse's name was Pie. The horse had hurt some people and was sort of mean. I noticed that he was a nice-looking but a small horse. I found out he was quarter horse and thoroughbred, and I asked to ride him. It was almost a human thing between us. I think we liked each other.

I really talked to this horse and I know he understood. One night, we're filming. I'm coming into a town and I have a little bell on the horn of the saddle, and this sort of identifies me. The bad guys are in the saloon, they're going to get me, and they hear the bell and they say, 'Here he comes.' Now, what Pie had to do is, the camera goes on Pie's leg and then cuts to the bad guys as Pie is rocking, and then it goes up and there's nobody on Pie when he's walking. It was three o'clock at night and they said, 'How long is it going to take you to get Pie to walk down this long street all by himself?' I said, 'Well, I'll talk to him,' and I went back and said, 'Pie, this is tough because you're a horse, but you have to walk straight down there and I'm not going to be on you, you see, but you have to walk straight down and clear to the other end of the set.' And the fellow says, 'How long is it going to take? You're going to talk all night?' They rolled the cameras and Pie did it the first time. It was amazing. I loved the horse.

I'm a plodder. I'm the inarticulate man who tries. I'm a pretty good example of true human frailty. I don't really have all the answers, I have very few of the answers, but for some reason, somehow, I make it. When I'm at the head of the wagon train, for some reason we get across the river.

1973

David Niven

The best part David Niven ever played was being David Niven. This is not a slur on someone I regarded as a friend, but an observation about a man who was much more elusive and complex than he would have you believe. The debonair, charming English gentleman, with impeccable manners, was also a commando during the war. He was a marvellous raconteur, with a comedian's sense of timing, and yet during the telling, his eyes were alert and watchful. When you were laughing, he was assessing. It was no surprise, therefore, that his two volumes of memoirs were both funny and perceptive. He satisfied that particular affection the English have for the man who succeeds effortlessly without seeming to stop smiling.

A long time ago in New York, I was broke and selling booze for some ex-bootleggers. An old society lady, called Elsa Maxwell, gave these great big parties and I tried to sell her some booze, and she said, 'This is not a good thing, you should marry a rich wife.' I said, 'Well, how do I do that on $40 a week?' That was what I was getting from the booze people. She said, 'I tell you what. I'm running a thing for the milk fund. I want you to be one of the professional dance partners. You'll wear a green carnation, and charge $20 a dance.' Well, I made about $40 for the fund, and then the awful thing happened. They wheeled on this sort of imitation section of the New York Stock Exchange, and people bought shares for the most popular man in New York. Now they had all these names of all these people they all knew and at the bottom was 'David Nevins', and they thought I was a man who'd made the microphone or something. Nobody bought anything, and it was the most awful day of my life. You saw thousands of dollars going against everybody else, and poor 'David Nevins' at the bottom. Awful.

I was almost fifteen – that was my excuse anyway – and we lived in London. There wasn't room for me in our small house, so I was farmed out into a room up at St James's Place some-where, and we lived in Sloane Street. Every night after dinner, this creepy stepfather I had used to give me tuppence for the bus, and I used to get off at the Ritz Hotel and walk down to my ghastly burrow, with a pot under the bed and all that horrible stuff. Then I got more adventurous and I used to walk on up to Piccadilly and look at all the lights – the Bovril and Owbridges Lung Tonic, and all those lovely things. And then I realised that lots of girls were walking about at the same time. I once saw a spectacular pair of legs and I followed this girl, just to look at her, and she seemed to have an awful lot of men friends and she'd talk to people. So I went to my room and I kept on thinking about this girl. The next night I couldn't wait to get up to Piccadilly again, and I walked around and I couldn't find her. And finally I did.

I saw her with a very nice-looking man and I thought that's her father, a man in a dinner jacket. She took him into a little house in Cork Street, and I hid and waited to see if she ever came out again. And she came out quite soon as a matter of fact. After that I really thought of this girl all the time, and I used to go looking for her at night. One night the girl suddenly turned on me, and she was a lovely Cockney. She said, 'What do want? Do you want a piece, mate? What are you doing?' I thought, 'What is she talking about?' Then she said, 'Want to come home with me?' and I said, 'Yes.' So this dream took me into a flat, and I thought this is going to be the ginger beer and the gramophone records.

She gave me this ghastly book of photographs and said, 'Look, if you have any trouble, take a look at these,' and I couldn't believe it. Then she appeared with the usual thing, the pink shoes and nothing else, and I'm actually gibbering. She said, 'You can wash over there, dear,' and I saw this terrible sort of kidney-shaped table full of blue fluid. And I washed my hands. I didn't know . . .

It sounds corny and odd but I think I fell in love with her, very much. She used to come down and see me at school. She came from Hoxton, never seen the country before. She used to arrive with a ghastly tartan rug and potage fruit sandwiches. I was at Stowe, and the headmaster, called Roxborough, was marvellous. The cricket match was on, and she was really a dish, a real beauty, lovely girl. Roxborough came over and saw me sitting on the rug with this girl. Oh, it was agony. He said, 'May I join you?' and I said, 'Oh Sir, this is Miss . . .' – I won't give the name, even now – and she said, 'You don't look a bit like a schoolmaster, do you dear?' He knew.

I was put in the Army because we had no money. My father was killed in the first war, so my mother's ambition was to get me off the books as quick as possible, and that was the best way to do it. I hacked through Sandhurst. I enjoyed that. It was very tough in those days, and I think it probably still is. That's where I met Trubshawe – my best, best man. I've been married twice and he's been my best man both times, and my best friend. He's huge, six foot six, and has a moustache you can see from the back on a clear day. Fascinating character, Trubshawe.

When I got into the movies, I used to put his name into every one, if I could. It would send a signal back to Trubshawe from Hollywood, that I was still there and thinking of him. But people got to catch on. I was with Larry Olivier, we were doing *Wuthering Heights*, and William Wyler, the director, said, 'Now, David, Trubshawe's name does not come into the Brontes' script, we don't want any of this.' He was really watching, and I was determined to get it in. Finally, Cathy unleashed these two great dogs on Heathcliff, who was Larry, and I had to defend him. I said, 'Down, Trubshawe, down, down.' And that was cut, but I did get it in. I talked to the prop man, and when Merle Oberon was walking through the village churchyard, there was: 'Here lies my faithful friend Michael Trubshawe'.

Those days of Hollywood certainly were the great days. I mean between 1930 and 1960, and I had the great luck and good fortune to be there the whole time, except for the six and a half years of the war. Take the middle of that, the mid forties, 800 million people a week all over the world bought tickets to go to the movies. Of course, there was no competition then – no night baseball, no bingo, indeed no television. So they had it all to themselves and they'd built up these fabulous stars through the star system. When I started there, I worked in twenty-seven Westerns as an extra, and with this voice I wasn't allowed to speak. So I was silent and doing Mexicans and things. I used to work at MGM studios, and that one studio, at the same time, had under contract Garbo, Gable, Joan Crawford, Jean Harlow, John Barrymore, Lionel Barrymore, Norma Shearer, Hedy Lemarr, William Powell, Myrna Loy, W.C. Fields, Wallace Beery, Marie Dressler and the Marx Brothers. The same studio had, in the children's school, Elizabeth Taylor, Mickey Rooney, Ava Gardner, Lana Turner and Judy Garland. And they built these characters up, and then other studios had Fred Astaire, Ginger Rogers, Cary Grant and Carole Lombard. Paramount had Dietrich, Voyet, Gary Cooper. And the public really made gods and goddesses of those people.

In those days, it was not great talents, it was great personalities, and there were probably forty people who could support a picture. Today, there are probably four who could support any picture. It was a case of publicity building up grains of sand until they became sizeable hills that could be seen a long way off, and they got up to all sorts of tricks. The first publicity man came from Barnum and Bailey's Circus, a man called Harry Reichenbach. He was hired in the early days to publicise one of the first Tarzan pictures. He booked a room on the ground floor of a hotel right opposite the theatre in New York where it was to open. A large packing case was delivered to his room. And then he pressed the bell and ordered eight pounds of chopped hamburger for lunch. So the waiter tottered along with this great platter, and there was a large lion sitting at the table with a napkin round its neck. The waiter sued Harry Reichenbach under immense publicity. That was really the first publicity stunt, and it sort of backfired, because he got badly sued.

My favourite one of all the flops was Walt Disney of all people. For the opening of *Pinocchio* in New York, he hired twelve midgets, dressed them up as Pinocchio and put them up on the marquee of the theatre, to gambol about and cause a stir with the traffic down below. Everything went along beautifully until lunchtime when somebody sent them up a couple of bottles of bourbon and the midgets started playing strip poker. By three o'clock, they were all naked and belching and screaming about, and the fire department brought them down in pillow cases.

The columnists were immensely powerful – Hedda Hopper and Louella Parsons. One was short and fat, the other was long and thin, and they were mines of misinformation. They were very, very powerful because between them they covered every single newspaper in the United States. They had millions of readers. I don't think they could ever destroy anybody who had great talent – they both hacked away at Marlon and never destroyed him. They had terrific favourites and they had terrific enemies. Hedda's great enemy was Orson Welles because he made *Citizen Kane*. Hearst, of course, was the prototype, and Hearst was her boss. Hedda took against Chaplin because she was very politically minded. She thought he was very left-wing and commie and all that stuff. They were very rough, and the studios used them. I remember I was under contract with Sam Goldwyn for fifteen years and something happened. I had a contract coming up for renewal or dissipation, and Goldwyn decided to soften me up for the kill, to get me to settle for less money. I was rather popular, I thought, at the studio. I'd been there as a beginner. And I picked up the paper and saw the headline: 'Niven Unbearable Say Fellow Workers'. The article said that I'd got so swollen-headed that no one could work with me, and that I hated Goldwyn. Louella put it in to help Goldwyn. That sort of thing did happen.

We did a little thing once. Ida Lupino was a great friend of mine and she was married to a very rough man called Howard Duff – she still is. My wife, Hjördis, and I loathed Hedda and Louella at this point. All four of us had had problems, so we made a plan. I called up a rather chic night-club and booked a table for two. The head waiter said, 'Oh yes, Mr Niven, just you and madam?' And I said, 'Just give me a quiet corner table in the dark.' And then Ida and I arrived, and that caused terrific twittering – there were spies everywhere for the columnists, in all the brothels and in all the hospitals, everywhere. The next thing I knew, about fifteen cameramen arrived. Ida and I were sitting in one corner, she's nibbling my ear, the whole bit, and right in the middle of all this excitement, in come Howard and Hjördis, and they go to the other side of the dance floor. And Ida, she overdid it, said, 'You must flee!' Howard, who was reputed as a brawler, spotted us and kicked over his table – crash! Everybody in the place was watching, everybody's waiting. I pretended to be a bit gassed. I got up and we took our coats off. All the photographers were getting into position for the kill. The dance floor's cleared and we circle round, looking at each other – the classic Western ending. And then finally we grab each other, kiss each other on the mouth and waltz all round the room! Louella called me in the morning and said she would not be woken up for false alarms.

1972 and 1975

Jack Lemmon

Jack Lemmon was not so much indifferent to the siren song of fame and fortune as he was immune to it. The world regarded him as a mighty film star. He saw himself as a jobbing actor. The *New York Times* defined his film career by describing him as: 'The brash young American Everyman who evolved into the screen's grumpiest old Everyman during a movie career that lasted half a century.' He was also a consummate comic actor, as he proved in his partnership with Billy Wilder in films such as *Some Like It Hot* and *The Apartment*, and later by co-starring with Walter Matthau in delights such as *The Odd Couple*. Matthau once described his co-star as: 'A clean-cut, well-scrubbed Boston choirboy with quiet hysteria seeping out of every pore.' Some of his performances, like some of the films he appeared in, will be seen and admired as examples of Hollywood at its very best.

When I got my first film with Judy Holliday, *It Should Happen To You,* I had never met Harry Cohn, who ran Colombia Films, but had heard he was a very tough, tyrannical man – one of the last of the great studio heads, who ran it with an iron fist. I'd finished the entire film and had yet to meet him, and was about to be on my way back to New York where I still lived. I got word on the set when I finished my last shot that Mr Cohn wanted to meet me. I went up to the office and he had it arranged so the venetian blinds were completely closed at one end and wide open at his desk, so he sat there with this sort of spotlight effect on him. Not only that, it was a long office and I swear it felt like you were walking up hill to get there. I was petrified by the time I got in front of his desk. He had a riding crop, and I stuck my hand out and said, 'How do you do, Mr Cohn?' I got my hand up about halfway and he lifted his up but had the crop in it, and he went wham on the desk. He said, 'The critics will use it like a ball bat, they'll kill you, boy!' And I said, 'What, what?' He said, 'That name – Lemmon. It's got to go!'

He went on for five minutes and said, 'How could I put a name – Jack Lemmon – up on the screen as a supposed leading man opposite this girl?' The first thing I said was, 'Why did you wait till now to bring all of this up? It's all done, you see, and I don't want to change it.' He said, 'Well you're gonna change it!' I said, 'No, I'm not.' Then I said, 'What do you want to change it to?' He said, 'Lennon,' which meant I would have ended up John Lennon, now that I think of it! And I said, 'Lennon?' Jokingly, I said, 'You pronounce it Lennon, they'll think I'm a Russian revolutionary.' He said, 'No, that's Leneeen!' Anyway, I said 'No, forget it, I'm going back to New York and you can forget the whole thing. Don't even give me billing' or whatever. So he previewed the picture, gave me a bigger billing, and I think he respected me because I did stick to my guns and we got along just great.

I was one of those terrible snobs who thought the theatre was it. I was going to save the American theatre, which, for some peculiar reason, they wouldn't let me do, and had absolutely no thoughts whatsoever of going into the movies. I thought movies were for curly haired, pretty little boys or something. I did enjoy certain actors and so didn't have a total disrespect for it, but personally had no desire whatsoever. It was just that lucky happenstance on my first film with Judy Holliday. When I read the script, there was one scene, and that did it. When I read that scene I said, 'Wow, that's a ripper.'

I met Billy Wilder about four years after I started working in film. My first film was in late 1954 and *Some Like It Hot* came along in 1959. We had met socially and I had admired his work from the time I was a kid, but I didn't know him well. He came up to me in a restaurant, to where I was sitting with my wife, and I said, 'Hello Billy,' and he said, 'Listen, could I sit for just a moment? I want to say something very quick.' And I said, 'Sure.' So he said, 'I got this thing here, there are a couple of guys, they're musicians, they see the same Valentine's Day massacre, all the gangsters, and you run and you've got to hide, because they're going to get you. And so you are going to be in an all-girl orchestra, which means you're going to be in drag for about three-quarters of the picture. Are you going to do it?' For some reason, I thought for one split second and said, 'Yes.' He said, 'OK,' and walked away. About six months later, the script showed up, and I thought it was the most brilliant farce I'd ever read.

I'll tell you something very funny that I realised shortly after we started filming. Once we'd gotten the make-up right and the hair right, my mother came to the set to visit us. I suddenly stood beside her, in front of one of those wardrobe mirrors, and God, I looked just like her! She had her hair done like mine and she always had a sort of slight bee sting with her lipstick. So I had a couple of pictures taken of us together – we looked like sisters!

I don't know how well we analyse ourselves, and I have not been analysed because I've always been afraid of spilling the beans and upsetting the apple cart, finding out what makes me tick, in case everything goes out the window. There's an old story about the comic who was the funniest man on earth and the biggest hit in the world. He went to the analyst, found out what was wrong, and finally became happy. Then he killed his analyst because he never got any laughs after that. I genuinely love acting and think it is a noble profession. We're very fortunate if we can make a living and become successful in it, because you cannot just entertain people but you can touch them, move them and enlighten them. And we don't, as people, get that opportunity all the time in everyday life.

1972 and 1987

Tony Curtis

Tony Curtis is the classic example of making the best of what the good Lord gave you and then some. His almost feminine good looks, his Bronx accent – 'Yonder de castle of my fadder' – made him both an object of desire and ridicule in almost equal parts. He not only survived, he triumphed in a career during which he showed the world that Bernard Schwartz, as he was born, had talent as well as beauty. Nowadays he paints more than he acts, but he will always be a significant part of Hollywood history because of his part in that perfect comedy *Some Like It Hot*, and the movie that first demonstrated his potential, the sadly neglected *Sweet Smell of Success*.

My father and mother were born in Hungary and they came to America in 1923. I was born in 1925, so I was brought up in a Hungarian environment with Hungarian Jewish parents, and those early days in Manhattan were spent with that group of people. I've never felt like I was an American or like I am an American. I never really felt part of that environment. That doesn't make it bad or good, it's just my observation. I travel a lot. I don't feel like I have roots in that sense. Wherever I can make a house for myself, that's where I live.

I loved the movies. In those days we always went to the movies, right from the time I could remember. It made no difference to me what the picture was, I just loved going. I liked going into a dark room and being amused and entertained, and it still has a wonderful ability to take your mind off your personal problems maybe for a few hours. For a couple of hours it's not bad to just lose yourself in someone else's environment and be drawn along by it, to get all excited and then you go out and it's still snowing and your wife's left you and everything. That, I think, was what provoked me to want to be a movie actor.

To me, any guy who made it in the movies was a hero, because how you could take somebody and make them a movie actor was incredible. I didn't even know the mechanics of it, I just saw them – Cary Grant, Clark Gable, Jimmy Cagney, Humphrey Bogart, Burt Lancaster, Kirk Douglas, Frank Sinatra. I've worked with these people – Yul Brynner, Jack Lemmon and Sidney Poitier – and I find that to be part of that family, to be part of that profession, is about as nice as I can have it.

At the beginning I liked Cary Grant very much and I still do, but then as I started to watch the other actors work, I realised each one had his own very special way of bringing a little magic to each moment that he played, and that's the name of the game, that's the ballgame for me. How each person can bring his own little imperfections that kind of fill out a scene – it's like blowing up a balloon, it gives it a three-dimensional quality. You see people's weaknesses, their strengths.

What you have to avoid is acting. You mustn't act. The words do the acting. When the guy says, 'I love you,' that's acting. I've transmitted some information. That's not acting to me, that's just a matter of reading a line well. A lot of people imagine and for years have always thought, and rightly so, that Shakespeare was a wonderful tool to work in, but it's very restricting. And you are bringing to those parts really the author's intent, which is very strong and powerful. But some actors can bring those little unfinished moments that give it a mystery that I'm sure Shakespeare meant at the beginning, and I think that's what acting should be – things left unsaid.

I've been able to create myself. I didn't change my name from Bernard Schwartz to Tony Curtis because I wanted to get into the movies, but because I wanted to be my own man. I wanted to be a creation of myself. I didn't want to be part of a background, of someone else's wishes and ideas and morays and religions. I wanted to be my own fellow, and that's what I started to try to do. And it's because of the audience that I made it.

I've had a lot of wonderful experiences. I'm really privileged. It's been an extraordinary life I've had. People are so gentle and so outgoing and giving, and if you observe them, it's just stimulating. A girl once saw me in the street and said, 'Tony of the movies.' I really liked that. 'Tony of the movies.'

1972 and 1976

Henry Fonda

David Shipman, in his invaluable book *The Great Movie Stars: The Hollywood Years*, described the appeal of Henry Fonda thus: 'He is honest Joe, deliberate, intelligent, slow to anger, chary. As a Western hero, brother to Gary Cooper, the antithesis of men of action like Gable or John Wayne. He really is that dependable, likeable actor that so many others have aspired to.' Henry Fonda was nominated for an Academy Award for *The Grapes of Wrath* in 1940 but had to wait until 1981 to win the award for his last film, *On Golden Pond*. The award was accepted by daughter Jane. Henry Fonda died five months later.

It never occurred to me to be an actor. I didn't have any background in my life or my family in any way. I did not grow up going to movies and thinking, 'I want to be a movie actor.' I studied journalism at college – I thought I was going to be a writer. Anyway, a very good friend of our family, Dorothy Brando – who later had a son named Marlon – was very active on the board of directors of a little theatre, the Omaha Community Playhouse, and I'm home from college and they're evidently hard up for a juvenile.

They'd cast somebody and he decided he didn't want to do it or left town or something, and they were suddenly stuck. It wasn't that Doll thought I had talent, I was just the right age. She literally just pushed me and I was too shy to say, 'Don't do this to me.' And that's how it happened.

In the meantime, my family didn't object in any way. The season lasted from September till May. I did a play about every month. Finally, the season was over and I'm home and my dad said, 'I think it's time. You're out of college, what are we going to do?' And I didn't know. I wasn't prepared for anything.

I answered an ad in the paper and got a job as a file clerk in a retail credit company. I got it in June, and the following September the playhouse director called me. He said, 'We're going to open with *Merton of the Movies* and I want you to play Merton.' I didn't know what this was, but I said, 'Fine,' because I'd had so much fun before. My dad said, 'No way. You've got a very important job, important in the sense that there is a chance for advancement. You can't do justice to both.' I was determined that I was going to do it, not because I had an ambition to be an actor, just because I'd had so much fun the year before. I had the only argument I've ever had with my father. My mother was the diplomat, but my father didn't speak to me for a month.

Opening night, the family came – my two sisters, my mother, my father. Eventually, I've got my make-up off, I've left and I'm home. Now, my father is sitting in father's chair and my mother and sisters are sitting in a group. He doesn't speak to me so I pass him and join my sisters and my mother, and they just went on with extravagant praise. Then my sister started to say something that sounded like it was going to be less than extravagant. She said, 'There was one point I thought if only . . .' She got about that far and Dad said, 'Shut up, he was perfect.' I've always felt so lucky that I was brought up by the parents I had. And three years later, when I learned you got paid for this in New York and I decided to go to New York, no quarrel at all.

In the end, it's funny because I kept that job with the retail credit company, and when I went to tell him I was going to quit and go to New York, the manager was absolutely stricken. He said, 'But Fonda, I was going to send you to the home office in Atlanta.' If I hadn't gone to New York, I might be the branch manager of the retail credit company.

I've done about eighty-five films altogether and I don't think more than fifteen of them are Westerns, but I do have a reputation of being a Western actor. I've done my share and I guess I've been lucky that some of those were the good ones. I'm not Western, even with my accent. I'm from the Middle West of the States, but cowboy – forget it. I don't like horses, I don't like riding. They have to pay me a lot of money to get me on a horse. It's dangerous. A man can get killed!

Both of my children, Jane and Peter, went through what is known as a classic rebellion. When a child is asked to go into the father's business, whether he's a banker or in show business, there has to be a kind of rebellion. You don't want to feel that your father made it possible for you, or you're a success because of your father, so they both went through it, and I like to think that I was smart enough to recognise it for what it was. Also, they both did well almost immediately, so I didn't have to hold my breath too long. We couldn't be more friendly or happier together. I couldn't be more proud.

I'm in awe of both of them. Jane is one of the most incredible actresses I've ever seen, and I have to say that I'm not surprised because I saw her do things early, before she'd committed herself. I thought, 'If she ever does want to, she's going to make it.' But when I saw *Klute*, as an example, I couldn't wait to sit and talk to her, and this was not father/daughter, this is actor/actor. Where did that come from? How did that happen to you? We were talking actor talk, and I realised the scene that had knocked me out was an improvisation, which I couldn't do if I was paid money to do it. I have to have the written word and a director to help me a lot. They got to this scene and the director knew what he wanted but it wasn't written. He talked to Jane about it and she says, 'Just give me a moment,' and this came out as an improvisation and just tore you apart. Anyway, she's not only this incredible actress, but she's the activist that you know her to be, and I'm in nothing but sympathy with her.

I did see a lynching once, when I was eleven or twelve years old. My father's printing business was on the second floor of the building that overlooked the courthouse square in Omaha, and he came home one night and told about this lynch mob that had started to form during the afternoon, and after supper he put me in the car and we drove back downtown – it was very unusual for my dad to be taking me at my age, and turning lights on and unlocking doors and going up the stairs. It's not like doing it in the daytime. I remember walking across the empty office to the window that overlooked the courthouse square, and this was where the riot was happening. My father never talked about it, he never preached about it, we were both just observers.

I watched an out-of-control mob of several hundred men drag a young black boy out of the jail and the courthouse, overpower the sheriff to get him out, string him up on a lamp-post, riddle him with bullets, drag him round back of a car or something like that. The mayor – this is how long ago – was on horseback. We did have automobiles but evidently he could get into the courthouse square away from the streets easier. He was on horseback trying to stop it and they damn near lynched the mayor – that was how out of control these bastards could get. It was a traumatic experience for me, I'll never forget it.

My father never told me but I would like to think that he realised it would be a lesson. I had to grow up and move away from Omaha to appreciate that my father was a Liberal Democrat in a hotbed of Republican reactionaries, and that's another reason I feel lucky to have had the parents I had. Oscar Hammerstein said, 'You have to be taught to hate, and you can also be taught you don't have to hate.'

1975

Fred Astaire

George Axelrod, the American script writer, once observed Fred Astaire walking down the street and invented a new verb, 'to Astaire', which he defined as walking while floating. Stanley Donen, the film director said, 'He even chews gum in time.' Gene Kelly remarked, 'If I'm the Marlon Brando of dance, he is Cary Grant.' Even now, a viewing of Astaire's musicals, particularly those with Ginger Rogers, is to experience a sense of aesthetic satisfaction as complete and fulfilling as inspecting any great work of art. Less obviously, he was also rated as one of the most influential singers of all time, maybe not so much by the general public, as by those who know about these things, the songwriters. They would do anything to get Astaire to sing their songs. For Irving Berlin, he was the infallible test of quality. Berlin said, 'He's as good as Jolson, Crosby, Sinatra. He is just as good a singer as he is a dancer, not necessarily because of his voice but his conception of projecting a song.' What was he like in real life? Modest, self-effacing, a hero when I first saw him on the silver screen, an even bigger hero after we had met.

Fred: I started at the age of four and a half, appearing professionally, and if you add that up to now, I have been performing professionally for seventy-one years. It woke me up when I thought about it. 'Oh my gosh, this can't be.'

But it is actually so, because I was born in 1899 and I went to New York when I was about four. And then there was some kind of a professional appearance that occurred around that time, so I added it all up and that's what it is.

Michael: I interviewed Bing Crosby recently and he thought he was a veteran. He's only been fifty years on the stage.

Fred: He's a child, for heaven's sake.

Michael: Were you reluctant to go on the stage, in the sense that you didn't have any ambition? You were more or less forced into it, weren't you?

Fred: I don't remember. I wasn't forced. My sister, Adele, was going to New York, to dancing school and stage school, so I went along too and the first thing you know, I was in it. I didn't know what I was doing at all.

Michael: It's staggering to think that somebody who has contributed as much as you have to dance really had no blinding ambition?

Fred: Oh no, at that point. I didn't know what show business was. I found out pretty soon, though.

Michael: What was it like, in those days of vaudeville? Was it fairly rough?

Fred: We played in some pretty crumby dumps when we were in small-time vaudeville. I do remember that we were on the bill with a dog act. The dog act had the star dressing-room and we had to climb a ladder to get the dogs up there. They couldn't climb it.

Michael: One of the most extraordinary periods in your career was the twenties when you came to London with a series of magnificent musical comedies, Gershwin numbers and the like, and literally took the place by storm, didn't you?

Fred: Oh, we had a very happy thing there with that success. We were very excited about that, and we were scared to death when we arrived, I can tell you that.

Michael: I suppose that the men you admired most, out of everyone you've met throughout your long career, would be those great writers who wrote songs for you?

Fred: Cole Porter and Gershwin, Jerome Kern – I admired

them tremendously. There are four or five top men who did wonderful things for me, and wrote songs for the pictures I was doing, and for me it was great.

Michael: Not just Kern and Berlin, who always believed you were the best interpreter of their songs, but a lot of jazz musicians nowadays rate you as one of their favourite singers. What is the quality do you think?

Fred: It's very flattering and I love it. It makes me very happy. I really don't know. I know Mel Tormé has always got something very kind to say to me. Sinatra and Tony Bennett, they all like what I do and those fellows can sing. They've got pipes, which I ain't got, but I throw a fake note there somewhere. I think what they like is that they know I mean what I'm doing and I'm trying to do what the composer's got there, and if I vary it a little bit, it isn't too much.

Michael: For a lot of the numbers you danced, you were dressed up in what became your trademark – the top hat, the white tie and tails. How much is that really you?

Fred: I don't like wearing a full dress suit. I had so much of it that people thought I was born in one, but it was necessary for what we were doing then. I actually haven't worn one in a film for quite a long time. I had to wear one to a couple of shindigs I went to recently, but I just don't like it. It's stiff.

Michael: A question I'm not going to ask you is who was your favourite dancing partner, because you're not going to give me an answer to that, are you?

Fred: Well, I can't, because I've always said my favourite dance partner is Bing Crosby. That gets me out.

Michael: Gene Kelly's the same. You won't talk about your dancing partners. Why is that?

Fred: Well, it's difficult because the gals are all so good and you just don't want to say, 'Gee whiz, I like that one better than the other one.' He had the same viewpoint. Each one had something special and to say which is the best – some are more effective than others and all that. When it comes to actual dancing, there are certain ways and styles and techniques that do show, and I could list a whole lot of names, but I don't want to get any priorities in here because I don't want to hurt anybody's feelings about it.

I must say, Ginger was certainly one – the most effective partner I had. Everybody knows that. It was a whole other thing, what we did. I want to pay tribute to Ginger because we did so many pictures together, and believe me, it was a value to have that gal. She had it. She was just great.

Michael: There were all sorts of rumours about you and Ginger in Hollywood, weren't there?

Fred: We were fighting, huh?

Michael: Yes, you were fighting.

Fred: Yes, that was the biggest nonsense ever. Before, you told me there was somebody who said that there was a twenty-five-year war with my girls, my dancing partners. Ridiculous, absolutely nothing like it. Ginger and I never had any fight. When Ginger kicked me down the stairs, I loved it! And she was just the same way. She could hardly wait for me to kick her in the ankle!

No, seriously, we never had a fight. Never. There were questionable conversations about material and I'd say, 'Oh, I don't like it,' or 'I do like it,' or 'I think you should know . . .' but you don't fight. I can't fight with the people I work with, I just couldn't do it. It didn't happen, but the press would have liked it that way, so we laughed about it.

1976

Shirley Temple

Shirley Temple's mother would constantly tell her daughter, 'Sparkle Shirley,' and she did as she was told. She twinkled and sang and danced throughout the Great Depression. Franklin D. Roosevelt said of her, 'It is a splendid thing that for just fifteen cents an American can go to a movie and look at the smiling face of a baby and forget his troubles.' Others took a more critical look at this precociously talented child. Graham Greene wrote of her, 'Infancy with Shirley Temple is a disguise, her appeal is more secret and more adult . . . watch the way she measures a man with agile studio eyes, with dimpled depravity.' Today she would be a sensation on one of those television talent shows. She was the biggest star in movies when she was aged four and her career was finished at the age of twenty-one. The showbiz child went on to become a woman of substance. She had a remarkable diplomatic career becoming US Ambassador to Ghana and Czechoslovakia, and US representative to the United Nations. She was the prime example of a mixture of intelligence and common sense overcoming the madness of juvenile celebrity.

I was in a neighbourhood dancing school, and there were ten little children all about three years old, and a producer came. He was looking for some children for some short subjects. I was a short subject at the time, and he told us all to line up and do a time step. I lined up, looked at him, and I didn't like his face. So I broke out of the line and went and hid under the piano. And he said, 'I'll take that one.' That was my start.

My father was a banker, and it was during the Depression so he probably was very grateful that someone came along to help out a bit. And my mother was a regular, nice home-maker, and made all of the clothes that we wore. They were very difficult times. And they didn't really have any ambition for me or anything, but it just happened. My mother is mostly German, with a little English blood, and my father is Pennsylvania Dutch, so we had quite a disciplined household. A lot of fun, but we had rules and regulations. So if people crowded around and said, 'Isn't she cute,' or 'Isn't she horrible,' or whatever, mother would say, 'Isn't it nice that you can make people happy?' She just let it go at that.

My mother worked hard. I couldn't read at the beginning,

and she would sit by my bed at night and read the scenes for the following day. I would listen to them and maybe repeat a couple of times, go to sleep, and I'd know them in the morning.

There's a law in the United States, that if anyone uses any word of profanity around a minor when they're working in television or movies, the child has to be sent home. And I used to consider this great punishment, because I would get to work and someone like Lionel Barrymore – who was in terrible pain, I don't know quite what was wrong with him, but it was just before he went into his wheelchair – would let off with a string of strange and very interesting sounding words. This was a Civil War picture, and I got into the costume, the hoop skirt and the pantalets, the bonnet and the whole thing, and I'd get sent home. And I couldn't figure out why this was.

Another time I was sent home, Lionel Barrymore got terribly angry because he never knew his lines. He had a slight drinking problem I think, too. So they brought the blackboard in and put his lines up on it, and he tried to read them and didn't do well. I kept correcting him and there's nothing worse than a child correcting an adult. So I was sent home again shortly after.

I had a [dental] plate and they'd have to keep it ready for which tooth would fall out. When I met President Roosevelt, I wouldn't smile at him and he kept asking me, 'Why won't you smile?' I was ten and finally my mother said, 'Well, she's lost her front tooth today and she's embarrassed about it.' And he said, 'Oh I had trouble with my teeth all my life. Let's just be friends.' So then the ice was broken.

The time I spent at the studio was different, but then I had my neighbourhood gang, and I was a tomboy. As soon as I got home I would put on blue jeans and a T-shirt and climb trees. I wasn't really – I'm probably still not – what I'm thought to be. For instance, I shot Eleanor Roosevelt with a slingshot when I was ten.

I retired from films in 1949 and married Charlie Black and we moved to Washington DC. I wanted to become more involved in the real world as opposed to the film 'real world'. For me, it's more important to try to contribute to peace for the world and to better health.

I got a very interesting reaction in Cairo, about a year ago. I was there as a guest of the Egyptian Government, the Foreign Ministry, and the night before I left, President Sadat invited me to come up to his home. I went out and he said to me, 'Well now you're an international politician,' and I said, 'Thank you,' and we talked about some of the really great problems in the Middle East – which is a worry for all of us in the world, a passionate problem, and I hope it can be resolved. After we'd talked a bit about that, we were going over various things in my UN charter, which I had with me, and he looked off into space and said, 'You know, when I was a boy going to school in London, I saw my first film, and it was your film. It was titled *Heidi*.' He said, 'I loved that film.'

1972

Bette Davis

When Bette Davis sat down, crossed her legs, lit a cigarette and challenged you with a stare that made you feel like a specimen in a bottle, you knew she was capable of giving you a bumpy ride. She, more than anyone, made it clear she was there to plug a product, not because she was, or ever would be, your buddy. With Ms Davis it was strictly business and the interviewer who presumed otherwise might suffer the kind of rebuke that made her a thousand enemies in Hollywood.

Her feud with Joan Crawford lasted a lifetime and produced many outstanding insults. My favourite was an interview when Davis said, 'I hate Joan Crawford. She couldn't act, she was a whore.' The interviewer begged to differ, pointing out that, apart from being a great star and a great lady, Crawford was dead. The interviewer said, 'You should never speak ill of the dead.' To which Bette Davis replied, 'Just because someone's dead doesn't mean they've changed.'

Bette: I started out in the theatre, and then talking pictures came along and they wanted everybody from theatre to come and see who would be good on the screen, so we all just went. It was a new adventure and one felt one should try it. In my case it worked out that I never went back.

Michael: If you'd looked at Hollywood at that time, you were hardly somebody you'd put the money on to succeed, were you?

Bette: None of us really were the same type. We were great puzzlements. We weren't beautiful women, we didn't behave in that Hollywood way off-screen, and we were not glamorous women in the theatre.

Michael: How much puzzlement did you cause to the people in Hollywood?

Bette: Quite a few years of puzzlement. It took a long time for them to recover.

Michael: When you first went there, did they ever try to tart you up? Glamorise you?

Bette: Oh yes. In the film *Fashions of 1934*, they made me up as nearly as possible to look like Miss Garbo, which of course is utterly impossible. They gave me the lovely long bob, and the nice beautiful wide mouth and the long, long lashes. It was sickening because it wasn't my type, and thank God I had brains enough to know that, and I never let them do that again. I just said, 'Either fire me or let me be what I personally am.'

Michael: As a contract artist, I would imagine that took a certain amount of guts, didn't it?

Bette: Well, yes. I was a meddler for my own good, but it becomes self-preservation. I continued that way, and they did that with so very many theatre actresses they brought out – changed all their teeth, changed their noses, changed everything. Those who had any individuality just never made it, because they looked phoney. I didn't feel so terrible challenged as regards working in front of the motion picture camera in the beginning. I didn't know then whether I had a real challenge or not. I knew I loved it but I didn't know if it would work out.

Michael: When did you know?

Bette: I worked in a film with George Arliss at Warner's, which was the beginning of the Warner contract. He gave me a marvellous part. I'd been fired by Universal, we were going back to New York, and he was my mentor and really saved my Hollywood life. I owe him all that.

Michael: Was there anybody at that time in Hollywood who gave you advice about acting that you've remembered?

Bette: Oh, Mr Arliss. A marvellous thing, he said to me – 'Don't ever worry about any of the publicity, don't worry about getting in columns and things. Do the work and that will come.' We had to do things out of continuity very often, and he would say, 'Every time you play a scene, remember what comes before on the screen and what goes after, then it will all match.' I was a fortunate girl really.

Michael: I'm going to ask you a question about a quote from your autobiography, which was written in 1963 and in which you said, 'All my marriages were a farce.'

Bette: In *The Lonely Life?* Well, that was a strange thing for me to say. There must have been something before that quote and after it.

Michael: It was in the last chapter, where you were summing up your life and talking about the difficulties of being the career woman, the star, and at the same time maintaining the marriage status.

Bette: Yes. It is difficult, no question, so that's why, I must admit, they seemed like farces, because they did not turn out to be either successful or real marriages.

Michael: It's not the institution itself that bothers you?

Bette: Not at all. I envy everybody who has had the good fortune to have a marvellous long marriage. I think it's a very important part of your life to have a good marriage.

Michael: Is it a price you think you've had to pay for the career you had? You've been married four times, haven't you?

Bette: Yes. You can't have everything. I've been more than fortunate. I've had the good fortune to succeed at the thing I love the most, and to have three marvellous children, so I've been more fortunate than some people.

Michael: What's the question you get asked most of all?

Bette: There is one question I am always asked – did I name the Oscar? Fascinatingly enough, the only night I was not asked this question was in Pittsburgh, Pennsylvania, the night of the Oscar show, which was very strange, because I'm always asked that.

Michael: What's the answer?

Bette: Well, I feel I did. My first husband's middle initial was 'O' and he never would tell me what it was, because he detested the name. So I found out that his middle name was Oscar, and the rear end of the Oscar looked like him, and I always called him 'Oscar'. That's my memory of it. Of course, it was a long time ago.

1975

Bing Crosby

I have thought hard about the verb to describe how Bing Crosby walked. 'Lollop' is the best I can do. He possessed the same unhurried almost languid method of perambulation as he demonstrated in his phrasing when he sang. Whenever I met him, I thought of Tom Watson's golf swing, Federer's graceful movement around a tennis court, Astaire dancing to a Gershwin tune. He was so laid back, you imagined interviewing him in a hammock. Yet he was the quintessential professional with a significance in the history of movies and popular music so important it places him in the same company as Frank Sinatra and Fred Astaire. Bing Crosby invented the art of crooning, demonstrated the craft of using a microphone. He changed the way people sang. As an actor he was typically self-deprecating. 'I do two kinds of acting, loud and soft,' he once said. This 'meagre' talent earned him one Oscar and the kind of popularity we can only imagine nowadays. His radio show alone had an audience of fifty million.

I lived in a little town called Spokane, Washington, and there was a syndicated comic strip called 'The Bingville Bugle'. One of the characters was a guy named Bingo. I was about six years old and they thought I looked like Bingo, so they started calling me Bingo. Then they dropped the 'o' and from then on nobody called me Harry except my mother. And it's stuck ever since.

I sang around the house a lot and mother took me down to a vocal teacher one day, Professor Kranz, and he gave me some scales to run up and down and taught me a few songs. I left his tutorage because my companions teased me – they thought singing was kind of sissy. It was a rough town, Spokane, a mining town, a lumber town, and they thought anybody who took up singing had to be very much of a sissy. I learned something from him, how to vocalise, but I don't think I went back to him more than four or five times. Then I sang, inevitably, at the little parish and school entertainments. Whenever they wanted somebody, why I'd get up and sing a song, and I was about twelve years old then.

My mother and father were both musical. Father played the guitar and mother played the piano. They both appeared in the local theatricals, *The Mikado* and other Gilbert and Sullivan things, and we always had a piano in the house. We had the first phonograph in our neighbourhood. We had the Fearless Quartet and Philip Souza's Band. Later, when they got out the disk, we had one of those. There was music in the house at all times.

I liked John McCormack, he had a beautiful, lyric type of

voice and sang with great sentiment. He sang some beautiful songs, like 'The Rose of Tralee' and 'I Hear a Thrush at Eve', and so many of the great Irish and English songs. And then later on, I was very keen about Al Jolson. He was a great singer, a great performer. When I was sixteen or seventeen, I used to go down and work in the local theatre whenever the great touring shows came through town. I was an assistant with a property department, and whenever Jolson was in town, I always managed to get a job and watch him. I'm sure I picked up a lot of hints from him, not only from his singing but his stage performance. When he came on the stage, he generated an electricity I've never seen duplicated, unless it would be by Frank Sinatra. No one else ever achieved that in my opinion.

I studied for the law. I had a little dance band at the time. I was a singer and the drummer, and I was studying at Gonzaga University. I was studying law part time and going to school part time and playing the drums and singing part time. I thought I could be a lawyer, because I'd been in a lot of elocution contests and belonged to the debating society, and I thought I had a facility for saying things on my feet. I lulled myself into the belief that I could be a great criminal lawyer and the drama of the courts appealed to me. But I found out after I'd been working for this lawyer about six to eight months that I was making as much money playing the drums as he was pursuing the law. So I gave up the law and enlarged my entertainment career.

The piano player in our little band and I worked up some duets together, took off from Spokane and drove all the way to Los Angeles. His name was Al Rinker and he had a sister, named Mildred Bailey, who was working in a Los Angeles nightclub. In my opinion, Mildred was one of the great singers of all time. She'd established herself in a very substantial fashion, and we thought we'd just move in with Mildred and she'd get us set. And that's exactly what happened.

We played all up and down the coast, in the Middle West,

and vaudeville, then finally wound up in Los Angeles. Paul Whiteman was playing the Million Dollar Theatre in Los Angeles, we were playing The Metropolitan. At that time, we'd done pretty well, and he sent a representative over to hear us. He was reasonably pleased with our performance and so we joined Whiteman a week later in Chicago and spent almost three years with him.

I'd been involved in a little automobile accident. I was driving home one night with a young lady. I'd had a few toddies, and a fella ran into me with his car, quite an accident. I took the young lady into the lobby of a nearby hotel to see that she was administered to, and the police arrived and said, 'You appear to have been drinking.' I said, 'Yes.' They said, 'Well come along.' They took me down to the station, locked me up.

The next day, Whiteman got me out on bail because we were right in the middle of a picture. I had to go down about eleven days later for an appearance in front of the judge. I'd been playing golf – I had on golf knickers and loud socks and a loud sweater – so I went down feeling very gaily dressed and sure that there'd be nothing to it. The judge says, 'It says here on the complaint you'd been drinking.' I said, 'Yes.' He said, 'Don't you know there's a prohibition law in the state, in the country?' I said, 'Yes, but nobody pays any attention to it.' 'Well, you'll have thirty days to pay a lot of attention to it.' And there I was for thirty days. The last half of the sentence, though, they let me go out to the set with a policeman. He had the time of his life.

I recall one time they said my ears stuck out too far – looked like a taxi with both doors open – and so they got the make-up man to study them and he glued them back. Then I looked like a whippet in full flight. The glue used to itch and, of course, in those days they used a lot more light when they were lighting a set than they do now and it was very hot. That made the glue come loose and they'd pop out and it'd be 'cut' and back to the make-up department, big glue job again. One day they popped out and I said, they're gonna stay out. By that time, I'd made a few pictures that were moderately successful, so they let them go on that way, sticking out.

Bob Hope and I were both in vaudeville. Oh, he was a gay one then. He had the straw hat and the spats and the cane. And we also belonged to an actors' club called The Friars in New York, where everybody congregated when we weren't working. We started palling around together and then I went on the radio and so did he, and I went out to Hollywood first and then he came three or four years later. I used to work on his radio show and he worked on mine, and the writers on the radio show used to cook up these gags about how fat I was or how hammy he was, niggling one another. From that, the people at Paramount thought, why don't we put these two guys together in a movie? And that's how it developed.

We'd made a picture here at Shepperton Studios and we both liked to play golf, so we found a house in the country and the golf course was right between Shepperton and the house. One day we were doing a scene – it was supposed to be in a harem and the villains had captured us and they decided on a soirée, a big orgy with dancing girls and wine and everything going on, because they thought they were sending us to our death on a moon capsule, and we'd never return. Bob Hope was stretched out on a chaise longue, and girls were curling his hair and another girl was painting his toenails red. I was laying on another chaise longue and they were squirting the wine into me and covering us with oil and frankincense and myrrh – all those things.

We finally finish the scene, the director says 'cut' and we whip over to the golf course, play thirteen holes, and come back in the locker room at Wentworth. We're sitting down and Bob takes off his golf shoes and socks, and I notice two gentlemen sitting on the bench across from us – typical British country types, with the 'tache and the tweed coats. One of them – his eyes looked down to Hope's feet, then he turned to his companion and nudged him, and his companion looked down. They looked at me and I shrugged, and they looked down again at these red toenails. Finally, one of them said to me, 'Mr Crosby, sir, is your friend with the ballet?' And Hope put on his shoes and socks, went out and said not a word.

1972

Memories of Marilyn Monroe

Tony Curtis

Marilyn Monroe was very, very difficult. Her personal madnesses were so destructive that it made her unhappy, and anyone who surrounded her. Consequently, it cost her her life and it had nothing to do with the picture business. Dear Marilyn was a fruit cake, and a fruit cake caught in an environment, in an establishment, in the system, the society – call it what you will – that demanded certain things from her that she was not capable of giving.

The fact that she was a very beautiful woman and had an interesting quality about her only enhanced, I think, that tragedy, because if she hadn't been, people would have left her alone. Somebody would have put her away somewhere, or she'd have been settled down some place where these terrible tensions and drives and power struggles would have just bypassed it. Consequently, she made her life, and everyone else surrounding her, miserable, but that's the way it goes.

I've heard that Billy Wilder, who directed *Some Like it Hot*, said she was a mean seven-year-old girl, and I've got a feeling that's about as good a description of Marilyn. But she could bring to a scene a lot of power. It was difficult for her to put them together, to make moments last.

Takes would be thirty-five for one line, or two lines, and Billy Wilder said to Jack Lemmon and I when we started the picture, 'Now look, as soon as Marilyn gets it right, that's the shot I'm going to print.' He said, 'You guys better know what you're doing. Don't be caught with your finger in your ear!' Well, Jack and I would get in at seven thirty, eight o'clock in the morning. We'd get into our trusses, get into our silk stockings, into all the under-garments, into the make-up department, forty-five minutes in make-up, thirty minutes in hairdressing – by the time we got done, it was two and a half hours. We'd get on the set ready to shoot at ten.

And she wouldn't show up till eleven thirty or twelve. There we were in these shoes – we tried to find places to sit down and kick off our shoes. We had to stay like that all day long, and then finally Marilyn would show up, and we'd go and rehearse it a couple of times, and she'd say, 'I'm ready.' Well, we had to do it. We'd come clobbering in trying to get our make-up in order, because we had to look fresh and we'd been like that now for twelve hours or something ridiculous, and we'd do the scene. And in one of the takes, Jack tripped, just stumbled, but we printed it.

1972

Jack Lemmon

Marilyn Monroe was difficult, but she was divine. She was not temperamental, she just was very late and would be fully made-up but, until she was psyched up and ready, she couldn't come out and face it. It did not bother me as much as it bothered Tony Curtis, but in the second half of the film he had very long scenes with her. I was off dancing with Joe E. Brown with a rose in my teeth. It was just the only way she knew how to work.

One time I won a lot of money from Tony because he said, 'We'll get it by take 40,' and it went up to 47, so I won. She would just stop a scene in the middle, even though it was going fine as far as the director and the other actors went, but if it didn't feel right to her, she would just say, 'Sorry,' and she'd shake her hands to loosen up and relax and we'd do it again. And all she had to do was come in and say, 'Where is that bourbon? Oh, there it is,' and Tony and I were standing there with our wigs and stuff on. And we got up to about take 42 or 43 with, 'Where is that bourbon? Oh, there it is.' That's all there was to it. Billy had given her 85,000 different ways to do it, and nothing had really taken. One of the world's greatest directors, he was at his wits end as to what to do with her now. And finally, just before we did get it, she stopped again, he said, 'Now, possibly, if you . . .' and she said, 'Don't talk to me now, I'll forget how I want to play it.' I have never seen Wilder stopped cold before. But I say this not in any derogatory sense, because nobody was like Marilyn, she was a wonderful comedienne and had a charisma that nobody has had before or since.

1987

2 Comedy

Billy Connolly

Someone once said: 'Billy Connolly is many people, all of them fascinating.' He was the welder in the shipyards of Glasgow who could play the banjo and tell funny stories between songs. Then he became the comedian who occasionally broke into song, and was commercial enough to get into the Top Ten charts. He went on to become the television actor, Hollywood film star, documentary film maker, author and, best of all, God's gift to the talk-show host. Over thirty years of *Parkinson* he appeared fifteen times, always delighting the audience and terrifying the management – never mind the host. I remember the managing director Bill Cotton fretting over Billy's early appearances on *Parkinson*, worrying in case he used four-letter words. 'He's too canny to do that on telly,' I told him. And he was. The fact is Connolly possesses great charm – most of the truly gifted comedians do, if you think about it, which means they can get away with saying just about anything they please. He is the master raconteur and, of all the comedians I interviewed, the one possessed of the greatest array of gifts. He has never appeared on a *Royal Command Performance*. I would love to be present if ever he was asked.

Michael: People say about the Glasgow you come from, you have to be a comedian to live there. Would that be true?

Billy: You have to be able to take a joke if you live there. It's a very grey place. If you've never been there before, it would be depressing. That feeling I get coming into Newcastle – I should imagine people coming to Glasgow get the exact same feeling. But it's a funny place. There's good patter in Glasgow, better than the comics on stage. A guy came up to me in the street – I hope I can get away with this, it's a beauty – he said, 'Hey, Big Yin!' In Scotland they call me Big Yin. He said, 'Did you hear the one about the guy who done his wife in and that?' And I said, 'No.' 'This guy was going up to meet his friend in the pub. He went down and said, "Oh how's it going? How's the wife?" He says, "Oh she's dead." He said, "When?" "Dead, I murdered her," he said. "You're kidding." He said, "No, no, this morning. Dead." And he said, "Look, I'm not talking to you if you keep on talking like that." He said, "Oh, please yourself. I'll show you if you want." So they went up to his tenement building, through the close, into the back green, into the wash-house, and sure enough, there's a big mound of earth, and there's a bum sticking out of it. He says, "Is that her?" and he says, "Aye." He says, "Why'd you leave her bum sticking out for?" He says, "I needed somewhere to park my bike." '

****

Billy: Going into the shipyards was a perfectly natural thing for me. It was like somebody from Aberdeen going to a fishing boat, or somebody from Yorkshire going down a mine. I wanted to be an engineer, and had an engineering certificate when I left school. So I went up to the shipyard and said, 'I'd like to be an engineer,' and he said, 'Yeah, sit over there and Mr Hughes will come and get you.' I sat waiting, and they had welding gear and I went, 'Oh this is great.' He said, 'Just start there and see if you can stick them together.' 'Sure.' After about four days I discovered I was an apprentice welder.

Michael: You joined the Army as well didn't you?

Billy: No, I joined the Territorials. I was fed up with the normal humdrum and there was this big straight guy always marching about the place. He said, 'You should come and join the paratroopers, make you a man,' and I said, 'Fair enough.' I went and got the king's shilling, and away we went. It was a bizarre episode in my life. At one point we were in the Kyrenia mountains, they took us to Cyprus. So for about three days over these mountains, we were chasing a regiment called the Green Howards. We caught one guy, and he worked beside me in the same shipyard. We were sitting up a mountain. I could have ambushed him in the canteen. They were quite humorous these guys, they had a great trick when you were parachuting. A wee light goes on, action stations, and you all stand up in the plane, check your own front, and the back of the guy in front of you. And – it happened to me once, the animals – they wait until it's almost time and they get a hanky, put it inside your parachute and pull it out a wee bit and say, 'Hey, what's that?'

****

Michael: Since last I saw you, much has happened. You've made a lot of movies, including one with Sharon Stone.

Billy: Yes, Sharon, she's nice. She's very good in bed.

Michael: You did a sex scene with her, did you?

Billy: We had a love scene. Incidentally, we were getting along famously, and she's such a big star. She has an entourage and I found the whole thing a bit strange, but in the scene she was really upset. She'd lost her children and was crying, and I'd calm her down. Then, I had to kiss her, which was very pleasant. That scene led to bed and there was no Egyptian PT going on. And I hate that. I've done a sex scene before and they're rotten because the whole thing, it seems to me, is based on hiding the man's genitals and exposing as much of the woman's as you can. You often hear of people with dungarees and crew cuts saying, 'It's because directors are men and they hate women.' Bullshit!

The reason is, if you see the man's willy and it's flaccid, they say, 'He's not shagging at all! This is nonsense! We've been conned! Look at that thing flopping around down there, this is seven bucks I paid here.' But if it's erect, 'God, he's actually giving her one!' And she's on talk shows for the rest of her life denying it, inventing things. 'Oh no, we made a pouch at the side, and he's banging away at the pouch.' This woman I'm supposed to be making love to, she's kneeling on the bed – you get the picture. The director comes over, because you know, sex is an animal act and the British just get it wrong all the time. They take the manners of the dining room into the bedroom, and you can't do that. Except for foreplay. It's good to remember to start at the outside and work your way in. You don't go straight for the money.

But when we came to the bed scene, sex was supposed to be finished, but at that time she had kind of fallen out with me. A wee bit, not serious. She was in a bad mood and she kind of deserved to be. Through no fault of her own, things had gone a bit adrift, and so she was not talking to me, and the director says, 'How do you feel about this scene?' I said, 'Oh I'm fine.' He said, 'You don't mind being in a bed with a woman who's not talking to you?' I said, 'I've been married for a long time! I've been on the road for thirty years, I've been in bed with people whose name escapes me.'

****

Billy: I love *Brief Encounter*.

Michael: What about those accents? I can't get over those.

Billy: 'Oh darling, yes, darling.' My wife and I used to do this thing. Instead of saying, 'Excuse me,' I'd say, 'Excuse one.' And then when we were lying in bed I would say, 'One loves one.' And she would say, 'One reciprocates with ardour.' And then my line is, 'One would love to give one one.'

Michael: How is Pam, by the way?

Billy: Oh Pam's great. She's a shrink now, Dr Connolly. She gets to analyse me on a daily basis.

Michael: She's a sexual psychotherapist?

Billy: She's a psychotherapist, and she specialises in sexual trauma. She speaks dirty to men all day. It's a brilliant job.

Michael: Does she do any field research with you?

Billy: She does research on me, but I'm kind of boring sexually. I would love to be more weird. I've got a sex life like a pigeon. It's a very quick affair. I always wondered about the guys who wear handcuffs and whips and suits of armour. 'You'll get used to my little idiosyncrasies,' he said, while heating the branding iron in the fire. I couldn't. I'd laugh. The one thing you mustn't do in sex is laugh, I've always found. And I think sex is an unnecessary stress and strain on men. We hear about women, usually somebody with a crew cut and in a boiler suit, saying, 'I'm fed up being treated like a sex object.' What? I thought you were a plumber! Whine, whine, moan, moan, 'Typical man.' The stress on men to bang away for days! You look at your watch, your tattoos are sliding onto the floor, you're praying for daylight. Trying not to ejaculate seems to be the whole business. Men have many methods. Some people think of the FA Cup team of 1953. You mustn't think of sex or poof! It's all over. I do the nine times table. I got to 81 once. I did a lap of honour round the bed.

****

Michael: I read that you once said you're an ordinary nutter working out his problems on stage.
Billy: I do that all the time.
Michael: Is there a kind of therapy involved?
Billy: I'm usually telling the truth – exaggerated out of all context. I did a thing about my father taking my picture at the seaside. I could never work the camera, I could never see him in it, and he would say, 'For God's sake, look in it properly.' And I'd look at it and go, 'Oh Christ, I can't see.' And he would be with my sister and he'd go up and whack me. 'Now take the bloody picture!' and I would cry. I would explain to the audience that I used to do that yodelling crying, you've probably heard children, or maybe you've done it yourself. And your father says, 'What's wrong with you, what the hell's that sound, what're you saying?' I was doing it on stage one night and I burst into tears. I was too close, I was doing it too well. I had forgotten to step back a wee bit. It's like singing the blues, you should be doing it from the outside looking in.

****

Michael: You've talked about your childhood, which was poor, but also funny.

Billy: It was great.

Michael: It can't have been great.

Billy: Well no, there was misery involved, but you can leave the house. You're not stuck there for your whole life. I had great pals and we dived around doing great boy things. And another thing, I refused to do my homework for many years and kept promising I would do it. I got beaten every day and I grew to really like it. It was a real high-noon situation every morning with the teacher and me. The worst thing that can happen to you in a tough situation like Glasgow, or Liverpool, or those towns, was a good punch in the nose, and you realise it isn't all that painful. You go, 'Oh, that will do.' So you want to fight all the time.

Michael: I can see the point you're making about that kind of physical abuse, but what about the other kind of abuse that you suffered?

Billy: The sexual abuse?

Michael: From your father. That must have been a terrible thing to have dealt with and understood as a child – you were ten years old when it happened to you. You kept it secret all your life until you told your wife about it. First of all, tell us how you told Pam.

Billy: It was the day of my father's death. He was about to die and we were downstairs for a minute, and I said, 'Look, I don't know what to do,' because I'd never confronted him and I felt very, very guilty. It wasn't until later I read that very few victims – though I don't see myself as a victim – confront the person who did it. He's your dad, you're desperate for him to love you and you try your whole life to do things he would like. If he loves football, you try, and you're not good. You want to be a cyclist but he calls cycling a 'Jessie sport' and says you run like a girl. So I'll be a mountaineer, I'll do something. And your whole life, you try to impress him and it never really comes because as you get older, his attitude towards you gets stranger and stranger, and he expects you to confront him and you're not going to do it. This silence develops between you, which is very odd – the great unsaid. And it goes from there to the guy giving you moral lectures about how to behave and how you're letting the side down.

Michael: Precisely. You should turn round and say, 'You should bloody well talk.'

Billy: No. That's what you think you would do, but what happens is this. You're young and it gets kind of confusing, and you think, 'Did it happen? Am I inventing the whole thing?' And then later it comes back. Of course it was real. Don't be stupid. The bit I always remember was the relief when we went on holiday, because we were in different rooms then.

Michael: Yes, and you were freed from it.

Billy: I was dying to tell people. I was dying to try to make fun of it, because I'd made fun of the violence. And I broached it a couple of times, I threw out a couple of little feelers.

Michael: Yes, I know.

Billy: But there's no colder subject on Earth.

Michael: It's interesting, the way you edited your life on stage. One of your funniest routines was going on holiday and wearing those . . .

Billy: Oh, the Big Willy swimming trunks! Swimming trunks that get jealous of seaweed. The wool gets heavy and the whole thing starts to sag and, oh God, it gets huge.

Michael: You live in Australia now, you see these macho guys strutting up and down the beach, and they've never swum in the north.

Billy: They've never swum in the North Sea. They've never made that noise as the wave hits your testicles – 'Whoa.' I remember that so very well.

****

Billy: Don't go! Please don't go. It's the only television I get. Nobody else wants me.

Michael: Is that true? Wherever you go in the world you're rejected by talk shows?

Billy: Rejected by everybody except you.

Michael: Ah bless. Well that's my job, we take in stray dogs. First of all, happy birthday.

Billy: Thank you very much indeed. I'm sixty-five. I'm an old age pensioner, which is very weird. People keep congratulating me as if I've done something. It's like you've just finished the marathon, and I just stayed awake for sixty-five years. But it's weird getting old, weird things happen to you. My nose hair has accelerated. All my other hair grows at the same old speed but I used to trim my nose hair once every fourteen years. Now it's three times a week. You take for granted your body knows what it's doing, so you think what's going to happen to me that I'm going to need long nasal hair? Tie it on top of my head or something? Or maybe it's the ultimate comb-over.

Michael: Are there any virtues to growing old?

Billy: Yeah. I used to think about going to bed to have sex and now I just think about going to bed. But the biggest terror I have of growing old is smelling of pee.

Michael: Are you at that stage yet?

Billy: I don't smell of pee but I live in terror of smelling of pee. I often wonder if you can smell it when it's you. When you go to a farm, you think, good Jesus, how can these people live with this? Ten minutes later, you're going, 'Oh, that smell's away. It must have been in a breeze.' You get used to it.

Another thing is I've started making involuntary noises, straining. I pick things up or get out of a chair and go, 'Ahhhh!' My cure for that is to change the conversation so as they don't hear you doing it. You think, I must get out the chair so you start a conversation. 'What about Iraq, isn't that whole thing a dreadful mess?' And they say, 'Aye, it's terrible.' And then you go, 'Ahhhh, the whole thing's a disgrace if you ask me!' And don't get into a beanbag chair. You mightn't ever get out. After you're thirty-five, don't go near a beanbag. You'll be flopping about like a turtle on its back. You have to make excuses. You say to the kids,

'Oh, off you go to bed. I want to watch Discovery Channel here. There's a great programme about bats shitting in a cave.' And when they've gone, you can roll on to the floor.

1975–2007

Bob Hope

In the days when stand-up comedians wore tuxedos, shiny shoes and slicked back hair, Bob Hope was the defining figure. He had the poise, the polished delivery and the best jokes gag writers could supply. Most of all, he had a comedy persona recognised worldwide because of his success as a movie star, in particular his partnership with Bing Crosby in the *Road* films of the forties and fifties. It was a blessed pairing, with Crosby the amiable contrast to Hope's treacherous, scheming, avaricious, double-crossing, lecherous buffoon, a man so conceited he would purr at himself in the mirror. He was a fascinating man to interview because his story was so rich. An immigrant from England, he went through vaudeville, radio, Hollywood, and continued working in his eighties and nineties. He died in 2003 aged a hundred.

I left England when I was four – something about girls and I had to leave. I remember being hit on the head when I was trying to protect my dog in Bristol, and I still have the mark. My mother was a concert singer in Wales, and I sang and then I danced. I had to announce an act in New Castle, Pennsylvania, a Scotsman I knew, Marshall Walker and his Whiz Bang Review. I got out there and I said, 'He's coming on, he's a Scotsman, I know him. He got married in the backyard so the chickens could get the rice,' and the audience laughed at that. The next day I said, 'And he also shot his wife because she bought vanishing cream,' and they liked that, too, and so I kept adding jokes. I was doing five or six minutes of material before I finished the three days, and I decided then to start doing single monologues.

In those days, if you had anything at all, you could get work, because there was so much vaudeville. You had it here in England. You could get a lot of weeks here in all kinds of theatres. You had a lot of music halls where a young guy could really get started. I wasn't known, of course, when I started, and I starved for about a year.

I was working for $5 a night. I was out of town, and trying to get going. Then I changed my name, from Leslie Hope to Bob, because I thought that was chummier and maybe somebody would like me that way, but I was wrong for a long while. I finally did get one date and it made me – it was for $25 at one theatre, and from that time on I got very lucky and moved on.

There were some tremendous acts. This fellow had a great alligator act but he had a very tough time for a while. They finally booked him for three days in Patterson, New Jersey. He used to wrestle an alligator in a tank, and he was such a sensation when he opened in Patterson that they decided to hold him for the full week. The manager of the theatre was just so happy, but he noticed on the holdover that he wasn't getting the same excitement, and so he called the act's agent and he said, 'I'm sorry I held him over. I'm not getting the same excitement.' The agent said, 'Well, I'll come over and see him.'

He looked at the show on a Thursday night, went backstage and said to the guy, 'You know, you had a great chance here with this act where you wrestle the alligator in the tank, and everybody was talking about you being held over. Marvellous. Now the manager's disappointed because he's not getting the same excitement,' and the actor said, 'He's disappointed? You should think how I feel. The alligator died Tuesday night.'

We did a lot of things. We danced with the Siamese twins, Daisy and Violet Hilton. They were joined at the hip. They were wonderful gals, and very romantic, by the way. It's a true story, at one theatre she fell in love with the stage manager and they went out. She came back a couple of years later, walked in and said to the stage manager, 'Remember me?' They got married. All four of them, and they worked it out.

How did I get into movies? I was in a show called *Ziegfeld Follies* at the Winter Garden Theatre in New York, singing a song called 'Can't Get Started With You' with a red-headed showgal, who later became Eve Arden. A producer and director saw me and they wanted me to do a juvenile lead in this broadcast. So there I was and I went in, and that's where I sang 'Thanks For The Memory'.

How did I meet Bing? I was a boy scout and I saw this old lady waiting for the traffic lights, and I helped her across and it turned out to be Bing. No, I met Bing I think around 1932, and we played the Capital Theatre, New York, and luckily for me, we did an act together, like two farmers meeting on the street – the president of the Coca-Cola company meeting the president of the Pepsi Cola company on the street. When I went out to Hollywood, before the *Road* pictures, I went down to the Delmar Turf Club bar, which Bing owned, part of, and we did our act together. The boys from Paramount saw us and said, 'Boy, these guys really work good together, let's put 'em in something,' and they put us in a picture called *Road to Singapore*. And that's how the whole thing started.

We entertained the troops from 1941 to 1972. It's the most exciting part of my life, and the most emotional. There was more gratification connected with that than with anything, because of the response and the feeling about it – the feeling about getting out with these guys who were making the sacrifice and doing a great job for the country. We played here in England in 1943, twelve weeks, came back in 1945 and played another twelve weeks. You'd have to go to understand it with those type of audiences and the feeling about it.

Do you know the idiot cards we used to take material from, alongside the camera? Just the fact that the idiot cards were late in Saigon probably saved us from really getting hurt. We were supposed to stay at the Brinks Hotel and the idiot cards were late coming off the plane. We didn't want to leave them out of the convoy, so we waited for them for fifteen minutes. Five minutes away from the hotel, the hotel was blown up – ninety-nine people injured and two killed, and we were supposed to be there. When they found out later, when they captured the rubber plantation outside of Saigon, the communiqué said that the bombing of the Brinks Hotel missed the Bob Hope Show by ten minutes due to a faulty timing device. I'm kind of in love with idiot cards.

People come up and tell me jokes all the time. Somebody told me the other day about an Italian who wanted to join the Mafia, and they sent him out to audition to blow up a car, and he burned his lips on the exhaust pipe.

1975

George Burns

George Burns was another vaudevillian who lived to be a hundred. With his wife, Gracie Allen, he formed a long-standing comedy partnership, which triumphed in radio, television and movies. His relationship with his wife is a wonderful love story, which he recalled with the marvellous humour that made him such an engaging interviewee. He was eighty when we met and had just won an Oscar for Best Supporting Actor in Neil Simon's *The Sunshine Boys*. He worked until he died. The *New York Times* said: 'Even as he aged he seemed ageless.'

We were seven sisters and five brothers. We were very poor but we didn't know we were poor – we thought everybody was poor. We lived in three rooms and slept on the floor, but my mother once said, 'You're very fortunate, you kids, there's a lot of people have no floor to sleep on.' I don't know what they slept on? And my father was very, very religious – very orthodox, which I'm not. And he had a beard that went from the fourth floor down to the street. I never would use the steps. I used to shimmy down on his beard.

I sang with three other kids – the Peewee Quartet – at saloons and on ferry boats, and we'd pass the hat around afterwards. On ferry boats, fellows used to take these rides to make love to their girls. They didn't want to hear us sing, and the songs we sang were ridiculous.

I loved show business all my life. Even though I didn't work, I always tried to look like an actor. I smoked a cigar, and I once found a pair of pince-nez glasses with a big ribbon. I wore those. I had no money, and I'd put on a little make-up to have people think I was in show business. Then I'd go to 42nd Street in Broadway, where the agents were, and I'd ride up and down the elevator. I thought that maybe some booker might see me. I might get a job. And the elevator boy said to me, 'Don't you play anything but this elevator?'

I did anything. Anything you'd ask me to do, I would do. I couldn't get a job with the same name twice. I was doing this act as Harry Pearce, and somehow I was booked into a little vaudeville theatre on the Lower East Side of New York. In those days, the contract had a no-cancellation clause in it, which meant the manager couldn't cancel us. I got $15 for three days – $5 a day. I went on and did my act, and the manager was waiting for me when I left the stage and he said, 'Look kid, that act of yours could close my theatre. You're booked here for three days for $15. Here's the $15 and go home.' I said, 'Not me. I'm booked for the three days, I'll play the three days.' He said, 'I'll give you $20 to go home!' I said, 'No. You didn't like my first performance? For my second show, I'll change my songs. I'll open with "Tiger Girl" and then I'll sing "In the Heart of a Cherry" and then I'll do my big closing number.'

He says, 'I'll make it $25!' And I said, 'No, I'm booked for three days. I'm a performer. I'm going to stay the three days and not only that, I've got cards printed.' He says, 'OK kid, you can stay, but you give me back the key to the men's room,' which was kind of bad, because that's where I was dressing. And let me tell you something, when you don't go to the men's room for three days, it doesn't help your singing. In fact, after the second day I didn't dare to do my yodelling finish. Those were the kind of acts I did.

I did all kinds of acts. I did a skating act. I did a ballroom-dancing act. I worked with a seal. I worked with a dog. The seal wasn't really my act. I was living in a little boarding house on 45th Street then. This man was living there, and he worked with the seals. He was booked into the Dewey Theatre in 14th Street and he got sick and asked me to take his place. I told him, 'Don't be silly.' I said, 'I've never worked with a seal. I wouldn't know what to do.' He says, 'You don't have to worry about it, the seal does the whole thing.' He says, 'The curtain goes up and the seal goes on a little platform and you're standing there with a ball in your hand and your pockets full of fish. And you just throw the ball to the seal, and the seal flips the ball. He juggles it, and throws it back to you and you throw him a piece of fish and he applauds with his flippers. And at the finish of the act there's a rack of horns and he goes to the back of the horns and he blows into the horns and plays "Yankee Doodle".' He says, 'At the finish of "Yankee Doodle", he presses a lever and two American flags come up and you throw him a piece of fish and as he's applauding with his flippers you're taking bows, and the curtain comes down.'

And I opened at the Dewey Theatre and got away with it. But that night I had a date with a very pretty girl who was also in show business. I was afraid to meet her because when you do four shows a day with your pockets full of fish, you don't smell too good. But I met her and she never noticed it because she was doing an act with Fink's Mules. In fact, she complimented me on my aftershave lotion.

I was very bad until I met Gracie. I was bad when I went with Gracie. Later on, I stole some of Gracie's talent, and I amounted to something. But I went with this girl and we did a ballroom-dancing act. And it was really a bad act. To give you an idea how little I knew about show business, our opening number was a Russian mazurka and we were dressed in Spanish clothes. We thought it was a Spanish dance! And she used to wear a big comb in her hair that pressed on a nerve and eventually took her away. I never loved her and she never loved me, but we were booked for thirty-six weeks, and her father wouldn't let me take her out of town unless I married her. I wasn't going to cancel thirty-six weeks. I was in love with show business! So I married her, we played thirty-six weeks, we were divorced and that's when they took her away. She was a nice girl, but the only thing is, she was a Jewish girl, came from a very orthodox family, and in those days they didn't shave under the arms. And she used to do a pivoting finish, and I'd step on her hair. It would hurt her! I lie a lot, but you know.

OK, Gracie! So I'm playing in New Jersey, and there was a girl on the bill who was the headliner. Her name was Rena Arnold. There was Gracie and Rena Arnold, and another girl. They lived together, these three girls. They were all in show business. Gracie was a dramatic, Irish actress. She was not a comedienne. She came backstage to see Rena, and Rena told her that 'Smith and Lorraine are going to split up'. So she went out to see us work and she says, 'Yeah, I'd like to work with that fella Smith,' who's me.

We met, and three weeks later we did an act together. I had an act in my pocket that I took from college humour and Whizz-bang. I could always switch jokes and I had this act where I was the comedian. I had on wide pants and a short coat and a red tie that used to swivel around, and a turned-up hat, and I'd skip out on the stage. I was funny. And Gracie came out. She was nicely dressed, and she was the straight woman. Everybody laughed at the questions and nobody laughed at the answers. So I gave Gracie all the funny stuff after that, and that's how we got started.

I'll never get married again. Our marriage was a big success because we never worked at it. Gracie didn't marry me because I was a great lover. She married me for laughs. I got more laughs in bed than I did when I played Las Vegas! We never argued about marriage, that was not our business. Our business was show business. And they say that marriage and work can't mix – it's not true. And don't forget that while we were married for thirty-eight years, we lived together, we dressed together, we ate together, we were on the stage together. We were not together thirty-eight years – we were together three times that. And it worked fine, there were no problems.

1976

Ken Dodd

If I had to give advice to any aspiring young comedian, embarking upon a career of trying to make people laugh, I would advise them to seek out Ken Dodd in concert and sit, marvel and learn. They would soon discover the most important lesson of all – that being a funny man is not the same as making a career in comedy. It helps but it is only the beginning. Dodd is a master of comedy because he has worked at it, and dissected it to the point of creating a map analysing which jokes work where. On stage, when he demonstrates the full repertoire of music-hall comedy, he becomes an orchestra of laughter. First, he tames the audience; then he titillates their 'chuckle muscles' until they can laugh no more. Only then does he let them go.

At the age of eighty-two he is still working, still brightening the lives of the audience, who leave the theatre convinced that in the morning the sun will be shining. Ken Dodd is a bringer of joy who ought to be available on prescription – ageless and irreplaceable.

Michael: Were you a funny man at school?

Ken: Yes, I was teacher's pet. I used to sit in a cage at the back of the classroom. I went to a mixed school – I wouldn't drink anything else. When I was three, I used to read *The Wizard*, *Hotspur* and *The Rover* and that's how it all started. One day in *The Wizard* I read this advertisement: 'Fool your teachers, amaze your friends. Send sixpence in stamps.' So I did and got this book on how to become a ventriloquist. It had a little bird warbler you put in your mouth, and months later, through going in the woods and lying in the long grass, I became an ornithologist. People say it affects your eyesight, but it never has with me.

Michael: Your first job wasn't in show business, was it?

Ken: I worked with my father in the coal business and then I was on the knocker – going round selling pots and pans and tickling sticks. I think that's where the 'missus' bit started. All my life I've sold things and served. I try to be of service to the public. At one time, I used to have a bucket and pan round; now I have a tickle round.

Michael: When you started making people laugh professionally, what kind of places did you work?

Ken: You can't make people laugh – you can only give people a reason to laugh. Laughter is inside you, and as a comic, all you do is touch the spring of laughter. You're all born with a chuckle muscle in the middle of your diagram. It works its way up, past your clack and out through your titter-box. It's like an attack of wind. As a baby, you're born with a chuckle muscle and if you don't use it, it will wither and drop off.

Michael: How did you begin making people laugh?

Ken: I got some jokes, and whenever I used to play a club, I'd go in and ask the steward for a cork. It wasn't that I was a nervous performer. I used to burn it and put a big moustache on, because at fifteen I didn't think I had the authority to tell gags to grown-ups. I'd seen an advertisement somewhere that said, 'Arnold Ramsbottom, plumber and artificial leg maker'. That tickled me, so I called myself

Professor Yaffle Chuckabutty, Operatic Tenor and Sausage-Knotter, and I used to go round telling gags at clubs.

****

Ken: My dad always used to say to me, 'You must be original. There can only be one of everything.' I'm a one-off. The doctor said, "There's nothing you can do about it.' So I capitalised on the teeth and the hair, and I used to say, 'I'm the only one who can eat a tomato through a tennis racket. I'm the only one who can kiss a girl and nibble her ear at the same time.'

Michael: What sort of performer were you in those young days, because today you've got the most extraordinary control over an audience. You know exactly how to play to them.

Ken: What I lacked in skill I tried to make up for in enthusiasm. I love enthusiasm. I love anybody who really gets stuck in to a job. You can be the world's greatest dancer, singer, impressionist but the things you need more than anything else in show business are enthusiasm and heart. You've really got to love your audience and love what you're doing.

****

Michael: You've analysed the regional difference in humour, haven't you?

Ken: When I turned professional, common sense told me the thing to do was to find out what you're selling. Are you selling happiness? Are you selling laughter? Are you selling jokes? What is a joke? So I used to go to all the public libraries and I read everybody who'd ever written anything about comedy and laughter, from Aristotle to Freud. I started touring all the halls and kept notebooks with different gags listed. You can tell a joke in Glasgow but they won't laugh at it in Manchester. They can't hear it. There are differences. The Scots like their humour crisp, and won't stand any long jokes, particularly from an

Englishman. I played the house of terror, the Glasgow Empire, and the first time I went out the manager said to me, 'Right, no football gags,' because he didn't want the place taken apart by rival Celtic and Rangers fans. Scots like quick jokes, and Londoners love their comics. If you go well with a London audience, they'll take you on for life, like Max Miller, or the Crazy Gang.

Michael: What's the worst kind of audience for a comedian to play?

Ken: The hardest audience? The one that hasn't paid. I always feel very honoured, very privileged, when people pay good money to see me doing something that, if they saw me doing it in the street, I'd get locked up for! I remember watching you on this programme, interviewing Dr Bronowski, and at the end of the show you said to him, 'You're one of the world's wisest men. How would you like to see the future of the world?' He said, 'I would like to see a world in which everybody enjoyed their job.' I enjoy mine, every second of it. But I would never want to give offence. I love sexy jokes. One of these glossy magazines rang me up when the pornography debate was on and asked, 'What is your description of the word "pornography"?' I said, 'Pornography is anything that degrades the human spirit.' There's nothing wrong in being sexy. If God invented anything better, he kept it for himself. I'm sure he doesn't mind us having a few laughs now and again. I prefer to say that I celebrate honeymoon jokes: 'By jove, Missus, this hotel caters specially for honeymoon couples. You can see the scorch marks on the blankets.'

****

Michael: How do you go about constructing an act?

Ken: The first thing you have to do as a comedian, you have to learn a bit of humility and let people laugh at you. One of the most difficult things is to take that. When you're good-looking like me, it's very difficult to do, so you have to have funny props, funny hats and things like that. The most important thing for any comic on stage is to make friends with his audience. After all, when people have come to watch you and be amused, you have to get yourself in with the audience and build a bridge between you and them. Gracie Fields used to say, 'It was like an invisible silver thread between you and the audience.' Actors may talk about rapport, but with me, I'm going to build a bridge.

****

Michael: There's a lot of anger in a lot of comics and comedy, but you are very benign. How would you describe yourself?

Ken: I'm optimistic – by jove what a beautiful day! What a beautiful day for putting your kilt on upside down and saying, 'How's this for a shuttlecock?' What a beautiful day for ramming your cucumbers through the vicar's letterbox and saying, 'Look out, the Martians are coming.'

Michael: Comics observe things, don't they?

Ken: There are all types of comedians. I'm a patter man, a sort of jolly Uncle Joe. My heroes were people such as Charlie Chester. And then you get the clowns who are very visual, but I've always been cursed with these good looks. You want to watch ageism. When you get to fifty, you've lived too long!

Michael: But you're still working.

Ken: Age doesn't matter unless you're a cheese. People retire when they stop what they don't want to do and start what they do want to do. I love it – I'm stage-struck. I can't wait to slave over a hot audience.

****

Michael: What ambition do you have left after fifty-four years on stage?

Ken: I have two projects. One of them is to persuade people to have a national archive of humour, and the other is to play every theatre in Great Britain.

Michael: You've done that, haven't you?

Ken: Not quite. I've been to the Shetlands twice, right down to the Channel Islands. All British audiences want to do is laugh – they're with you all the way. One thing humour does teach you is that the secret of happiness is to plant a seed and watch it grow. You can grow a family, a show, a business, but you plant something and see it grow. And you must feel you're necessary. When you're not, off you go. And these words of wisdom contribute to comedy: when things look black, take them to the laundry. Never put off till tomorrow what you can do today, because if you do it today and like it, you can do it again tomorrow!

1980 and 2007

Tommy Cooper

In his biography of Tommy Cooper, John Fisher observed: 'For most of the time to be in his company was to bask in the sun. To walk through the street with him on the cloudiest day was to experience the glow manifested towards him by passers-by, as if a hurdy gurdy were playing and a fun fair lurked around the corner.'

He was a comedian of great gifts. Again Fisher (and he knew Cooper better than most) is allowed an opinion on the subject: 'At a combined level of skill and technique, innocence and cunning, wisdom and wonder, eccentricity and human fallibility, there has been nobody in British show business quite like him.' Maybe the most attractive fact about a very remarkable human being was that he never knew why we loved him so much. He never understood how funny he was. Sadly, when he died, he was still wondering.

Michael: Where did the fez come from?
Tommy: The fez?
Michael: The fez, yes.

Tommy: The fez came when I was in Egypt. I was in the Army and we did a show at the YMCA. I used to wear a pith helmet and one day I forgot to bring it with me. These waiters used to walk around with fezes and long white beards, so I took one off a waiter's head, and I've worn one ever since.

Michael: Well, I'm amazed that you were in the war. Which war was that, the Boer War?

Tommy: Boer War? No, it wasn't, no. The Cod War. You've seen me, haven't you? On a tin of sardines?

Michael: You were actually in the Horse Guards, weren't you?

Tommy: That's right.

Michael: What was that like?

Tommy: Very good.

Michael: You enjoyed it, did you?

Tommy: Yes, I was in the Horse Guards and I was stationed once in Pirbright – that's in Surrey. We were under canvas, and then we used to get up and gallop over the mountains, and then we'd gallop up the other mountains and down and over the waters, through the fences, and gallop along the fields and over the mountains again and straight back to camp. And the next day I went out again and I took a horse with me.

Michael: It's hard to imagine you on a horse. How do you manage?

Tommy: Well, they're big horses – seventeen hands. No feet, just hands. It was very good, really. As a recruit I didn't know this, but when you put the girth around the horse, the horse blows itself out because it doesn't want the girth to be tight. So what you're supposed to do is just wait for a little while. He looks like he's ready but he's a little bit suspicious. Then, all of a sudden, you've got to tighten it, quick. But I didn't know this, so he had his stomach blown out and I thought the girth was tight. So we're on parade and they said, 'Right, in front of your horses.' We do that. 'Right, prepare to mount.' We put our foot in the stirrup and they said, 'Mount.' I pressed my foot in the stirrup, and the saddle and I went right underneath the horse.

Michael: They're very strict with discipline, the Guards, aren't they? Did you have any trouble with that at all?

Tommy: Well, as ever, we had a sergeant, and they used to call him 'Caller of Horses'. We were under canvas and they used to call us out for roll call. But at four o'clock in the morning, pitch black, the corporal major used to come out with a hurricane lamp and he used to say, 'Good morning, men,' and we used to say, 'Good morning, lamp.' We couldn't see him. And this corporal major, big man he was, hated anybody with a face. The sergeant used to come round to wake us up in the morning, and he used to say, 'Good morning! Good morning! Good morning!' with a bayonet in his hand.

Michael: Let's talk a bit about your act. Have you ever used animals?

Tommy: Yes, as a matter of fact I have. I've got one here. I brought this back from Africa.

Michael: What is it?

Tommy: It's a mongoose.

Michael: A mongoose.

Tommy: A man-eating mongoose.

Michael: I didn't know there was such a thing.

Tommy: You won't see it. As a matter of fact, it's very unpredictable. Sometimes it's friendly, sometimes it's not. I got this when I was in the middle of the Congo jungle and a friend of mine was there, stationed with me. He used to write home to his mother, and I remember one day he wrote saying, 'Dear Mum, I'm out here in the heart of the Congo jungle, eating bananas and coconuts all day long. I'm getting brown as a berry. Incidentally, the tribe are head-shrinkers. They can shrink your head to the size of a small orange.' And he puts, 'PS, can you get me a bowler hat size one and a half, send it over.'

1979

Eric and Ernie

It is difficult nowadays to explain to people who were not around at the time the bond between Morecambe and Wise and the British public. They didn't just make the nation laugh – they comforted and reassured us that, so long as they were around, everything was OK. No comedy duo, not before and certainly never since, used the medium with the inspirational technique invented by Eric and Ernie. You felt they were in the room with you, and even the plays wot Ernie wrote, for all the big names and epic grandeur of events, portrayed a sense of intimacy. And when Eric and Ern shared a bed, even the most sensitive prude and outraged bigot found nothing to complain about.

It helped they were pleasant and amicable men as well as great entertainers. In 1973, we booked Eric and Ernie and Raquel Welch on the same show. We thought the lads would have some fun. So did Miss Welch and she wasn't playing, so I interviewed them separately, Raquel first. I asked her if she had always been beautiful. She said not until her 'equipment' arrived, which caused a stir and accounts for what follows.

Eric: I was fifteen when my equipment arrived. I was forty when it left. I'm forty-five now. I think it's coming back again.

Michael: There's hope for us all.

****

Michael: How young were you when you first went on stage?

Ernie: On stage? Do you mean professionally? Or actually right at the beginning?

Michael: Yourself.

Ernie: Oh seven. I used to perform with my father, do a double act in clubs all over the country.

Michael: Really?

Ernie: It's what we used to do, yes.

Eric: Around Leeds. You didn't do it all over the country.

Ernie: Well, we used to go in the country and in Leeds as well. That's what I meant.

Eric: It was like a joke.

Ernie: It was, yes. Not much like a joke.

Michael: What were you doing? What kind of double act was it?

Ernie: It was a very good double act.

Eric: It was. I never saw it but I've heard about it. It was very nice.

Ernie: What used to happen was I used to . . .

Eric: He used to work with his dad, you know.

Ernie: This is very sentimental, and very dear to me. My dad and I used to go round the clubs.

Eric: What was the name? You used to have a name for the act.

Ernie: Used to be called Bert Carson and Kid.

Eric: Yeah, he was Bert Carson. He was a midget, you know.

****

Michael: When was the first time that you met?

Eric: What? Him and I? Yesterday morning, wasn't it?

Ernie: Yes it was, actually.

Eric: I wish you'd introduced us. I've no idea who he is.

Ernie: Where did we first meet?

Eric: My audition.

Ernie: That's right. I saw him give his audition.

Eric: I won the Lancashire and Cheshire Contest, in Hoylake. The first prize was an audition – no money – just an audition, which I gave. He was with Jack Hylton at the time, and saw my audition.

Ernie: But what did you do?

Eric: I did double acts in those days, didn't I?

Ernie: Yes.

Eric: It was Flanagan and Allen, I used to do.

Ernie: Flanagan and Allen he did. On his own.

Michael: By yourself?

Eric: Yes.

Michael: How did you do that?

Eric: I had false legs. True! No, I just used to put this battered top on and sing.

Ernie: You used to do that a lot.

****

Michael: The only time you've been separated in thirty-four years, in a professional sense, was during the war, wasn't it?

Eric: That's right, he was on their side.

Ernie: Yes we were.

Michael: You were a Bevin boy.

Eric: I was down the mines.

Ernie: And I was in the merchant navy.

Michael: Good lord, what was being a miner like?

Eric: Dark. It's quite frightening quite honestly. I was eighteen and in for eleven months altogether. I was twenty-eight when I came out. It's a frightening thing. I never saw the pavements dry. Six to two I was on that shift. And no pit had baths. I used to go home and fill the tub. And black sheets.

Michael: Black sheets?

Eric: My landlady had black sheets for miners. Seventeen and six a week I used to get.

Michael: Really?

Ernie: And he was overpaid.

Michael: What about the merchant navy, what did you do there?

Ernie: Went up and down the coast.

Michael: Doing what?

Eric: He was on the collier.

Ernie: On the collier, I was. He was digging coal, I was moving it.

Michael: So you're still together really.

Ernie: I found him among the lumps one day. 'What are you doing here, Eric?'

Eric: Not a lot.

Ernie: We used to go down to the Gas Light and Coke Company. I was on the boat.

Eric: Sounds like a juggling act, doesn't it?

Ernie: What?

Eric: Gas Light and Coke.

Ernie: It's been very lucky for us, coal. I always get a feeling with coal. I bought my wife a coal ring. It's always been lucky for us.

****

Michael: The act was almost brought to a premature end four years ago, when you had your heart attack?

Eric: I'll do anything for a laugh.

Ernie: How are you feeling?

Eric: Oh, great.

Michael: It seems a daft question, but I wonder was there a funny side to it, Eric?

Eric: What, the illness? Well, in a way there was. We were working at this club in Blackley. I got a bit of a twinge in my arm and I happened to say to Ernie, 'I don't feel too good. I might go home tonight.'

Ernie: So, 'I'll sign the autograph,' I said.

Eric: 'You sign the autograph.' I drove home in the car towards Leeds, and the pains got worse and worse. I had both arms across the chest and I started to come out in a sweat. Funnily enough, I didn't realise it was a heart attack. Had I thought it was a heart attack, I'd have had a heart attack and died. I thought, 'Well, I'd better put myself into a hospital.' It was getting worse, and it would have been about half past one in the morning, so I stopped a fella in Leeds and said, 'I don't feel very well. Do you think you could take me to a hospital?' A fella called Walter Butterworth, I'll never forget him. It wasn't his real name, but I'll never forget him. And he said, 'Yes, oh aye. Hey, you're Morecambe and White!' And I said, 'Morecambe and Wise, yes.' He looked at my car and said, 'Oh, I've never driven one of these. I'm in the Territorials. I've only driven a tank.' I got to the stage where I couldn't have cared less.

So, he took me to a hospital and it was locked. There

Bing Crosby was so laid back you imagined interviewing him in a hammock.

Dorothy Parker said meeting Orson Welles was like meeting God without lying.

James Cagney was more than a film star – he was the Statue of Liberty with a gun in his hand.

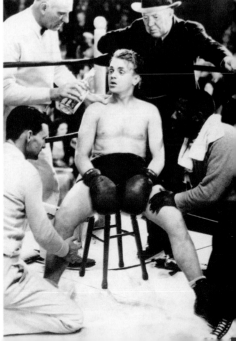

Kirk Douglas shared with James Cagney the physiognomy of the all-American dream.

No one represented the Wild West, the American frontier spirit, better than John Wayne.

Jimmy Stewart: 'I'm a plodder. I'm the inarticulate man who tries ... When I'm at the head of the wagon train, for some reason we get across the river.'

David Niven satisfied that particular affection the English have for a man who succeeds effortlessly without seeming to stop smiling.

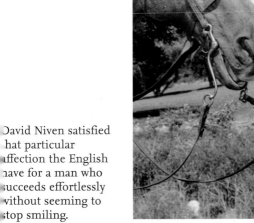

'I don't like horses. I don't like riding. They have to pay me a lot of money to get me on a horse. It's dangerous. A man can get killed!' Henry Fonda.

Franklin D. Roosevelt said of Shirley Temple, 'It is a splendid thing that for just fifteen cents an American can go to a movie and look at the smiling face of a baby and forget his troubles.'

'He even chews gum in time,' Gene Kelly remarked of Fred Astaire.

Sisters in suffering, Tony Curtis and Jack Lemmon had to endure up to forty re-takes a scene when filming *Some Like It Hot* with Marilyn Monroe.

The formidable Bette Davis, who is said to have christened the Oscars after her husband's rear end.

I first met Peter Kay when he was the warm-up man on *Parkinson*. He once told me, 'One day I'll walk down these stairs. You'll introduce me on your show.'

Someone once said, Billy Connolly is many people, all of them fascinating.'

Bob Hope found international movie stardom in the 'Road pictures' with Bing Crosby and Dorothy Lamour – *Road to Rio* was the fifth out of seven. In the days when stand-up comedians wore tuxedos, shiny shoes and slicked back hair, Bob Hope was the defining figure.

Ken Dodd is a bringer of joy who ought to be available on prescription.

were some French windows and he was banging on the French windows while I'm stood at the side. The windows open and a fella in braces and a pair of pants says, 'You can't come in here. This isn't a proper hospital. You want the main one up the road.' He explained where it was and Walter drove me there. I got out of the car and he ran up a hill, went in there and tried to get me some form of wheelchair. He's there five minutes, and I'm waiting, so I start to walk up the hill like Quasimodo. I go in there and he's obviously said to the fella behind the counter, 'Eric Morecambe's out there and he's not very well, could I have . . .' and the fella wouldn't let him have a chair as far as I could make out. So I walked in and the fella looked at me and went, 'Ho, ho, yes,' and says to all the boils and cuts and slashes in the outpatients, 'Eh, 'tis him!' So I said, 'My real name is Bartholomew.' I never tell anybody that. He says, 'You don't look too good, son.' I said, 'No. I'd like to put myself into hospital.' He said, 'Right. Name?' I thought, well, I won't say Bartholomew, so I said, 'Morecambe.' 'Address?' which I gave him, 'Age?' which I lied about. He said, 'You don't look too well. You'd better lie down on that thing.' I lay down on the stretcher and the next thing I know I'm being injected. This Walter Butterworth is sat with me and I said, 'I'd like to say thank you very much for all your help and everything.' He said, 'Oh that's all right. My mates won't believe this.' And – these are the exact words he used – he said, 'Will you do me a favour?' And I said, 'What?' 'Before you go, will you sign this?'

1972 and 1973

Les Dawson

The problem I had interviewing Les Dawson was that I couldn't look him in the eye. There was something in his general countenance that made me want to laugh. Sensing this, he would wait until I had to face him and then he would gurn his features until I was looking at one of those toothless, pinafored, disapproving women of my youth, and I would be helpless with laughter. His use of words and his delivery might have been deep rooted in his Lancashire childhood but there was also more than a hint of, what one critic called, 'studied misanthropy'. Not surprisingly, his great hero was W.C. Fields, and I feel the master would have approved of his pupil.

Michael: It always strikes me that one of the things about your style is this aggression with the audience, and I wonder where that came from?

Les: It started in Hull. I was having a terrible time. I was dying everywhere. In India they were calling me the 'Fourth Prophet'. I got this booking at a fishermen's club in Hull and they came straight from the trawler, with salt caked on their faces and a sockful of money. They sat down and drank themselves to oblivion, and the act was superfluous. I died the death of deaths night after night, and one terrible night they were letting bottles go and tellies were being thrown.

Michael: How do you mean, letting bottles go?

Les: They used to shake them and take the cork off, so it was like an alcoholic El Alamein. It got to the Thursday and I couldn't face it any more, so I went to a pub in the Land of Green Ginger and got stoned. I went back and couldn't get off the piano. This makeshift curtain opened and I was on the podium, so I said, 'It's a great pleasure for me to be in this superbly decorated kipper factory,' which they'd just spent twenty thousand quid on, and suddenly I was getting laughs.

Michael: You had a lot of other odds and sods jobs before you made it big. What do you remember most vividly?

Les: I was a vacuum-cleaner salesman. A woman called me in, because I looked so pathetic at the door, and I had a suit that was so shiny I used to clean it in mirror gloss. She was in a hurry and I took the vacuum cleaner and was trying to show her how it worked, and me tie got caught in the agitator underneath. So while I'm choking to death near the spin dryer, and it was only inadvertently by crushing my legs I managed to cut the switch off, she said, 'You're not much bloody good, are you?'

Michael: I read somewhere that you once played piano in a French brothel. Is that right?

Les: Yeah, it wasn't a lot of money but there were plenty of perks. I was over there trying to be a writer, would you believe. I was full of these daft ideas. I firmly believed that you must gravitate towards Paris if you want to be a writer, which is the worst place in the world. I was living pretty rough, and the place was dreadful. My room was so small, when I turned the lights out I was in bed before it was dark. I used to get bed and breakfast and cramp pills, and to make ends meet I had to play the piano. I started playing piano in this place and thought I was doing great, and then I found out that it was to get rid of the customers.

Michael: You played them out, did you?

Les: Yes, to try and break the rhythm.

Michael: It's something you shared in common with another great comedian, W.C. Fields, because he played piano in a Pittsburgh brothel, didn't he?

Les: That's right. To me, he was the greatest, not because of what he said but how he said it, and he came out with the most immortal line I've ever heard. It was virtually a death-bed soliloquy because a fortnight later he died. He was a great drinker. He was laying in bed, reading the bible, and this producer came in and said, 'Bill Fields, you of all people reading the bible.' He said, 'I'm looking for a loophole.'

Michael: That's a great line. You're very much in the great line and tradition of the north country comedians, aren't you? Who's the one you admire most of all?

Les: Rob Wilton. I think one of the things that makes humour in the north is that it's based on adversity more than anything else, and people like Rob Wilton were steeped in this, and there was a great warmth and depth. One of the lovely things he said was: 'Things were very bad and a friend of mine said, "Let's buy a greyhound and win a few bob at White City." So we bought a greyhound called Flash. I wouldn't say it was slow but on its first race, the hare bit its leg. So I said to this friend of mine, "Now, this is ridiculous. It's costing a fortune in fodder. Let's get rid of it." He said, "My pal, you're quite right. I'll tell you what we'll do, we'll throw it in the canal." "No," I said, "there's no need to do that. Just run away from it." ' And that's the sort of humour that transcends the so-called generation gap. It's a funny remark with a lot of heart in it.

Michael: And humour out of adversity, because if you didn't laugh, you went under, I suppose.

Les: That's exactly it. I do a lot for the poor, you know – the wife, the mother-in-law.

Michael: You've got a mother-in-law, haven't you?

Les: Oh yes. She's very nice actually. She's got a face like a bag of spanners. We get on very well together. When we stay at her house, which she's decorated in early Dracula, she knows that I am personally very fond of pets, and you can bet your life, when I go to bed of a night, there's always a black widow spider in the corner. She's a very big woman. She has her knickers on a prescription.

It's something peculiar to Lancashire, the fact that when two women talk, particularly that age group, if there's anything at all that they consider risqué or referring to the female body, they never finish the sentence. 'I believe she's near her time. I believe she had a . . .' And they never finish the sentence. It was really most peculiar, and they used to get things mixed up. There's the one about the woman in hospital and this chap said, 'How are you?' She said, 'I've been very ill, you know. That's my time of life . . .' She said, 'It's a very serious operation. It's called an hysterical rectomy.'

I think, because of television, that this ridiculous differential between the north and the south is now gone. The people down here and in the north are the same. It's just in the north you have some peculiar sayings. If I dare quote this, there's also an old farmer, he said to me that courting couples are always at it. He said, 'I caught a couple the other day. They were at it like a frog up a pump.' It's a lovely descriptive feeling.

Michael: People must always ask you this question but it's one that interests me particularly about you – how do you see the function of humour?

Les: I don't know. There have been many. How can you analyse when something is funny? What is funny to one isn't funny to another because it's the reverse side of tragedy. If something happens to you personally, it is tragic to you. Other people will sympathise but it's your problem. It's the same with humour. What is funny to you is a personal thing.

1974

Peter Kay

If you hang around long enough, you are bound to witness the first flowering of a great talent, to be able to tell adoring grandchildren: 'I knew him when he had nothing.' When I first met Peter Kay, he was the warm-up man on *Parkinson*, deputising for the regular comedian, who had taken to his bed to ponder the nigh-on impossible task undertaken by all of his profession, namely endeavouring to persuade life into a corpse. What I noticed was the voice, the Lancashire accent, the homage paid to those music-hall comics of my youth. He told me, 'One day I'll walk down these stairs. You'll introduce me on your show.' And I looked into those eyes – full of what can only be described as crafty innocence – and knew he had spoken the truth. Peter Kay is now a huge star and I knew him when he was a nobody!

Peter: I worked at part-time jobs all me life. It's not that me mum and dad didn't encourage me to be a comedian, but I could never settle in jobs because after about four months,

I'd get sacked – not because I couldn't do the job but because most of the time, it was like I wasn't there.

Michael: What kind of jobs did you do?

Peter: I started off packing toilet rolls in Franny Lee's in Bolton. I used to stack shelves. I lasted about six months. I've had all kinds of jobs – theatre box office, cinema usher, bingo. I used to wash cups, and I got sacked for putting the wrong fluid in the dishwasher, and they come out dirtier than when they went in. There were some great stories at bingo. When they're playing, it's big money, and it's like a religion. I remember one night I were up and this woman, something happened, I don't know, she fell off a chair. It was, '4 and 1, 41!' '5 and 3, 53!' 'Supervisor, supervisor!' Well, the supervisor come over and helped this woman and they put her in the recovery position. So they carried on calling, but then she wanted another supervisor to come over and help her husband, because he were doing two books. He was doing his own and his wife's and he couldn't manage.

I'll tell you another one. I used to be an usher, £2.40 an hour and all the sweets I could eat. Once we had a guy come in one Saturday afternoon, and – God love him – he come in and said, 'I don't feel very well, and I think I'm going to have a fit,' and I went, 'Oh God, oh God!' I put him in a corner and he lay down. They went and got the manager and projectionist, Alan – he was from Job Club. He was the only dwarf projectionist you've ever met in your life. He had a pair of binoculars and a stool. They came down and saw to this man, put him in the recovery position.

We had two hundred kids in to watch *Toy Story*, so I said, 'What are we going to do?' because if they pile out and they see him here, there'll be pandemonium. They rang for the ambulance, and the manager said, 'Get that!' and it were a six-foot cardboard cut-out of Flipper. And they carried it over. I said, 'Oh, God, you can't do that, you can't do that! That's awful.' The paramedics come and said,

'Where is he?' I said, 'Over there, behind Flipper.' You could just see his head. I loved working in the cinema, because I loved film and then when the cinema shut, I thought, 'Well, I've two choices. I can either go and get another job or I can have a go at stand-up,' and I did and it just all went mental.

****

Michael: You don't drink, do you?

Peter: Yeah, it's funny really because I didn't drink, which is a blessing and a curse. It's a blessing because you can always drive home from everywhere but a curse because everyone wants a bloody lift! Especially on New Year's Eve when it's triple fare: 'Can you get another one in?'

Michael: It's strange when you think of the life you've had. When I knew you first, you were doing the warm-up for the show, and you were doing working-men's clubs and had been for a long time. That's a boozy culture isn't it? You must have been the only person there who wasn't drunk?

Peter: What happened was when I started doing it, I realised I could get up on stage – I were nervous but I didn't need a drink. Once you've got over that hurdle you think, 'If I can do this without drinking plus I can go home and don't have to waste half my money on a B&B, it's great.'

Michael: Working in those clubs at that time, do you look back with fondness? Did you enjoy them?

Peter: Oh yes, there's some brilliant stories about some people I worked with. I did Eccles Masonic Hall once and a guy said to me, 'How do you want your lights?' And I said, 'What are my options?' He went, 'On or off!' He had a light switch on the wall! I went on with a Cher lookalike who did Shania Twain songs! Shania Twain! And she'd taped *Stars In Their Eyes* off the telly, the beginning of it, and it'd come on: 'Tonight, singing live . . .' and she went, 'Cher.' I did another gig with another Cher lookalike. She was called Cher and Cher Alike, and I did one with a Shania Twain lookalike. She were called Shania Twin. She was supporting Pete Loaf, not Meat Loaf!

Michael: Pete Loaf?

Peter: A carpet fitter with a grudge! He had a Harley Davidson on stage and he did 'Bat Out Of Hell'. I did a gig last year – I've got to tell you this – at Blackpool Opera House. For some reason there were all magicians on in the second half and I came out at beginning of night and said, 'Hello!' And the curtains were shut, and I said, 'These should be open!' So I put them on my shoulder and pulled them open and there was a magician trying to put a woman in a box! Swear to God!

****

Michael: How's your nan?

Peter: Oh, she's great, she's fantastic. She's eighty-six now.

Michael: Is she?

Peter: Yes, she's cracking.

Michael: She still watches the programme?

Peter: Yeah, she watches you. She won't be next week because you're off, aren't you? She's fine, me nan. I've tried getting me nan Sky Plus because she's in a flat, like you'll be in. Have you got Sky Plus? It's up there with running water and electricity in my life. I said to get it and me nan said, 'What is it?' I said, 'You don't need videotapes, you just have Sky Plus, and you plug it in.' I said, 'You can pause it.' 'What? What do you mean?' I said, 'Well, if you want to go and have a brew or something, you just pause it.' She said, 'What about everybody else?' I said, 'No no, you're not . . . you don't control Britain!'

She broke her wrist. She fell in town, God love her, but they're made of a different strength that generation. She fell over and got up with a broken wrist, and she got on the bus with two bags of shopping. She went home and then walked from the bus stop to her flat and then rung me and said, 'I think I've broke me wrist.' I were driving up and said, 'Is it all swollen up? I'm on my way up. Have you any ice?' She said, 'No, no, I've no ice,' and I could hear her opening freezer. I said, 'Well, what have you got?' She said, 'I've got peas.' She said, 'But they're in a tin.' 'Don't put tinned peas on a broken wrist!' But she's fantastic, she's great.

****

Peter: This is your last show.
Michael: You keep saying so. I know that.
Peter: You've had 'em all on here, haven't you?
Michael: I've had 'em all on here.
Peter: Fred Astaire.
Michael: Yep.
Peter: Bette Davis.
Michael: Yep.
Peter: Rod Hull.
Michael: Yep.
Peter: Morecambe and Wise.
Michael: The two of them.
Peter: You're kiss of death, aren't you, when you think about it. How long have we got? You know what I mean?

2002–07

Peter Sellers

Apocryphal story: fan to Peter Sellers, 'Are you Peter Sellers?' Sellers, 'Not today.' Attributed story: Billy Wilder on being told Peter Sellers had suffered a heart attack. 'What do you mean a heart attack? First of all you gotta have a heart.'

Peter Sellers was a conundrum, mainly because he never quite worked out who or what he was. To the public, he was the man who, along with Harry Secombe, gave voice to Spike Milligan's dreams and imaginings; proved his formidable talent as a comedy actor in *I'm Alright Jack*, Blake Edwards' Pink Panther series and Stanley Kubrick's *Dr Strangelove*; and was courted and fêted wherever he went. He was a hero to many, including Dudley Moore and Woody Allen, as well as being the same man who told me, 'I hate everything I do.'

He didn't do many interviews, so the one we did in 1974 was a rarity. He was my only guest and it took some organising, including averting a last-minute potential disaster when, on the eve of the interview, he decided against doing it. Eventually, he walked on and fascinated and beguiled the audience with the kind of talent possessed by few. Afterwards, I knew how his directors felt at the end of making a movie with him. Priceless, but why, oh why, did it have to be so difficult?

We were in Southsea and Dad was appearing in a show, Mum was pregnant with me, and I was born in a nursing home. I think about two weeks after I was born, the comedian in the show took me on the stage and presented me to the audience because Mum was well loved in the show. And that was the first time I appeared on the stage.

My mum very much wanted me to go into the theatre, because my grandma was in the theatre as well – the whole family were. Mum used to stand behind a screen in white tights – it was a bit of a daring thing then – and they used to project slides on to her and she would depict various famous characters from history. As the slides changed, my dad would be playing the old Joanna in the front. And she was a character actor. She used to take part in sketches and things like that.

My grandmother, as a matter of fact, was the very first one ever to put a water show on tour – a German invented an enormous water tank, which filled the stage – and eventually drowned the band once because it broke, in Huddersfield I think it was. Some of them were drowned. And these girls used to dive into the tank and do all kinds, very daring then, in bathing costumes. The shows were called 'Splash me' and 'Have a dip' and whatnot.

I got a job in an uncle's theatre at Ilfracombe. My mother

used to say anybody in the theatre should never ask another person to do a job they couldn't do themselves, so I was sweeping out after each performance. That was the first job I had at ten bob a week, and then after that I used to take tickets on the door. And then from box office I went to assistant stage manager, front of house, lights, stage manager, and gradually progressed my way up to playing small parts – 'Your carriage is without,' or 'Hello!' You know – minor, diddly tiddily pooh things. I saw some very famous actors come to that theatre. Paul Scofield was one in *Night Must Fall*, years ago, with Marie Claire. Before that I used to travel round with my mother and father, all over the country, when I was a kid.

I really didn't like that period in my life. I didn't like the touring. I didn't like the smell of greasepaint – it used to hit you when you went in through any stage door – and baritones with beer on their breath and make-up on their collar. All these deep voices asking, 'Hello, little sonny, how are you?' 'Are you all right, little boy there, little boy?' I used to spend my time sitting in dressing rooms and whatnot, and so I didn't like that. This is why, probably, I hated being in the theatre.

It's a very dreary business, being a drummer or any musician, doing gigs around the country, or in one set place, because you get a lot of hooray Harrys who come up to you and ask you for songs. The typical musician's story – and this is probably true – is about a fellow who came up to a very well-known friend of ours, Alan Clare, a pianist, and said, 'I say, would you play "That's What You Are"?' Alan said, 'I'm sorry, I don't know "That's What You Are". I'll have a look through the book.' So he had a look through the book quickly and this chap is sort of dancing round a very tall girl, and he came back and he said, 'I say, there's a drinky pooh in that for you.'

And he came back, and said, 'Piano player! Piano player and kettle drummer!' – I was known as a kettle drummer, I don't know why – 'Aren't you going to play "That's What You Are"?' So Alan said, 'I'd love to play "That's What You Are", but

I don't know how it goes.' He said, 'Good God, what is the country coming to?' He said, 'I never thought I'd reach the day when somebody didn't know "That's What You Are".' Alan said, 'Well, if you sing it, I'll try.' He said, 'It goes like this: "Unforgettable, that's what you are" . . .' You can't win, you see.

I was getting nowhere fast and I noticed that Roy Spear was doing a show called *Showtime*. The compère was Dick Bentley and there were lots of new acts. I'd written in, I don't know how many times, to try and get on the show. No reply. But I'd got nothing to lose. I thought, 'Well, I'll phone up,' because I used to do these impersonations, and one of the big shows on the air was *Much Binding in the Marsh* with Kenneth Horne and Dicky Murdoch.

And you do things at certain times in your life – you've got to get ahead – so I thought, 'If I stay here, I'm dead.' Even if he kicks my arse out of there, it doesn't matter, as long as I make some impression. So I phoned up and I thought, being a senior producer, Spear would probably know Horne and Murdoch, who were very big then, and I thought if I click with the secretary, I'll get through, right? So I said, 'Oh, hello, this is Ken Horne, is Roy there?'

Now once she said, 'Oh yes, he is, Kenneth, I'll . . .' I knew I was right. So I got on there, and Roy said, 'Hello, Ken, how are you?' I said, 'Listen, Roy, I'm phoning up because I know that new show you've got on, what is it, *Showtime* or something. Dicky and I were at a cabaret the other night, saw an amazing young fellow called Peter. What's his name? Peter Sellers. I think it'd be very good if you probably had him in the show. Just a little tip, a little tip, we just go round with him, you know.'

He said, 'Well, that's very nice of you,' and then it came to the crunch and I said, 'It's me.' He said, 'What?' I said, 'It's me, Peter Sellers talking. It's the only way I could get to you, and would you give me a date on your show?' And he said, 'You cheeky young sod.' Then he said, 'What do you do?' I said, 'Well, I obviously do impersonations.' I was twenty-two at the time. And anyway, I went up there and I got a date on the spot and I got a write-up – the first write-up I'd ever had in my life. It was really nice.

Doing *The Goons*, it was the happiest time in my life. I mean, professionally in my life. We worked like one person. Once when we were living in Shepherd's Hill in Highgate, there was Alf Marks living upstairs, Spike and me down – I'd just got married and Spike had just got married. I was going away and I'd had installed in my flat a new alarm with personal attack buttons. And Milligan said could he stay in my flat, because he'd had a barney with his wife at that particular time, and I said, 'Great.' I was going away with Suzanne anyway.

Above the bed was one of these sort of pear-shaped switches that you normally use to switch off the light, but in fact it was a personal attack button. Old Milligan at that time was going through a bad period and he'd got a long grey and white and green beard and red eyes. I don't know what was going on, but he pressed this thing in the middle of the night and fifteen drunken coppers came knocking at the back door. When he opened the door, they knocked the hell out of Milligan. He said, 'I tell you, my friend Peter Sellers lent me this place.' 'Ah, we've heard all about that. Come on now.' What happens is, when you press the thing, a recording goes straight through to the police. And Milligan, he was taken to the police station, and I got a call up in Birmingham to say, 'Will you tell them that I was sleeping in your flat and I want to switch the light out!'

1974

Pete and Dud

Compared with Morecambe and Wise, Peter Cook and Dudley Moore were the bovver boys of British comedy during the sixties and seventies. They were a compelling double act in the great tradition of the tall thin one and the short plump one, but that was where tradition ended. Driven by Cook's anarchic personality, the two pursued a view of life described by one observer as 'beady, remorseless, hilarious'. Stephen Fry said of Cook, 'He had funniness the way that some people have beauty or dancers have line and grace.' His place in British comedy is guaranteed and is an important one. His creation of The Establishment Club was a key moment in the development of the sixties' satire movement in Britain.

Dudley Moore was also a man of exceptional talent. He left domestic comedy for Hollywood and, because of the movie *10*, became an international star and sex symbol – or 'sex thimble' as the wits defined him. But his real gift was as a musician. As the *Guardian* observed when he died in 2002: 'What other Hollywood comedian could claim to have sung in Gilbert & Sullivan, cut jazz albums, played the Brahms Triple Concerto with Itzhak Perlman and Yo-Yo Ma, and fronted a classical music series on television partnered by Sir Georg Solti?'

Sadly, they both died far too young.

Peter Cook

When we were about to do *Beyond the Fringe* in the West End, there was this great thing. Jonathan Miller wanted to be a doctor, and was torn between medicine and the stage, and they called him 'the doctor of mirth'. Alan Bennett was torn between going on the stage and being a don, or at least a teacher, and I had nothing. I kept thinking, 'I must invent something,' like 'I want to be a nun, should I go on the stage or not?' But I think both Dudley and I really wanted to do it, and have kept on.

There was one dreadful moment during *Beyond the Fringe*. I don't know if Jonathan has ever forgiven me. His first baby was born in America while we were on tour, and he was doing a sketch about philosophy. In the middle of it I came on with

Jonathan's newborn baby and said, 'Excuse me sir, the wife has just delivered this. What should I do with it?' and as far as I remember he said, 'Just put it in the fridge.' But he was furious because he thought I might have dropped it.

In America, they always ask you about Cockney rhyming slang and the Queen. I said, 'In Somerset we have our own rhyming slang.' They said, 'Sounds very interesting. What is it?' And I said, 'It's based on the word "fisherman", because there are a lot of fishermen there. So for example, if you're talking about the weather, you can say, "Well, tomorrow it's going to be a bit fisherman's." That can mean fisherman's net, which is wet, or else it can be fisherman's fly – dry.' I said, 'The wonderful thing about Somerset rhyming slang is that we use one word, and it applies to everything. If you fancy it, you can approach a girl and say, "I wouldn't mind a bit of a fisherman's," which is fisherman's rod.' They believed it completely. It's all a lot of fisherman's as far as I'm concerned.

Touring America was remarkably dull. You go from city to city and tell each one it's your favourite city and remember not to bad mouth it after you've left – otherwise the press gets back to you. I've never said a bad thing about any American city, apart from Detroit. We were there for five weeks. It has 35 per cent unemployed, it's freezing, nobody comes into the centre of the city because everybody who's got any money lives in the suburbs and you're inclined to get killed. Actually, the nearest I got to being killed was in Chicago.

I was in my bedroom at eight in the morning, which is unusual, and I woke up and felt a presence in the room. In fact, two presences. I looked down at the bottom of the bed and there were two men going through my suitcases. It was fairly obvious what they doing, namely robbing me, but I came up with the two stupidest remarks I've ever made. First of all I said, 'What the hell are you doing?' as if I thought they were giving room service. Then they rushed out of the room carrying with them a tape recorder-cum-radio, and I said, 'Drop that!' I've been watching too much TV. He dropped it on the bed, and I was fully armed with one soiled Kleenex. I ran down the stairs very calmly and said, 'Two gentlemen probably coming down the elevator or the side stairway, one about 185 pounds, six foot one, one lighter skinned, about 161 pounds, five foot ten . . .' I was reeling off all these figures from the *Streets of San Francisco*. 'Please apprehend them. This is Mr Cook, Room 5B.' I was totally calm, and they escaped.

When the police arrived, I was having a good time. I said, 'I really don't want to waste your time because I could be dead. Why not go and save somebody on the street or whatever,' and they said, 'No,' and took fingerprints. I was totally calm, then five o'clock in the evening, I fainted – delayed reaction that two people had been robbing me, and were probably armed. I think, if you're going to rob somebody, you might as well carry some guns, and do a good job.

The first thing I did when I arrived back in New York – I haven't been there for about six years – was to go to Times Square. I saw a sign saying: 'Live nude models, 25 cents.' I tried to calculate, and that's about 4p – better than Soho. So I gave them 25 cents, walked in through a door and there was a lady, naked, revolving on a small pedestal. She looked very bored, so I said, 'This must be rather a boring job,' and she said, 'It is.' I said, 'How long do you do it?' and she said, 'About five hours at a time.' I said, 'Do you just revolve?' She said, 'I occasionally yawn, but mainly I revolve.' 'This must be very tedious,' I said. 'How much do you get paid?' I was having quite a chatty conversation with this lady. Suddenly I was seized from behind by two enormous men who asked me, not very politely, if I wanted to be killed. I said, 'Not at the moment, no.' So they said, 'Get the hell out of here!'

I'd gone in through the wrong door. What I should have been doing was peeping in through a tiny window. As I left I saw these feverish eyes peering through tiny windows, obviously thinking they were going to see something more than they'd actually paid for. I left rather rapidly and the men followed me up Times Square. I was retreating to the safety of my hotel, and they repeated their threat to kill me, very convincingly. I paused by a policeman and said, 'These two gentlemen are following me and they said they want to kill me. I think my best plan is to get back to the hotel.' And he said, 'Yeah, don't for Christ's sake involve me in crime.'

1972–82

Dudley Moore

Michael: Did you always want to be a comedian?

Dudley: No, it was never an ambition. It was a survival motive. When I was a boy, I was bashed up a lot.

Michael: Because of your size?

Dudley: Because of my size and because I had a dodgy foot. Well, that's what I thought. I think it was just because I was one of those people temperamentally set up somewhere in childhood for being bullied. There are people who are set up for bullying and some for being bullied. At the age of thirteen, having had my trousers pulled down every day, not with delightful consequences, I suddenly decided in an English lesson to make a joke. I was tired of this treatment and had to neutralise myself.

Michael: You what?

Dudley: Castrate myself. It was a form of castration in a way, because it took the guts out of me and gave birth to something else. I made a joke, and everybody looked round saying, 'Is he making a joke?' From that moment I became a clown, and dropped all the subjects I wanted to study, including maths and physics, because it took too much time and I had to devote a lot of time to falling about. Therefore, I fell back on things that I did naturally – music and French. And that was the beginning.

Michael: Were you shy with the opposite sex then?

Dudley: I was, yes. It was a constant frustration. I went to a mixed school and I never was able, except maybe once or twice, to pluck up the courage to say, 'Can you come out to the pictures tonight?' There was one girl, Shirley Powell. I still love her – she used to wear striped sweaters and that makes everything look wonderful. And when I was a prefect, I felt I had more reason to hang around the girls' cloak-rooms, saying: 'Come on girls, out of there.' Shirley Powell came out and I said, 'I really like you,' and arranged to meet her at the Cherry Tree pub in Raynham at eight o'clock on a Tuesday night. I waited for about two hours, and she turned up and said, 'Hello.' I said, 'Oh, hiya,' and she said, 'I can't come out, I'm going to see my friend,' walked round and went off. And then there were girls who were terribly sexy at the age of sixteen. They knew they had you by the nose hairs and could do what they would and you wouldn't know what to do. I didn't know what to do. There were some boys who used to go into barber's shops and ask for unspeakable things. They were well away in the long grass during the cricket matches, but me – nothing. Nothing!

Michael: Until when?

Dudley: Until today! Oh, do you know, I was twenty-four.

Michael: Twenty-four?

Dudley: I was out of Oxford, I was twenty-four and I made an assignation. I arranged to meet this lady, who was a bit of a raver, in a hotel, and she said, 'I've come on the midnight train.' I'd booked us in as 'Mr and Mrs Moore', trying to look like a husband, and she got on the milk train about six o'clock in the morning. We went to this hotel and it was disastrous, really.

Michael: Was it?

Dudley: Oh, yes. After all that expectation, twenty-four years, the six o'clock milk train comes in, and you don't really feel . . .

Michael: 'The six o'clock milk train'. That's magnificent. That's one for your collection, 'The New Language of Erotica'.

Dudley: It seems a very good time of the day, six o'clock.

Michael: It didn't put you off, though?

Dudley: No, not at all. Wondrous thing, sex, but it's terrible to think that all those early years, which were probably the most colourful of my life – the most difficult, most passionate – were absolutely squandered in fear and guilt and trembling. That's terrible. My son is seven months old. I'm telling him the facts of life now.

Michael: I'm delighted about your success in Hollywood, but how do you feel to be a Hollywood star at this stage in your career?

Dudley: Well, I suppose that answers it, in a nutshell. They don't know me out there. They hadn't known me before, so I am a discovery of sorts, even though I've been twenty years in the business. I felt I was a star years ago in '59, '60, especially when I was in the airport. I was at the airport once and John Gielgud was there, and said, 'Where are you going?' I said, 'Portofino,' and he said, 'You must see Lily Palmer,' and gave me a note. I was curious on the plane and opened it up. It said, 'Darling Lily, this is to introduce the young pianist from *Beyond the Fringe*, Stanley Moon.'

I was a little embarrassed, so I didn't go. Years later, when I was trying to get rid of an awful apartment in New York, he came to the door and the first thing he said was, 'I'm so sorry about that awful mistake I made. I must have told it to so many people.' The worst thing was in a restaurant, years later, and there was Sir John. The place was completely deserted, and I got a note, which said, 'Dear Stanley Moon! So nice to see you again,' signed Sir John. I thought, 'That's nice he's remembered it.' So I went across to him. He was very engrossed in his meal, and I was just about to bash him on his shoulder and say, 'How are you?' and so forth when I felt a tap on my shoulder. It was a waiter, and in another corner of this deserted restaurant was my agent, who was in fits of laughter – he'd sent me the message, and I almost disgraced myself with Sir John.

1976 and 1980

Spike Milligan

The problem when preparing for an interview with Spike Milligan was you were never quite sure which Spike would turn up. Would it be Spike on the verge of a nervous breakdown, Spike convinced the world is at its end, Spike Milligan saviour of the rainforest or the white rhino, Spike driven to the brink by the Gas Board, or best of all, Spike, the most surreal of our funny men letting us aboard his carousel of laughter.

In other words, he could be an interviewer's joy or worst nightmare, a delight or a pain in the arse. I speak from experience. Over time, I interviewed Spike on many occasions without ever managing really to pin him down. On the other hand, I became a friend as well as an admirer, and to stand in the shadow of the man who created *The Goons* is to visit the pantheon, which is where he resides and where his companions are no doubt as confused as I was.

Michael: Was your childhood in India a golden period?

Spike: Yes, magnificent. It was the last throw of the dice for the British Empire. It was like the Romans about to leave Hadrian's Wall. I saw staggering arrays of soldiers, troops, Bengal Lancers, Ghurkhas, Irish Guards – the whole lot. And I thought the whole world was made up like this, a sort of 'new' England. It was an absolutely stunning childhood in that vivacious sunlight.

Michael: And what about your early comedic influences? Who were the people who first made you laugh?

Spike: Well, my father was a comic clown actor and dancer, so I was in the wings of the theatre when I was very young. My mother used to play the piano for him and he was quite a funny man. Being Irish, he told me outrageous stories. It was only later in life I suddenly realised, 'Dad, you never really killed an elephant with your bare hands, did you?' He said, 'No, no, it's a lie.' 'Why didn't you tell the truth?' He said, 'Would you rather have an exciting lie or a boring truth?'

He was a dream man. He came from Ireland and at the age of fourteen they forced him to join the British Army. He didn't want to – he wanted to go on the stage. All his life he regretted it and instead lived in the dream world of the stage and used the Army as a way of making money. He was terribly romantic and it annoyed him that he went bald at eighteen and had piles when he was eleven. He used to call these the 'extremities of torture'. He used to say things to me like, 'You know Chopin? If he was bald and had piles, he could never have written the nocturnes. You can't write nocturnes with a sore arse.'

Michael: Did he wear a wig, if he was bald?

Spike: He wore a wig. I thought all dads wore wigs. I remember one time in Rangoon. He wanted me to be a good shot, so he took me out with a blank cartridge gun and said, 'Now, I'm going to run behind these rocks and shoot this pistol at you. You've got to fire back at me.' The crows and eagles in Rangoon are notorious for being aware of people shooting at them. So my father went behind a rock and hid, and suddenly an eagle came down. Next thing, it came up with this wig. He threw his boots at it, rocks and everything else, and he wrote away to England for a new wig with more powerful glue. Years later, Burmese naturalists were amazed to find a nest made out of a wig. Couldn't work that out.

****

Michael: Wasn't your dad a bit of an inventor?

Spike: He must have been. He didn't make a good job of it, though, did he? You know the eternal cry in the world to invent the perfect mousetrap? He said, 'I've got it, I've got it!' This was in Rangoon. He said, 'Come and look at it.' So he took me to a room, we looked through the door and there's a pile of cheese and eight mice. I said, 'How do you get rid of them?' He said, 'Easy.' He got a gun and went bang, bang! Took us months to eat them all.

****

Michael: You've written five books about your war experiences. It must have been a deeply traumatic time for you?

Spike: It was traumatic, but at the same time I had the benefit of meeting blokes who have been my friends ever since. And there were some extraordinary things. Heroism's a strange thing. I'll give you an example of what a British squaddie is like. I don't think any British squaddie's quite brave, but he doesn't like being beaten. Our cook in Italy was getting dinner ready, we were all in the camouflage nets and they were bringing up ammunition lorries with the covers on. He got the dinner laid out, and the Germans lobbed in about ten 88mm shells. The cover of a lorry caught fire and it had this ammunition on board. So with great courage, I ran into a slit trench, and suddenly I heard the lorry start up. And this was the chef! He'd got into the lorry and he drove it down to the bottom of the hill. Fortunately, it didn't explode. He came back and I said, 'God, what did you do that for?' He said, 'I didn't want to cook the bleeding dinner twice, did I?'

Michael: Did you have much contact with the Germans?

Spike: Well, there's a famous story. The English officer always baffled me. I didn't know whether he was brave or acting brave. There was a nice officer called Beaumont Smythe, and he said we're going to go. We'd just advanced on an area, we were looking for an observation post, and we'd gone past the German lines into enemy territory, but we didn't know it. I was driving him. He got out and he's standing with this map when I heard a noise behind me. I looked round and there were three German paratroopers, standing with their hands up. I started to look for my Tommy gun and the book of instructions on how to work it. I got out, and said to them – very silly because they had them up all ready – 'Hände Hoch!' 'Hands up,' I said. The officer didn't look around. He said, 'What's going on, Milligan?' I said, 'There are three German paratroopers here, Sir.' He said, 'Well ask them what they want!' "They want to surrender, Sir.' He said, 'Well, tell them we haven't got the facilities.' How did we win?

****

Michael: Why did you like the Army? You've said subsequently it was one of the happiest periods of your life.

Spike: Well, I got away from my mother and father for a start. My father was a lunatic – so is my mother, now I come to think of it! It was hell. She's a very good Catholic and how can I explain it? Before you could eat your meals: 'Bless us, Oh Lord and these thy gifts, which we are about to receive, Christ The Lord – no, not yet, no!' Then she'd pray for the soul of all the family, for the soul of grandfather and so on. By the time she'd finished . . . I never ate a hot meal in the house! She thought it was sinful of me, blowing the trumpet. And I used to go into an airing cupboard with a sock in it to learn. That's why I was glad to get into the Army! I had to get away. Thank God for Hitler, I'd never have made it.

****

Michael: You are officially a stateless person, aren't you?

Spike: Apparently, when the Commonwealth was being re-arranged, they passed a law that said anybody whose father was born in Ireland before 1900 was no longer British, but stateless. So I didn't know what to do. I felt deprived. I'd just been in the war, and they said, 'Well, you'll have to apply again.' I thought, 'Oh well, my father's Irish.' So I phoned the Irish Embassy and I said, 'Can I have an Irish passport?' They said, 'Oh Jesus, yes, come round. We're very short of people.' So I went round, and I'm Irish now! This is the best part of the Home Office, though – I wrote to them and said, in the light of the fact that I was stateless, what passport would you advise I get? They said I could have become a Hindu and had an Indian passport.

Michael: They wanted you to become a British citizen in the end?

Spike: Well, they said I could apply again, and that would entail taking an oath of allegiance to the Queen. And I thought, 'I've never been disloyal to the Queen! You ask her!'

****

Michael: Did you know at the time, how influential *The Goon Show* would be?

Spike: I had no idea at all. It was just a burst of energy. We all compacted together and I never knew it would be what it was. I suppose it did make a breakthrough.

Michael: You didn't enjoy those days very much, did you?

Spike: The pressure was so great. I didn't know it, but I was killing myself, really. I had mental breakdown after mental breakdown – six or seven times. It destroyed my first marriage, so it wasn't a very happy time in that respect.

****

Michael: Tell me Mr Milligan, what is your next publishing venture?

Spike: I think true stories are funnier than when you make them up. I don't like dirty stories, but this is a true story, about the waist downwards. A friend of mine, who shall remain nameless, primarily because he wasn't baptised, got dysentery. Things were getting a bit bad and people in the office were sort of spreading around, and they suggested he went home early. He had to walk to Waterloo, about twenty-five minutes before the rush hour started. On the way to the station he had a terrible accident, and he thought, 'I can't go on like this.' He saw a supermarket, rushed in and said, 'Look, I've got a disease of the legs. Can you give me a pair of underpants and a pair of trousers, medium size?' The woman says, 'Got them,' so he took this plastic bag with the trousers and things in, and rushed up for the train. By then it was almost rush hour and he thought, 'My God, I can't go in a compartment.' He was just reeking by now. So he thought, 'Ah, the loo.' He went in, locked the door, and waited for the train to start. He took his trousers and underpants off and threw them out of the window. Thought, 'Thank God for that.' Then he opened the plastic bag and there was a lady's pink cardigan. It is a true story.

Anyhow, he's got to get off the train, so he's wearing a trilby hat, a jacket, collar and tie, and naked from the waist downwards with a lady's pink cardigan. In desperation, he pulled his legs into the arms and suddenly realised, where the neck was, all his wedding tackle was hanging out! So, the train is coming up to the platform and – this is the English at their best – he took off his trilby hat and he tucked the brim all round! This is not a lie, I didn't make this up – this is a true story!

****

Michael: What would be your idea of paradise?
Spike: Having Debussy and Ravel at my beck and call, to play for me any time of the day I wanted them to.
Michael: It's a lovely thought, isn't it?
Spike: Because neither of those are bald or have piles!

1977–87

Barry Humphries

Barry Humphries is a man of fastidious appearance and perfect manners. He would be as welcome at Court as he would be suited to the surroundings. Being an Aussie, he might regard that as an insult, yet I have little doubt he should be knighted for his services to jollity. His relationship with Dame Edna Everage alone is worthy of the highest honour. Her position as one of the world's most iconic women is entirely due to Mr Humphries' handling of her assets. Similarly, if an old ratbag like Les Patterson gets a 'K', the case for Sir Barry is indisputable. I have interviewed all three during my career and each and every encounter proved unforgettable in that I cannot get rid of the memory, try as I might.

I was the only person at school who never told dirty stories. I never liked them, and I didn't like the people who told them. I was about thirty-five when I started being filthy, and I've enjoyed it thoroughly, I might say, ever since.

The acting started, really, by accident. I was given parts in school plays and invariably I played eccentric parts, or housewives. It seemed that, very early on, I was cast in the role of the housewife in school plays. For example, in plays about miners being trapped, I was usually at the pit-head with a bundle. But I always felt uncomfortable in these clothes of my mother's, as a matter of fact, because they never fitted very well. Later I went to university where I studied philosophy and law – it was decided I should be a lawyer – and it was in those years that I started creating theatrical happenings.

I think I realised I was a frustrated performer. I invented practical jokes, which weren't meant to be filmed or ever talked about. They were entirely for my own pleasure. What I liked to do, for example, was to have breakfast served to myself on the train into town so that at the first station, a grapefruit would be presented to me as I sat there, reading the morning paper. At each station, incidentally, I had an accomplice waiting. The next station, cornflakes, then toast, and by the time I got into town, a cup of coffee. Of course, the other people in the compartment were totally mystified. This was many years before *Candid Camera* so no one quite knew what was happening. It was kind of street theatre before street theatre had been invented.

I like to introduce elements of the extraordinary into everyday life. And if I can disgust a large number of people, it gives me almost as much satisfaction as it gives me to amuse them. And so I always carry a large tin of Russian salad somewhere about my person. Now, I was on a plane, and the airline sick bag is something that all air travellers are familiar with – it's tucked in there between *The Bulletin* and what to do if it crashes.

However, I'm sitting there thinking, 'Why not empty this tin of Russian salad?' Just one of those things that crosses your mind. Here I am with a tin of Russian salad and an empty sick bag, why not bring these two elements together in some way? I also had a plastic spoon. Now, how to introduce the plastic spoon into the scheme of things was the next problem. It seemed at that point that the air hostess was sick. I don't know quite what it was. I was just eating Russian salad out of the wrong receptacle. Was there a chip of carrot on my lip? The result of course . . . you know people overreact. I think that is a term used by amateur psychologists, but the airline overreacted and I was asked not to travel on that airline again.

Edna is a very real person. In fact, when you said that I'd been on the show, I had to think twice about that because I quite honestly don't feel I've done a *Parkinson* show before. This is my first *Parkinson* show, and it just happens that I am an agent, an impresario, and I have a very talented artiste called Dame Edna Everage. She was on your show, and so I heard all about it from her. In a sense, she does take over. I still hold the majority of shares, but from time to time the personality of Dame Edna is very strong.

I met Edna on a bus. I was in a production of Shakespeare, because at university I drifted into amateur university theatre and then into professional theatre. I toured in a production of *Twelfth Night*, and on the bus trips between one town and another, every member of the cast had to do a turn. Someone sang a song, someone recited a poem, and I used to sit on the back seat of the bus and impersonate the Lady Mayoress of the next town – everywhere we went, the Lady Mayoress would always stand up and say what a wonderful thing it was that these people were bringing Shakespeare to the Australian bush. And then she'd get the name of the play wrong.

I had this falsetto, which I'd learned from school plays, and I would sit on the back seat and do this voice, which amused everyone greatly. At Christmas time, when we had to do the pantomime, the producers said to me why didn't I do that character? And I said, 'Well, I could do it in the wings. I could do the funny voice and one of the actresses could impersonate this person.' We christened her Edna, because it was possibly the dullest name we could think of.

So I was Edna, and I wrote a sketch and once again borrowed some appropriate female attire. I resembled a pantomime dame more than anything else, but the character was born. It seemed suddenly that I'd hit upon a vein of humour that no one had tried before, certainly not in Australia. So on and off in the years that followed, interrupting a pretty busy life as a character actor, I did the part of Edna. It always surprised me the character became so popular. It had always just been a pastime of mine.

I would phase out the character of Edna if she was destructible. You would think someone like Edna would self-destruct, wouldn't you, intricate missile that she is. I would stop doing her if she ceased to amuse me, or if I felt there were no enlightening and funny things that I could say about my own life and background, and about Australia, through the character. But since Australia is growing and developing and getting funnier and funnier, I feel that I can still bring in a new audience. I look down into the stalls and I see kiddies being brought along by their doting arty, crafty, misguided parents, gazing up awestruck and disgusted at this bird of paradise, which thinly disguises a vulture.

Les was created because, in Australia, we have clubs, and the clubs have a big audience, and the people who go to the clubs don't always go to the theatre. Although for many years I played conventional theatres in Australia, a friend of mine said, 'You haven't got to the real Australian audience. You haven't done the clubs.' So I was persuaded to do one of the biggest in Sydney, and I had to invent someone to warm up the audience. So I invented Les Patterson. I made Les Patterson the entertainments officer for the club. I made him very drunk and he staggered, and it hadn't occurred to me he exactly resembled the secretary of the club. I hadn't consciously based him on anyone, but apparently he was absolutely identical.

I'm totally teetotal. I drink huge quantities of liquid but it's non-alcoholic. That hasn't always been the case. I discovered, about twelve years ago now, that I was allergic to the chemical ethyl alcohol, which is the important ingredient in that wonderful invention, booze. For very many years I'd used alcohol with great success. I was always very nervous, as a lot of people in my profession are, and I found grog was wonderful. It was a miraculous discovery for me. It wasn't until I was in my early twenties that I started drinking at parties, and I found that I drank differently from other people. I was the last person in the world who thought I had a problem. I found out later, when I stopped drinking, that a lot of people were quite worried about the amount that I drank, or what happened to me when I drank. I just felt I was more confident and more amusing. In fact, I was deeply unamused by my own behaviour. I was a very despairing person.

I got to the stage where I needed the morning drink. I found myself at some of those pubs in Covent Garden that open very early – you'd be surprised at some of the people we know who were there. It's amazing how one feigns surprise – 'Oh fancy seeing you here!' 'Oh yes, you know, just happened to be passing, old boy.' And you have to wait until their back is turned to get the vodka up.

The awful thing about alcoholism is that the last person to know about it is the practising alky. He thinks this is normal behaviour – doesn't realise he's insane. A few people I know have died with those views. Luckily, with quite a bit of help from a lot of other people and a very good doctor and an excellent hospital in my home town of Melbourne, I managed to put the last drink down, and I haven't picked up a drink in twelve years. To me, it's one of the great things of life, but it's out of the beverage class and in the poison class for me.

I was, in fact, such a boozer that I was offered a senior job at the BBC, and that shows you how bad I was. I thought I wouldn't laugh again in the early days, and it is a glum topic to bring up, but you can pick up the gift of life again, and life is very, very funny sober. It's not all doom, gloom and ginger ale I can assure you.

1980 and 1982

Dame Edna

Dame Edna: They'll adore you in Australia, they really will.
Michael: You think so?
Dame Edna: As a conversationalist, I'd love you to go and see my husband Norm when you're out there.
Michael: How is he?
Dame Edna: Very far from well. I've only got one husband, but he's like seven. He's got this terrible condition, at the moment it's quiescent, but he's got what's called a rumbling prostate. That means anything could happen, and so we have been advised by one of the greatest Harley Street prostatologists that a transplant is in order. And we're just waiting for a donor. Mike, you might step off the plane at just the right moment. I shouldn't say this – I know my husband keeps a very low profile with regard to his illness. He never mentions his prostate, and when he does, he only mentions it in passing. As a matter of fact, that's the only time he ever feels it.

****

Michael: Now, talking of managers, what about your manager, Mr Humphries?
Dame Edna: I don't speak of him I'm afraid, he's terrible. You have a manager I suppose? Watch him like a hawk. It's terrible, Michael.
Michael: What's happened?
Dame Edna: I trusted that Barry Humphries and he helped

me early in my career. He was a talented but smooth-talking person. He was wearing a short-sleeved shirt and I saw these scars on his arm. I thought, 'Oh, he's been doing something a bit silly.' And then I realised what had happened – the drawer of the till had slammed on his wrist. He's had his hand in my money! Look at the figures yourself. Don't trust anyone in the matter of your own money.

****

Dame Edna: Don't pussyfoot around Michael Parkinson, we've known each other too long. I have a dysfunctional family, there's no two ways about it.

Michael: Drugs?

Dame Edna: Nightmare. I don't know what they get up to. Substances of some kind. My daughter Valmai, who was a lovely child, she's into shoplifting in a major way. In Waitrose. I said, 'Look, you're bringing shame on the family. Can't it be Harrods?' And she's been frisked by the same heavily built security officer so many times. And now they're living together, isn't that awful? This woman's name is Frankie Clitheroe. One minute, Michael, she's wanding my daughter in a back room at Waitrose. Wanding her, frisking her, patting her down, and the next minute they're shopping together in Ikea, can you believe that?

Michael: What about your son, Kenny?

Dame Edna: Kenny?

Michael: Yes, Kenny.

Dame Edna: He designed this dress, he's so talented, Kenny. He's a practising homeopath, as a matter of fact. I'm pretty sure that's what he said he was. My darling, let's face it, I'd had two Valiums and a big mug of Ovaltine and I was in bed, a bit woozy. Kenny came home very late after a Stephen Sondheim tribute, and he said, 'I'm a homeopath, Mum, and so is my room-mate.' He is a lovely boy.

Michael: Oh, he is.

Dame Edna: My son's room-mate you would adore. His name

is Clifford Smale. He's American. He's from the Boston area, quite religious. He was an altar boy, as a matter of fact. He toyed with the priesthood, you know.

****

Dame Edna: Sexuality, it's never been an important thing in my life. But I have drives, I have juices. My gynaecologist looked up this morning and he said to me . . .

Michael: He said what?

Dame Edna: He said I was still capable of breast feeding.

Michael: Oh dear.

Dame Edna: Mind you, sometimes, if we were a little bit lonely, sometimes we'd lean on the spin dryer. We'd kick it into that fast cycle. It's called white goods abuse, as a matter of fact.

****

Michael: I believe you gave some advice to Calista Flockhart?

Dame Edna: Calista Flockhart, isn't that a great name? It's vaguely pharmaceutical I think. Can you imagine going into the chemist and saying, 'I'll have a little soap and a little toothpaste and . . .' look left and right and centre, 'a small tube of Calista . . . with applicator.' As you know, I am a serious actress and was given this role in *Ally McBeal*.

Michael: Yes, I know.

Dame Edna: And that brought the series to a complete close. But I got to know little Calista, who was a skinny little thing, and lonely. And I found a man for her, because Harrison Ford is also a carpenter. He was doing work for me, making some bookshelves and things. And I don't like to mention this, because this is a family show, but the thing that brought them together was crack – have you heard of that?

Michael: What, crack cocaine?

Dame Edna: No, no. Carpenter's crack. He was bending over fixing these bookshelves and her eye fell on that little groove above his jeans and that was it I'm afraid. It's been a lovely story. I was Cupid in that relationship.

Michael: How wonderful. Now, you've had this job as advisor to Laura Bush?

Dame Edna: Oh yes, I've been a bit of a spin doctor. But I helped little George, I must say.

Michael: Did you? How?

Dame Edna: I have and I gave them a lovely present last Christmas – an atlas. And little George called me up in the middle of the night – he's not aware that there are different time zones in the world, bless his heart – and he said, 'I love my atlas, Edna. I've got it open at the index but I can't find Overseas.' He said, 'I'm looking and Laura tells me to look under A for Abroad, but I can't find that either.' Isn't that delightful?

****

Dame Edna: Talking about icons and legends, Lauren Bacall said you can't be a legend unless you're dead. She can talk. I mean, look at me. I'm alive and I'm a bit of a living legend.

Michael: You are.

Dame Edna: And she criticised Nicole Kidman.

Michael: Ah.

Dame Edna: This Aussie bashing, you know, it's dreadful. Nicole is lovely. She's young, she's talented in all sorts of roles. I don't think it was right for her to attack our icons. Mind you, I don't want to be an icon. Have you ever been to Greece?

Michael: Yes.

Dame Edna: Have you ever been to Greece and seen an icon? Horrible, and cracks all over their faces. Oh, I'm sorry, Michael.

****

Dame Edna: Michael's being good. Viewers, Michael is being good, because when I was on his show last time – if you could call it a show – I told him, 'Stop touching yourself.' He's got this habit, when he says something, he explores the little bits of his ears and flicks his nose. Horrible. But you're not doing it now – he's clenching his little hands together . . .

Michael: Absolutely.

Dame Edna: Don't touch yourself inappropriately.

Michael: No, I won't!

****

Michael: Well, thank you for talking to me and giving us all . . .

Dame Edna: Talking to you! I'm here. What would be the point of coming here and not talking?

1979–2004

Sir Les Patterson

Sir Les: Good luck to you. And hello there, ladies and gentlemen.

Michael: How are you feeling?

Sir Les: I'm not feeling too great. Oh dear. Oh sorry, Mike.

Michael: What is it I've got on my hands?

Sir Les: Sorry, it's an ointment I'm supposed to use. I was just giving myself a quick application before the show. I'm supposed to use an applicator but I generally don't bother. You'll be all right on your next trip to the Philippines. Are you with me? No worries.

Michael: Now this thing about image is totally important and a large part of your job. What is the image that you're trying to project?

Sir Les: I think you'd better phrase that again, Michael. I think it's, 'What is the image that I am bloody successfully projecting,' ladies and gentlemen. And that is Australia as a thinking organism. You know, it wasn't very many moons ago, what you did to old Brian Humphries was deadly, the poor bastard. I saw him out there, oh cripes you must have given him a rough time.

Michael: We talked about getting on the grog.

Sir Les: Get stuck into him. My mother always said, 'Never trust a man who doesn't drink,' and I don't. I like a drink, I'm not ashamed of it. As a matter fact, I'm as full as a Pommie complaint box at the moment. I mean that in a very nice way, too.

****

Michael: There is this question of girls being forward, being overwhelmed by your sexuality. How do you cope with it?

Sir Les: Oh, I do get a bit. I had an embarrassing experience in a London taxi. I had this little lass, and I was showing her the sites of London, you know – Buckminster Castle, St Paul's Abbey, Trafalgar Circus. We were driving around and, I kid you not, this little sheila done a streak in the back seat of the car. I didn't know where to look. We got to our destination and the driver says, 'That'll be so and so,' and he said, 'Are you going to pay me?' and she . . . I'm sorry, I can't say it, but she flashed the map of Tasmania. For those of you who aren't too crash hot on geography, Tasmania is a triangular continent, a bit on the bushy side. Anyway, to cut a long story short, the driver said, 'Haven't you got anything smaller?'

****

Michael: Do you have any artistic leanings? Do you write anything at all?

Sir Les: I write the odd poem, from time to time. I could be at an international airport, I could be on a TV talk show, like this, and suddenly I feel a stanza coming up. I feel the odd hexameter rising in me. Ladies and gentlemen, as you might have gathered from this bit of paper in my hand, I've knocked off a bit of a poem here and this is a propos of Mike's presence in my homeland of Australia recently. The odd critic got the knife out – what's new about that, Parky?

Michael: Nothing.

Sir Les: So the odd journo gets out the poison typewriter and I feel, because Parky can't defend himself – a lot of people in show business can't defend themselves, can they mate? You're comparatively defenceless, so I've written this poem and it's called 'An Ode to Parky':

> There's a bloke who's keenly watched and widely read
> Who always hits the nail on the head
> He kicked off modestly in the UK
> And he's a world celebrity today.
>
> If he gets nervous, well, it's never showed
> His face is like a mile of rugged road
> His crows' feet are the dried-up beds of smiles
> And his best friends are aware that he's got piles –
> Of charm, pizzazz and British spunk and phlegm
> Of TV interviewers, he's the gem
> He could interview a Zulu or Iraqi and make it interesting
> His name is Parky.
>
> Australian critics are all chippy guys
> They tried to chop old Parky down to size
> Some even said, 'Go back where you come from –
> We won't be taught charisma by a Pom.'
> But he knows the average Aussie journalist
> Is following orders, jealous or half pissed!
>
> He smiles, he does his job, he doesn't care
> When you're the top, where do you go from there?
> So raise your glass of lager, rum or saki
> Whether you be Hun or Nip or Darkie
> And drink the health of my old cobber – PARKY!

1982

Three Pythons Take Flight

There was such a to-do at the TV Centre when *Monty Python* went to air, with executives flapping like a flight of eagles. It was not quite the end of the world, but certainly the end of light entertainment as we had known it. Michael Palin, Graham Chapman and John Cleese were creators of Python and much more besides – think of Palin's sublime *Ripping Yarns* and Cleese's unequalled *Fawlty Towers* – as well as being bemused observers of the impact their meteor had as it crashed into the TV Centre. Here the three of them reminisce about that time and their lives after Python.

Michael Palin

If you look at the Python shows, some are absolutely awful! Some were just totally embarrassing, whereas there were other little things I'd forgotten all about, for instance, a wonderfully silly sketch called 'The Fish Slapping Dance'. All it involved was me in explorer shorts and a pith helmet, with John Cleese, by the side of a canal. The music plays and I go up to John and slap him very lightly on the side of the face with these little pilchards. Music stops, I bow, John gets this great pike from behind his back and thwack – knocks me straight into the canal. Now, when we rehearsed it, the canal was full. When we actually filmed it, a boat had gone through and the lock was empty. I fell fifteen feet! My pith helmet filled with water, I thought that was it. What a way to die! My whole life flashed before me.

I managed to persuade the Pythons that if we wanted to get some really good locations, we shouldn't use Dorking all the time, and instead go up to the Yorkshire Moors. I don't think they really liked it. They thought it was a bit of a plot by me to get them up there. John got particularly testy. I remember one day we filmed in a nightclub in the early morning and they hadn't cleaned it from the night before. John went into the toilet and there was a lot of stamping about, came back and said there was not a single basin without vomit in it! All six basins!

Anyway, we did some quite nice things up there. We did one sketch called 'The Batley Townswomen's Guild Re-enact the Battle of Pearl Harbor' – a ridiculous thing set in a muddy field, high up on the moors. We're all in drag with handbags, little hats and scarves, and we all rush in and beat the hell out of each other, grappling in the mud. It's very silly and nothing really happens. We got to the end of it, and John asked, 'Where do we go now? Where do we clean up?' They said, 'Oh, back at the hotel.' The hotel's two hours away. He said, 'Look, we're filthy, I'm covered in mud, where on earth am I going to clean this stuff off?' Of course, he forgets he's got a handbag and lipstick and make-up. Someone goes off and finds a local farmer and asks if he would mind if some actors came and used his bathroom, just to clean up a bit? He said, 'Oh no, that's all right.' Then he sees six big lads in drag coming along, their tights in tatters, their skirts the wrong way round, bras ripped, going into his bathroom!

Within the group there were various layers of anger. John and Graham Chapman were quite angry about things. In Graham's case it could be because he was gay at a time when it was very difficult to be gay. John has always found life difficult. I think John had a perfect view of how life could be and it made him very, very cross. Some of John's best performances are based on anger – brilliant stuff, but very intense.

We never really knew the extent of Graham's drinking, and he didn't tell us until after he gave up, which was just before *The Life of Brian*. I remember I was deputed to give Graham a lift into work, because we lived nearby. I'd drive my car there and hoot the horn. Sometimes he'd come down within five minutes, but sometimes it was twenty minutes. I don't know what was going on up there. The window would open up and someone I'd never seen before, some young Malaysian waiter, would say, 'He coming in minute.' But when he came down there was a very strange smell. I was so naïve, I just thought he used an odd kind of toothpaste. It was only much later, when he'd given up drinking, that Graham said, 'I couldn't face the day without a couple of vodkas, and when I heard you hoot that horn, I had to make sure I had a couple of vodkas before I could even get down. Then I'd clean my teeth.' He was a lovely guy and extremely funny and inspired, but I could see he was difficult to work with. John wrote with him and I remember John saying he probably wrote 95 per cent of the material, but the five per cent Graham put in was absolutely what made it special.

John came to me with *A Fish Called Wanda,* saying he'd written this wonderful story about a gang heist. One of the members has a stammer, so at the vital moment it's very difficult to get the information they desperately need. He knew my father had a stammer, so he asked me about the technique of stammering. We talked about various things, like the fact that my father could sing perfectly well but had a terrible stammer when he spoke. It coloured his life completely. It made him rather aggressive and cantankerous. He was a man with a good sense of humour but if you've got a stammer, you can't address a meeting very well, and he was in management.

After I'd finished doing *Wanda* a lot of people wrote and said either I should or shouldn't have done the character, and some people who were developing a form of therapy for stammering children got in touch and said, 'Would you be interested in helping us out?' I said, 'Yes,' and we now have the Michael Palin Centre for Stammering in Childhood. It's been a great success, and I think if my father had had that sort of treatment and been able to go to a place like that, his life would have been immeasurably changed.

I'd been fascinated in most of the world since I was a boy. I always wanted to be an explorer. The idea with the travel series is to embark on the sort of travel where you'll meet people. So if you can get on a train or a boat, it's much better than going by four-wheel drive. And, of course, that also applies to camels in the desert. I don't have a way with camels, and it's been a real embarrassment. First of all, the first time we went out in the Sahara, we went to a refugee camp in Algeria, where they eat camels. They looked after us, lovely people, but they felt we had to have a meat course for breakfast, lunch and dinner, and it was always camel.

It has a sweet, slightly muttony, taste. It was perfectly good but after you've had it for five days, three times a day, you begin to think, 'Oh, I'd just like a bacon sandwich,' but, of course, you can't have a bacon sandwich out there. On the last day, there was camel for breakfast, and it was little bits of camel kidney. As soon as I put it to my nose, I knew this was a camel kidney past its sell-by date. But I couldn't not eat because she was so pleased, all this hospitality was for us, so I put it in. Within twenty-four hours my stomach turned into a Kenwood mixer. Really awful. For twenty-four hours it was camel's revenge.

When you're travelling like this, you have to eat what's offered to you – often it's a matter of hospitality. I remember in a small village in Peru, there was a festival on and a very old lady came up and handed me this gourd. In it was a pink, sort of yoghurty substance. I looked at it, drank it and it was quite nice, slightly acrid and all that. I said, 'Very nice, thank you very much. Lovely, thank you.' I then asked the guy what it was and he said, 'Well, it's a special palm wine that they make for this festival.' It's so important to the villagers, they cut down the entire sugar crop just to ferment this palm wine. And, of course, in places where there aren't any sugar groves growing, they ferment it with the saliva from old ladies. So if someone had said, 'Have a saliva yoghurt,' I would probably have said, 'No,' but by that time it was too late.

Most of the world – or at least, on the journey I recently did around the Pacific – still is a Python-free zone. The trip started very badly on a little island between Russia and America. It was extraordinary, just a bleak rock sticking out of the water, where they hunt whales. They've been asked if they want to move, but no, they want to stay on this island. We filmed with the Eskimos all day and I thought, 'I've really gone to the ends of the earth here.' Then, a little Eskimo group shuffles up to me. I think it's going to be a sort of traditional Eskimo farewell, and they said, 'Are you the guy from *Monty Python and the Holy Grail*?' I thought, 'Well here, in the middle of the Bering Strait, they've seen the Knights Who Say Ni!' So you can't get away.

1982–2007

Graham Chapman

I think I became a doctor because it seemed the simplest course for me at the time. Writing essays and doing anything artistic in school, for me, called for a little more effort, whereas anything to do with science meant I had to learn things. I was a little afraid of creating things, in a sense. I think medicine is a good training ground for anything, because you meet all sorts of people naturally in very strange predicaments.

I think it was the early radio shows that drew me into showbiz. I was an avid listener to radio shows such as *Take It From Here, Jewel and Warriss* and *Hancock*. Then later, when I was about thirteen or fifteen, it was *The Goon Show*, which was not like any other show. It didn't even like the medium that was putting it out particularly, it didn't like the BBC – wonderful. That was something I could relate to, and I suppose that's influenced us. Harry Secombe was kind enough once to say that *Monty Python* did for television what *The Goons* had done for radio, and maybe we did . . . I don't know.

I did a lot of drinking, a very great deal. Deep inside, I think I was insecure. I didn't really feel I deserved the success I'd achieved. I think that was it. After all, I was the one of the group who hadn't . . . I wasn't public school. I'd managed to get to Cambridge and felt a little bit out of my depth there. I never seemed to have to do a great deal of work, and yet managed, which made me insecure, so I drank.

At my peak, I was drinking four pints of gin a day. That was only during the last month and a half or so. I stopped because I noticed that it was beginning to affect my work, when I could remember my work. The very first day of filming *The Holy Grail*, we were halfway up a mountainside in Glencoe, and I hadn't got my daily dose. It was seven o'clock in the morning when we left the hotel. The bar wasn't open. I wasn't prepared, as I should have been if I'd researched my drinking properly.

I had the DTs on the mountainside, while having to try to remember lines and stand up. It was then that I decided next time I do a job like this, I'm going to be clean for it. It's not fair to the other chaps, to me, to what I've written, and it's very stupid. So, when I next had a patch of time that I thought I would need to recover, I took it and recovered, after three days of hell.

Once the decision had been made, it was easy, except for the three days of unpleasantness – having things crawling all over me and hallucinating, that sort of thing. One of the worst things, strangely enough, was not being able to remember whether I'd slept or not, if I was dreaming or awake. It was completely disorientating. I didn't know where I was. Objects seemed to threaten me – an angled lamp by the bedside. I would be just lying there, saying, 'Argh!' It was rather like W.C. Fields always acting that part. After that, a week in hospital, just cooling off on Valium, I've been fine ever since.

I came out because I didn't like being dishonest. I thought I had to be, because I didn't think people around me would understand. It took *me* some time to understand. This was when I was about twenty-four or twenty-five. I was thinking about getting married. I had a steady girlfriend, we'd been together for about a year, and then I found that wasn't quite what I wanted. To explain to John Cleese, my best friend at the time, a very upright gentleman and very English in many ways, was tough. He was not the sort of person, I thought, to take very kindly to a little piece of news like that about a friend of his, who used to smoke a pipe and play rugby and climb rocks. He was rather shocked, but his girlfriend was much more understanding. She explained to him that it wasn't necessarily the end of my life.

Telling my parents was pretty horrific, and difficult to do, but they were marvellous. It was difficult for me, but it needn't have been. They were very understanding. I told my mother first and she was upset, largely because of the effect she thought it would have on my father, so she insisted that I didn't tell him, and I insisted that I should. She prevailed and I didn't. They left the apartment where I was living and went home, and a week later I happened to ring my father and he said that Mother hadn't been sleeping at all for the last week. Eventually, he'd prised out of her what it was that had been bothering her, and he said, 'Don't worry, she just doesn't understand about these things,' which was wonderful.

1980

John Cleese

In Weston-super-Mare, we were all going to be accountants. My dad said to me, 'You know, my boy' – he used to get a little bit grand when he was talking – 'what you don't realise is if you go into the accountancy office now, by the time you're twenty-one, you'll have the initials ACA after your name and the world will be your oyster,' which is why we used to do those poisonously rude sketches about accountants. I was getting it out of my system.

He never quite got it. In 1967, when I was doing three programmes a week with David Frost and *I'm Sorry, I'll Read That Again* on a Sunday, I got a letter from him saying, 'Have you ever thought about going into the personnel department of Marks & Spencer?' I told this story a few years ago and somebody from Marks & Spencer sent me an application form.

My dad was witty and off the wall. If Dad couldn't get a

meal in a restaurant, he'd call the waiter over and say, 'I'm awfully sorry but I've got an operation to perform at three o'clock.' Once, we were driving down a little windy Somerset lane and some lunatic came round the corner much too fast. We both had to slam on our brakes. The guy jumped out of the car and came over, shouting, and when he'd finished, my father said in a French accent, 'Ah, you are a fine old English gentleman, no?' The guy looked at him for about thirty seconds and said, 'As a matter of fact I am, yeah.' That was my dad's sense of humour.

My mother's sense of humour was extraordinarily black. She'd ring me up and start going though all the things that were bad about her life. It was frustrating because you want to make her feel better and you can't say, 'Well, have a double scotch and shape up.' So, one day when she was saying that her leg was worse and two of her friends had died, I said, 'Well look, you've reached the point when you've had enough, Mum, and I know a little man in Fulham and he'll come down and kill you.'

I think I said it out of a kind of desperation. There was this stunned silence on the other end, and then she starts howling with laughter. So from then on, if she started getting depressed, I would say, 'Shall I call the little man in Fulham?' One day I said the little man in Fulham has died so I'm going to have to find somebody, and she just went on and on.

I went up to the Footlights stall in my first term at Cambridge and said I'm sort of interested, and they said, 'Oh, are you? Good. Do you sing?' I said, 'Sing?' I was in a Broadway musical and I had to mime, that's how good I can sing. Then they said, 'Well, it doesn't matter. Do you dance?' They said, 'Well, what do you do?' I went bright red. I said I try to make people laugh, and I just ran away and I didn't go anywhere near Footlights for two terms. Then my oldest friend, who knew someone in Footlights, was invited to go along, and the two of us did something together, and then it kind of happened. I liked the Footlights because they were the most interesting bunch of peers I came across at Cambridge – a wide variety of all the subjects they were studying, a variety of class. They were just fun people.

With Python, we knew we wanted to do something different, but I always remember saying to Michael Palin when we were in the changing rooms, just before we recorded the first show, do you realise we could be the first people in history to do a whole comedy show to complete silence? And he said he was thinking exactly the same thing. Then we went out. We heard Jonesy and Chapman doing the first sketch and ever so slowly people started to giggle and I looked at Michael, and we sort of thought maybe we'd be all right.

The Life of Brian is my favourite of the Python films. I think it's the best, and also we were making jokes about important subjects. It's best when jokes are about something important. It's wonderfully silly and makes people terribly cross. They were all protesting outside the New York cinema when it opened, all the established churches – the Lutherans, the Catholics, two lots of the Jewish faiths and Calvinists, I think. We were all condemned. And Eric Idle said, 'Well, at least we've brought them together for the first time.'

Basil Fawlty was real. I had lunch with Jimmy Gilbert and he said, 'What do you want to do?' I said that I'd like to write something with my then wife, Connie, and he said, 'Fine, write a pilot.' We sat down and said, 'Well, what are we going to do?' We looked at each other and I said, 'There's the hotel we stayed at in Torquay.' She said, 'Yeah, OK,' and we just started. We knew it was that.

He – Mr Sinclair – was the rudest man I've ever come across in my life. It was as though the hotel would run really well if he wasn't constantly bothered by these guests. There are so many stories. I remember we were having dinner early on, because all the Pythons were staying there, and they decided to leave because they couldn't put up with it. For some reason, I stayed on and Connie came and joined me, which is how we actually observed the man. At dinner, Terry

Gilliam, being of the American persuasion, was doing what Americans do – he cut up the meat, put down the knife, took the fork in his right hand and speared the meat. Mr Sinclair was walking by, trying to avoid people's eyes and look lofty, and he said, 'We don't eat like that in this country.' We were so astounded.

Then everything was too much trouble. He was one of those people who'd stare into space and the moment he saw a guest coming, he'd busy himself. So you'd come up to the desk and just stand there for a bit, and eventually you'd say, 'Excuse me, sir?' 'Oh, what?' 'Could you call me a taxi?' 'Call you a taxi?' 'You know, call me a taxi?' 'Oh, all right!'

We used to ask people for hotel stories. I had a friend in the restaurant business and I knew he'd worked at the Savoy, so I asked him what was the worst problem he'd had there. He said, 'Getting rid of the stiffs,' and your heart leaps with joy because he's just given you a thirty-minute episode with one comment. I asked, 'What happened?' He said, 'Well, the trouble was trying to get them into the service lift before any of the guests saw.' It's all absolutely true. I'm afraid what he told me was that a lot of elderly folk, who didn't have any relations left, would go in to the Savoy, take a few pills and not wake up in the morning, because they knew that the Savoy would handle it beautifully. That's rather touching.

2001

Michael: Did sex play a part at all in your life, as a young teenager?

John: You have to be joking. We're talking about Weston-super-Mare!

Michael: Well, that was the second line of my enquiry – was it available? Did you know about it? I love it when we get to this subject.

John: I was such a late starter sex wise that I'm embarrassed by it. I will write down how old I was. Anyway, it was in the Station Hotel, Auckland, New Zealand that I broke my duck.

Michael: How old were you?

John: I will never be able to live this down!

Michael: Go on.

John: Twenty-four! You bastard!

Michael: The Station Hotel, Auckland.

John: Oh dear, yes. And some newspaper found out and went and took a photograph of it.

Michael: What, the building?

John: Yeah. And it was like the hotel in *Psycho*.

Victoria Wood

Whenever I think of Victoria Wood I imagine someone almost sidling into the spotlight and performing with an eye on the exit. There is something diffident, shy even, in her manner, which is not what you might expect from someone as gifted as she. One critic said she chimes with the people because she is 'extraordinarily ordinary'. In her plays, sketches, situation comedies, one-woman shows, Victoria Wood constantly demonstrates her right to be regarded as a glorious and, maybe, unique talent. Speaking personally, anyone who created the barmy Mrs Overall, as played by Julie Walters in Acorn Antiques, can claim one of the highest positions on my list of favourite comedy writers. What looked like a demotion of Victoria's Christmas Show in 2009 must have been a mistake by BBC planners, or else they are in favour of something better, which, as yet, I haven't seen, and nor has anyone of my acquaintance.

I wanted to be famous. I don't know why. I was sitting in the garden by a hedge at our house in Tottington Road in Bury, and I remember thinking, 'I want to be famous,' and that was it really.

In my family there were four of us, and we lived in this huge bungalow on the top of a hill outside Bury in Lancashire.

It was like a prefab on steroids. It had been a students' holiday home for the poor children of Bury. They were so poor, they had to have a holiday home in Bury. It only had about four rooms but my mother divided it into lots – twenty little rooms – with little bits of hardboard that she'd nicked off building sites. Whenever you slammed the door, three walls would fall down. We stood there like Buster Keaton in the middle. And we all had our own room and we all did our own thing. My mother was in the big office full of wool. I don't know why. She didn't do any knitting. She was just in a room full of wool, and my father was in an office typing, eating Thornton's toffee, the sort you hit with a hammer. We had a TV set but we only rented it. I was obsessed with the television and it was always a disappointment when it went back to the shop in the summer.

At school I couldn't do a thing right. I was a liar and a thief. I stole charity money. If I hadn't done my homework, I used to steal half the homework pile because I thought, well, the teacher will never think it's been stolen. She'll think she left it somewhere.

I knew I was funny. I thought I could be funny and I could play the piano, and somehow I'd do something with that. I didn't know exactly what it would be, but I just had a feeling inside that I could do it. I was really lucky because my sister couldn't spell and so she couldn't go to the grammar school, so she went to another school in the next town, Rochdale, where they didn't care if you could spell or not. As long as you could spell Gracie Fields, that was enough. And Rochdale, compared with Bury, was groovy. Bury had black puddings and the Lancashire Fusiliers. Rochdale had poetry and sculpture and a drama festival, and there was a youth theatre in Rochdale. She went there and I went there with her in the summer holidays, and that was my salvation when I went at fifteen.

I didn't have the bottle to apply to the big drama schools, such as RADA and Central, so I applied to these ones that were behind sweet factories and two flights up above a dry cleaner's. In fact, I went to one and the woman said to me, 'Well, I'm sorry, you'll never be an actress because you have a deformed jaw.' 'Oh, thanks very much.' So that was me finished. But I auditioned at the Manchester Poly School of Theatre. It's got a proper drama school and Julie Walters was a first-year student when I went there. It was an all-day audition and a very sad day, because I was so nervous I threw up. And I was all dressed up. I had this big green cardigan and a green midi-skirt – went down to the length a nun has a dress now if she's a bit raunchy – and a big, dark green PVC maxi-coat. I looked like a bottle bank, actually.

I couldn't do anything because I was so overcome by nerves. Just at the end of it I started to feel better, and I looked around and suddenly noticed the girl who'd been showing me in and out of all the rooms. She had these little sparkly eyes, and she was doing a stand-up routine. She was talking about when she used to be a nurse in Birmingham, and I thought she was the funniest person I'd ever seen. She said to me, 'I hope you get in.' Seven years later, I'm in this revue at the Bush Theatre in Shepherd's Bush and one of the actresses was Julie Walters. I suddenly looked at her and said, 'Did you used to be a nurse and did you go to Manchester Poly?' and she said, 'Yeah. Did you used to be a bottle bank, because I've got some jam jars left.'

That show at the Bush Theatre was the first time I ever wrote a good joke. Now, that was a bit sad because that was 1978 and I'd been working for four years. I'd written a sketch for Julie about someone who thinks they're pregnant. I remember the joke. A woman says to her, 'Where are you in the menstrual cycle?' and she says, 'Taurus.'

While I was a student, I was a barmaid at a pub where a lot of BBC producers used to drink – BBC producers were all drunks in those days. I went to a party where they were, too, and I must have been drunk because I played the piano and sang, and they said, 'That's bloody marvellous. You must come down to Pebble Mill tomorrow morning.' The next morning the phone rang in my bedsitter and they said, 'We're all here, where are you?' I said, 'I didn't know you meant it.' They said, 'Yeah, come down, we're waiting.' And I went and there was a piano and I auditioned. Then I started to get little bits of work for the BBC on local programmes, and I got my Equity card.

I'd have been very sad if I'd been born in Basildon. All the comedians are from Lancashire, Yorkshire, Scotland or the North-east. There are a few Cockneys, but not counting them. I think it's the disrespectful attitude, a sort of bolshieness. It's partly a way of speaking, partly the vocabulary, partly being very flat and not impressed by anything. You need that attitude to be a comedian. I was once in a chip shop in Morecambe and a woman came running in and she said, 'The pier's just burnt down,' and this other woman said, 'About time.'

I do a thing in my show about how I couldn't be in a sex show in Bangkok, because I'm from Greater Manchester. Bangkok is the sex capital of the world and Greater Manchester is the chip capital of the world, which is why all the sex shows are in Bangkok and all the chip shops are in Greater Manchester. If all the sex shows were in Greater Manchester, there would just be girls with their coats on with chip pans, going, 'Because I'm not in the mood, now leave it.'

2000 and 2001

Dawn French

It was always a reassuring and joyful moment to see Dawn French walking down the stairs. You knew you were in for a good time. There is joy in her performance – whether in her partnership with Jennifer Saunders, her sitcoms or her appearance on a talk show – which intoxicates her audience, and this interviewer in particular. She is a funny woman as opposed to being a woman who simply says funny things. She is intrepid in her search for adventure and fun, as she proved when she threw her knickers at Tom Jones and snogged George Clooney. The perfect guest.

I've wondered what it was that gave me confidence from an early stage, and I can only put it down to my dad. There was a night when I was going to go out to a disco, and I was really ready to have sex with anybody who wanted to ask me. I had hotpants on, and thought I looked great. My father called me into his office, and I thought, 'Oh, I'm going to get the lecture.' But instead, he just said to me, 'You are the most precious thing in our lives. You are beautiful and worthy of anybody who shows you any attention. You shouldn't feel grateful for the scraps that any other girl leaves behind. You should have the best.' And I was just beaming, big and chested that I am, and in fact no boy came within ten feet. I wouldn't allow any of them to come near me that night, because they were beneath me. He gave me a bit of self-esteem and reinforced something I think I already felt, and I think a lot of big women would feel if they were allowed to – if they weren't constantly shown images of anorexic women as something to aspire to.

Jennifer Saunders and I weren't friends instantly. We met at college and Jen had already been there for a few weeks. My dad had just died so I was late to arrive, and they already had gangs set up – not horrible big LA gangs. She sat with some quite posh people, and I had no one to sit next to. However, both of us happened simultaneously to need somewhere to live and a mutual friend had a newly converted flat, so we both moved in. I remember thinking I really wanted to move into that flat, but I really didn't want to share with her. And I'm sure she was thinking exactly the same thing. She was not tidy – up to her knees in pants. The classic thing happened – there was a burglary in our house and the police came and said it was a pretty awful burglary but the worst area was the top room of the house. Of course, that was the one place the burglars hadn't been and that was Jennifer's bedroom.

Neither of us intended to do any acting, and certainly not any comedy, but we made each laugh a lot in the flat. We were on the teacher course, but a lot of the actors at college used to show off at the end-of-term cabaret, and we thought, 'Well, they're just showing off. We can do showing off quite well.' So we had a go at it, for the craic really. And then it became a real opportunity. There was a thing called *The Comic Strip* and they were looking for girls to be part of it. They only wanted women, because they didn't have any, and that's where it started.

I'm not good at big, showbiz bashes. I'm extremely incompetent at them, actually. For instance, Jennifer and I were out for supper and a chap came over to us and said he represented a big make-up company. They had provided make-up for us before and they could do with some help at a little bash they were having the next night. They didn't have enough people coming and would we go along to bump it up a bit? Jennifer immediately said, 'No.' I said, 'Er . . . no, don't think I can, but if I'm in town I might do.' Anyway, I was in Soho and I'd finished work, came out on to the street, no make-up, just my bag with some scripts, and I was looking for a cab to get back to the BBC. There were no cabs but suddenly round the corner comes a man on a rickshaw. I waved him past and he said, 'Oh come on, Dawn, give a bloke a chance! Where do you wanna go?' And I said, 'I'm going to the BBC. You don't wanna go all the way there, do you?' And he said, 'Hop on! Do you a deal.'

I hopped on and that was such a mistake! I don't know if you've had a rickshaw experience, but as the guy is pedalling, he's trying to talk to you over his shoulder. 'So Dawn, how's it going?' And that draws everyone's attention to you sitting in the back there, like the Queen of Tonga! It's very embarrassing, very cold and uncomfortable, and I thought, 'I've got to get off this rickshaw.' We'd gone about a hundred yards and that had taken about an hour and the guy was really failing, so I thought, 'I'll just nip into that party, because that's quite close. Then I'll come straight out and get into a cab.' I said, 'I've had a thought. Go round that corner. There's a party there I'm going to go to.' As he came round the corner, I could see this was not a small party. There were fifty paparazzi, with laser lights arching and supermodels in backless dresses, and I'm on a rickshaw with no make-up and my work coat. So I'm walking up the red carpet completely by mistake. I went into the party anyway. I was glad to be off the rickshaw.

Once Jennifer and I were in a play and we went out for lunch with the writer, who, incidentally, was the woman who wrote *Beaches*. We took her out for a treat and she chose to go to the Ivy. We were having our lunch, and Terry Gilliam came in. He came over and gave us a hug and told us he was working on something called *Twelve Monkeys*, which I thought was a porn film. He sat down and then Brad Pitt walked in, a sort of angel really. He walked past our table, fool, and sat down with Terry Gilliam. I went to the loo soon after and I got a piece of paper from one of the waiters and wrote a note to Terry saying, 'You will make Brad Pitt kiss me or I will kill your family.'

I saw the note being delivered and Terry winked at me, and I thought, 'Oh yeah, he's just enjoying the joke,' and I got involved with my food, as you do. Somewhere near the chocolate pudding, suddenly there was Brad Pitt, kissing me. He was so brilliant, he said, 'Hey Dawn, looking great, can I take you out, call you?' and then he went off. Jennifer Saunders' chin just hit the table, and I was so excited by it that I couldn't actually hold on to the lie for longer than about five seconds. Lenny knows that this sort of thing has to be done. If, I don't know, Julia Roberts wanted to kiss him, I wouldn't get in the way of it, frankly. You've got to take your thrills where you can get them.

1999–2007

Joan Rivers

If I could hire someone to insult and discomfort an enemy, I would phone Joan Rivers. She is lethal because she is fearless. There are no taboo subjects, no part of the anatomy she will not describe, no area of human behaviour she will not subject to explicit examination.

Her apprenticeship was performing stand-up in New York strip clubs. Anything after that was a stroll. She was a perfect guest for a talk show in that she didn't mind whom she sat next to, providing they could take a joke. For a while, she was an acclaimed replacement for Johnny Carson on the *Tonight Show*, which demonstrates the American predilection for talk-show hosts to be funnier than their guests. She is the world's most hilarious and endearing bitch.

Joan: I hate old people.

Michael: I know you do.

Joan: The only good thing is – two good things I should say. One is you lose your hearing, so you can't hear the doctor say you're going to die. The other thing is, you get into cinema half-price, because they know you'll forget and see it twice.

Michael: You don't like being old. Is that the reason for the plastic surgery, to arrest the march of time?

Joan: Well wouldn't you? Oh, every woman out there for God's sake – pull it up and snip it off. And just make another person have it walk beside you.

Michael: But . . .

Joan: I think plastic surgery is great. You can overdo it. My very good friend is Cher, we went for bikini waxes and they start at her forehead . . .

****

Michael: Now, we were talking earlier about plastic surgery, and you've had a bit of that.

Joan: Why me? How dare you. I will do it when I'm ready. Excuse me, I've gotta take out some stitches. Keep talking.

Michael: What about your family when they see you? How do they react?

Joan: Well, they don't recognise me, so that's good, because every time it's like a first. My grandson has never, ever seen me without a bandage somewhere. My daughter said they were watching *The Return of the Mummy* the other night. He ran up to the TV and went, 'Grandma, Grandma!' So excited. 'Oh, Nanna New Face!' Look, if it makes you feel good . . . You want to be beautiful and if that's the way you want to go through life, it's your choice.

****

Joan: You know why my generation were never told the facts of life?

Michael: Were you not?

Joan: Never. My mother said, 'The man gets on top, the woman gets on the bottom.' That's all she told me. I bought bunkbeds. I had no idea. I shouldn't tell you this, because it's a funny show I know, but my first sexual experience . . . well, it was a rape. So you know . . .

Michael: A rape?

Joan: Yeah. Luckily, he didn't press charges but . . .

****

Michael: Was there what could be termed a golden period in your life, as far as it went, for men?

Joan: People think that when you get older, sex is over. And I have a very active sex life. I would just like a partner! You can't have everything, right? I can still have full orgasm, as long as a man knows where to touch me. Which is Tiffany's. But what men like . . . when a woman is attractive, she can be a moron, it doesn't matter. You've had them on this show.

Michael: This is true.

Joan: There was one starlet, who will remain nameless, and she saw a sign saying 'wet floor' and she did! And all the men thought it was cute. It doesn't matter if they're attractive.

Michael: You're still dating, are you?

Joan: I am. I still date. I date older men, so that leaves me God! And I look at my body and I go crazy. I don't like dating younger men. Cher is my good friend and she dates them. She's going out with a foetus now! She goes to Toys R Us to pick up guys.

****

Michael: You've been quoted as saying how unattractive you were as a young women.

Joan: Darling, you had to be funny. When I was born, the doctor looked at me and looked at the afterbirth and handed my mother the afterbirth! They found me, luckily, in a garbage can two weeks later.

Michael: Did it have a scarring effect?

Joan: A scarring effect? You silly man! A scarring effect? My whole life. Well, we're not going to go here but my gynae-cologist examines me over the phone! Flies wouldn't sit on me if I was in sheep-shit! It just doesn't work!

Michael: Did it have an effect on your sex life?

Joan: Sex life? I put a face on my vibrator! There is no sex life and there should be now with these older gentlemen, because of Viagra. Viagra Plus – do you have that here? You have Viagra, but Viagra Plus? I'm not making a joke. In the United States it's thirty-six hours of erection, so you can be ready when she is! These poor old wives. There's these ninety-year-old guys and these dry wives, and they are in and out, setting them on fire! In California now, you've been hearing about the fires? The Malibu fires were started by my neighbour! Harry Schwartz, ninety-two! 'Come here, baby!' Malibu is in flames because he had Viagra Plus! Just awful, bodies go, you know.

****

Joan: I've been fired. I've been thrown out. I've been told I'm over. So you keep coming back. I think that's why you come on the stage, you just want to have fun. If there are four gay men in the audience, I'm gonna have a good time. God bless the gay men, and may I say one thing?

Michael: Please do.

Joan: I am all for gay marriage.

Michael: You are?

Joan: Yes. Because why should only straights suffer divorce. It's so unfair.

****

Michael: It's interesting because I watched you this week on television, talking very movingly, actually, about your widowhood. That was a fascinating programme. Six different women dealing with a situation, and I was fascinated by your story.

Joan: My husband committed suicide.

Michael: And you were angry about it.

Joan: Angry? Angry! That son of a bitch, if he came back I'd kill him now! You ruined my daughter's life, you son of a bitch! Take this, bang! You want to die? Come over here! It was horrible. Suicide is something that should not happen, and when people are struggling so for life . . . I work with paediatric Aids and we do all this stuff and then you see . . . But the pain is so intense. I understand that, too, because I work on suicide prevention. My poor husband. And it was my fault because we were making love and I took the bag off my head! One step from the bed to the window, he's like SuperJew!

Michael: But you deal with it how you deal with everything.

Joan: I do. I deal with everything with humour because it's horrible.

****

Michael: You're seventy-one now, aren't you?

Joan: I don't think we have to go into that.

Michael: Well . . .

Joan: They bought out my cake. It took me a year to blow out the candles, because you have no breath left. You lose your breath. And you know what happens?

Michael: What?

Joan: Can we really talk?

Michael: Yes.

Joan: At forty you begin to lose your eyesight. At fifty the mind starts to go. At sixty you start to fart, it is just terrible. And you don't lose your sense of smell till seventy. You're so alone!

****

Michael: What are you hitting me for?

Joan: You're going off the air, you son of a bitch.

Michael: Why are you upset?

Joan: Because I love to come over here and do your show. I have been doing your show, on and off, for years.

Michael: This is true.

Joan: And I've been keeping everything you ever gave me in the closet, right next to Tom Cruise, and, oh, grow up! Allegedly! You know, every guest gets gifts. I don't know if the audience knows this. There's always little gifts.

Michael: Yes.

Joan: And they've always been shitty. You would give a welcome mat to Anne Frank. You know me, but a T-shirt? One year I flew six thousand miles. A T-shirt. Winona Ryder wouldn't shop with this. Oh, and the cookies. They gave out German cookies. I'm a Jew. They fed them to Jews at Auschwitz, they were so terrible.

2004–07

Paul O'Grady

What you look for in an interview with a comedian is a lot of laughs. That's what they do for a living. Best of all, you want a life story that is as dramatic as it is funny. Paul O'Grady gave me what I wanted. I have heard many remarkable stories but none as fascinating as his account of a child born to poverty in Birkenhead; making a living as a social worker in Camden; earning an extra few bob as a drag act in pubs; and becoming a great television star. A singular and inspirational member of the human race.

Michael: You came from Tranmere, a fairly rough old area?

Paul: A little bit, to say the least.

Michael: And your mum had it rough, didn't she?

Paul: They had a terrible life, me mum and her two sisters. They were born in extreme poverty in Birkenhead, in the depression. It was really grim. When they were kids, they all went into domestic service. My mum was the tweeny maid in between floors, my Auntie Chrissy was the cook and Auntie Annie was the nanny. They hated their jobs. One day, there was a dinner party for fifteen, so they're all sat there, and the lady of the house is having her dinner. They served the first course and Auntie Chrissy said, 'Right, come on, let's bugger off!' They got the kids, gave them a big jar of jam each in the kitchen, got off out the window and vanished. I've often wondered what the lady of the house did, when she rang the bell for the next course, called 'Savage!' – because that was me mother's maiden name – and they'd gone. They'd just left. They were really fiery.

Michael: The person who appeals to me in your background is your Auntie Chrissy. You could build a TV series around her.

Paul: Oh, easy. She was a clippie on the buses, and she was the captain of the Lord Exmouth Public House darts team. You wonder where Lily came from – this is my childhood. No wonder I'm half crazy! She's a big blonde woman, full of one-liners, with a fag in her gob. She used to sit on the lav when you're in the bath, with the lid down, flicking the ash in the palm of her hand. And when she'd finished the fag, she'd wipe it on her skirt. She had a heart of pure gold but was tough as old boots. I got a letter – this is Lily – off an old lady to say are you any relation to a Chrissy Savage she worked with in the war? I wrote back and it turned out they were in the war together. Auntie Chrissy was on the ack ack guns – she was only nineteen. She'd lie in bed, the sirens would go and I believe the language would turn the air blue. She'd get her Woodbines, head full of rollers, put a great coat over her nightie, and she'd get on this ack ack gun, spinning around like a maniac. Pregnant, too – she didn't know she was pregnant! And the language came because it disturbed her kip, not because she hated the Germans! They'd had the nerve to disturb her beauty sleep. If Hitler had heard her, he'd have vanished.

Michael: How do you go from there to working for Camden Council?

Paul: I worked in a kids' home in Birkenhead first, and I went from there.

Michael: So you wanted to be a social worker, basically?

Paul: I wasn't so bothered about what I wanted to do. I'd like to sit here and say I've been driven by various ambitions, but I haven't. I've just floated in and out of things. I'd leave a job on a Friday, start a new one on a Monday, and I'd leave that on Tuesday and go on the dole.

Michael: But you didn't pick easy jobs. You went into social services in Camden, and were looking after battered women and their children. You were living with them, weren't you?

Paul: Yeah, they've stopped it now, which is a shame, but it was called the peripatetic team. Say a parent went into hospital, we'd go into the home and look after the kids to save them from going into care. Nine times out of ten, you're dealing with real squalor, and often drunken boyfriends would turn up in the night and think I was the new fancy bit and go for me. We'd be having fights in Camden High Street at three o'clock in the morning, with babies under me arms. I'd be thinking, 'I'm twenty-five, give us a break. I should be having a life!' But I really enjoyed it. I'm painting a bad picture, but it wasn't all bad.

I met some really great people, people I'm still in touch with.

But you saw too much squalor and too much heart break, too many sick children and too many women getting murdered by these pigs of husbands. We weren't allowed to hit them. We were supposed to show our card and say, 'Camden Council.' I shouldn't tell you this really, but some fella came to the door once and said, 'I want me baby,' and I hit him over the head with the dustbin. 'Do ya?' Boff! And I had an official in the front room. I said, 'He's collapsed on the step!'

Michael: You're bound to get involved.

Paul: You can't help it, you really can't. You've got kids to look after and that's your main aim, and all I cared about was protecting them. I used to think, 'Well, I'm not playing this by the rule book. Four o'clock in the morning and a drunk on the step with a broken bottle – I'm going to take whatever steps I have to.'

Michael: What kind of view has it given you of the world?

Paul: Quite warped! No, it didn't, I see good and bad now, in everything. Now, nothing bothers me, nothing fazes me. It really doesn't. *C'est la vie.*

Michael: It seems an extraordinary leap from what you've just described to the pubs of South London.

Paul: Ah, there's a reason. We got lots of time off in lieu, so I got a job. I used to work in pubs, behind the bar, to supplement me income, because it was lousy money. I worked in drag pubs. I was in all sorts of little drag acts, and I used to think, 'I could do that.' We were always playing Liverpool housewives, shouting out of windows to imaginary kids, 'Go to the shop for us,' just to amuse ourselves. So it was an extension of that, and because all the acts in those days, or most of them, were in sequins and it was Shirley Bassey orientated – very glam – I went the other way with Lily. She had a tattoo and a love bite, scuffed heels and holes in her tights. She was a divorced prostitute with two children and a fondness for booze and drugs.

Michael: Just a normal, everyday woman. But it was a very tough apprenticeship, wasn't it?

Paul: Oh, you're telling me. The Vauxhall Tavern on a Saturday night, late show, they'd eat the young live. It was really rough, you had to be able to control them. And often, if they got too lairy, I'd get off the stage and belt them – boof, shut up – and get back on!

2002

Paul Merton

Paul Merton, taking off on one of his fantastic flights of fancy, is like watching a great jazz musician at work. His ability to improvise enlivens *Have I Got News For You* and is a major reason for the longevity of the show. His partnership with the acidic Ian Hislop is perfect casting. His deadpan delivery punctuated by manic outbursts is a clear homage to his heroes, the masters of comedy in silent movies, in particular Charlie Chaplin and Buster Keaton.

I knew I wanted to be a comedian from a very early age, about three or four years old, which I admit is very bizarre. I went to a circus and saw clowns falling over, and I hadn't seen adults behave like that before. I thought it wonderful that adults should have great big shoes, ginger waistcoats, hair that went up at the side, and threw buckets of whitewash over each other. Nobody told them off. They were allowed to do it and I thought that was wonderful.

I was a funny boy at school. I was one of those at the back of the classroom who used to make other kids laugh. I would collect jokes from *Beano* and *Dandy* and as I got older I started to make up my own jokes. I used to love writing English essays – you got into compositions where you could invent other people's stories.

I was taught by a mixture of nuns at first. When I was about eight years old, I had to write an essay at school called 'What I Did During the Summer Holidays'. I had gone to Great Yarmouth with the family. I was young, I had no money, no source of income, it made sense to go with them, so I did. I started writing this essay, saying we went to Great Yarmouth and it was very nice, the beach was very sandy. Then a spaceship landed, I got on the spaceship and we went to the moon. I just didn't want to write about sandcastles, and she was really annoyed about this, the nun. She said, 'You can't write that. That's not true, it didn't happen.' I thought, 'This is rich, coming from a nun,' what with the Garden of Eden, and the snake says to Eve, 'Don't eat the apple . . .' A spaceship landed in Great Yarmouth, and I'm told that didn't happen. I think she maybe thought I was trying to start a rival religion.

It was annoying. When you're young and a teacher tells you you've done something wrong and it doesn't feel wrong, you wonder why she's saying it's wrong. She read this essay out as an example to the rest of the class of the sort of thing not to write. The following week all the other kids thought, 'Well, we can write about spaceships. Instead of "A Day in the Life of a Supermarket", we can write about anything.' She made me stand up in front of all the class and humiliated me by saying, 'This is all your fault.'

I auditioned at RADA simply because I was nineteen, and if you don't know anybody in show business, to say you want to be a comedian is as daft as to say you want to be an astronaut. So with RADA, what I wanted to do was find out what it would be like to stand on stage. I'd read that you go along, stand on a stage, and about four or five people judge you. I did a piece from *Richard III*, the 'Now is the winter of our discontent' thing. I had no ambition to get into RADA but what it proved to me was, as I stood on that stage, I wasn't scared of it.

****

I was working on *Sticky Moments* with Julian Clary and *Whose Line Is It Anyway*, writing the first series for Channel 4, and everything I wanted to happen was happening in the space of about three or four months. For the excitement, I was working about eighteen hours a day, and if you're spending that much time just thinking, eventually you overload. I went on holiday to Kenya and I took these anti-malaria pills, which have since been found sometimes to have a side-effect on the brain. It was quite harrowing at the time. I had a manic episode. It wasn't a depression, it was the opposite really, and so I went to the Maudsley Hospital for treatment. It was a career move basically. I thought this would make a very interesting chapter in an autobiography one day.

It was difficult because *Whose Line Is It Anyway* was being shown at the same time, and I said to my psychiatrist one day, 'There are some other patients in the hospital who are bothering me a bit.' He said, 'Well, why?' I said, 'They think they know me.' He said, 'Oh yes, why would that be?' I said, 'Well, because I'm on television.' 'Oh, really?' He didn't watch Channel 4 at all. In the end, I had to get a tape to show him it wasn't a delusion. One patient came up to me in the canteen and said, 'Are you Paul Merton?' I said, 'Shh, I'm not supposed to be here.'

The disturbing thing was they had this system where the nurses and doctors would be dressed just like the rest of the patients. We had a group therapy session every morning and everybody would sit around and there would be terrible stories. Someone over here is a schizophrenic, someone over here lost their house and their family, and all these kind of things. One particular woman was having a very bad time. She used to be in tears and I found out after about three days that she was a staff nurse. I saw her in an office going through all the files. What sort of thing is that to do to a nutcase? It was very, very bizarre.

Before I went in, I was trying to do three or four things at a time, and since then I've only ever concentrated on one thing. For example, while I'm sitting here talking to you, I'm not eating a kebab. That would be two things. If I was riding a bike, eating a kebab and talking to you, that would be three things, and the Maudsley would be a short step away. So I have to concentrate on one thing. Show business is just a job. It's a great job if it works and it's successful and you get lots of money. That's fine, but that's all it is. Once you finish the job, you go home and the job is over. I think that's what I learnt, rather than taking the job home with me.

1998

3 Sport

Muhammad Ali

I first encountered Muhammad Ali in 1971 and I have little doubt the hour-long interview did more than any other to establish the reputation of the show. In 1971 he was the pretender to the title but he looked and talked like a champion. He had great physical beauty and grace as well as a wonderful sense of the absurd. He was irresistible. I didn't know then I was to chart both his rise and sad decline in three more encounters.

The man I met again in 1974 had jettisoned some of his charm. This was a religious warrior. As he told me, 'You are facing a holy war when you fight me now!' At the time he was world champion, having just spectacularly beaten George Foreman in Zaire. He was angry but invincible.

Our last meeting was in 1981 and signalled an end to a career without parallel in any sport you care to mention. He brayed at the moon and we all listened. Sometimes he spouted dangerous nonsense and we forgave him. He brought to a brutal sport a new and adoring audience, and those who saw him will never forget him. I cannot watch our final interview without feeling both sad and angry. Sad because the man who had truly been the greatest could be so betrayed by the sport he loved, and his life would become a misery. Angry because people who should have known better let it happen. *Time* magazine got it right, saying Ali was 'coaxed into fights by his manager long after he should have retired, and perhaps because he loved the sport too much'.

Round One – 1971

Michael: I think one of the things undeniable about you, Muhammad, is that you've got this flair for publicity. You attract it. Have you always had this gift, thinking right back?

Muhammad: No. I trained for a fella named Duke Saberdong. He was a Hawaiian fighter and he was a giant, about six foot eight tall. I was due to fight him in Las Vegas and I was on a television show. Gorgeous George – a famous American wrestler – was there talking before myself and I came on after him. During the time he was being interviewed, he was saying, 'I am the prettiest wrestler. I am great, look at my beautiful blond hair. If that bum even messes my hair up, I'll annihilate him.' He said, 'George, what if you lose?' 'If I lose, I'm catching the next jet out to Russia. I want everybody out there to know, if I lose . . .' He just got mad, said, 'I'm sick and tired, I'm getting off of this show,' and he ran off the show.

I was so nervous, I said, 'Boy, he sure talks a lot!' I had to go to see what he would do. Would he win or would he lose? When Gorgeous George came down the aisle, he had these two blonde, beautiful girls carrying his robe so it wouldn't get dirty. Real conceited and arrogant. And I was there in astonishment, just twenty-one years old and nobody knew me yet – Olympic champ, but I hadn't started talking yet. And I looked at him, and I said, 'Boy, he needs a good whooping.' I just wanted the other man to give him a good whooping. And he reached over and he took a can of beer out of the fellow's hand, he was arguing with him, and threw it in his face, and messed the man's suit up. Later, I found out this fella worked with the show, but the people didn't know.

He got up to his opponent's corner before his opponent got into the ring, he took some deodorant and sprayed the fellow's corner. He won the first fall, he lost the second fall, he won the third. But when I saw all of those people come to see Gorgeous George get beat – and they all paid to get in, that's the thing – I said, 'This is a good idea!' And right away I started talking – 'I am the greatest! I am beautiful! If you talk jive, you'll fall in five. I cannot lose!' In America, they've got a little saying – they said, 'The nigger talks too much!' And we sold everything, they lined for miles, coming to see me get beat. And I went to the bank laughing every time!

Michael: Can I go back to your childhood? When you were a kid in Louisville, did you get involved in fist fights and things like that?

Muhammad: A couple. I can remember a couple of those fights when I ran, because it's kind of dangerous. One fellow was going for a rock and another one was picking a stick. There weren't no referees or no judges and I got out! I've been in a couple of scuffles, but not too many.

Michael: When you were twelve and in your early teens, did you ever imagine yourself as being world champion?

Muhammad: Right, it happened one night when I heard Rocky Marciano – 1954, 1953 or sometime. He had beaten Walcott or somebody and I was in the rain on my bicycle, leaning over listening to a fellow's radio in the car. I got there too late and I heard the fellow saying, 'And still the Heavyweight Champion of the World . . . Rocky Marciano!' A little skinny kid from Kentucky, about eighty-five pounds and small, and I rode off in the rain on my bicycle, and I could just hear the man saying, 'And still the Heavyweight Champion of the Whole World, Cassius Clay!' I heard it as I rode off in the rain, and I said to myself, 'The champion of the whole world can whoop every man in Russia, every man in America, every man in China, every man in Japan, every man in Europe!' The champion of the whole world! So I kept working until I did. I was going to be not only champion of the whole world, but better than all of those before me.

Michael: I'm not gonna argue with you.

Muhammad: Then you're not as dumb as you look!

Michael: Can I turn the conversation a little bit because you're as much now a political figure as you are an athlete.

Muhammad: I don't call myself a political figure. I'm seeking the peace.

Michael: But you're involved in a political struggle, in a power struggle between black and white, and you're a leading member of that. Can I ask you when you were first aware, when you were a child, of the differences between black and white?

Muhammad: No, I've got to get that thing straight. I'm not involved in a power struggle, I'm not between black and white. I'm involved, I would say, in a freedom struggle, do you understand? I wouldn't say power struggle. We're not trying to get that type of power, to rule nobody. We're just trying to get out from under the legal rule.

Michael: But what I asked you was when was your first recollection as a child of being a second-class citizen, being treated like one?

Muhammad: Second-class? No, more sixteenth-class. They used to say you're a second-class citizen, and I'd say to my mother, 'Momma, how come we're second-class citizens?' The Chinese can go where I can't go in America, the Englishman – you can come into white America and set up businesses and do things I can't do, and the Puerto Rican, the Hawaiian, and just about everybody came before the black people, more respected. So I said if we were second-class citizens, we'd be doing all right, but we were way down from second. If we were second-class citizens, we'd be driving Cadillacs and living good. First-class would be driving a Rolls-Royce, but we'd still be doing good. Now we're way under that.

I'm not just a boxer. I do a lot of reading, a lot of studying, I ask questions, I go out travelling to these countries and watch how their people live and I learn. And I always asked my mother, 'Say mother, how come is everything white?' I'd say, 'Why is Jesus white with blond hair and blue eyes? Why is the Lord's supper all white men? Angels are white.' I said, 'Mother, when we die, do we go to heaven?' She said naturally we go to heaven. I said, 'Well, what happened to all the black angels? They took the pictures?'

I said, 'I know, if the white folks was in heaven too, then the black angels were in the kitchen preparing the milk and honey.' She said, 'Listen, you quit saying that, boy!'

I was always curious, and I always wondered why I had to die and go to heaven. How come I couldn't have pretty cars and good money and nice homes now? Why do I have to wait till I die to get milk and honey? And I said, 'Momma, I don't want no milk and honey. I like steaks.' I said, 'Milk and honey's a laxative anyway. Do they have a lot of bathrooms in heaven?'

So I was always curious. I always wondered why Tarzan is the king of the jungle in Africa – he was white. I saw this white man swinging round Africa with a diaper on, hollering! And all the Africans, he's beating them up and breaking the lion's jaw, and here's Tarzan talking to the animals and the Africans have been there for centuries and they can't talk to the animals – only Tarzan is talking to the animals. I always wondered why Miss America was always white, with all the beautiful brown women in America – beautiful suntans, beautiful shapes, all types of complexions – but she always was white. And Miss World was always white, and Miss Universe was always white. I was always curious.

And this was when I knew that something was wrong. I won the Olympic gold medal in Rome, Italy. Olympic champion – the Russian standing right here, and the Pole right here. I'm defeating America's so-called threats and enemies, and the flag is going up, and I'd have whooped the world for America! I took my gold medal, thought I'd invented something. I said, 'Man, I know I'm gonna get my people's freedom. I'm the champion of the whole world, Olympic champion. I know I can eat downtown now.'

I had my big old medal on, and in the restaurants at that time, black folks couldn't eat downtown. And I went downtown, I sat down, and I said, 'A cup of coffee, and a hot dog.' The lady said, 'We don't serve negroes.' I was so mad I said, 'I don't eat 'em either, just give me a cup of coffee and a hot dog!' I said, 'I'm the Olympic gold medal winner. Three days ago I fought for this country in Rome, I won the gold medal, and I'm gonna eat.' I heard her telling the manager. Anyway, I didn't raise nothing, they put me out. And I had to leave that restaurant in my home town where I went to church and served in their Christianity and fought in all the wars. I'd just won a gold medal and couldn't eat downtown. I said, 'Something's wrong.' And from then on I've been a Muslim.

Round Two – 1974

Muhammad: I should have this show, shouldn't I? Let me tell you something else, you are intelligent. See, you're not as dumb as you look. When they told me I was gonna do your show, I was, 'Oh no!' People like you – David Frost, David Susskind – I like people who make me think, and you talk, and this is a brainy man, he's not just an ordinary fella. You think it's easy. Come take his position. You'll find out that I'm a witty person and it's kinda hard to talk to a man like me. And I need people of wisdom such as myself to make me think, keep me going.

Michael: I'm glad you can remember what you're saying, because I can't. Well, you made a takeover bid for the show, but I don't see why you should do that because you've done it all right, twice. Let me ask you something else. You're a great athlete, as I see it, one of the greatest athletes I've ever seen. You're certainly one of the greatest boxers that there's ever been. Why do you fight people who are quite obviously not in your class?

Muhammad: Like, for example, who?

Michael: Well, let me put an even better question to you.

Muhammad: See him go for that? Let me put it another way, ah? Things are getting hot, you see him drinking that water.

Michael: I want a medal for coming on your show, don't I? Well, let's take Joe Bugner as an example. Now, I've seen Bugner fight . . .

Muhammad: Now somebody told me something, that they don't like the way you write about Bugner. They say you put that man down. That's a shame. The British can't even unite. Look, you've got a good white hope, you can build the man up, give him some confidence and might make him be better than he is. You can't attack him and all the other people attack him. He's representing England. You need to stand up for him, he's your chap.

Michael: That kind of thing cuts no ice at all. The fact is the man's got no class, right?

Muhammad: He's got more class than George Foreman! Joe Bugner's a better fighter. I didn't knock out Joe Bugner. He went twelve rounds with me. He went twelve rounds with Joe Frazier. Joe Bugner's a good fighter.

Michael: There have been a lot of people you've not knocked out.

Muhammad: He must have stole your girlfriend or something. I'm trying to figure out why you're getting on Joe Bugner like that.

Michael: Because, you see, in boxing like in any other sport, I admire grace and I admire skill, more than anything else. And I'm not putting Joe Bugner down at all. I think Joe Bugner's a very nice man, a decent fella and all this. But I don't think he's got any talent in the ring. And I think to ask Joe Bugner to fight . . .

Muhammad: That mean's I'm nothing. You mean the man who did twelve rounds with me ain't got no talent? I hit him with everything.

Michael: You didn't hit him with everything!

Muhammad: Who didn't hit him with everything? That was a hell of a fight, me and Joe Bugner.

Michael: So how good do you think he is?

Muhammad: He's good and – how high is he ranked in the world? I don't know.

Michael: About number four.

Muhammad: He's that good. The top ten best heavyweights in the world, he's the fourth best.

Michael: But what's the gap between number four and number ten, or number three and number ten? It's a big gap. Because if you go from three to ten downwards, there's some right dummies in that lot, isn't there?

Muhammad: Yes, so what are you trying to say?

Michael: Well what I'm saying . . .

Muhammad: Can you box?

Michael: No, no.

Muhammad: Have you ever boxed?

Michael: No.

Muhammad: Well why would you know so much about boxing? You have a good television show, and you're a good script man, but won't you stay out the ring?

****

Muhammad: Have you always been on this television show? You were the little old hustler running round before you came up here one day. Now look at it you. Supposing I told you, you would never be nothing and you're not as good as David Susskind and you're not as good as Eamonn Andrews, or you can't make it like Harry Carpenter? And now you're about number-one man round here. But you had to work up. You're destroying the man, and talking about him. See people like you are good. It's people like you that make Joe Bugner train hard. Because one day the curly haired, handsome Joe Bugner is going to be the champion and you're going to say, 'Joe, would you come on my show?' And Joe will say, 'Didn't I tell you? Because they told me I didn't have a chance with George, that made me fight. They told me I didn't have a punch, didn't they? They told me I'm no good for nothing. He don't know what I'll do, he's scared. No, but it's people like you, you're a good man, you speak your piece and I'm sure that you wouldn't say what you say if you didn't mean it.

Michael: Do you think you'll retire as world champion?

Muhammad: I hope to, I can't really say but I hope so. I don't think I'll be beaten in the next five years.

Michael: Next five years? Well, you'll be thirty-seven then.

Muhammad: Right. Sugar Ray Robinson fought when he was

forty-two, Archie Moore fought when he was fifty-one. I'm greater than all of them. Thirty-seven's young. Jersey Joe Walcott won his title at thirty-seven.

****

Michael: How much do you think you help your people?

Muhammad: I don't really know. It's up to the individuals and you can't ever see it. The man who truly does something from his heart don't look for thanks, nor do he look to see the results, he just do it. And if I say something, beauty is in the eye of the beholder, then I would say whatever people think of me is in the eye of the beholder. So people look at different things. You say something, some will see it this way, some will see it that way, some will take it as good, some will use it to help them, so it's just up to you to take it.

For an example, I would say look at our religious leader in America, Elijah Muhammad, leader of all the Muslims in America, who is converting our women, cleaning up our people and giving them high morals, teaching them their names, their language, their culture, where they were from before they were made slaves. His teachings are so powerful they have now reached here in London, England. He said something that helped two black sisters from near here. They took off their pants, they took off the mini-skirts, they wear the long robes now, the head pieces, they're just like the Muslims in America, and they follow him to his word. So what I'm saying to you is what I have heard. I mean what I'm saying, I don't know who I'm influencing until they themselves stand up.

Michael: What's wrong with the mini-skirts, what's wrong with hot pants?

Muhammad: Well see, this is a European design thing. You go to Saudi Arabia and tell the women to put on a mini-skirt. Go to Zaire, Africa, have the women put on short dresses. They'd be fined or locked up. Go to Pakistan, all throughout the black Islamic Muslim countries. Number one, I have a wife and she's walking around with a skirt up to here and then what's happening? Why would I want anybody to see her? People look and they're weak and they're lusting for her, all kind of freaks and no good people on the streets. Horses show their behinds, cows and animals and mules. Human beings don't walk around with their behinds out. Savages walk around with their behinds out. And my wife's behind ain't for every man to look at. You understand what I'm saying? Makes a lot of sense.

Anything God made precious, nature hides it. You cannot find diamonds easy, you have to dig and dig and dig. You cannot find gold. Everything God made valuable, he made hard to get. Pearls, rubies, oil, you have to dig and half the time you don't strike. Everything God created that was valuable, he made hard to get to. Ain't a woman more important than some diamonds or some oil or some gold? What do you mean, what's wrong with walking around half naked? That don't look bad to you because you're of the European nature. The black people are righteous, and the Europeans have made them unrighteous.

****

Michael: Let me put a point to you. This is a book written by a friend of yours, Budd Schulberg . . .

Muhammad: Hold on, he's an associate, not a friend.

Michael: Well, an associate.

Muhammad: Not a friend, an associate. I've got a lecture on friendship. Friend is a big word, he's an associate. You are an associate. I can't say Michael Parkinson was my friend. That's a lie, you are an associate.

Michael: But a man who has known you for a long time.

Muhammad: Yeah, right, not for a long time. He's known me for the few minutes he's around me every so often.

Michael: And wrote a very good book about you.

Muhammad: Who?

Michael: Schulberg did.

Muhammad: I never read the book.

Michael: You didn't read the book? Well let me tell you it is a very good book indeed. But he points out one or two things that interest me about you. I mean all the contradictions in you that are fascinating, that people forgive you. Now can I just put one to you that he says? He says, 'He's devoted to a religious movement that looks at the white race as devils whose time of deserved destruction is at hand, and yet keeps in almost daily touch with white friends like Gene Kilroy and Al Conrad. In fact, he's got more genuine white friends than almost any black fighter I've ever known.' Now isn't there a contrast there? You belong to a faith that teaches separatism, which we talked about before when you came on my programme. Yet here, you have white friends.

Muhammad: You say I've got white friends. I say they're associates.

Michael: You don't have a single white friend?

Muhammad: No.

Michael: What about someone like Angelo Dundee?

Muhammad: No, he's an associate. And I don't have one black friend hardly. A friend is one who would not even consider giving his life for you, that's a friend. The one who would not even think about it. A friend is one who has always got desire to give and keep back nothing. Always a desire to give and not look for nothing in return. Everybody you name are with me for money. And for what they can get. I don't have no friends. I wrote a poem that says:

> Friendship is a priceless gift,
> That cannot be bought nor sold,
> But its value is far greater than a mountain made of gold.
> For gold is cold and lifeless,
> It can neither see nor hear,
> And in time of trouble it is powerless to cheer.
> Gold it has no ears to listen,
> No heart to understand.
> It cannot bring you comfort or reach out a helping hand.
> So when you ask God for a gift,
> Be thankful if he sends,
> Not diamonds, pearls or riches
> But the love of real true friends.

See friends are very rare. So what I'm trying to say is this: I've got a lot of white associates. Elijah Muhammad, the one who preached that the white man of America, number one, is the devil. He's been preaching, he's never mentioned England. England's people have never lynched us, raped us, castrated us, tarred and feathered us, burned us up, stuck knives in pregnant women's stomachs, enslaved us, robbed us of our name, our knowledge. Elijah Muhammad's been preaching that the white man of America – God told him – is the blue-eyed, blond-haired devil. No good in him, no justice. He's going to be destroyed, his rule is over. He is the devil. Now Elijah Muhammad preaches that, and I follow him, and the white people of America know Elijah Muhammad. They tap his telephone, they know we're there, we're two million five hundred thousand strong, we're all over America and nobody yet attacks us as being liars. No white man says, 'We are not a race of devils. Come to court, Elijah, you are lying.'

Now are you telling me that I believe that the white man's the devil? We do believe that. We don't believe it, we know it. You understand? Now, I'll tell you this, since this is true. We are in the country. We work with people, we serve people, we're still intelligent, we're civilised. Our goal is to separate and have our own country, clean up ourselves, quit fighting, quit killing one another, quit disrespect for all men. The Muslims in America, we're the most respectable people in America. We're the cleanest. We're trying to be righteous and we're tired of begging white people. We want to clean up ourselves and have our own country, have our own land and rule ourselves and quit forcing ourselves on people who don't want us. Now, what's wrong with this? Just because I'm in this civilisation, I'm living in there. I have an associate who works in my camp, happens to be white. White people don't love black people. It's a fact that white people hate the black people. Listen, listen. What you mean it's not true?

Michael: Well it's not true.

Muhammad: You're the biggest hypocrite in the world if you go on nationwide TV and tell me white people like black people.

Michael: I don't dislike black people.

Muhammad: Oh you don't, I know you're all right. I'm not saying you dislike them in the way you want to show it, but the white people give black people jobs. Black people died in hospitals, white people operating on them. American black people been there for four hundred years and white people feed us, they clothe us, we don't make shoe strings, we don't have our hair combed, we totally rely on the white man and the white man is good to us, the white man has done a lot to help us, and to make a way for us, and still it's the same white man talk about us and no one likes us.

Michael: No, no, no . . . you're missing the point.

Muhammad: No, I ain't. I came on – you ain't used to no black man, and mainly no boxer, having no sense. I'm not just a boxer, I'm taught by Elijah Muhammad, I'm educated. Even Oxford University, your biggest seat of learning, offered me a Professorship in Philosophy and Poetry to come in and teach. I'm not just an ordinary fighter. I can talk all week on millions of subjects, and you do not have enough wisdom to corner me on television. You do not have enough – you're too small mentally to tackle me on nothing that I represent. I'm serious. You and this little TV show is nothing to Muhammad Ali. You've got some more questions, then ask them and I bet you I'll eat you up right here on air. There ain't no way you can tackle me. All of you are tricking. That's how you, John Hawkins, the white Englishman, tricked us out of Africa to America. You get me on your show and ask me all kind of trickery. You're ready for me. Budd Schulberg said . . . this is a big bomb he's going to drop on me now.

Michael: What are you talking about? What's a bomb?

Muhammad: 'Budd Schulberg says you've got white men working in your camp and you're teaching to white men, the devil.' I'm supposed to be trapped now and look bad.

How're you going to trap me? You're a white man and your knowledge ain't nothing to a Muslim. How're you gonna get on your TV and trap me? Ain't no way. You can't beat me physically, nor mentally. You are really a joke. I'm serious. This is a joke! You can read this damn book all you want. My leader's Elijah Muhammad who preaches the doom of America, and the biggest white people in America, who are wiser than you here, they don't tackle us. Now how are you gonna get on your TV show and get something ready for me? You had to have it all planned. I didn't know you had a book waiting for me and you were gonna ask me all this. Behind stage you're so nice and you're so, 'Oh, we'll have a nice talk,' and then you get me on the TV. This is a serious thing you got me with. You're contradicting – you're attacking my religion. You're turning white people who are associates, making like I'm thinking they're devils and I'm bad, and you got me on a TV show to say this, and this is the death question. Suppose I couldn't answer that and you had me cornered?

Michael: A likely story.

Muhammad: Yeah, you laugh now because I caught you.

Michael: Must have been a good question I asked you because you've been talking for about fifteen minutes.

Muhammad: I'll talk for twenty more.

Michael: That's right, I know that.

****

Muhammad: I had to be a fighter.

Michael: You would have been something else, would you?

Muhammad: If I could of went to school and got an education and could speak say three or four languages fluently, and got a good trade in life, I'd forget all about fighting.

Michael: Would you?

Muhammad: Yeah.

Michael: When you were at school, I mean did you miss out on education?

Muhammad: No I didn't miss out, I wouldn't learn. I didn't know the value of it. I was a little black boy in Kentucky, didn't know nothing about I'd be on your show, didn't know nothing about I'd be a world champion. Playing hookey, playing with the girls – just go into recess and eating lunch and joking, not knowing the value of education like many children don't today. Never thinking that one day I'll have to feed myself, didn't have no idea of profit and getting out and making money, like lots of children do, and time went by and I graduated and I went to the Olympics and they put me out just because I could fight. And my mind was mainly on sports. They just let me go. Now all of a sudden I found myself having trouble reading things, looking at contracts, I've got to hire lawyers and watch lawyers, and I knew the value of education then. So I'm going to brainwash my children now. My daughter's six years old. She speaks Arabic, English and Spanish.

Michael: In fact, when you left school, Muhammad, were you semi-literate in the sense that you had difficulty reading? Could you read?

Muhammad: No, not that type of literate. I have a wisdom that can make me talk to you or an educated man on any subject, and if the audience or the people listen, they say I won. Now, I'll say this. I'm serious. I had the type of knowledge that Jesus had, Moses had, Abraham, Elijah Muhammad – men who are illiterate according to your educational standard. Moses was so illiterate he couldn't talk. His brother Aaron talked for him. Jesus was a carpenter, Noah, Lot – all of God's prophets were uneducated men. This is why he chooses them, because he don't want nobody to take the credit for his success. He's God, he takes them empty and teaches them. So I've been taught by Elijah Muhammad. I studied life, I studied people, and I'm educated on this, but when it comes to reading and writing, I'm not. I may be illiterate in that. But when it comes to common sense, when it comes to feelings, when it comes to love, compassion, heartened, for people, then I'm rich. I wrote something once that says where is man's wealth?

His wealth is in his knowledge. For if his wealth was in the bank and not in his knowledge, then he don't possess it, because it's in the bank. You know what I'm saying? My wealth is in my knowledge, see? I'm a boxer and I challenge. I love to come on your show because you ask me good questions and I like, I really like, a man like you. You ask me a question here – that was good. But you didn't write that, it was already in the book. You just brought it out, you found that. See, ain't nobody else wise enough to go find that. See, I like people like you, you make me think, you keep me sharp, because I'm a spokesman for my people.

****

Michael: Do you feel that we missed the best of you as an athlete in the three years or three and a half years that you were banned?

Muhammad: No, you see the best now.

Michael: You think you're a better fighter now than you were then?

Muhammad: Right now. I don't run, I don't dance all the time, and I'm strong. I was the young man two years ago. Now I'm the old man, now I'm more seasoned. I still took everything George had. I'll be here five more years before there's a threat of me being beaten.

Michael: And when that threat comes along, it's a real threat; would you pull out before you take the gamble of going out as defeated champion?

Muhammad: If I'm the champion, I've defeated everybody and the real thrill is up, and I really believe I can't win, it'd be wise to get out while I'm on top.

Michael: Yeah. What, in fact, if you could build the fighter now who's going to defeat you. I mean what qualities would he have to have?

Muhammad: He'd have to be about my height, a little taller. He'd have to be about one tenth of a second faster. He'll have to hit me real hard. He'll have to be faster than me on his feet. He'll have to be more experienced. I mean you add it all up, there ain't nobody who's just going to come along like that. They've got to build themselves up and I see them while they're building. Nobody's going to start fighting tomorrow and have these qualities.

Michael: No, they're going to take some time.

Muhammad: It takes time and I don't see nobody on the horizon. If I'm not in condition, if I'm not serious, there's quite a few of them might win. But if I'm serious, with Allah, God in my heart and I'm fighting for a cause . . . See, I bring God into my fights. I'm not fighting for me, see? I'm not on this show talking just for publicity. Anything I do, there's a purpose involved. I'm serious. So that's why I fight. So now you know, from now on in, Muhammad Ali signed to fight is for freedom of black people. Now God is involved. You're fighting a spiritual holy war when you face me now.

Round Three – 1981

Muhammad: I'm getting old now.

Michael: Do you feel old?

Muhammad: Yeah, I feel like I'm about seventy-three – your age.

Michael: Do you?

Muhammad: No, I feel pretty good.

Michael: I tell you why I said it's good to see you looking good, because, as you know, there's been a lot of speculation about your condition after the Holmes fight, particularly in this country. There was a suggestion, for instance, that there was brain damage.

Muhammad: Well, I'll tell you what – your brain controls what comes out of your mouth. I'm doing this interview and you check me out, and after, you tell me if I've brain damage.

Michael: I'll let you know at the end of the interview, shall I?

Muhammad: I went to a place called the Mayo Clinic. It's the world's best clinic. There were reports about me having brain trouble, kidney trouble and speech defects, so I went to the Mayo Clinic and got a physical. Stayed there for about two days and one hundred per cent check out.

Michael: But I mean, I suppose the questions people ask about you – and I think it's out of the love they have for you – are because they don't want you to go on getting hurt in the ring.

Muhammad: I never get hurt, it's strange.

Michael: Oh, you must have got hurt in the ring?

Muhammad: When?

Michael: Well, I saw you fight Joe Frazier.

Muhammad: I didn't get hurt.

Michael: You didn't?

Muhammad: No.

Michael: You're a very good actor.

Muhammad: Are you calling me a liar?

Michael: No, no!

Muhammad: I've been hit a couple of times but I've never been knocked out. I've never been stopped like Joe Frazier and Ken Norton and Leon Spinks, Earnie Shavers. I mean out to the count of twenty-five, if they counted that long. I ain't ever been hurt. Had a broken jaw once but otherwise I've never been beat – even in the Holmes fight, I was just beat up bad. They stopped the fight because I wasn't looking good and it wasn't feeling right.

Michael: Are you serious about wanting to fight Holmes again?

Muhammad: I shall return.

Michael: You shall return.

Muhammad: First, I want to prove that I'm qualified. Holmes has said that if I can prove myself qualified and I still can fight – I looked so bad that night, until it looked like I couldn't fight no more. I couldn't move, I didn't hit him, I wasn't perspiring, I was dehydrated. Eleven rounds in 110 degrees heat and no sweat came out of my body.

Michael: But would it be different next time, Muhammad?

Muhammad: We shall see. That's why I want to go back. And let's say I don't do right the next time, I'll just have to admit I'm finished. I would hate to do it.

Michael: Why do you need to go back again, because you've done everything – more than any other boxer's ever done?

Muhammad: I realise I have more fans, same as I had before the Holmes fight. But it's myself. I want to prove to myself that I can beat Holmes and I can win my title back. For instance, I'm the only man who had a chance to go four times. No man has ever won it three times. So why do we go to the moon? Because it's there. Why are we trying to go to Mars? Because it's there. Columbus wouldn't have discovered America if he didn't take a risk. So he who is not courageous enough to take a risk will accomplish nothing in life. I'm a risk taker and the four-time championship is there and I'm the man who got that close to it. So it's something I've got to do.

Michael: But you're taking a risk, you see, with more than just your physical wellbeing. You're taking a risk with the fans, the reputation that you've built up throughout the world and the love that you feel wherever you go. What they don't want to see is you being badly beaten again, ever.

Muhammad: Badly beaten?

Michael: Well, that's what it's about.

Muhammad: Forget the Holmes fight, I was not badly beaten.

Michael: Well you looked badly beaten.

Muhammad: I saw the film, I watched it myself. I didn't take a bad beating. I took a few punches, but not a bad beating. But I know what I'm doing. See, I've been fighting twenty-seven years.

Michael: That's the point as well.

Muhammad: I know more about boxing than you.

Michael: That's true. You have been fighting for twenty-seven years and you've seen . . .

Muhammad: Look at my face.

Michael: You're still pretty good.

Muhammad: Almost as pretty as you!

Michael: But you've been round the fight game, as you say, for twenty-seven years and you've seen what can happen to fighters. You've seen the shambling wrecks that go around, you see them at every boxing occasion. And what people are frightened of is . . . they don't want that to happen to you.

Muhammad: What, to be a shambling wreck?

Michael: That's right.

Muhammad: I'm a long ways from a shambling wreck.

Michael: Oh, I'm not suggesting you are now. I'm saying that's what they're frightened might happen.

Muhammad: Let me tell you why they're frightened. Some people can see farther than others. Some people are pressed with limitations. We all live in a long world of limitations and some people can see farther than others. So therefore, when people judge what I'm doing with their logic, it can't be done. Their reason says it shouldn't be done. Their knowledge of history says it can't be done. So their reasoning and their knowledge and their logic clashes with my superior belief. Therefore the result is they don't believe. My thinking is so superior and my knowledge is so positive and my logic is so wise until it clashes with the mentality that is down here, and I'm up there. So by me being so high, I can see more and see farther than you. And you're looking at me saying, 'Ali, don't do it! Don't do it! Ali, please stop, you're gonna get hurt!' And you're in a job making sixty, seventy pounds a week, never been out of the country, not known in his own neighbourhood – 'Ali, don't do it.' I'm at just such a high level until I don't think like you, I'm not like you.

Michael: But you know why they say that. It's for the best possible reasons.

Muhammad: Because they fear and they are wary. It looks dangerous to them, but it's not really that dangerous to me. It's just another day.

Michael: And it's the affection they have for you. They've never felt about another boxer like they've felt about you.

Muhammad: Oh, that is so nice.

Michael: Ha ha, there we go. Round four.

Muhammad: Take this interview for an example. Look how we're talking and how I'm handling you. You're a wise man. And boxers can't do this, even boxers who don't take beatings, even young boxers. This is knowledge and wisdom, this is brain. Look how we're talking. It looks like my show.

Michael: I can't be wise, mind, it's the third time I've interviewed you.

Liam Neeson on Muhammad Ali

Michael: I know of your profound love of boxing and I didn't realise until this interview that we met before, in 1981, in the company of Muhammad Ali. We were in his suites at the Dorchester.

Liam: I remember that indeed. I was there with my girlfriend at the time, who was invited for his film *Freedom Road*.

Michael: It was an awful movie.

Liam: It wasn't very good. And yeah, we were up in his suite and I remember children being there. Ali, he's famous for it, went straight for the kids and we were all ignored for a few minutes. Eventually, we formed a semi-circle and he was coming round, shaking hands with everybody. My knees were genuinely shaking. You're going to meet your hero, and I thought, 'I have to say something to him, because I'll never get the chance in my life again.' And as he came up to me, I just went, 'Man, I love you!'

1998

George Best

George Best was the Godfather of the modern footballers. The first pop star of soccer. The Fifth Beatle. He wasn't just back-page news; he was a front-page headline whenever he stepped outside.

He was the prototype of the kind of modern celebrity that found its apotheosis in David Beckham. He was also one of the greatest players of them all. The sadness is we will never know how good he might have been, but the ultimate tragedy is neither did George Best. All of us who loved him, and those who tried to care for him, didn't understand the one fatal truth about George – he didn't want to give up drinking. On the other hand, whenever I think of him, which is often, I only remember what he did on the field of play, particularly before the booze dimmed his great gifts and eventually destroyed him. I have chosen two of the interviews I did with him, which provide something of a mirror of each other – the first in 1973 when, aged twenty-seven, George quit Manchester United and football; the second in 2001, when he had sought treatment for his alcoholism.

1973

Michael: Are you really not ever going to play football again, George?

George: No. People keep asking me, saying well you must come back and you're going to come back. I made a decision almost a year ago and I changed my mind then, but this time I won't.

Michael: You won't? What makes you so certain?

George: I don't know. I made a mistake the last time. When I said I was going to quit, I should have stayed out of it. I came back and faced the same sort of problems. So this time, I don't want to face any more problems.

Michael: George, I've known you for a long time. Is it possible – I don't believe it is, you see – for you to live without football?

George: Well, so far. I don't know how long it is since I've played – it's three or four months I think – and I haven't missed it.

Michael: You haven't?

George: Not in the slightest, no.

Michael: Let's go back, then, to the point where you took this decision to end your career. What really was the reason?

George: It was a mixture of lots of things, in the game and out of the game. I wasn't enjoying playing as much as I had done. I wasn't as fit as I should have been. It was my own fault.

Michael: Why was that? You were drinking?

George: Generally things, yeah. Night life and drinking, I suppose. Too many late nights. And I wasn't enjoying training as much, which I always had done. Even if I'd been out late, I always enjoyed the training part of it. But even that was becoming like a job, which it never had been before, to be honest.

Michael: What about the things in the game that got you down? What were they specifically?

George: Basically, my own fun, and the fun of the team – I wasn't enjoying the coaching side of it, the training side of it, that was just the general thing around Manchester United at the time.

Michael: Would you have been any different had you gone to any other club?

George: It might have been, but I wouldn't have let anyone take a chance on paying a lot of money for me and gone to them and maybe done exactly the same things, especially after they'd paid a quarter of a million pounds for me.

Michael: But that's an interesting thing, because what you're really saying is that you can't guarantee your own conduct?

George: Exactly, yeah.

Michael: Really?

George: Well, I do things on the spur of the moment instead of sitting down and thinking about them. I tend to run off and try to think about sorting them out somewhere else, usually in a different country.

Michael: Yes. But this time you've sorted it out, you've come to the conclusion, no more soccer – finished?

George: Yeah, definitely.

Michael: Are you comfortably well-off?

George: Reasonably. I've played since I was seventeen until recently, and that was nine years. I was earning good money and I didn't spend it all, so . . . I'm not well-off. I haven't got a lot of money, which is why I'm going to work and make more.

Michael: The more you look at it, George, the more daft it becomes, you see – because here you are with this extraordinary talent, you could have worked till you were what, thirty-two, thirty-three, thirty-four, something like that, and then retired. You'd have made a fortune, man, and you just jack it all in!

George: I might make more now that I've jacked it in!

Michael: I hope you do, but I don't think so. The sad thing is that you deny us the pleasure, actually, of watching you play. Do you have no regrets about that at all? Do you have no instinct as an entertainer, which you've always said you were? Do you have no loyalty towards the audience?

George: I don't know, a lot of people have asked me that and said, 'Don't you think you owe the public something?' I'm not sure whether I do or not. I like to think I've given them something for ten years, but I just couldn't take what was going on outside of the game. People say, well how can you have pressures and strains when you're doing something you're getting well paid for, which I don't think we do. You're training, you're keeping fit, but I think to be a British footballer, to play sixty-five, seventy games a year, sometimes two and three times a week, and at the end of it look forward to what – three or four weeks' holiday?

And certainly you've got to do what you're told for eleven months of the year, and you can't sort of go mad. You've got to be in bed at reasonable hours and you can't relax completely, and I think there's a hell of a lot of strain on professional footballers. When I first got into trouble, or when they started talking about me being under pressure and strain, at the same time there were three or four other first division players who were having troubles. And if they'd been single as I was, and not married men with responsibilities, I think they would have done exactly the same as I did.

Michael: Yes. Why don't you get married?

George: I can't afford it!

Michael: No, really, a serious question. You're, what, twenty-seven now, aren't you?

George: Twenty-six.

Michael: You've been out with more birds than I've had hot dinners – considerably more! Have you never found anybody who you really wanted to marry?

George: Not really, no. If I had done, I'd have been very pleased because I love children. I love kids and I'd have been the happiest man in the world if I could have found someone. But it just hasn't happened. I've taken a lot of girls out and if I'd have met the right one I would have married her, but I just haven't.

Michael: But what's the problem? Is it that they're after Georgie Best, superstar, rather than Georgie Best, ordinary Joe?

George: I don't think so. I think it's pretty easy to spot the ones who are after you for your name – well, I like to think I can. I think it's only common sense. I don't know what it is really. Maybe I'm too hard to please, I don't know.

Michael: Yeah, yeah. Are you going to go on looking?

George: Oh, of course, yeah!

2001

Michael: When I say, 'How are you?' to you, it has a real meaning, doesn't it?

George: It does these days, yes.

Michael: How are you?

George: Still here, still here.

Michael: And what's the latest medical bulletin?

George: I'm still on a load of medication, and Alex and I decided . . . we took what I suppose you'd call a drastic step of having the Ant-abuse put in, the tablets I tried many years ago.

Michael: What made you decide to go into hospital? Because, in the past, you've always resisted those temptations, George.

George: I think what it is, Michael, we kid ourselves. Sometimes, you think, 'Right, OK, I'll stop drinking for three months, or six months, or a year,' but at the end of it the good old liver recovers, and I can go and have a drink. But that's not the way it is, and I got seriously ill. It was Alex who called the medical people. I was on my floor in Chelsea, and I couldn't move. She called the ambulance, and they had actually to pick me up and carry me into hospital. They took me to Chelsea and Westminster, and they probably made a mistake. They gave me a jab that made me feel like I was on drugs or something, and I recovered very quickly and went home, that night I think. But obviously it wasn't right, and I was very seriously ill. I went through a spell where I thought, you know, I couldn't be bothered any more, really.

Michael: You wanted to top yourself?

George: Yeah, I thought it would just be easier. I had nothing to live for, or I didn't think I had.

Michael: Did you plan it?

George: Yeah, yeah.

Michael: What were you going to do?

George: I was going to go and get a bottle of Louis XIII brandy. I was going to get a nice bottle of Dom Perignon and take a few pills, and get a hammock in Jamaica or the Bahamas somewhere, and that was going to be it. But funnily enough, in a way, the fact that I almost died sort of changed my whole look on life.

Michael: The book you've written, you've called *Blessed*. A lot of people would think, the last twenty-seven years of your life have been far from blessed, haven't they?

George: I believe that a lot of people are born with gifts. We have to work. I think you have to work at it, but you've also got to be very lucky in life at times, to be born with something. And I was born with something. I really didn't have to work too hard on it. I did, because I enjoyed training, contrary to what people used to think, and I used to love being fit.

Michael: What's interesting in your book – and we've known each other for, well, a lifetime, and you've written about twenty-seven books about yourself, in my reckoning – but what's interesting about this book is that for the first time you've confronted yourself. You've always backed off facing up, haven't you? In a sense, run away from things?

George: I have. I tended to hide in corners, whether I didn't want to face reality or I just couldn't be bothered facing it. The effect it has on your family when you become famous. My poor old mother couldn't handle it. My dad is strong, he's strong as an ox, and he's got a strong character, but my mum couldn't handle it, and it ended up costing her life at the end.

Michael: She became an alcoholic.

George: Yeah, and for a long time I found it difficult to talk about. It's still difficult to talk about.

Michael: I'm sure it is.

George: For a long time I blamed myself, I thought it was me. But then I realised that whatever I had done, it might not have changed one way or another. It might have been a little bit easier for her, but I'd been away from home since I was fifteen, and I certainly couldn't look after her, because I was having enough problems looking after myself, and failing most of the time.

Michael: But when was the time it started affecting you? You write in the book about when you're twenty-two, you start having blackouts.

George: Yeah. We all laugh and joke about it, you can't remember where you parked your car the night before, and it seems funny at the time, but at the end of the day when you can't remember days and weeks it's slightly different. And when you're drinking fourteen pints of vodka a day, it doesn't help. But there wasn't one point, it was gradually getting worse, obviously, because it almost finished me off.

I think the worst period was when I was in America, and I was so far away from home. It sounded quite exciting, because it was a new league, and all the best players in the world were there. They were bringing in big crowds, and it was quite exciting. I was living down on the beach in Los Angeles, I had a very successful business, and on the face of it, everything seemed perfect. But I was so bored. I was becoming a beach bum. I always had plenty of money, and the sunshine and everything else, and of course Calum was born, but for some strange reason, even that didn't pull me out of it at the time.

Michael: In the book, you do put your finger on it, because you have to confront things as an alcoholic. You confront the moment where you're at your lowest point, which was in America, when you went to the bar with a girl. Tell us what happened.

George: Well, I got to the stage where . . . in this country it was easy. I could walk in a bar, like most people who are well-known, and someone will send you a drink over. You just sit there for five minutes and someone will buy you a drink eventually. You don't need money here. But in America it was slightly different, and I was desperate for a drink one night, and I stole from a girl's purse at the bar, when she went to the ladies' room. Then I knew it was something a little bit serious, because I've never been a dishonest person, or I hope I haven't, in my life, and I made up for it.

Michael: You went back.

George: I went back and gave it back to her, but the fact that I'd done it in the first place, really, I thought, 'What am I doing here?' Stealing for some stupid craving that was killing me.

Michael: Ten bucks, yeah. But that didn't stop you, you see. And the other thing, too, which is interesting, was what you went through, it seems to me, for other people, not for yourself. You went to Alcoholics Anonymous, and you couldn't face it there, could you? You never got on with that.

George: No, I tried everything. I went, but it's a little bit difficult for me to go to Alcoholics Anonymous. I made efforts, and it works for a lot of people. A hell of a lot of people go to AA and it saves their lives, but it didn't work for me.

I tried private counselling, but like I used to do with dear old Sir Matt, I used to sit there and just nod, and agree with everything, thinking, 'I can't wait to get out of here, so I can go and have a drink.' But yes, I made efforts. I was hospitalised twice in America, and had a lot of help from a lot of people. But I don't know. I remember once in the hospital in America, and I think it was an Irish guy who'd become a counsellor and had been dry for something like twenty-odd years. He said to me, 'We all need a crutch, but you've got to realise that one day it might not be there.'

Michael: Yes.

George: And he said, 'The way I looked at it was it's like you've got a choice of switching the light off or on.' He said, 'It sounds over-simplified, but that's it.' I said, 'Monday?' He said, 'You've got to decide whether you want the light to keep shining, or whether you want to switch it off.' Luckily, I made what I think was the right decision, and at the moment life is just – compared to what it was just a year ago – it's amazing.

Michael: You were the first soccer superstar – front page, back page – and I remember you very well. I remember you being totally, in a sense, naked, because nobody knew what was happening to you until it was too late. Your agent, I remember, used to live in Huddersfield. There's nothing wrong with Huddersfield, but if you have the biggest super-star in football . . .

George: It was a bit weird. My dear old agent – I'd just come into the game and he was stuck in a little office in a square in Huddersfield getting ten thousand letters a week from

Tommy Cooper
never understood
how funny he was.
Sadly, when he
died, he was still
wondering.

Eric and Ernie
didn't just make
the nation laugh –
they comforted
and reassured us
that, so long as
they were around,
everything was OK.

Above: Peter Sellers was a conundrum, mainly because he never quite worked out who or what he was.

Left: The problem I had interviewing Les Dawson was that I couldn't look him in the eye

Below: Peter Cook and Dudley Moore were the bovver boys of British comedy during the sixties and seventies.

Spike Milligan, the most surreal of our funny men, drew us aboard his carousel of laughter.

I have little doubt that Barry Humphries should be knighted for his services to comedy.

Dawn French is a funny woman, as opposed to being a woman who simply says funny things. She came on the show with long-standing partner in comedy, Jennifer Saunders.

Michael Palin (*above*) and John Cleese (*below*) found fame as Pythons. There was such a to-do at the TV Centre when *Monty Python* went to air, with TV executives flapping like a flight of eagles.

If I wanted to hire
someone to insult and
discomfort an enemy, I
would phone Joan Rivers.
A regular guest on my
show, on this occasion
she entertained Stephen
Fry and George Michael.

Paul O'Grady is a singular
and inspirational
member of the human
race.

I first encountered Muhammad Ali in 1971 and I have little doubt the hour-long interview did more than any other to establish the reputation of the show.

George Best was the Godfather of modern footballers, the first pop star of soccer.

Bobby Charlton is much more than a hero; he is part of our cultural heritage.

I found David Beckham to be a modest man, professional in every way and unfailingly charming.

Shane Warne is the Aussie ultra male in action – bold, brash, confrontational.

all these girls sending him knickers. It aged him very quickly. And obviously there's a lot of protection now, hopefully people have learned that you have to look after your superstars. You need good back-up and I have it today. It's a little bit too late from a football point of view, but from my life point of view, and earning a living, things are . . . I live every day at a time.

Michael: The question I've always wanted to ask, I'm going to ask you now because I know the answer, it's in the book. You had a reputation with the ladies, second to none. What was the nearest to kick-off that you made love to a woman?

George: I think it was half-time actually. No, there was this story – a very famous story – when Wilf McGuinness was in charge. I saw Wilf on Tuesday night and he reminded me that he actually caught me in a lady's room just before we left for a Cup semi-final. But he only caught me in a room, he didn't actually . . .

Michael: Oh, he did.

George: No.

Michael: No?

George: I wouldn't dream of doing something like that before a game. The problem was, as he was leaving, he said, 'You better play well today.' And the first time I got the ball I fell flat on my face.

Michael: I won't ask you the obvious question!

Bobby Charlton

As well as being a truly great player, Bobby Charlton represented everything that was once required of a sporting hero. He was as modest as he was talented, as sportsmanlike on the field as he was courteous off it. He understood the importance of a game that brought colour, vivacity and excitement to people whose lives were often a struggle in a sombre landscape. Bobby Charlton represented the game's traditional values. He still does and even now, when he's in his seventies, people doff their caps and pay respect as he passes by. He is much more than a hero. He is part of our cultural history.

When I eventually got into the first team, and Sir Matt Busby gave his team talk, he said, 'We're in Trafford Park, the largest industrial estate in Europe, and the people who work there, when they finish work at the end of the week, they want to go and see something a little bit different and a little exciting. So you have the responsibility. The people on the shop floor, they've worked really hard, so you have to give them their little bit of entertainment.' And ever since Matt Busby was there, we've tried to play attacking football.

I'm very flattered when people mention the Best, Law, Charlton era. I used to think, 'Wow, that's me, I'm in there.' Denis was unbelievably brave. He would put his head in front of anything. He was sharp, and if the goalkeeper dropped it, even a few inches, it was in the back of the net. He was electric, and people thought, 'We must go, if Denis Law's playing.' And then this little lad George Best came on the scene as a junior. The coaches had been saying, 'There's a really good young lad, a great young player coming through, a little lad from Belfast,' and I thought, well, they were laying it on a bit thick. I thought nobody can be as good as that. Then he came on the field and he played on the left wing against a friend of mine, John Angus, and he humiliated him. This little lad was so brave and so tough and his control – he did things that people were so excited about. Sometimes I used to think he was a bit selfish. Sir Matt Busby's assistant, Jimmy Murphy, said, when I was fifteen and first arrived at Old Trafford, 'Bobby, you're now a professional. You can't play for yourself any more. If one of your players gets the ball, you have to give him the option to pass to you. Make it easy for him. It's a team game this, not an individual game.'

I remembered this through the whole of my early career, and then when it came to George – he would pick up the ball and my instincts would tell me, 'Go and help him, go and make yourself available,' and then George would look at me and go in another direction. He was so infuriating, but at the end of the day you had to hold your hands up and say, 'Well, you're never going to change him, you might as well sit back and enjoy it.' George was George. He had this phenomenal gift and, unfortunately, he finished very early, and the great tragedy, I thought, the great tragedy of it all was that you don't get players like George Best very often. We were lucky, and unfortunately he went the wrong way and didn't really give as much to the public as he might have done. But it's not a criticism.

I didn't want to talk about Munich and offend some of the relatives, or friends, and then eventually it got to the stage when almost everybody was asking me to do it, and I thought, 'Well, I'd better just get this off my chest.' So I wrote about it in my book, and I really felt better after I'd done it.

Manchester United was such an adventure, you know. Going to play in Europe, we were going to play in places we'd never heard of. We didn't know the players. There was only one club, Real Madrid, who had Di Stefano, that you really knew. All the others were strange, and Matt Busby said, 'We have to do it,' and even against the wishes of the Football League, he went into Europe. He said, 'It's the future. This is what the public want to see.'

And of course, on one of the journeys back the accident happened. Had it not been for the accident – the team itself was so good and the club had so many fantastic players – Manchester United would probably have won the European Cup a long time before we did.

After the crash, I'd think, 'Well, why me? Why am I here, with nothing happened to me other than a little gash on the head, and all these other friends killed?' I felt, 'This is not fair. Why should it be me?' It took a long time for me to feel good about it – feel better about it, certainly.

It was such a momentous event for so many young people

to die, on the verge of the great success that was ahead of them, and I just couldn't understand why, but it was because of the design of the aircraft at that particular time. Half the seats were facing forward and half the seats were facing backwards, and the ones who had their back to the front of the aeroplane were the ones who survived, pretty much.

We walked away and we couldn't believe it. I couldn't believe it. I maybe had a bit of concussion, but a few days later, when you realised exactly what had happened and the enormity of it, then you start thinking about how lucky you've been.

I went to the first match after Munich. When I got home, they were preparing for the next round of the FA Cup, against Sheffield Wednesday. My Uncle Tommy had a car, and Tommy, my dad and myself, we came down to see the match, because they had told me, 'Just stay away as long as you wish, Bobby, come back when you're ready.' When I got to the match and I saw the effort put in by all the young players, and Harry Gregg and Bill Foulkes, I thought, 'Well, what am I doing? There's nothing wrong with me.' So I said to Jimmy Murphy, 'I've got to go back to see the doctor tomorrow but I'll be back on Friday.' And I came back.

It was left to us to make sure that their names were remembered – the players who died – and the only way that you could satisfy everyone, really, was to win the European Cup for them. They'd been trying their best to win it, and we would have won it with them, and the win was just momentous for so many great young players.

2007

David Beckham

It's not very often a footballer attracts the attention of the Poet Laureate. When David Beckham was ruled out of the last World Cup because of injury, Carol Ann Duffy wrote the poem 'Achilles' in his honour. She explained, 'He is almost a mythical figure himself, in popular culture.' In comparing Beckham to a Greek God, she showed more sensitivity than wife Victoria, who told me she called him 'Goldenballs'. The red tops were in no doubt which description was worth the front page.

David Beckham is a good footballer and a great global superstar, which has as much to do with fashion as soccer. If the way to a life of glamour and riches was paved by George Best, the first 'pop star' of the game, then there is no doubt who got the better of the deal. George advertised pork sausages. David modelled Armani. Beckham earned $42 million in 2009, George died with very little in the bank.

There is much to admire in the way David Beckham has faced relentless scrutiny and often cruel and hurtful comments about himself and his family. I found him to be a modest man, professional in every way, and unfailingly charming.

My mum and dad have always been there, since I was seven or eight, when I first started playing Sunday League football. They've been to every game from then up until now. I think my dad's missed two games in my whole career and that's the sort of support any youngster needs to get to the top. Having my mum and dad behind me has got me where I am today.

I was always asked by my teachers at school what I wanted to be when I grew up, and the only thing I used to say was a footballer. I'm sure they had their doubts but I never had my doubts about becoming a professional footballer and I love every minute of it.

Sometimes at school I used to get kicked all over the place, and come home with bruises from head to toe. I used to get quite a bit of stick. I'm never one to sort of turn round and say, 'I was really good at football when I was ten, eleven.' I left that for other people to say. My dad, he had never really told me I was that good, but I think deep down he knew I had a bit of ability.

When young kids ask me questions, the first thing I say to them is that practice gets you to the top, most of the time. Obviously, you have to have a certain amount of ability, but that's something my dad always drummed into me, since I was eight, nine, ten. A lot of my friends at school used to go out to parties on a Saturday night, and go down the corner shop with a bottle of cider, and I used to be tucked up watching *Match of the Day* with my dad, and looking forward to the Sunday game, so I was always dedicated in that way.

There have been ups and downs and it's been a roller-coaster ride, but I've loved nearly every minute of being a professional footballer. When I moved up to Manchester at the age of sixteen, obviously it was daunting for me because of moving away from family, but then again, my mum and dad were up there every weekend, supporting me, so that made it a lot easier.

I was scared of every manager I've ever had in my career, from my dad at seven or eight years old, to Stuart Underwood, who is like a sergeant-major figure for Ridgeway Rovers, then Eric Harrison, and Nobby Stiles, who used to coach us at Manchester United. And all the youngsters who went through Manchester United were scared of Sir Alex Ferguson, and that's how he got the best out of all of the young players.

Leading into the World Cup [2006], six months before that, I'd decided that I was going to stand down as England captain. I'd had six years of being captain, the biggest honour any footballer could ever hope for, and it was a big decision for me. No one knew about it apart from one of my best friends and, obviously, my wife. It was a decision that I'd come to and I had to get used to it. I'd not told anyone because I felt that leading up to the World Cup, I didn't want to affect anything that was going on with the team.

We got knocked out and it was another disappointing World Cup for us, and that morning I remember waking up and I cried because I knew what I was going to have to do. I went into the press conference, cried all the way down to

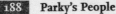

the press conference, got through it, and cried all the way back to the hotel.

Football has changed a lot since 1966. It was an amazing team that won us the World Cup and it's truly incredible we haven't won it since, because of the amount of money that is in football. But it's what we work towards. It's not as if we go on the field thinking, 'I can't wait to get off the pitch, go home to our big houses and nice cars.' Once you're on that field, all that matters is winning.

For me, and for the players I've played with in my career, money's never had anything to do with playing football. Of course, people are going to say, it's easy for you to say that because obviously you've got the money. But for me, when I was a young kid growing up at Manchester United, I was lucky to have played under *the* best manager in football. He was the one who controlled everything. And these days I think it's a lot easier for sixteen- and seventeen-year-old footballers to earn a ridiculous amount of money. Having the Academy in London and the one in Los Angeles, I get to work with some amazing kids. You'll say, 'Is there anything you want to ask me?' Even the eight or nine year olds, one of the first things they ask you is, 'How much money do you earn?'

I keep myself as family orientated as I want to be. I've got three beautiful boys, a beautiful wife and we're very family orientated. We do everything for our boys. They come before anything we do in our careers, anything that we do in our lives. Everything revolves around them. If I didn't keep my feet on the ground, I know there are many friends, and my dad, who would knock it out of me.

2000–07

Michael: Do you feel that David has, perhaps, a better public persona image than you have?

Victoria: I think he does have now. I don't think that he did a few years ago. And I think that sometimes, when you can get down and think, 'Why don't people understand me?

Why are they saying this, why are they saying that?' what better person to look at than my own husband, to see how somebody can turn all that around. David is . . . I call him 'Goldenballs', you know.

Michael: Goldenballs Beckham, eh? It's a good one that one, isn't it?

Victoria: That's one of those things I shouldn't have said, but . . .

Shane Warne

The thing about Shane Warne is he likes being the centre of attention. This is no shrinking violet. This is the Aussie ultra male in action – bold, brash, confrontational. He also happens to be the greatest spin bowler of them all. Due to the nature of their craft, spinners can be whimsical, sometimes philosophical, cricketers. If they were musicians, they would favour the oboe. By contrast, Shane Warne is a brass band. As much by personality as by skill, he transformed the philosophy of spin bowling while also challenging the way opponents dealt with it. His eventful life has encompassed scandal involving women, bookmakers, diet pills and lurid headlines, all of which he has dealt with in an open and straightforward manner and without resorting to tearful recriminations or sympathetic spin. Most rare and commendable of all is that he was the very best at one of the most difficult trades in all of sport. How many can claim that?

I never sat there thinking, 'I'm going to do this. This is what I want to do.' I never had those feelings with cricket. I wanted to play Aussie Rules Football, but I wasn't good enough. I tried out at St Kilda Football Club, and played a couple of years of under-19s, and in the reserves. I never made the seniors. I just played cricket in the summer because most of my buddies did. I was a batsman. The bowling never interested me because I was getting whacked around. It's tough being a spinner when you're no good, and it's embarrassing as a youngster when your ball goes over the fence and they can't find it, and say, 'Can someone get us another ball? We've lost that one.'

You know those concrete posts you have at school, near the entrance. I was sort of bending down by one, someone jumped on my back and pushed me into it. My legs broke, pretty badly. The doctor did what he did and I was in plaster from the neck down, with a couple of holes in it. I got round on a trolley on my hands for twelve months. I think that might be one of the reasons I've got strong wrists. It might have actually helped me.

Once I left St Kilda footy club in 1988, or they got rid of me, I went to England and played league cricket down in Bristol. I put on nineteen kilos, had a bit of fun. My dad didn't recognise me when I walked past. Every night we were just drinking pints. I came back to Australia, got into the Cricket Academy and I was picked to go to the West Indies on a youth tour in 1990.

I thought, 'I just want to go along with it, this seems like a bit of fun.' I still wasn't taking it seriously because I didn't think I was any good. I played my first Test match and got smashed, played the next Test, got smashed against India, got dropped. I went back to the Academy with Terry Jenner and Rod Marsh, and got back down to seventy-nine kilos. I got super fit because Terry Jenner asked about what sacrifices I'd made to keep getting selected for Australia. 'You're not taking it seriously. A lot of people would give anything to play Test cricket for Australia.' He said, 'A lot of us,' including himself, 'have done a lot of good work. You've done nothing and you're still getting a game. You don't deserve it and you haven't made any sacrifices. Look at you, you smoke heaps, you go through the bottle shop and grab twelve beers and just sit in front of the telly and drink them. And you're still playing for Australia. You don't deserve to.'

I said, 'Yes I have, of course I've made sacrifices.' And he said, 'OK, tell me what.' I said, 'Oh you know, lots of stuff,' and I was trying to think of what sacrifice I'd actually made, and I hadn't really made any. So I thought, 'Right, I'm going to get super fit, I'm going to learn as much as I possibly can,' and the only way to learn is to make some mistakes, but the overriding fact was that I listened. For the first time, I actually started to listen to people – as youngsters we all think we're pretty good, and we know anything.

When I first started, I used to wait for the batsman to make a mistake, and I didn't have a plan. But as I got on and understood the game a little bit better, I realised that I needed a plan, I needed to get the batsman out, and no matter what the situation, you always say, 'How am I getting them out?' That dictates my field no matter what. So my attitude always is to get them out, not to stop runs.

When you actually want to put someone off their mark, you generally try to pick on him. I tried a few wrong ones at the start – I picked on Sachin Tendulkar, and now he's one of my best friends. You've got to pick on someone who is trying to make a name for himself on the team, he wants to impress people. I think to put someone off, it doesn't have to be by swearing or calling him an idiot. Sometimes it might be, but most of the time the best sledge is the clever one, or the ones that have some truth and just might hurt a little bit.

I remember a time in Sydney, when a gentleman got an MBE. He didn't really do much to deserve that MBE, and I just let him know that he might want to hand it back. I can lend him some stamps if he wants. I dish it out so I've got to be prepared to cop it, which is fine, but I'm very lucky in that the more I get sledged, the more it makes me concentrate. When I'm batting, I'm hopeless, but if I get sledged, that actually helps me. It makes me concentrate and not play a silly shot.

Allan Border was the bloke who taught me that if you feel like you're not quite there when you're bowling, or batting, the one thing he found that worked for him was to sledge someone – just choose someone in the opposition and pick a fight with him. He said if you pick a fight, it's him versus you, so it makes you switch on, gets your competitive juices going and makes you concentrate. So I tried that a few times and I liked it. It kind of worked.

Daryll Cullinan played his first game against us in 1994. It was the first time Australia had played South Africa in a long time, and he had just broken the record for the highest first-class score made by a South African. So we said, 'When he comes out, we'll see how he goes against spin straight away.' So I bowled a leggy, bowled a flipper and knocked him over, so that was that. Second innings, I bowled a wrong'un to him as the last ball of an over. I've got my hat, walking back to slip, and as I was walking past I sort of lingered to hear what he was saying. He started laughing and said, 'Oh, how easy was the wrong'un to pick? I picked that wrong'un quite easily.' So the next day, I set him up for a flipper again. Bang, got him out. I just reminded him where the changing rooms were with a few words before that, and it ended in 'off'. Once I'd done that we said, 'Rightio, let's really keep it on Daryll.' So any chance we had we said, 'The flip is now called the Daryll ball.' We really tried to build up the pressure on him.

The series finishes, he gets dropped for the next series. Four years later, he gets called back. I pick up the paper and there's a big double-page interview with Daryll Cullinan about how he's been to see a psychiatrist, he's been playing the man and not the ball. And I'm reading this and thinking, 'Come on!' So he comes out to bat and Mark Taylor says to me, 'Come on, get back to your mark.' I'm saying, 'In a minute, in a minute,' and just looking around the ground, asking Daryll Cullinan, 'What colour was the couch? Were they hourly sessions? Half hour? Do you pay by the hour?' And then I walk back. The crowd got into it and I ended up getting him out stumped. So that was pretty good too.

I've been lucky enough to have the opportunity to play cricket for Australia, and I'd like to think that I've repaid the fans, the public, the selectors for choosing me and sticking with me. I didn't think I was good enough to take 700-odd wickets, make 3,000 runs and play over 100 Tests. It's been an amazing journey and I've loved every minute of it. And I wouldn't have changed it. I wouldn't have changed the spanking I got at the start, because that made me more determined, that made me have a taste for it, and I think as a young kid working out what you want to do in life, some people never have that opportunity. I had a taste of international cricket, the carrot was dangled, but then I was proud of what I did. I wanted to become the best I could, and I put in a lot of hard work.

The one thing about being Shane Warne is that everyone's got a comment, and whether it be good or bad, everyone wants to hear it. Sometimes I think it's a bit harsh, but a lot of it I bring on myself, so you have to expect that. A lot of it's been a bit too harsh, I think, and a bit unfair, but it comes with the territory, so you've just got to live with it, move on. There were times when I let it get to me. I used to be annoyed with it, but I suppose I've had plenty of practice, so I've become a bit stronger now, and whatever they want to write, or judge me by, they can.

A role model? I think I have been. I think there are a lot of kids who would like to be like me, and hopefully they won't make the same mistakes I have.

2006

4 The Stage

Richard Burton

Peter O'Toole

Richard Harris

Sir Alec Guinness

Dame Judi Dench

Sir Ralph Richardson

Sir John Gielgud

Sir Ian McKellen

Richard Burton

They will tell you Richard Burton squandered his priceless gifts in Hollywood, that we will never know how great an actor he might have been. My question is, if that be true, how is it every contemporary revered him and none would deny him his place in the pantheon? He lived his life as a Hollywood epic but that is not to deny the great intelligence and perception he brought to the craft of acting; nor his love of words, and his ability to read a gas bill and make it sound like poetry. *Time* magazine once described his voice as possessing 'A tympanic resonance so rich and overpowering that it could give an air of verse to a recipe for stewed hare.'

When I interviewed him in 1974, he had just come out of rehab in a Swiss clinic in a vain attempt to stop drinking. There are moments in your life you treasure. This was one.

Michael: Have you ever felt yourself going towards the precipice and pulling back?

Richard: Yes, I have. Yes, I think we all do, we Celts.

Michael: Would you care to tell me how? In what circumstance?

Richard: Well, there was a second or two I think, perhaps about a year ago, when I didn't fancy much staying alive.

Michael: Really? You contemplated suicide?

Richard: Oh, no. No, I wouldn't kill myself in the ordinary sense of the word. I wouldn't take pills or drugs, or anything really. I suddenly woke up one morning and found how splendidly rich and extraordinary the world was, and that I couldn't bear its richness and its beauty, and in order to obviate the idea of the richness and the extraordinary beauty of the world, I thought, it's best to leave it.

Michael: How do you leave it if you don't top yourself?

Richard: You can kill yourself any second. I don't mean by any obvious means, but you can, of course, drink yourself to death. That's rather pleasant.

Michael: It's better than falling on a sword, that's for sure. Is that what you tried to do? To drink yourself to death?

Richard: I had a go.

Michael: How acute did this become and what amount were you drinking?

Richard: Pretty bad. The doctor in California said that if I kept on as I was going, I only had two weeks to live, which was rather fascinating. If you examine the idea of two weeks – every second, every minute, every hour, every day, two weeks only – I was absolutely fascinated. I wasn't frightened at all, but fascinated. So I thought, 'Here we go again, boys. We're on the edge of a terrible precipice.' Anyway, I decided to withdraw from the precipice, which I have done, and now I can bear the richness of the world and its many effronteries.

Michael: And tell me, how difficult was it having embarked on this business of drinking? You drink what, how heavily? Some people might think that four gin and tonics are too much for them, and they'd be on the floor.

Richard: I was a champion. I'm told – because, of course, you don't remember if you drink that much – I was up to about two and a half to three bottles of hard liquor a day, which is a lot.

Michael: Strewth! I like drinking but I think that might blow my head off. To have drunk that amount, you must have started in the morning, at breakfast?

Richard: You start at midnight, and you keep on from midnight, and you go on and on and on. You don't eat. You don't do anything very much except drink. Fascinating idea, the idea of drink on that scale. It's rather nice to have gone through it and to have survived, because I suppose that we all know we're going towards an inevitable doom. It's rather interesting to go towards it deliberately and then withdraw, because nobody else has been there and withdrawn, but I've been there. I've seen that dark wood, I know how terrible it is, how frightful it is and how frightening it is. But I went there and came back.

Michael: What brought you back from the edge?

Richard: I think I refused to die. I may drop dead this second for all we know, but at least I'm not inviting it.

****

Michael: I suppose the part you've been playing latterly is one of the most challenging – Winston Churchill in a new documentary, *Walk with Destiny*. Did you ever meet him?

Richard: Yes, many times.

Michael: What kind of an impression did you form of the man? Was he formidable in the sense that he was frightening?

Richard: Yes, I think I was a little frightened of him. There are about four or five people in the world, whom I've met, who actually put me in awe, and I would say that Sir Winston was certainly one of them.

Michael: There is a marvellous story I know, about you playing Hamlet and Churchill being in the audience. Peter O'Toole came on the programme and said that the trouble with doing 'To be or not to be' is that everybody joins in. You found this to be true?

Richard: Certainly it was true in Sir Winston's case. He came to *Hamlet* and sat in the front row of the Old Vic with his wife and detectives, whatever they were. I came on stage feeling absolutely diabolical, but I was told that the old man was in front. Of course, there was only one old man, and I started to speak the first lines: 'A little more than kin and less than kind,' and I heard this extraordinary rumble from down below and I wondered what it was. I thought, 'Have I got a hangover? What's going on?' and it was Sir Winston, speaking the lines with me, and I could not shake him off, whatever I did. I don't know quite what he was trying to do. I suppose he was rather upset that he wasn't on stage. It was really quite extraordinary. With Sir Winston joining you in a duet, it's not the easiest thing in the world.

Michael: Did he go backstage to see you?

Richard: Yes, he came in the interval. He went back to see the rest of the performance and came back. I thought he'd gone home because I watched through the spy-hole at the Old Vic and thought, 'Ah well, we've lost him. He's gone.' I thought I might as well have a drink then, since he's gone. You know, get sloshed. So I sat in the dressing room and I was just about to put a whisky and soda into my mouth when the door opened and suddenly there was Sir Winston. He bowed very graciously and very courteously said, 'My Lord Hamlet, may I use your lavatory?'

1974

Peter O'Toole

For someone who loved talking, Peter O'Toole had a fear of talk shows. He told me of an appearance on a Johnny Carson show in America when he was so terrified he fainted on set. 'He asked me a question, and I woke up in a dressing room, my glasses broken. I'd fainted. And I was replaced by a talking dog.' As an actor, he had the capacity to be glorious. His swan song was in Keith Waterhouse's marvellous play *Jeffrey Bernard is Unwell*. He performed a scene from it at Keith's memorial service in 2010 and, at the age of seventy-eight, demonstrated, stylishly and effortlessly, that he was still a great actor and a star undimmed by the passing years.

I have great affection for a lot of my childhood. We were a very tightly packed little Irish Catholic community, so one became much more Irish than the Irish. The expatriate Irish are always so.

Then came the war and evacuation, the usual thing – the little tickets and gas masks full of sandwiches. Then I went to a Protestant school and then back to Leeds to complete my education. I didn't really have very much. It truly didn't interest me at all, and I managed to escape from it when I was about thirteen.

Not only was I from Hunslet – I didn't have a Yorkshire accent – I also had blond curly hair, and I was known as 'Bubbles', and that cost me a lot of lumps. But acting came . . . well, you absorb it, I suppose. There's no immediate process in it. It's an accumulation of things. I left my little warehouse where I'd started work and went to work on a newspaper. The newspaper led to night school, with my need to improve myself, and free tickets to the theatre.

Bit by bit, I got involved in local amateur things and by sixteen or seventeen I was onions deep in theatre. At that point, his Majesty felt it was vital to the security of the nation that I joined the armed forces, which put a temporary halt to things. I vomited over every cubic foot of the seven seas – well, if not seven, at least two or three of them anyway.

I felt ridiculous, creeping around in bell bottoms, and they obviously felt I was ridiculous as well. I recall once being in Hampshire in a very high priority secret radio station, and the trick was to get the weather forecast in code and decode it. I couldn't be bothered with all that, and I'd made the acquaintance of a Wren via the teleprinter. What I used to do was to nip up through the pig sty, stick a couple of coppers in the telephone and ring the Wren, who would give me the stuff neat. Alas, this initiative wasn't felt to be initiative at all. The poor girl got the sack.

I went to RADA when I left the Navy. Well, I thought I'd been a good boy, died and gone to heaven. We were outnumbered – it was four to one pretty ladies, hundreds of them. Oh, it was bliss, and nothing to do, no work as such, not as I understood the word work – no picks, shovels and stuff like that.

I'd made a film called *The Day They Robbed the Bank of England*, in which I was, of course, invited to play the Irish tearaway. I've always carefully avoided playing Irish if I could. I played a Guards officer, and a friend of David Lean's, an

Indian gentleman, had seen it, rung up David and said, 'Lawrence is on the screen.' David went to see it, rang me up and said, 'You're Lawrence of Arabia.'

I'd met Mr Spiegel before. The phone rang – Sam Spiegel Advertising, and would I go and see him? I'd just been clearing my dressing room and I'd half a bottle of whiskey in my pocket, and when I went in the door and took off the coat, the bottle of whiskey fell out and smashed on the floor. Now, the idea of meeting him was to replace a rather unreliable actor in a film he was making. I did some sort of test with him and I made a joke, which, alas, he didn't think was very funny. He nearly died when David said he wanted me to play Lawrence because he wanted Albert Finney or Marlon Brando. I was one of a long, long line.

To give you an idea of how we got on, Richard Burton and I, we pulled a terrible thing together. He used to go to watch my rushes and I would go to watch his, because neither of us particularly liked seeing ourselves on the screen. And we got into an awful scrape. We used to toss up to see what wine we'd have, toss up to see who could do what scene and everything. He was having his problems at the time, and one day we were hiding in a pub at lunch and he said, 'Let's do *Hamlet*.' I said, 'No, no, never. I've done it – so have you.' He said, 'Let's do it again, just to be perverse.' I said, 'Oh no, no, it's the worst play in the world, I won't do it.' He said, 'Go on.' So, I don't know, I'd had too much red ink, or whatever. We tossed coins. We decided that we'd have Olivier and Gielgud to direct, and tossed up to see who got whom, and to decide between New York and London. I got Olivier in London and he got Gielgud in New York – and we did it!

You know, no matter how things go, there's a thick vein of pure farce that runs through everything I do – even playing Hamlet, this huge honour to open the National Theatre. I came up from the bowels one day and while I was on stage to being or not to being, I could hear slight titters. It was an afternoon performance, and I thought, 'What are they laughing at?' Of course, when you do that soliloquy, everybody knows it, so they all join in anyway. They should lower a song sheet. But I'm not used to too many titters. I did some fine gesture and realised I was wearing my bloody glasses. I'd been down below with the stagehands picking out winners! I just sort of trudged through as far as I could and thought, 'How do I get rid of these?' The only thing I could do was to sling them at Ophelia, and poor Rosemary Harris got a pair of horn-rims slung at her.

Katherine Hepburn – I'd have broken Spencer Tracy's fingers thirty odd years ago. I mean it, I would! When I met her, she came to see me, and I was pissing in the sink, actually. Theatres are not well equipped, and my dressing room was a considerable distance from the lavatory. And that voice! A voice suddenly said, 'My name is Kate Hepburn,' and I was pissing – at the sink! So I did all sorts of fine things of washing my hands and all that. Oh Jesus! I got through that and then the phone never stopped – she became a press agent for me. She was partially behind *Lawrence of Arabia*, I know she was. When there were some ditherings with Spiegel and David, Kate was there. She came to Aqaba to wish us luck. She's an incredible lady. I mean, I love her.

1972

Richard Harris

I've always thought of Richard Burton, Richard Harris and Peter O'Toole as names of typhoons bringing shock and awe to Hollywood, Broadway and the West End of London. The popular press christened them 'hellraisers', which meant they drank too much for their own good and paid the price. Peter O'Toole once tried to explain the carousing. He said, 'We were young people who had been children throughout the war. You can imagine what it felt like in 1945 to be free – not to be bombed, not to be rationed, not to be restricted. There was a tremendous amount of enthusiasm. We weren't solitary, boring drinkers, sipping vodka alone in a room. No, no, no – we went out on the town and did our drinking in public.' As well as being gifted actors, they were possessed of compelling personalities, and their memories were of lives led at full tilt.

I interviewed Richard Harris twice – in 1973 and 1988. The early one was the hellraiser in full spate. Fifteen years later he was off the booze and different.

1973

My family was very rich. My great-grandparents were extremely wealthy. We had flour mills and baking powder mills and bakeries and so forth. I wasn't extremely successful at school. There was a special class in my school that was invented for eleven boys. I was brought up a Jesuit Catholic. They're very proud of their sort of academic honours and the students they send out into the world, and there were eleven of us at this particular time in this particular school who they didn't want to send out. They couldn't kick us out, and they didn't want us in the school, so they invented a class just for us.

When I left school, what was I going to do? My father said, 'Well, go into the business.' There wasn't much I could do, but they had huge big barns and lofts and I spent my day going round with a stick, frightening the mice away from the flour. I remember when he finally got rid of me. I felt that all his workers were underpaid, so I brought them out on strike against my father. They paraded outside with signs like, 'Your son said we should have more money'.

If I had my life to live again, I would not wish to erase this period, in which, unfortunately, or indeed fortunately as the case has turned out, I got tuberculosis. I was three years confined to bed, and then I began to study and read an awful lot, and devour books. I studied acting and Stanislavski. Then, I think, the whole sort of inventiveness came to me. I don't mean to be morbid or sentimental, but illness is a great burden upon your friends. The first week or month they all come and say, 'Ah, you'll be up in a month, you'll be up in a week.' They pour in, and then after a couple of months you've got fifteen friends. In another couple of months you've got six, and then you've got three, and then you have one, and then you're on your tod. From that moment on you're alone. And so I was put on my own and eventually thrown on my own resources. I used to invent people out of light bulbs. I used to have conversations with people in light bulbs, and invented hundreds of people coming in and talking. I was the king of England or the pope or whatever. The pope, can you imagine? Harris the pope, wouldn't it be fantastic? Instant sin, instant absolution.

I've got great theories about women. I think women should have lots of opinions, but should not be allowed to express them. I always say to a woman, 'Now look, you're very beautiful and we're going to have a little date, but I don't want you to speak. You just nod your head.' I remember once asking this beautiful woman a very important question, and she nodded her head so fast, she almost dislocated her neck. And then the next morning, they wake up and you say, 'Well . . .' 'Ooh, good morning, it's wonderful,' they say, and you say, 'It's not, you shouldn't have spoken. You've ruined the joke.'

The only time you miss a woman is when you haven't got one. I have ghosts in my house in London. I have a family of ghosts in my house, I swear to you. I don't tell the girl about the ghosts yet. A woman lives with me for a bit in the house, and then I'm getting a little bored. Women become extremely demanding after a while. A woman would always like you to be involved with another woman rather than a career. If it's another woman, there's something for her to touch or fight or talk about, but when it's your career, it's not tangible. It can't order her out, you see? So I've invented a marvellous reason for her to go.

What I do is this. After about a week or ten days, when I'm getting bored, I tell her about the ghost in my house. I say, 'Well, there's a little ghost here. You know that, don't you?' The sounds of the house, they think that's a ghost. So what I do then is that one day I say, 'I'll be back at nine. I'll pick you up, and we'll go out for dinner.' Then I won't come back at nine o'clock, and she'll be stuck in the house, and the stories of the ghosts will start coming into her head. 'What do you think of this ghost in this house? It's two o'clock and he isn't back yet . . .' There'll be little creaking noises and things begin to move round the house and she says, 'Oh, my God, oh my God, this is terrible.'

Now, when I get back around 7 a.m., I find a little note saying, 'Dear Richard, left, gone. Didn't like your house guests.' She's disappeared. But the house is full of clothes, all for the jumble sale one day. It's full of dresses and coats and shoes and socks belonging to various women.

1988

I love Peter O'Toole. I think he's the best actor in the world, and we had a fantastic growing up together in the theatre, one of the best. I worked with Peter down in Bristol and this year he was on Broadway doing *Pygmalion*. I went back to see him. I hadn't seen him for fifteen years and I wondered how he'd receive me. He'd gone a bit peculiar, I think, but he thought I'd got a bit peculiar, so we kind of avoided each other. So I saw him in the middle of the theatre, and I said, 'Peter.' He put his arms around me and looked down at me, because of course Peter is very tall. He speaks with this kind of wonderful lisp, and he said, 'Mixer, ya haven't changed a bit.' He always called me 'Mixer' because I mixed things up for people, got into rows and that. I looked up at him and I said, 'Peter, we're two wrecks.' He dropped his glasses and looked me straight in the eye, and he said, 'We should be dead.' And it's true.

We had the opportunity years ago of actually re-enacting one of the greatest stories in the history of the theatre, which evolved around two separate actors, not O'Toole and I. O'Toole and I did a play together and we had time off during the second act. We were down in Bristol and we went over to the pub and threw back pints of beer. Obviously, we mistook our cue and the stage manager came rushing in and said, 'Harris, O'Toole, you're off.' I said, 'Good God,' and we drunk down the beer. We were out in the street finishing the beer – nothing in the world would ever make us give up the beer – so we finished the beer, dropped the glasses and ran. O'Toole's got big long legs and I'm running to keep up with him, but I caught up because I'm the first one to go on. So I came through the stage door, ran out, just made my entrance to cue, and tripped over a wire across the stage. I landed right at the footlights. A little Bristolian woman sitting there looked into my face and said, 'Good God, Harris is drunk!' I looked down and said, 'Madam, if you think I'm drunk, wait till O'Toole makes it.'

I think that not drinking – I stopped in 1981 – I'm probably more myself now than I was when I was drinking. I dunno why I drank. There's a whole theory in therapy in America, which is very dangerous, I think. Americans are pre-occupied with why, why? I got up this morning. Why? Because the sun shines. I put on my clothes. Why? Because you can't walk around the streets naked. Everything they ask you is why, so they discover that there has to be a reason why you drank. I didn't drink because I was running away from anything. I was having a flourishing career. I drank because I loved it, and they couldn't understand that. I really loved it. I really loved not knowing where I slept last. I really loved getting engaged to people I'd never met. It was wonderful.

I remember in the Beverly Hills Hotel, I was very drunk and very happy and looking forward to my hangover. I went to the desk and there was no one behind the desk in this famous hotel, so I took the key to my room, but I'm dyslexic I found out later in life. Instead of taking key 32, I took key

23. It happened to be a married couple on their honeymoon, and the suites in the Beverly Hills are all identical. So I put the key in and the door opened, obviously. It was the right key. It was the same sitting room, and I took all my clothes off, as I do in the sitting room, and then I opened the bedroom door and I threw myself into bed, but there was a screaming and a howl. I said, 'What is it?' and suddenly the light went on and there was a naked man on one side and a naked woman on my other side. I got right between them, which was perfect.

Suddenly, he throws the Arctic freeze, and I can see why, because I was naked and that was something quite spectacular there, right? I laid on the bed and suddenly, when he unfroze and came back to reality, he said, 'What are you doing here?' I said, 'I have no idea, but if you get a good idea in the middle of the night, wake me up.' It's a true story. They never put me out, and they never called the manager. I woke up the next morning and they're having the wedding breakfast. I'm still lying there, and they said, 'Are you all right? Can we get you . . . you're Richard Harris, yeah?' 'Give me your Bloody Marys, straighten me out . . .'

I remember what I did last night, which makes my life very full. Richard Burton and I did a picture together called *The Wild Geese* and we came to the conclusion that for one-third of our lives we were drunk, for one-third we were getting over a hangover, and for one-third we slept. So we thought we lived our lives for everybody else. They thought we were great fools. We were kind of foolish. When we were sitting up there, reciting Dylan Thomas and Shakespeare for their benefit, if you can't remember it, then you haven't lived it. Life is a series of memories. What you can't remember, you didn't do. So I've only lived half a life. I've got to live a long, long time before I can make up for the life I've lost when I was drunk.

I said to Richard one day, 'You've gotta stop drinking,' because I had stopped, or kind of stopped. Richard Burton said to me, 'How did you do it?' I said, 'It's very simple. The impulse to drink only lasts one minute. If you can survive the one minute, you last another hour, and maybe there'll be twenty impulses during the day.' He said, 'What do you do for that one minute?' I said, 'You just jump for one minute and the impulse goes away.' Well, I can tell you, every time I looked at Burton he was doing that. I swear to God, every time I looked at him, he'd say, 'It's not doing any good!'

I made it very difficult for my wives. For instance, I remember a great story about Elizabeth, my first wife. I'm very friendly with her. She's a fantastic woman, a really courageous survivor. I said to her, 'What was I like when I was drunk?' She said, 'Well, magnificent really, sometimes. But then a look would come over your face, and I'd think, "Oh dear, here he goes again," and everything would flash off the table. That was very difficult.'

I remember once saying I was going to buy a newspaper, and I was gone eight days. I thought, 'How am I going to get back? What am I going to say to her?' and at this stage I heard she was going to file for a divorce. She'd really had it. The poor thing really suffered a lot. 'I gotta go back and see her. How many days am I going to run? Eight days? What am I going to say?' So I arrived back and knocked at the hall door at Bedford Gardens, and I heard her coming down the stairs. I thought, 'What's she going to say?' She opened the door and I looked at her and I said, 'Why didn't you pay the ransom?' And, of course, having a wonderful sense of humour, she fell on the floor laughing. So we patched it up that time, but in the end I ran out of excuses and ran out of jokes and she ran out of humour, so she threw me out. Quite right.

Sir Alec Guinness

Comparing Laurence Olivier, Ralph Richardson, John Gielgud and Alec Guinness, one critic observed that what set Guinness apart from the others was anonymity. What he meant was he possessed the ability to obliterate himself within each character he played. He was like that in real life. We shared a tailor – Dougie Hayward – and it was Doug who introduced us. Sir Alec was an enigmatic man, who seemed to possess his own means of camouflage. I never saw him as soon as I entered the shop, rather he would emerge from somewhere or other. Then, when you looked again, he had gone. He told me once that the greatest lesson he learned as an actor was watching a bird in a zoo. Alec said the bird stood still as a statue, unmoving and unblinking, until he looked away and when he looked back again, the creature had assumed a very different pose. That, he said, was what he sought – to act without being observed. He was a mysterious and fascinating man.

I'd done *Great Expectations* with David Lean and we'd got on very, very well. I owed him a lot. When I heard he was going to do *Oliver Twist*, I fancied the part of Fagin. I don't think they wanted me at all! I thought, 'Well, I'll blow a little cash on this and try this out.' David and I were very friendly by then and I said would he come and have supper with me at the Savoy? So I took him out and counted out the cash. I said I would love to have a shot at playing Fagin, and he said, 'No, no, no. You're too young and you're not . . .' I said, 'Well, this is what's wrong with British films. You don't want actors, you just want types. Where are you going to find that type who can throw in a performance?' Finally, I bullied him so much he said, 'Well, all right, you can do a test for it.' I did the test and, fortunately for me, got the part.

I went into an advertising agency when I was about eighteen, as a copywriter. No use at that. Then they tried me out at layout and put me back to copywriting again. I did it for about eighteen months and cost them a lot of money. When I was doing the layout business, there was something four inches by four inches to go on the front page of the *Daily Mail*, and I'd unfortunately marked to the block makers four foot by four foot, which is rather larger than the *Daily Mail* was, even then. I waited and kept telephoning about this block and finally a taxi arrived and two chaps came in, lugging this great thing. Well, that was that. There was a lot of copper. And the *Daily Mail* appeared next day with a very nice little empty space and a notice saying, 'Reserved for Mullard's Valves'.

When I went into advertising, I knew I wanted to be an actor, but I didn't know how to become one. I didn't know anyone in the theatre, but one of the girls at the advertising agency said, 'Why don't you try for a scholarship at RADA?' It had to be a scholarship. I had no money. Finally, I thought, 'Well, I'll try for that.' I phoned up John Gielgud, whom I didn't know at all. I think I had some sort of crazy idea that he might give me lessons in his spare time! He said, 'Oh boy, I should try someone like Martita Hunt. She'd be glad of the money.' Typical Gielgud.

After I'd been to Martita about four times, suddenly there was my money, which I'd paid in advance – collected, borrowed I think – and she said, 'Take the money, dear. You're no good, go away.' But she became one of my dearest friends, and when I persevered she was absolutely behind me all the time.

I got a scholarship – not to RADA, because when I turned up there, I was met by someone who said, 'I'm very sorry, we're not giving any scholarships this year.' I'd had the appointment and paid the entrance fee and all that, and I was in a terrible state. I ran into a girl whom I'd known when I was a child in Eastbourne and I wept on her shoulder a bit. She said, 'You'd better bus it along, because in Baker Street there's the Fay Compton Studio of Dramatic Art and I know they're holding auditions tonight.' I went along with no appointment, rushed in, got the scholarship and that was that. I lived on about 27 shillings a week in a little Bayswater attic. Friends were very good to me.

John Gielgud was at the height of his romantic success

then. I was supposed to be at the Fay Compton Studio for two years, but I stayed just six months. I simply had to earn my living, couldn't go on like that. At a public show I'd won whatever the prize was, and one of the judges had been Gielgud. On the strength of that, I thought, 'I'll see if Gielgud remembers me.' I went to see him at Wyndham's Theatre, not thinking I'd be shown in, but I was shown straight in to his dressing room after a matinée, and for four or five days he sent me after various jobs.

He sent me, rather madly, to see if I would get the job of understudy to Douglas Fairbanks Jr, of all people, in a play called *Moonlight is Silver*. I was obviously the wrong type for that. I was gangly and hopeless. So that was no good. He sent me down to the Old Vic, where they were auditioning for *Antony and Cleopatra*. I was ushered on to the stage, got out about two lines of my little audition piece and the director – can't use the language here I'm afraid – said, 'Get off the . . . stage – you're not an actor. Get away, get away!' I used to report back to Gielgud each evening, saying, 'No good, failed.' I think that night, he was getting a bit depressed at seeing me coming in each evening. There was a pile of very crisp pound notes on his dressing table. He said, 'You're far too thin. I'm sorry you haven't got the work but go and eat. For God's sake, go and eat, and take this,' and he handed me £20, which I was too proud to take.

I said, 'I'm perfectly all right for money.' I had fourpence left in the world, and I think I was light-headed from lack of food. He said, 'The next time I do a play, you shall be in it, I promise you.' Anyway, I went without the £20, had no job and faced struggling back to my digs. On the way I passed the Piccadilly Theatre, where I saw there was a new play coming on, *Queer Cargo*. Instead of going to the stage door to see if there was anything, I went to the box office, but it coincided with the stage manager arriving, and they all looked at me with astonishment. 'What do you want?' I said, 'I'm an actor and I want a job.' The stage manager said, 'Are you a good actor?' Rather rashly, I said, 'Yes, very good.' And he said, 'Well come and read to me.'

I went into a room with him and I read him bits of things he stuck in front of me, and I ended up understudying the five leading male parts and walking on in the first act as a Chinese coolie, in the second act as a French sailor, and in the third act as an English sailor. I was offered £2 a week, but having secured the job, I was very mean and said, 'No, no, I shall report you to Equity. I want three.' And I got the £3.

A short time later I went to see Maurice Evans playing Richard II at the Old Vic and saw Gielgud in the stalls. I deliberately went out of my way to buy a cup of coffee very close to him, just in case he noticed me. He suddenly did and said, 'Where have you been? What have you been doing? I want you to start rehearsals in two weeks.'

When I first went to Hollywood, there was a party at the Beverly Hills Hotel. Enormous party. I hadn't been asked. It was being given by John Wayne and he suddenly heard I was in the hotel and very kindly, about midnight, phoned up and said, 'Put on a black tie and come on down.' I was thrilled and went down to this great gathering. It was the first time I'd met Betty Bacall. I was talking to her, and she was ravishing and marvellous, when a well-known Hollywood agent came up and dragged her away, saying, 'Oh, you mustn't be seen talking to that Limey, come on.' I was so furious. I've never clocked anyone ever in my life, and I clocked him.

I flew out in a rage, back upstairs, ripped off my black tie and went back to bed. I was ashamed of myself but also very angry with this chap. The phone went. It was John Wayne again saying, 'Come down again, you've got to make it up!' So I put on my black tie and thought, 'I'll behave very well.' By then, of course, it had become something of a scandal and a lot of people had gathered round. He said, 'I want you to shake hands with this man.' So we solemnly shook hands, rather coldly, and there was a lot of applause for that, where-upon I clocked him again! It was something he said. I don't know what it was, but it drove me mad. John Wayne was marvellous about it, very kind of comforting, and I got a huge box of cigars the next day from someone. I don't know who it was.

My very first night in Hollywood I met James Dean, and it was a very odd occurrence. I'd arrived off the plane and been met by Grace Kelly and various people, but I found that I was alone for the evening. A woman I knew phoned up and said, 'Let me take you out to dinner.' We went to various places but she was wearing trousers and they wouldn't let her in any of the smart Hollywood restaurants. It was 1952 or 1954. However, we finally went to a little Italian dive but that was full, and so we got turned away. Then I heard feet running down the street, and it was James Dean. He said, 'I was in that restaurant. You couldn't get a table? My name's James Dean, will you come and join me?' So we said yes. It was very kind of him.

Going back to the restaurant he said, 'Before we go in I must show you something. I've just got a new car.' And there in the courtyard of this little restaurant was some very smart little silver thing, all done up in cellophane with a bunch of roses tied to its bonnet. I said, 'How fast can you drive in this?' He said, 'Oh, I can do 150 in it.' And I said, 'Have you driven it?' He said, 'No, I've never been in it at all.' And some strange thing came over me. In some almost different voice, I said, 'Look, I won't join your table unless you want me to, but I must say something – please do not get into that car because if you do . . .' and I looked at my watch, and said, 'It's now Thursday, ten o'clock at night, and by ten o'clock at night next Thursday, you'll be dead if you get into that car.' Nonsense. So we had a charming dinner, and he was dead the following Thursday afternoon in that car. That was one of those odd things.

1977

Dame Judi Dench

Dame Judi was once asked if there was any award left for her to win. 'There's still Cruft's,' she said, which explains the soft spot I have for our greatest actress. She's a Dame but nothing like theatrical Dames used to be. Dame Edith Evans was imperious, demanding attention both on stage and off it. Dame Judi is more demulcent in her approach to life and her profession. She once told me, 'Acting is not so much what you say as what you don't say.' She also confessed she couldn't bear to see herself on screen because she imagined she was tall and glamorous, and she didn't like what she saw. She might not be six foot tall but I think she is beautiful, and empathic as well, with a ribald sense of humour. But then I'm biased. She sang 'Thanks for the Memory' to me on my last show, a serenade that sent me into retirement a happy man.

My brother always wanted to be an actor and I trained as a theatre designer. That's all I wanted to be, really. I was much encouraged by my father and mother, who were not anything to do with the business. My father was an amateur actor and a doctor, and my ma joined in as well – made a lot of costumes.

My best memory of my father, and the best way I could sum him up, would be that he was an ordinary GP. I used to go with him in the car sometimes when he was visiting patients, and he would turn into a road and the children would come and hold on to the car and run with him. He was a family doctor *par excellence*.

We used to go to France for holidays in the fifties. You were only able to take something like £25 – something absolutely amazing – and I saw a pair of shoes that I liked a lot. He said, 'Well, I think we could probably get you the pair of shoes.' Then we went in to a restaurant and I have a passion for seafood, lobster and large prawns, so I said, 'Look at this, look at this!' He said, 'Would you like some of those?' I said

I'd absolutely love them. So I had five of these great big prawns and finished them with enormous relish. He said, 'You've just eaten your shoes.' There was absolutely no question that there was enough to go round.

My parents were wonderfully supportive of both my brother and me. When I played Juliet for Zeffirelli – his very first production he ever did before films – in *Romeo and Juliet* at the Old Vic in 1960, and came to the line, 'Where are my father and my mother, nurse?' my father, a very sane, calm man, said loudly to at least twelve people around him, 'Here we are darling, in row H.'

I did *Hilda Lessways* for Granada. We used to do it live and at the end of one episode Bill Squire said to me, 'Will you marry me, Hilda?' and I said, 'I'll think about it George, I'll think about it.' The credits rolled and we all breathed a sigh of relief, and the phone rang in the corner. We went across to the man who'd answered it and he said, 'It's your father.' I said, 'My father?' He said, 'Yes.' My father said, 'Hello darling, absolutely wonderful. We know it's a story and we know you know the end, but the man's a bounder.'

I don't read scripts. My husband Michael always knew. He wouldn't tell me to read the script but he would read it and just say, 'Why don't you read this line?' And he would be right, he would always be right. So I still don't do it. I read recently that Richard Eyre said it's to do with freefalling and I think that's exactly what it is. I didn't realise but it is real fright – it's being pushed out of the plane. You can get caught in a branch or something, can't you, at the last minute! I like to feel real fear.

I read recently in the *New Yorker* that ours was a volatile marriage. It was a volatile marriage in the way that, I expect, yours is or anyone's is. People kept saying to us, 'You're such an absolutely perfect couple,' and we were. I was so lucky to meet somebody like that and I knew him nine years before we married, so I knew Michael for nearly forty years. And lightning doesn't strike twice in the same place. He would have been my best friend if I hadn't married him, and I feel incredibly lucky that we met and worked together and had our rows.

We had a wonderful row once. It was coming up for Christmas time. We were appearing in *A Pack of Lies* at the Lyric Theatre in Shaftesbury Avenue and we had a really terrible row about the boiler going. We once had a terrible row about milk bottles. That lasted the whole way to Pembrokeshire in a small car. We were furious about the boiler – I was so angry and so was he. Never spoke. We hadn't spoken for twenty-four hours. It was on a Monday and we were going to the theatre to play in *A Pack of Lies* opposite each other. We were sitting in the car, I was looking out of the window this side and he was looking out of the window that way. And at one point in Shaftesbury Avenue we stopped in the traffic, and a woman passing caught sight of us and said, '*A Fine Romance!*' It made us laugh. He was the best. I miss everything about him.

When I was being wooed by Michael, he was doing a film with Sir Ralph Richardson and Sir John Gielgud out in Yugoslavia. Michael said to me that 'at coffee time in the morning, we all have coffee and Sir Ralph has what he calls Mr Gordon', which was a huge gin. He said, 'When he drinks it, he will drink it straight. He doesn't sip it.' And I was standing there one day, and everybody had their coffees, and then Sir Ralph got his gin and it went straight down, didn't even touch the sides of his mouth. We all went out to dinner that evening and he said to Michael, 'May I whisper something to her?' and Michael said, 'By all means.' So he bit me on the ear. I said, 'Sir Ralph, that wasn't a whisper.' He said, 'No, that's a bite between friends.'

When doing *All's Well that Ends Well* at the Gielgud, I couldn't resist the fact that I came on for the second half and had one small scene and then I was off till the very end and I used to get quite bored sitting in my dressing room – nobody to play with, they were all on stage. Suddenly, I thought one night, 'I know what I'll do, I'll go and appear in *Les Mis* next door.' And so I did. They got me a costume and I raced along the street and then sat down in the middle of an actor's nightmare because I'm stood with a whole group of people that I'd never seen before in my life, all dressed up. I went on and did the whole of 'The Barricades'. And then I raced back for *All's Well*. Jonathan Pryce wrote to me and said, 'There's a very nice part of a dead goat in our second act if you want, at 9.20 p.m.!'

2002 and 2004

Sir Ralph Richardson

Ralph Richardson once said to a lighting cameraman, 'Don't come too close, you'll see through my talent.' It was a typically unforgettable remark from a most singular man. When he first came on the show, he walked down the stairs and told me he would like to 'inspect' the house, whereupon he joined the audience for a chat. He did the same with Russell Harty, walking on, ignoring Russell and inspecting the set until he came upon a badly painted picture of the River Thames and the Houses of Parliament. 'Lovely view you have here,' he said. He liked to set the agenda, play the game according to his whim. I was fortunate to get to know him over the years, and it was a rewarding experience. He was, of course, a great actor but the greatest, funniest, most beguiling part he ever played was himself.

My first job was in the Liverpool and Victoria Insurance Company as an office boy in Brighton. I must tell you this. I started at school in the most unhappy way – I hated school. Nobody liked me and I didn't like anybody. It was a dreadful start in my life really. However, I did get this job when I was about sixteen, as an office boy at ten bob a week, and then my happiness and luck started. Everyone there was so nice to me.
    I enjoyed myself, but whether they enjoyed me is quite

another matter. I don't think they did. I behaved rather badly, as a matter of fact, because I did run a little magazine in office time and produced it on the office Roneo. And I used to pull the leg of the manager rather badly. I invented a kind of character for him. He was a very nice manager, but I used to change his blotting paper continually. I'd come in when he was busy and say, 'Sir, we must change the blotting paper.' He'd say, 'I don't think – oh, we must change the blotting paper.' Then I'd wait, and then I'd bow to him. I had to do it very carefully because I hadn't got to be found out about pulling his leg. Then I would say, 'Sir, have we fresh ink?' And he'd say, 'What?' And I'd come in with a bottle and say, 'We must have fresh ink, Sir.' However, that's very silly. I didn't attend to my work as well as I should have done. I was looking after the post. I was responsible for the cheques going out and I was perhaps more interested in pulling the boss's leg and running this magazine than really attending to my duty, which was very dull. And cheques went to the wrong people. It was awful! It was worse than anything! A chap would get a cheque for £600 and then they'd have to get it back again because the wrong man had got the money!

A little bit on in my disastrous life, I was an art student and didn't get on very well at that, either. That was in Brighton, and I used to go to see all the great actors in the music hall and on the stage. One day I went to see Frank Benson playing Hamlet, and he did just one thing that struck me. As Hamlet saw the ghost, the ghost said, 'Revenge!' And Hamlet took his sword out of his scabbard and sharpened it on the floor in the most extraordinary way, saying, 'Revenge,' and making a weird noise. It struck me, perhaps that's the job for me – not as an artist drawing things but perhaps drawing or illustrating Shakespeare, and that's where it suddenly occurred to me that I might be an illustrator of literature.

When I saw Benson, I lost no time. There was a little repertory company in Brighton run by a chap called Frank Grocott, and I got his name. The next morning I banged on his door. He came down, he was just having breakfast, with a cup of tea in his hand. I said, 'Great news for you, Mr Grocott – I believe your name is Grocott, Sir – I've decided to become an actor.' And he said, 'What? I don't understand. Have you ever done any acting before?' 'No, no,' I said, 'I haven't, but I've decided to become an actor.' So he said, 'You're talking nonsense. What could you do? What have you been doing?' 'Well,' I said, 'I've been at the art school.' He said, 'Could you paint the scenery?' And I said, 'Perhaps I could. But look here, Mr Grocott, if you take me on, I could pay you a small premium.' Grocott said, 'Come inside! Come in and have breakfast!' So I stayed with Grocott for quite a long time, and he was very, very nice to me.

Grocott's company was a very small little theatre, almost an amateur theatre, but Charles Doran, whom I was with for many years, had a proper big touring company in those days. I wrote to him and he answered and said, 'Come and see me.' I cycled over to Eastbourne where he was playing. One matinée, I got this appointment. Oh, it was the great moment in my life. After the show – he was playing Shylock in *The Merchant of Venice* – he said, 'Now the governor will see you,' and opened his little dressing room.

He looked at me and asked me what I'd done. He said, 'Could you show me anything? Could you recite something for me?' I said, 'Yes, Sir, I could. I'll do you a speech from Marc Antony from *Julius Caesar* if you like.' So he said, 'Well, go ahead.' I started: 'Friends, Romans, countrymen, lend me your ears. I come to bury Caesar, not to praise him . . .' *et cetera*. He was taking off his make-up and watching me in the mirror. On the wall he had a lot of things hanging, including his street clothes. He was listening very nicely and politely, and then I came to the death of Julius and I said, 'Do know this mantle?' and I took something in my hand, and I was getting rather excited about it. I said, 'Look, see what a gash the envious Casca made! Look where Brutus . . .' He let me go quite a long time, until it came to the will. I said, 'The will! The will! We will have Caesar's will!' Doran said, 'Do stop it, Richardson! Do stop it!' 'Oh,' I said. 'Sir, is it no good?' He said, 'It's all right but look, you're stamping on my trousers!' I stayed with Doran for many years at the theatre, and he was a great patron to me.

When I think about what I have learnt, I think it is really what I may have unlearnt. I went on the stage when I was young. I had a huge make-up box. I had every colour under the sun. I had coloured powders. I had liners. I plastered myself in make-up because I think I was a bit nervous and it was a kind of shield for me. I wasn't so frightened if I had a lot of make-up on. Of course, I spoke in a very loud voice, but I think I've slightly unlearnt insofar as if I look at my make-up table now in the theatre, I've got one pencil and one pencil sharpener. Whether that's an advance or not, I don't know.

1971

Sir John Gielgud

Sir John Gielgud made his first appearance on the London stage at the Old Vic in 1921 and for eight decades he was a dominant presence. In the 1930s he was the unchallenged master in classical roles before he handed the crown to Sir Laurence Olivier. He starred in silent movies in the 1920s and more than fifty years later won an Oscar for playing a butler in *Arthur*.

Throughout his life he seemed to play the part of the absent-minded eccentric, blundering across a minefield of social indiscretion. He once told Elizabeth Taylor, 'I don't know what happened to Richard Burton. I think he married some terrible film star and went to live abroad.' On the other hand, he often gave good, if slightly unexpected, advice. Asked by a young actor how he should approach playing King Lear, Gielgud said, 'Pick a light Cordelia.'

He appeared on the show with W.H. Auden, the poet creased and crumpled, the actor sitting to attention in his chair, face shining like a polished apple, the voice, as Alec Guinness described it: 'Like a silver trumpet muffled in silk.'

I walked into the Old Vic in 1921, when I was a student at Lady Benson's school, and I wasn't even paid anything for doing it. I carried a spear in two or three plays and giggled a good deal, in the wrong places. But I remember, years ago, when I was in my prep school, having been isolated because I had mumps, or some infectious disease, and walking up and down the steps of the terrace in the garden, with a rug draped round me, thinking I was a king or a monarch of some kind. I suppose this is my first sneaking desire to act. There wasn't anybody looking, fortunately, or they would have had a fit.

I had two brothers and a sister, and we all were very fond of the theatre and acted together. We had toy theatres and went to all the plays we possibly could when we were young. It wasn't really certain which of us would take to it as a profession, and it certainly wasn't mentioned. My father didn't approve of it very much. When I said I wanted to be an actor, they said, 'Well, you'd better work at architecture if you want to be a designer,' and I said, 'Oh no, let me not go to university.' I was just going up to Oxford. 'Let me go on the stage for three or four years, and if I don't make a success of it, then I'll go into an architect's office.' And I got enough jobs in that short time to get a start, but I was a terribly bad actor at that time. I don't quite know what encouraged people to go on employing me because I was self-conscious and very inept, and everybody laughed at me. And several actors and companies told me better not do it.

I was rather pleased with myself and I don't think I knew anything about it. I just thought it was a kind of exhibition business, and it took me a long time to discover that you had really to reveal something of yourself. I wanted to put on something to play a part, to be kings and queens and all that. I suppose that anybody can get up and perform – we all have a streak of exhibitionism in our nature – and one is mixed in being ashamed of it and being delighted with it. Of course, you like coming into the room and everybody laughing at you or saying you're clever, or something. I was a bit of a show-off. And then I met Noel Coward at a party and thought *he* was a total show-off, before he was a success. And sure enough, it was very ironic, because then he became an enormous success in the twenties, and the first real chances I had were to follow and understudy him in two plays, and take over his parts. By that time, he'd become a skilled and brilliant actor, and I was still a great show-off. I thought he was awfully conceited, probably because he was taking the limelight away from what I thought I ought to have, at that early age. But after that we became great friends, and I learned an awful lot from him.

There is a very marvellous story about Noel Coward and the Coronation. We were all sitting in the rain watching the procession. It was a terribly cold day, we all had rugs round our knees, and most of the carriages were closed. Churchill came by and all we could see was his feathered hat being waved out of the window, and everybody was getting rather disappointed. And then in an open carriage came the Queen of Tonga, who was a magnificent looking dusky lady, in a green turban and a great green sari, and she had an enormous success with the crowd because the rain was pelting down and everybody was delighted to see her, and she got an enormous reception. Sitting next to her in the carriage was a very small man, dressed in black, and somebody said to Noel Coward, 'Who is that little man sitting next to the Queen of Tonga, do you think?' and Noel said, 'Her lunch.'

I have a great reputation as a brickdropper. I make terrible gaffes, and people forgive me because they know I don't mean to be malicious, but sometimes they do sound very bad. When Clement Attlee was Prime Minister, I met him and his daughter at a dinner party in Stratford on Avon after a play, and I was trying rather gaily to say that I so enjoyed living in Westminster because it was so near the theatres, and I said to Miss Attlee, 'Where do you live in London?' and he said,

'Number 10 Downing Street.' It didn't occur to me that she might live there, too.

I had a terrible moment once in *The Vortex*. We were playing in a theatre called the Little, which was very tiny, in St John's Street. In the last big scene with Lillian Braithwaite, when the son is haranguing his mother and taking dope and it's a tremendous, melodramatic scene, a cat came on to the stage. Of course, the audience screamed with laughter and Lillian Braithwaite, keeping in the play, said, 'Oh Nicky, for God's sake, put that cat out of the room.' So I took it up, very gingerly because I disliked cats very much, and threw it out of the window. It immediately came in again at the door, and I was so distracted and despairing that I threw it into the audience. Fortunately, it was a flat stage and I don't know what the front row thought, or where it landed. We never saw it again. It was really rather desperate.

1972

Sir Ian McKellen

Sir Ian McKellen is that rarity, the great classical actor who is also box office both on stage and in the movies. His presence in international movie franchises such as *X Men* and *Lord of the Rings* introduced him to a huge international audience while at the same time his *King Lear* and *Waiting for Godot* drew adoring crowds as well as huge critical acclaim. The boy from Burnley, who never trained to be an actor, drew his inspiration from watching weekly rep, and variety stars including Jimmy James and Jimmy Wheeler. He will also be remembered as one of the founders of Stonewall, the organisation formed to fight for gay rights. His calm and persuasive manner and clear enunciation of the need for change did much to alter the law as well as public opinion. In the following interview he talks movingly about how coming out changed him as a man and an actor.

In America they're very impressed and very confused at the same time. Most of them think I'm a Lord and now related to the Queen, and I don't disabuse them. But you do fall down with a bump when you arrive through customs. I arrived at Heathrow, fresh from the Oscars. I'd been seen by a billion people all over the world and I'm signing a few autographs, and I arrived in London and it stopped. As I went through the green channel I was beckoned over by a couple of heavies. I had to take out everything I'd brought back from America, and I kept saying, 'I'm just back from the Oscars, you know.' So I opened up all the cases and they said, 'Well, you don't seem to have much with you. You have cigarettes?' 'Yes.' 'Any gifts?' 'Oh,' I said, 'yes, when you're up for an Oscar you get a lot of gifts.' Well, you do. I was offered a mattress for a start. A mattress company who were sponsoring the Oscars said I could have a mattress, did I want a king size or a queen size? What a stupid question! I said, 'I don't need a mattress, I've got an emperor at home.'

So they gave me lots of jewellery, a couple of watches, alarm clocks, lots of make-up and this suit I'm wearing tonight, which I had made by a tailor in Los Angeles. And customs pounced on this and asked how much would it cost if I'd bought it? I said, 'I'm not in the habit of asking people who give me things how much they cost.' So they impounded the suit. I said, 'I've got the opening of my movie. I've got to wear this suit.' I finally got it out. The tailor had to send a fax over saying how much it would have cost!

Stonewall was founded in my kitchen. I'm looking forward to a blue plaque, or a pink plaque! Mrs Thatcher's government was putting through a nasty bit of legislation called Section 28, which was designed to protect children. And the way she was going to protect them was she wasn't going to allow people to mention the word 'homosexuality' or teach children that people like me existed in the world. So people like me were offended by that, thinking that we're all equal in this world and we're not all the same and let's be grown up about it and proud of our differences.

In discussing this and debating it on the radio with a rather right-wing homophobe, as we call them, he was talking about 'them' all the time, and I said, 'Well "them" is me. I'm gay.' And I came out, almost without meaning to. I suppose I'd been thinking about it for forty-nine years because that's how old I was. And there wasn't anyone in my life who didn't know. I'd never hidden it from them but I'd never talked about it.

I may appear to be self-confident, as we all appear to be fairly self-confident people – actors I'm talking about – but only because we're speaking other people's lines and we've rehearsed what we're going to do. Many of us, like me, are sheltering from the difficulties of life by going into this pretend world where everything's all right, and if it's not all right you can do a re-take or there's somebody there to help you – there's a prompter in the corner. Life ain't like that. And I think if I'd been confident enough to say to the world, as I always said to my friends, that I was gay, then I would have had a self-confidence that would have held me in good stead in the part of my life that wasn't organised.

It changes you so utterly inside. I wasn't aware of the mill-stone that had dropped, but it freed up my emotions enormously in life, and blow me, it freed up my emotions on stage and in film. I find I can cry now. I never could cry before, when the part called for it. Everything started flowing properly. I became a normal person at last. You find this odd because you've been a normal person all your life. I wasn't allowed to be normal. Now I feel I've joined the human race, and it's wonderful.

If you've done as much Shakespeare as I have, it's just assumed that as a lad you play Hamlet and Romeo. And then when you're a bit older you play the middle-aged parts and when you get into your late sixties it's now or never for King Lear. Ralph Richardson, the wonderful, wonderful actor, said to a friend of mine, 'You're going along one day and the sun's out in the sky and the birds are tweeting and there's nothing wrong in your life at all. You couldn't be happier. You're singing a merry song and then, oh, you find you've got your foot caught in a Lear.' And that's what I've got. I've got my foot caught in a Lear.

You're playing a man in his eighties so you're imagining yourself into that frame of mind. But he's an old man who is discovering life for the first time, the reality of life – what it is to love his family and love the people he's been bossing around all his life, as king. Shakespeare, who was an actor, knew that with *King Lear* he'd written a hard part, and you're stretched not just physically but emotionally and mentally. And after the storm scenes, he gives you a rest. You're off stage for about half an hour while other actors get on with other parts of the story. It's a very welcome break. *Hamlet* has one as well. It's even better for me because we have our interval at that time, so I had fifty minutes off stage. It's wonderful, you can sit down, you can have a chat.

One night, I thought, I'll have a little kip, because there was a very inviting sofa in the dressing room. And I had a local dresser who was far too polite to interrupt me when he sensed that my cue to go back on stage was getting near. And I'm under blankets so the Tannoy won't interrupt me with the sound of the other actors getting on with it. I'm fast asleep and the management realised McKellen's not here. So they come to find me. The dresser says, 'I don't know where he is.' Well I'm under the blankets. They look in, they can't see King Lear, so they think, is he out having a cigarette? What's he doing? He said, 'Oh he's gone wandering around . . .' No, no.

But the cue comes and there's a pause, and poor old Bill Gaunt and Ben Majors are just sitting on stage with nothing to do but twiddle their thumbs and they're thinking of leaving when the stage manager takes on his responsibilities and says, 'Ladies and gentlemen, I'm afraid we must postpone the performance just for a moment because there's been a technical hitch,' at which time he heard me racing down the steps to get on to the stage, so he says, 'Oh, no. Here he is.'

1999–2007

5 Music

Paul McCartney

When I first met the Beatles, they were about to board the rocket ship that blasted them to the kind of stardom not even the drug-induced imagination of the hippy generation could have dreamed. It was Manchester in the sixties, the epicentre of a cultural revolution that embraced the world. In those days, we all shared the same limelight. Paul McCartney asked me for an autograph for his mum. He was a happy lad with a guitar and a gift for writing unforgettable tunes. When I interviewed him in 1998 he was a legend of rock'n'roll, and his song-writing partnership with John Lennon produced songs to last forever. The boy, McCartney, had long gone. John Lennon had been murdered, Paul's beloved wife Linda had died. This was a reflective, mature man looking back on an extraordinary life. Yet when he sat next to me and played and sang 'Yesterday', we both remembered how it all began and shared a smile.

Michael: Was this new record a way of working through your grief from the death of Linda?

Paul: I think so, a little bit, because she loved her rock and roll, and she'd always said to me, 'You've got to do that rock and roll album.' I'd say, 'Yeah, I'll do it, I'll do it.' So when she died, I thought, 'You know what, I've really got to do that rock and roll album.' I left things for about a year, just wanted to see how it was going to affect me, rather than jump into work and get busy and try to ignore and deny it all. Thirty years with such a beautiful woman – I've got to see how this is going to affect me. Then, when I was ready to work again, I thought, 'It's gotta be that rock and roll album.'

Michael: And how did it affect you? What was it like? It's an awful question to ask anybody.

Paul: Yeah, I didn't expect to be sitting here being asked that. We expected to be eighty years old on the porch in our rocking chairs. But it was very difficult, of course. I was very sad, because we fought against it. We did everything you could possibly do to the last minute. We thought we might have cracked it – there's always hope. So when she did die, it was just a terrible blow for me and the kids, and all her family.

Michael: Nothing prepares you.

Paul: I don't think you can get prepared for that, no. It's just horribly sad. And instead of saying, 'Right, that's it. I'm British. I'll get on with it,' I thought, 'Right, I'm gonna sit here and cry,' which I did. I just – anyone who came round – I just cried. I don't know you – waah!

Michael: That's not very British is it, but it's very Irish of course.

Paul: Very Irish. God bless the Irish!

Michael: In a sense, you'd been through this terrible grief once with your mother?

Paul: Yeah, that was one of the frightening things really, because as it was going along there were little echoes I remembered from my childhood – 'That happened to my mum.' One particularly is that I remember Mum getting tired and us kids didn't really know. I remember my dad saying, 'Go upstairs, love, and have forty winks.' So I made sure, when Linda got tired, I never said to her, 'Go upstairs and have forty winks.' You get a bit superstitious almost. It was not very nice at all because she was such a beautiful, strong woman. She was a difficult woman to lose.

****

Michael: There was this historical meeting, in the sense of the history of music, with John. Tell me about that meeting.

Paul: Well, we had a friend in common who went to school with me and George. He was called Ivan Vaughan, and he used to be in one of the little skiffle groups John was in. John used to jive with Ive, the ace on the bass. Ivan used to have one of those tea-chest basses – a bit of string on a broom handle on a tea chest. So he said, 'You should come along. This group's playing and my mate John's in it, at the

Woolton Village Fête.' So I did. I went along and saw this group on the little stage there, and the singer – John – just looked to me like he had something.

Michael: That was the start of it. Was there one single image, one single moment that, when you look back, sums up Beatlemania for you?

Paul: Beatlemania? The single image, I suppose, would have to be arriving in America for the first time, because we'd kind of crept out through clubs and dance halls – The Cavern, theatres and things like that, a little bit of telly when we saw you, radio and stuff. Then eventually, a thing came to go to America and we weren't sure how big we were there, so we got off the plane and there were millions of people. We said, 'Who's this for?' They said, 'It's for you!' And we rode in a big limousine and all the DJs were saying, 'And the Beatles are arriving in New York, it's official! They've landed . . .' So we were thrilled.

Michael: You liked each other, didn't you? There was a kind of brotherhood?

Paul: We did like each other a lot. You had to, or you couldn't get on. There was one time when – this is how much we had to like each other – we'd travel around all the time and we'd be in the ever-present van. We'd come up from London – we'd never stay in London, we'd always go back home for the night – so we're coming back and I think the heater had gone off in the van, and it was a bitterly cold winter's night. So we hit upon this plan of lying on top of each other. It was the only way. You had to do that, didn't you? It was a Beatle sandwich – isn't that a nice thought? And the person on the bottom, that was the least favourite position to get because it got a bit heavy. So you had to keep swapping, you know – I'm on top now!

Michael: And where did the inspiration come from? How did the two of you used to write? Was it a formal, 'Let's write a song now, John'?

Paul: Yeah, it was like that. We'd go home, normally to my house because his Auntie Mimi wouldn't have us at hers.

My dad was at work, so we could sneak off school and go there, and it was, literally, just 'let's try and write a song'. We wrote a few quite bad ones at first, but then we started to get a little better and the inspiration just came. It comes through all sorts of different places.

Michael: The inspiration – it's now legendary that you dreamed that phrase up in your mind and then sat down and called it 'Scrambled Eggs' or something, the original title of 'Yesterday'. But since that time, it's become the song you're most associated with. Have you really thought where the song came from?

Paul: I don't know. I dreamed it and woke up one morning with the tune in my head and didn't believe it was mine really. I just thought, 'It can't be because I've got the whole tune.' It'd never happened like that – very strange that it should seem the most successful. I didn't even write it, really. My subconscious kind of wrote it.

Looking back on it now, people have suggested it might have been to do with the death of my mum, because it has got, 'why she had to go, I don't know, she wouldn't say,' and, 'I believe in yesterday . . .' and stuff. So it may have been subconsciously something to do with that, but I don't really know. It's nice to have written it. And it's kind of magic – I believe in those magic moments. They sometimes just happen to you. I don't talk about it too much in case the magic doesn't happen again.

****

Michael: It's still amazing that all these years after John's death, there's still this debate about the two of you, about history being rewritten, revisionist history – John's this and you're that. First of all, for people who didn't meet him, what was he like?

Paul: John? He was beautiful. Very beautiful. He was a very complex guy because he had a lot of tragedy in his life. His dad left home when he was three and he didn't see him till he got famous. He went to live with his auntie and uncle, and the uncle died. I remember John telling me he started to think he was a jinx on the male side. John's mum lived with another guy. We used to visit, because he doted on his mum, but then she got run over by an off-duty policeman, I think, one night in front of Aunt Mimi's house. Then his first marriage ended in divorce. He had a lot of tough breaks really, John, so I think he was very guarded. And I think the wit and everything was always the shell that came down. But that was one side of him. He was a very loveable guy, very warm-hearted and a great friend.

Michael: How upsetting was it when the split occurred? Not just the Beatles, but you and John had this rift when some very cruel things were said, particularly about yourself by John.

Paul: We kind of had a war in the newspapers. There was a lot of that went on. And it was very upsetting. It was terrible. But what can you do? I could just say, well I think you're a load of bloody this and that, and all that we could do was to have the war in public. That was really upsetting, I think, for both of us. I think he had to clear the decks in order to give Yoko space. This was now his new relationship and, being a good, loving guy, he had to get rid of the old mates in order to give her what he thought a woman needed. But the great thing about it was that after all that warring, before he died, we did make it up.

Michael: What was the first approach? Was it by accident?

Paul: There were all sorts of approaches. I would come to New York and say, 'Let's get together.' 'Yeah, what do you want?' 'What do you want?' 'Well, I don't want . . .' 'Oh sure, pull the other one.' There was a lot of that. Eventually, I think, it was when he had Sean. When he had his baby, he mellowed a lot, and I remember then I was able to ring him up and say, 'What are you doing?' And he'd say, 'Oh, I'm baking some bread actually.' I said, 'Baking bread? I've just baked a loaf here. We've had a bread strike . . .' So we could talk about babies and baking bread and stuff. We had some really good conversations and, thankfully for me, we were really good friends by the time he died. I'd hate to have left it on the other note. It would have been the ultimate tragedy for me.

1999

John Lennon

I can't add much to Paul McCartney's tribute to John Lennon except to wonder if, had John lived and come to maturity, he would have spoken so kindly of his friend and collaborator. If Lennon and McCartney had been cast as cops in a TV series, Paul would have been the good cop and John the enforcer. I interviewed John and Yoko Ono in 1971 in the very first series of *Parkinson*. It had been two years since the break-up of the Beatles and relations between John and Paul were fractured. He said if I asked him about the Beatles, he would answer only if I pulled a black sack over my head. He called it 'total communication'. I was pleased to be part of this novel experiment in interviewing techniques – overjoyed not to be required to do it ever again.

Michael: Can I put something to both of you about this sort of creative phase that you're both going through at present? I think you've got to accept, John and Yoko, and particularly you John, that it's alienated you from the people who originally loved you in this country.

John: A lot of them, yes.

Michael: Yes, I think they don't understand any more.

John: When I left Liverpool with the group, a lot of Liverpool people dropped us, and said, 'Now you've let us down.' When we left England to go to America, we lost a lot of fans, because they begin to feel as though they own you. The people in Liverpool did, and they did until we decided to leave. And the same in England. A lot of people dropped us because we went to America, but of course we got a whole pile more, or a different audience. And it's the same now. I'm not going to gear my life just to attract an audience. I started out playing music because that's what I wanted to do, and in front of an audience is how you do it, and now it's not very different. Then I sang 'All You Need Is Love', now I might sing 'Power To The People'. The message is basically the same. It's just sort of slogans.

The alienation started when I met Yoko. People don't seem to like people getting a divorce. It's all right to do it quietly, but we can't do it quietly. So we fell in love and it's unfortunate. We fell in love and we married. A lot of people think that to be odd, but it happens all the time, and Yoko just happened to be Japanese, which didn't help much. And so everybody had this impression that John's gone crazy, but all I did was fall in love, like a lot of people do who are already married, who married somebody very young, and that's all we did.

Then we did 'Two Virgins', which didn't help much, but we were just trying to say to people that being naked doesn't mean a damn thing. I think it's those kinds of things that have done it more than anything else.

Michael: I think recently another reason for people taking a dislike to you, Yoko, is, of course, you've become known, again through newspapers in this country, as the woman who broke up the Beatles.

John: But that's not true. Listen, I'll tell you, people on the street, and kids, do not dislike us. It's the media, I'm telling you. It's not us. We go on the street and the lorry drivers say, 'Hello Yoko, hello John,' and all that jazz. And I judge it by that. My records still sell well, her records sell all right, so it's not people in general, even though they've had this propaganda.

Michael: Yes, but Yoko's presence, John, did it lead to tensions in the group? Was it part of the break-up?

John: The tension was already there, you see, after Brian died . . . I said we could talk about the Beatles, but you know I want you in the bag.

Michael: What do you want me in the bag for, John?

John: Because then it's total communication if you're in the bag. Are you going to do that?

Michael: Can we talk about the Beatles?

John: All right, fine.

Michael: In the interests of communication, John. Wait a minute, does the bag go over my head?

John: Yeah.

Yoko: You look very elegant, actually.

John: Nobody could break us off, we broke ourselves off, you know. When Brian died, we got a bit lost because we needed a manager. All of us are artists, so we can't manage ourselves or look after ourselves in that way. But it's a lot for four big-heads like the Beatles to stay together for such a long time, and in the early days there was the thing of making it big or breaking into America. And we had a goal together. But when we reached about twenty-eight or twenty-nine, it began to be all, 'What's the goal?' and 'We've made it.' We were getting more talented and George began to write lots of songs. We couldn't even make an album – you were lucky to get a track on an album. And then we all started to get more interested in our own music and going different ways. If you hear our separate albums, they're similar, but our personalities have developed, and they were a bit stifled in the Beatles. Between us now we sell ten times more records than the Beatles did individually. If you add them all together, we're doing far better than we were then.

1971

Elton John

Of all the rock legends, Elton John was the one most able, and willing, to tell it as it was. He was a regular on the show, a significant part of its history, and we became friends. Today, he is the bejewelled sage of rock'n'roll, the wise adviser to another generation about to make some, if not all, of his mistakes. Yet he was never more of an example than when he took on the tabloids and successfully fought against their grotesque distortion of his life. In the end, the music tells you all you need to know about the man. He succeeded because he never lost the ability to laugh at himself, nor to make light of his faults. Had he not been a musician, he would have made a wonderful stand-up comedian.

1976

Michael: When did you start to play piano? Can you remember the first time you played?

Elton: Oh yes. When I was about three and a half, I played 'The Skaters' Waltz' by ear, much to the delight of my parents, who grabbed me and said, 'We could make a fortune here.'

Michael: No, really?

Elton: No. They gave me encouragement, but I started and played by ear. We lived in a bungalow and, I remember, I was off school once, ill, and I was playing the school hymn but sort of jazzed it up, and the vicar came round. I didn't know he was there, and I was trying 'All Things Bright and Beautiful' à la Jerry Lee Lewis, and it didn't go down too well. But my parents always encouraged me to learn and I hated learning the piano, like scales and arpeggios, but you see, they won out in the end.

Michael: Your father wasn't too keen on you going into pop music, was he?

Elton: No, he hated me going into pop music. He wrote me a letter when I was sixteen saying, 'I think you're an idiot and you're better off in Barclays Bank because this thing you're doing is absolutely stupid and you're going to turn out to be a wide boy.' I was about sixteen stone, so I was a wide boy already . . . My parents divorced when I was about fourteen and my real father didn't encourage me one bit after that, which I found extraordinary, because he was a trumpeter with Bob Miller and the Miller Men. He used to be in a dance band and I think he still does frown a bit on what I'm doing. I still think he'd rather I'd been the head of the Air Force or something like that.

Michael: Did this parental objection make you more determined to do what you wanted to do?

Elton: Absolutely. I'm the most incredibly ambitious person – I don't let it get out of control – but I think you do have to be ambitious all the time, because if you settle into a rut and think, 'Well, I'm OK now, I can settle down for a couple of years and do what I'm doing,' I don't think it helps. I think you have to want to get better and you have to want more out of what you're doing, and I still feel that way. I've always been ambitious from the word go. I've always known what I wanted to do, which I think is an advantage. People I went to school with, left school, went to university and got all their degrees and they still didn't get a job because they didn't know what they wanted to do. I left school two weeks before my A-levels and the headmaster committed hari-kari. But at least I knew what I wanted to do. I started off as a tea boy in music publishing, but it was a start and I loved those days.

Michael: You also played piano in a pub, didn't you?

Elton: Yes.

Michael: What kind of training was that?

Elton: Fantastic. I used to play every Thursday, Friday, Saturday and Sunday for a year, at the Northwood Hills Hotel. First of all I just played the piano and didn't sing, and then I earned a little bit of money, saved up and bought myself a little amplifier and microphone, and then I started to sing.

It was all Jim Reeves songs in those days, and Cliff Richard, but I used to slip in the odd Jerry Lee Lewis number just to pacify myself. You'd get the drunken Irishman coming over to you with a pint of Guinness and saying, 'Play "When Irish Eyes are Smiling",' and you'd say, 'Well, I've got something else to play,' and he'd start pouring beer over you. A couple of nights I had to go out the window. I used to play right near the window – I'm not stupid, folks. I'd be playing the piano, the fight would start and out the window I'd go.

But they were fantastic years. I learnt a lot because all my biases were broken down. I thought, 'I'll never play that,' and in the end I did, because it meant I'd earn an extra two bob.

Michael: So you have never been a musical snob? You'd play anything that we ask you, provided you're sitting next to a window?

Elton: If someone's got a broken bottle, holding it to your throat, you'll play anything. 'Flight of the Bumblebee' even.

Michael: How much of a struggle was it for you in those days, when you were playing in the pub, and afterwards when you used to back other musicians?

Elton: I was in a group and we used to back people, American groups, soul groups, which I loved. We'd back people like Patti LaBelle and The Drifters for a sort of not-quite-honest agency. We used to get paid £15 a week and we'd travel up and down Britain, do three gigs a night. In fact, one day we did four – we played an American servicemen's place in London in the afternoon, then two ballrooms in Birmingham, came back and played the Q Club in Paddington, and we still got £15 a week, and humped our own equipment.

Michael: When you look back on those days, are you able to see that you knew perhaps you might get to where you are now?

Elton: Absolutely not. Those are the days when I thought, 'Well, this is it. After this breaks up . . .' and the group was at a point where it would be breaking up every other day, 'there's no chance for me here. What am I going to do? It's all down to me working in a record shop.'

Michael: Did you get very depressed about that?

Elton: Oh, terribly, because I was just playing the organ and I hate playing the organ. I wasn't very good on the old draw bars. I got very, very depressed. In the end, I was glad when the whole thing just fell apart.

Michael: You were suicidal at one point, weren't you, which was not so much to do with the music but other things as well?

Elton: I saw my royalty statement. No, that was later on when I was writing my own songs. It was over a romance, actually, a torrid love affair. It was just one of those things where I left home, got the flat in Islington and moved in with a lady, and it just didn't work out. She hated my music. She used to like Buddy Greco's 'Girl Talk' and that was the only thing she ever used to play. I'd come home and say, 'What do you think of this?' and she'd say, 'Rubbish!' So, she was very encouraging. In the end, I just called it quits. It was very emotionally draining and I did try to put my head in the gas oven, but I left all the windows open, thank God.

1998

Elton: It's very hard to say you need help, because you think you can solve your own problems. What happened was that someone naturally challenged me, face to face, and read out a list of what they thought was wrong with me, which was quite long. A bit like *Woman's Hour* really. And then my list of what was wrong with the other person lasted for about half a second – 'You don't put CDs back in the covers properly,' and the list about me was, 'He chucks up all over the carpet and . . .' It was then I thought, 'Oh yeah, this has gotta stop.' I was so unhappy. Let's face it, drugs were fine to start with, but when you record your own conversations on drugs, or on alcohol, it's just a lot of old rubbish, basically.

Michael: How bad was the drugs and alcohol situation at that moment we're talking about?

Elton: I did ring up the office one day to complain that the wind was too windy. Mayday! 'Oh, she's finally lost it.' I was staying at the Inn on the Park in London and I rang up to say, 'It's very windy, can you do something about it?' There were many incidents like that, unfortunately, I'm ashamed to say.

Michael: But how did you confront it?

Elton: I just had to go in to a rehab clinic and take notice of what other people said – do what I was told for about a year. I took a whole year off. I did six weeks in Chicago, came home and did what I was told, and I've changed. It saved my life, without doubt.

Michael: You reckon you'd have . . .

Elton: Oh, I wouldn't be here, without question, no.

Michael: Really?

Elton: Yeah, absolutely. It was a very unhappy time. That's what drugs do to you. They bring out the worst side of your character. Drugs and alcohol are really an escape from what's troubling you. I'm not very good with confrontation. I wasn't very good at expressing how I felt, so drugs were an escape, and of course then when you're on drugs, you think you're being so fabulous and truthful, and when you wake up the next morning you find you've invited people for dinner and then you stay in bed because you don't want to see them. It's that syndrome. It's an abortion syndrome. So I've learnt since to confront people and say how I feel, and it's the one thing I've never been very good at, ever since I was a kid.

Michael: But what I found difficult to understand was you always had this kind of low esteem, and that was the basic problem. You say you felt unattractive as a kid and all that, and yet there you were, this hugely glamorous superstar of pop. You walk out and there are 80,000 people in the audience going crackers . . .

Elton: Yeah.

Michael: For two and a half or more hours, you had them in the palm of your hand, you had all that adoration and adulation, you had all the money in the world, anything you wanted, and you came off and you felt worthless. I used to watch you and think, 'Well, what's the problem?'

Elton: I think that's true of a lot of entertainers. I think they know how to be comfortable on stage, but they don't know how to be comfortable off stage, and I think it was very difficult for me to live my life off stage and find a balance or a happy medium. Drugs were certainly the wrong way to go, but that's the route I chose.

Michael: What used to amuse and astonish me too – you must have a constitution of a shire horse.

Elton: Two shire horses. Sometimes it backfired. I remember once in Sydney, I hadn't been to bed and I went on stage, and it was the first night of a tour. We had a new keyboard player, and the rest of the band were as stoned as I was. He was completely straight, and I was playing 'Sad Songs Say So Much' and got to the point when you get to the middle 'A', and I couldn't stop playing the middle 'A'. I think I played it twelve times thinking, 'What comes next?' And the keyboard player thought we'd laced his drink with LSD but all the band was so stoned, they just followed. Those things give me nightmares, but you look back and they're very funny. You have to laugh at it, but on the other hand, you have to have a healthy respect for what it can do to you, and it was not pleasant.

Michael: But tell me, there is that wonderful story about your nan, about when you were in America and then you tried to . . .

Elton: Well, in 1975, I was playing Dodgers' stadium and I hired a whole Boeing 707 to fly all my friends and relatives over, including my grandmother, who at that point was seventy-five years of age. I had my house in Los Angeles and she stayed there with my parents. It wasn't a particularly happy time for me. I was in love with someone who didn't love me, and I just took a handful of sleeping tablets and threw myself in the swimming pool and said, 'I'm going to die.' I had this huge towelling dressing gown on, and I'm fighting for my life in the water, and my grandmother's sitting there, smoking away, and she said, 'Oh well, I suppose we'll be able to sod off and go home then.'

Larry Adler

Larry Adler was an exhausting man. He never stopped talking and rarely listened. He was an indefatigable, unstoppable source of anecdote and reminiscence yet rarely boring. Any man who inspired Malcolm Arnold to write a concerto for mouth organ, who knew George Gershwin, Duke Ellington and Louis Armstrong, and who played a doubles match at tennis partnering Charlie Chaplin against Greta Garbo and Salvador Dali, must be worth listening to. He came to England because he was blacklisted during the terrible McCarthy communist witch-hunt in America – their loss, our gain. He was responsible for one of the moments on the show I shall never forget when he improvised a version of 'Summertime' with Itzak Perlman, the poignancy of which will haunt me until the day I die.

I did study the piano. I was a lousy student, and wouldn't practise. I loved the piano and I admired people like Rachmaninoff, for example. I tried to emulate what he did, forgetting that it takes an awful lot of hard work to become a pianist, and I wasn't willing to do that. So eventually I was expelled from music school, because instead of playing agreed works, I didn't like the lady conducting the examination and I played 'Yes We Have No Bananas'. End of academic education.

When I was thirteen or fourteen, the *Evening Sun* in Baltimore, which was responsible for the career of a man you are probably a fan of, H.L. Mencken, ran a mouth-organ competition, I think as a promotion stunt. Something gave me the idea I could play it. I cannot tell you to this day what gave me that idea, but I bought a mouth organ, found that, in fact, it wasn't difficult to play, learned the piece, went into the contest and won it.

There was a bit of luck. I had known Beethoven's 'Minuet in G' simply because the notes lay close together and it made it easier to play, and the judge of the contest was a classical musician. All the other kids played 'St Louis Blues' and things like that. And I won. He said, 'We have given the award to Lawrence Adler with an average of ninety-nine and nine-tenths.' Then he says, 'No one is perfect.' So I was the champion, and three months later I ran away, quite literally, without telling my parents. I had the money to do it because I sold *Liberty* magazines, and I just bought my ticket to New York and went on the stage.

In 1973 I came to Israel, and just after the Yom Kippur War, I played in a hospital in Jerusalem. I was playing in the various wards when someone asked, 'Mr Adler, we would like you to play for one man.' He was about nineteen years old. They'd brought him down from the Golan Heights and he was in a state of shock. They said, 'You'll think he doesn't hear you because he won't react, but please play for him because we think it's liable to do some good.' So I played something and there was no reaction whatsoever, and this is unnerving. But then I played something else and when I finished the second piece, his lips moved and he spoke, in Hebrew. The nurse bent down and she said to me, 'He said will you play something of Beethoven?'

Now, of course, I had to react as if he talked all the time. I mustn't let him know that I was affected by this, so I said, 'Well, Beethoven wrote several things, which would you like?' So he smiled, and to watch this man smile – and I'll tell what he did. He said, 'Can you play part of Beethoven's Ninth Symphony?' So I played the finale, and as I played it, patients from other wards came in, in wheelchairs, and they were singing to it, and then he began to sing it. I tell you, it tore me apart. I'd never known a more dramatic moment in my entire musical life than when that young man started to sing.

I suppose the really tragic moments in one's life are the omissions, and I think of the great men, composers, whom I met, when I had a chance to say to them, 'Would you consider writing for my instrument?' and didn't have the nerve to do it. Rachmaninoff is the main one. The other was Ravel. I met Ravel in Paris. He asked me to play the 'Bolero' for him. He didn't like it, by the way. He made it very clear he didn't, too.

Paul Whiteman was playing at the Roxy Theatre in 1929 with his film *The King of Jazz*, and I used to hang around outside the stage door. When anyone came in or out, I'd start playing the mouth organ, hoping maybe here's a job. I still do that. Anyway, Frankie Trumbauer came out, the great saxophone player, and I played for him and he took me to Paul Whiteman, who was sitting there with a rather skinny young man by him. I played for Whiteman and Whiteman said, 'Can you play "Rhapsody in Blue"?' but I couldn't. I was fifteen years old. I wanted to tell him I was a sophisticated guy and said, 'I don't like "Rhapsody in Blue".' Whiteman turned to the skinny fellow. 'How do you like that, Gershwin? He doesn't like your "Rhapsody in Blue".' And, of course, I wanted to kill myself.

But later on in Hollywood, I not only met Gershwin but he and I were after the same girl – Simone Simon. Do you remember her? Well, I thought I was making a lot of headway with Simone, but in fact she was only using me as bait to encourage Gershwin. One night she invited Gershwin and me to dinner, and we sat across a table glaring at each other. Why did she do this sadistic thing, inviting both of us? After dinner, two technicians from Warner Brothers came in with recording machines. Gershwin sat at the piano, I played the mouth organ and she sang all the melodies from *Porgy and Bess*, which she wanted to record.

I never wanted to be an actor. I don't think I could. I was at Grauman's Chinese Theatre in 1933 and I did get signed for a film called *Many Happy Returns*. I was about sixteen then, and they signed me for $300. I didn't know whether it was $300 a day, week, month or year, but it was my first film. So I went out to the studio and they told me that I was going to do a number with Guy Lombardo and his orchestra. And I said no. 'What do you mean, no?' I said, 'I don't like

Lombardo's style.' He said, 'We didn't ask you what you liked. This is what you're going to do.' So I walked off the set. They called me back the next day and the director spoke to me, gave me a talking to, and I said, 'I'm terribly sorry. I don't want to work with Lombardo.' So he fired me.

It got all the way up to the head of the studio, William LeBaron, and he was very, very kind. He was really like a father, and he said to me, 'Now, Larry, you can't walk off a signed contract. This will be very damaging for you in show business. You must not do that.' And I said, 'Well, I'm sorry, Mr LeBaron, I don't like Lombardo's music and I don't want to play solo with that as accompaniment.' He said, 'But Larry, you're unknown. Millions of people will hear you if you do this.' I said, 'I don't want millions of people to hear me with Lombardo.' So he said, 'What do you like?' I said, 'I like Duke Ellington.' He said, 'So do I, Larry. We all like Duke Ellington. We can't hire Duke Ellington just to accompany you.' I said, 'No, I guess not.' So I went home. Three o'clock in the morning LeBaron called me. He said, 'Well, you no-good little schmuck, we got Ellington for you.' They hired Duke Ellington to accompany me. They paid him $5,000 to accompany my $300.

About four or five months later, Duke and I were at a nightclub called The Grand Terrace. Earl Hines was the big star there, and always on Thursday night he would have guests. So Duke and I were there and played 'Sophisticated Lady'. When we finished, Duke said, 'Larry, I want you to meet somebody.' He took me over to the ringside table and said, 'Larry, I'd like you to meet Billie Holiday,' and I started to say, 'How do you do?' And she said, 'Man, you don't play that thing, you sing it.' Oh, that moved me. I can't tell you what that did to me.

I think that anybody who was even making a left turn on a one-way street was accused of being a communist, and you were blacklisted. I do remember going to New Orleans and the American Legion picketing me so I didn't open my engagement. That night I got a call. I picked up the phone and said, 'Hello.' 'Larry Adler?' I said, 'Yes.' He said, 'This is a friend of yours.' I said, 'What's your name?' He said, 'Never mind my name, this is a friend of yours.' I said, 'Come on, you know my name but you're not telling me yours.' He said, 'Listen, you Jew bastard, you get outta town or we're going to ride you out on a rail.' Then I was aware. And of course in school, I was beat up about once a week because I had killed Christ personally. I had an alibi. I knew where I was. Nobody would believe me.

Chaplin was a neighbour of mine in Beverly Hills. I moved to Beverly Hills in 1944, to be psycho-analysed, and the man who was my analyst had analysed George Gershwin, and Judy Garland and quite a lot of people. He seemed to specialise in show people. I played tennis a lot with Chaplin and one day he called me and said, 'Larry, are you busy right now?' I said no. He said, 'Can you come over to make up a fourth at tennis? Bill Tilden's dropped out.' Well, Tilden was the greatest tennis player in the world. Of course, if Tilden dropped out, who do you call? Adler.

So I went up there and he was knocking up against two other people – it was a lady and a man. She had blue shorts and stringy hair, and she looked like a James Thurber drawing of a drunk. He looked a mess. The man had a rather weird moustache. Charlie just said, 'Get on the court.' So I came on the court, we started to play, and after a while the lady said, 'Shall we begin the set?' When she spoke, I realised it was Greta Garbo, and at that moment the shorts became white and the hair was perfectly groomed. I just fell for the Garbo legend. And the man was Salvador Dali. He had a way of swinging at a ball but never hit it. And do you know that Chaplin was the best player of the four of us? He must have been in his sixties then, and the way he covered the court made me quite ashamed of myself.

1975 and 1980

Tom Jones

As soon as you hear him singing, you know he is Welsh. The voice is the music of the landscape of the country of his birth. It is as identifiably Welsh as Richard Burton reading Dylan Thomas. He's seventy now and women still throw their knickers at him, but nowadays more out of habit than lust. Cosmetic enhancement has left him looking like a pensioner trying to appear as good as his voice sounds. When he met Dame Edna Everage on the show, she told him that too many people went into plastic surgery hoping to emerge looking like a Cadillac and ending up like a Ford Mondeo.

I was brought up in a family who all lived close together. My mother's brothers and sisters lived in Pontypridd, where I come from, and so did my father's brothers and sisters, so I had all these aunties and uncles and cousins living in the same town. We would always get together for birthday parties and at Christmas time, and it was always a big singsong.

Women in Wales carry babies in a shawl – 'Welsh fashion' they call it. They wrap the shawl around themselves and then the baby. My mother tells me that if an up-tempo song came on the radio, I would start to move around in the shawl. She says she couldn't hold me. It was a strange thing. She thought, 'What the hell have I given birth to here?'

In Wales, there are a lot of big voices. The only difference is that I liked popular music, whereas a lot of the big voices in Wales are traditional singers. A lot of the rugby players, and rugby followers, have great voices. If you ever see a rugby match at Cardiff Arms Park, you'll hear tremendous singers, but they're more of a traditional type. I think what set me apart was I was listening to pop music as a child, and then when rock'n'roll began, I started picking that up.

When I did *The Ed Sullivan Show* in 1965, I was told, if I

was going to move around like that, they would just keep the cameras on close-up and wouldn't give me a long shot, which had happened nine years previously with Elvis Presley. No sexual movement on stage. I thought that was weird because I was doing it in this country on television. Then I went to Australia and in Sydney my shirt ripped up, because it was hot there. The police said they were going to video tape the show and view it, and if they thought it was too much, they would cancel the tour. I thought, 'Christ!' I couldn't believe it. Growing up in Britain, you think Britain is a conservative place, and that America and Australia, all these places, would be more lenient, but it wasn't the case.

Every singer who was a teenager in the fifties was influenced by Elvis Presley. I collected his records and watched him – he was a big influence on me with the movement and everything. He was doing what I wanted to do. I met him in 1965, when I first went to the States, to find that he was a fan of mine. I had 'It's Not Unusual' and 'What's New Pussycat' and 'With These Hands' and one album, and he had all the records. I met him in Los Angeles at Paramount Studios. I was there to sign a contract for a song I was doing for a movie and he was actually making a movie there. When I walked in they said, 'Elvis is here today and he would like to meet you.' I thought, 'Oh, that's strange.' It was the first year of success for me. I was talking to him and was knocked out by him appreciating what I was doing, after all those years of watching him.

He used to like to give things to people, and he saw that I took one bodyguard around with me when I was in Vegas. And he liked me so much – I know he did because he took so much time with me – he was always trying to protect me. He used to say, 'You need more men, Tom, you need more.' He said, 'Somebody's gonna take a shot at you.' So I said, 'I don't think so. It seems to be OK.' One day this fella comes over with a box. He says, 'It's from Elvis and he feels you need to carry this gun,' because he always carried a gun – always, on stage as well.

He would never take drugs in front of me, although I knew

he was taking drugs, because people close to him were telling me that he was, but I never saw him take any in front of me. I think it was the fact he knew I didn't like it and I didn't do it. So, if we were in a suite in Vegas, he would pop into the bedroom every so often and come out like he'd had a swig of whisky or something, but he never used to drink – very rarely he would take a drink. I knew he was getting high on something but I didn't know what it was. Then there would be a change in personality with him. He would either be very docile or very up, and he would sleep at funny hours. I sleep in the day and I'm up at night, but he would sleep in spurts. And the fellas he had working for him would have to do the same because when he woke up, everybody was up!

I was told that Charles Manson was a songwriter and a bit of a singer, and he got very annoyed with people who had become successful. My TV show was on in the States at the time and it was very successful. He looked on successful people as a threat – if he removed them, he'd have a chance. So there were a lot of entertainers' names on this list that was read out in court when the trial was going on. The lawyer stood up and said he had this list, and here are the people, and this is the way he's going to do it. One of his girlfriend followers was going to come to a concert of mine and make sure she got to me backstage, and then get back to the hotel and finally get in the kip, and at the crucial moment she was going to cut my throat. That's a terrible way – that's taking excitement to the extreme, isn't it?

I really enjoy singing. I love performing. I don't know what life would be like without it. What happened to me was I turned a hobby into a profession. When I used to work on all kinds of jobs in Wales, my hobby when I finished work was to go to the local pub and sing. So, as I say, I turned it into a profession. Without it, I wouldn't know what to do. I would just be in and out of boozers all the time. It's the only thing I really love to do.

1987

Luciano Pavarotti

In a strange way, Luciano Pavarotti reminded me of Arthur Mailey, an Australian cricketer. Mailey was a gifted man, an artist and cartoonist, a compelling story teller and a spin bowler of rare quality. One day his skipper overheard him discussing the technique and finer points of bowling leg spin with an opponent. The captain chastised Mailey for divulging information to the enemy, whereupon Mailey dismissed his concern by saying, 'Spin bowling is an art and therefore belongs to the world.' Pavarotti also believed that his divine gift was universal and not the exclusive music of the cognoscenti. It made him a controversial figure, but no one did more to bring opera to millions of people who, before Pavarotti, believed it was not for the likes of them.

He was twice a guest on the show. In 1979 he was in full and glorious spate. In 2003 he was a grim parody of the man I first met. He was ill, overweight, surrounded by a multitude of minders, and miming instead of singing. He was perspiring so much he seemed to be melting. But when I think of the privilege of meeting him, I recall only the warm and generous man whose greatest gift was that when he sang, he made you believe his divine talent was for you alone.

I am very nervous before a performance and sometimes during. Especially when I have to speak! Five minutes before the time, I will not wish my worst enemy to be present, if I have one so bad. But the moment I put my feet on the stage, another person comes inside me and everything disappears if the voice is there. If the voice is not there, and sometimes it happens, then the trouble begins, and the brain must really drive you in that moment!

My father, until two or three years ago, was never happy. We were never to forget that he had a beautiful voice, and he did not succeed and was a little bitter inside. But more than bitter. He really understood that the work is very difficult.

When I was nineteen, we had to decide whether I would become a mathematics professor or gymnastic professor or a tenor. The family had a little discussion around the table and my father suggested that the profession is too difficult, and I should become a mathematics professor. My mother said she feels something – my mother has heart trouble, and she says that because of this, she is even more sensitive about other people. And that night she decided that I have to become a tenor, and of course, like in every other house, the wife wins.

I saw Beniamino Gigli live when I was twelve. I remember it very well because at that time I had already decided to become a tenor, and I went to the theatre where he practised in the morning. I waited for him downstairs and when he came down, I said, 'I would like to become a tenor.' He said, 'Bravo, bravo.' I asked, 'How long should I study? How long did you study?' And he said, 'I just finished now.' It was a very good answer and made me think about a lot, and I took this suggestion he gave to me to be an eternal student and to be never satisfied with myself. I think it's the only way to improve, or at least to stay at a certain level.

I think when somebody reaches a normal weight, he should put on, let's say, twenty pounds more to be a tenor – but under these twenty pounds, this body must be a real athlete. I was a real athlete. I played soccer until the age of nineteen and I was good but not good enough. But I am strong and muscular under this body. It is very demanding. First of all, you can't be sick, and I mean not even a little cold that everybody can have and still live very well. Plus you must have incredible power, because singing is a physical demand.

I have the feeling that the audience gives me back the love I give to them. I really am devoted to the audience – I think I am a servant of the audience. And this is probably the reason the public understand and they give me love back with applause.

A normal human voice is baritone. The tenor is different – it's a kind of artificial voice, which must be constructed. It's like all things that have something exotic about them – it's more exciting. There are people in my country who go to hear the voice of the tenor because they think it's the most exciting voice. Others prefer soprano. Very few prefer baritone or bass.

The perfect sound I want is a sound that probably doesn't exist. It's something I'm still looking for. But most of them please me and, more important, please the public and the critics. There is a certain kind of respect for people who become somebody in our profession, and that takes away the rivalry. I really respect my colleagues who reach the top, rather than being envious. There's no professional jealousy between me and sopranos – certainly not. Between sopranos and me, probably – but you'd have to ask them that!

1979

Sammy Cahn

One of the more constructive, as well as pleasant, consequences of doing *Parkinson* was meeting Sammy Cahn, who decided to adopt me and be my guide in Hollywood. No one knew that mythical place, nor its inhabitants, better than Sammy and his wife, the lovely and funny Tita. They introduced me to Frank Sinatra, Billy Wilder, Tony Bennett, Sydney Poitier, Kirk Douglas and many more. Sammy knew everyone from Al Jolson to Sammy Davis Jr. Of all the lyric writers, he was the one who explained it best in commercial rather than artistic terms. 'What comes first, the lyric or the melody?' was the question. 'The phone call,' said Sammy. No one understood Sinatra's genius better than Cahn. Along with Jimmy Van Heusen and Jule Styne, he wrote some of the great songs for Sinatra's comeback years. He was the best of company, a loyal and generous friend, and a significant contributor to the Great American Songbook.

Michael: Where do the ideas for your lyrics come from?

Sammy: Phone calls. If the phone rings and someone says, 'Will you write a song like . . .', that's actually how it starts – not with the words, not the music. The phone rings and someone says, 'Will you write me a song called . . .'

Michael: I see, and they give you a title?

Sammy: All the time. I can't think of a title.

****

Michael: You collaborated with a great number of people in your time. What is the kind of relationship that you have? Do they just write the melody?

Sammy: Well, for instance, I was in my apartment and my sister came to visit me. It was a Saturday night, and I was in my pyjamas and robe, and she said, 'Are you ill?' I said, 'No, I'm not ill.' She says, 'Saturday night, you're in pyjamas. Aren't you going out?' I said, 'If you're in show business, Saturday night you stay home. The civilians go out. If you're in show business, Saturday night is the loneliest night in the week.' They left, I went to the piano and I wrote what you call a lyric. And I figured when Jule Styne came home, he would listen to that and say, 'Are you crazy? I'll write a melody.' He liked it, and got paid for the melody as well.

Michael: God, it's a marvellous lyric. It's a beautiful song.

****

Michael: What about the lyrics that never hit the screen, that were rejected? Were they rejected because they were bad?

Sammy: Well, there are many, many reasons. One of the scores I did was for a film called *Pink Tights*. It was supposed to be the choice assignment of the year – Frank Sinatra, Marilyn Monroe and Dan Dailey in the very first cinemascope musical. Jule Styne and I wrote one of the most incredibly marvellous scores ever written.

Michael: Modest fellow.

Sammy: I only tell you that because you're never going to hear it. When this film was about to start, Miss Monroe ran off to Japan with some ball player called DiMaggio – gives you an idea how long ago that was. So there we were at the studio with nothing much to do, and one afternoon the door opened and in walks Sol C. Siegel, the producer, to say, 'Can you fellows write me a song called "Three Coins in the Fountain"? We happen to need a song called "Three Coins in the Fountain" because the New York office wants to call the film *We Believe in Love*, and we figure if you can come up with a song, maybe we can change their minds.' I said, 'Fine. Can we see the picture please?' He says, 'You can't see the picture please, the picture is all over the lot. They're dubbing the picture, they're looping the picture, they're scoring the picture. You can't see the picture.' I said, 'Maybe we could read the script then.' He says, 'You can't read the script unless you go to Italy. You wanna go to Italy to read a script?' I said, 'Do you think maybe you could give us a tiny clue as to what the film's about?' 'What's the film about? Three girls go to Rome, they throw coins in the fountain and they hope they'll fall in love,' and he left. So he left us with a title and a clue, and I went to the typewriter.

It's the longest walk I ever took to a typewriter, I'll tell you that. I put the piece of paper in the typewriter and started to type. The first line was easy, three more followed: 'Three coins in the fountain, each one seeking happiness, thrown by three hopeful lovers, which one will the fountain bless?' Now you would need a computer to estimate the various notations it would take to cover those four lines, but Jule Styne, being the composer he is, began to play. Having agreed that was the perfect theme for this film, he was three-quarters finished, because it repeats three times in the song. So he handed back the paper. 'You wanna know something, Jule? This song is finished. I've said everything I had to say in these first four lines. I don't know what else to say,' and, typically, he said, 'How about mentioning Rome?' That's fair: 'Three hearts in the fountain, each heart longing for its home, there they lie in the fountain, somewhere in the heart of Rome.' Now, this song is finished.

At this point, the door re-opened and back came Sol Siegel to say, 'How are you fellows doing?' I said, 'We have a song, but if you'll give us about one hour, we'll learn it and do it for you.' He said, 'Learn it? Didn't you write it?' What he didn't understand is after you write a song comes the really important work, preparing the demonstration of the song, the proper key, the proper accompaniment. He said, 'Look, if you have a song, let me hear it. We're fighting time,' and I sang for the first time: 'Make it mine, make it mine, make it mine.' He said, 'It's great. Let's go do it for Zanuck. Daryl, the boys have a song.' So I sang to Daryl Zanuck for the second time. Zanuck said, 'It's sensational.'

That song went on to become the title theme of the film. It went on to win the Academy Award and became the number-one song in the number-one picture in the world. Now, if this is not enough of a happy ending for you, we have what is known in the theatre as an epilogue. During all this excitement, 20th Century Fox forgot a small detail. They forgot to make a deal for the song. So the door burst open and Sol Siegel screamed, 'Fellows, we're in great trouble. We forgot to make a deal for the song.' And I said, 'That's right, *you're* in great trouble.' He said, 'You're going to have to give that song back.' I said, 'We're not going to have to give it back, and we're not going to give it back.' He said, 'Be reasonable. You can't own the number-one song in the number-one picture in the world.' I said, 'We do.' He said, 'Listen to me one more time. You cannot own the song in our picture, you just cannot.' I said, 'Pardon me please while I go talk to my partner. You know something, Jule? Fair is fair. If it weren't for Siegel and Zanuck, we never would have written the song,' and being the decent chaps we are, we gave back half the song. So from this day hence, whenever you hear 'Make it mine, make it mine, make it mine', you know half is ours.

****

Michael: Let's talk about some of the people you've written songs for. You wrote the song for Mario Lanza, 'Be My Love'.

Sammy: I must tell you, Lanza was the most incredible experience of my life. The phone rang and it was MGM's Hungarian in residence, Joseph Pasternak, and he said, 'Can you come out to the studio, I'm about to make a film to bring out a new talent, Mario Lanza, and I want you to meet a Hungarian composer named Nicholas Brodszky.' May I describe Mr Brodszky for you?

Michael: I'll try and stop you. Carry on.

Sammy: He was a short statured gentleman with jet black patent leather hair, and the kind of a shape, if you pushed him over, he rolled back up. Pasternak said, 'Nicky, will you go to the piano please and play for Sammy the love theme for Lanza.' Nicholas Brodszky went to the piano and he played the love theme for Lanza and Pasternak said, 'Can you put words to that?' I said, 'I could put words to it if I could hear it. This fellow plays like he has eleven fingers on each hand. I dunno what the melody is.' So for the first time in the history of Hollywood a pianist was hired to play for the composer. But luckily, Nicholas Brodszky had had operatic training, and this was very helpful to me because I made him sing every word as I wrote it to each note so I could have some idea of how it might sound when it came out of that enormous voice box of Lanza's.

****

Sammy: I must tell you a curious thing: the really great singers are actually the fellows who don't sing. I would say Rex Harrison is the single most incredibly great singer of songs and yet he doesn't sing. Just sit down and listen to

'My Fair Lady' quietly. It is the single best example of singing without singing.

Michael: He very simply talks his way through.

Sammy: It's really not that, because if anybody could just talk their way through, I would be with the Royal Family. No, he does something else. Fred Astaire does something else. It's an incredible kind of an example of making the word come with the note, which is what lyric writing is about. Fred Astaire probably introduced more song hits than any other singer. He's just an incredible, incredible talk-singer, but still it's singing. It's the best kind of singing.

Michael: Yes. What is that thing you just said about being like lyric writing, hitting the note? What does that mean?

Sammy: It's the marriage of the word and the note. The difference between a poem and a lyric, is that a poem is something read with the eye, and the eye transfers to the mind and the heart. A lyric is something that is heard. It goes to the ear and the heart, so you must be able to sing a lyric, and I fancy myself a fellow who puts words to notes that sing out of the mouth.

1974–82

Sammy Davis Jr

Some of the most disturbing and evocative images conjured up on the show came from performers who had personally witnessed the inhumane treatment of black performers, particularly in America. Natalie Cole's story of the treatment her father, Nat King Cole, and family received when moving house into a predominantly white neighbourhood; Julie Andrews telling me how, by simply holding hands with Harry Belafonte on a TV show, the sponsors wanted to cancel it; Muhammad Ali being told, on entering a diner in his home town, 'We don't serve niggers here', are all vivid in my mind. But the most compelling evidence of institutionalised racism came from Sammy Davis Jr and his account of life in the US Army. He was a truly great entertainer – maybe the most remarkable of them all – but he was also a gutsy and resilient human being.

I was singing and dancing at three. In those days, the tradition of vaudeville was, if you had a son, you brought your son on and he took bows at the end of the act, so my dad used to bring me out. We were working at a place called the Standard Theatre in Philadelphia. I was three years old and they had an amateur contest. I won that and I think the prize was $5, and from that point on they started sneaking me into the act.

I never went to school, not one day of formal education at all. I'm not proud of that, incidentally, but if I had a choice to make, being where I am now and using hindsight, I would probably do it the same way. In those days, they disguised me. When I got to be five years old I was a regular member of the act. They used to put burnt cork on my face – I used to black up and they passed me off as a forty-four-year-old midget.

The only time it became a job was when I would see kids playing baseball or rollerskating or bicycling and I couldn't do it. My dad and uncle wouldn't let me because I might hurt my legs. They were afraid that, if I went out and played baseball, I'd slide into a base and break my ankle. So the things that everyone takes for granted, including going to school, became pushed aside, and I focused purely on show business. And show business was totally my life. It consumed me and I wanted to consume show business.

I was in the Army. Don't ask me how, but they put me in the infantry. First I went to the Air Corps. I wanted to be an aerial gunner, and I figured, because I was small, they were looking for small guys for the turrets, and I wanted to go. And for two glorious months I was doing everything, but I could not write. If there was an exam that said check off yes or no, I'd pass like that. But when they had to have written answers, I couldn't do it. So finally even the bureaucracy discovered there's a cat here who can't write, and what's he doing in the Air Corps? And they weren't that thrilled about having black cats in the Air Corps anyway at that point, so the Lieutenant called me in and he said, 'Davis, you put down here Calvert's Correspondence School. How much schooling did you get?' I looked at him and I realised at that point it had come. The truth had to be said, but I didn't know how to say it. And I started to cry.

He said, 'You've never been to school, have you?' I said, 'No sir.' He said, 'You know that we are only taking Negroes who have had at least a high school education, and preferably a couple of years of college. I'm sorry but we have to transfer you.' I was never so heartbroken in my life. I'd found a camaraderie and I loved being in the Army because it was the first time I was on my own. Then they shipped me to the infantry.

Everybody in the infantry was bigger than I was. Everybody. And I'm talking about hard-bitten, tough guys. There were no integrated groups then, and every other word was a curse word. And they all seemed to start with mother. I'd never been cursed at, and I started to cry again. I tried then to prove I could make it, and I became kind of comfortable – I took basic training three times because every time I would get to the point of embarkation, they would send me back because I had what they called an athletic heart, but I went right back into the infantry.

Finally, the guy said to me, 'You're an entertainer.' I would get up Saturday nights in the service club and dance. I couldn't help dancing and singing to the juke box. And the guy said, 'Why don't you join special services, or at least apply for it?' And I did. So I started doing impressions, because in the Army they were so hungry for any kind of entertainment. And there were no black people doing white people at all, in the days I'm talking about – 1944, 1945. No black guy had ever dared to stand up and say: 'All right, schweetheart, the lot of ya's, up against the wall.'

About the second day I was in the Army, we were all lined up in the latrine, in the bathroom. In those days, everybody had their little kits, with their shaving stuff in it, and I had my little kit around my arm. A guy behind me, a big cat, turned to his partner and said, 'How come that nigger's in front of us?' And I said, 'Look, I'm not a fighter, I don't do that, cats.' I thought to myself, 'Just try to charm your way out of it.' I knew I could get no help – I had no protection, so I just ignored it. He said, 'Hey,' and he turned me around. He said, 'Where I come from niggers are never in front of white people.' And I'm thinking I've got to do something but I don't know what to do. I can't do it physically. I said, 'But I've been in line for a long time. I was at the end before I moved up.' And I turned back around. He said, 'Obviously, you don't understand me, nigger, do ya?'

When he said it the last time, I swung the bag and caught him square – pow! I knocked him to the ground, and when he was laying on the ground he looked up at me and said, 'I'm on the ground, but you're still a nigger!' And I realised there had to be something. There had to be another way, because violence wasn't it. There had to be another way to communicate with people. I had to find another way to tell him he was wrong.

Those who survive are those who realise that the stupidity of man still exists and we must deal with it, and everyone must use his own instrument to deal with it. I wanted to use my talent that God had given me. I can do a white man, I can sing like a white guy, so there must not be any difference. And that's what used to shock the audiences in the early days – 'Geez, he sounds just like him.' And even to this day, when I occasionally do impressions, people will still say, 'You know, you sounded just like Frank Sinatra.' But that was my fight. That was the way I fought it. And I think probably the reason why I tried to fight it with my talent, and have all during the years, has been the fact that I got my nose broken three times trying to be violent, and this

is it – I ain't getting it broken no more because I am definitely not a fighter.

I was a Catholic until I was sixteen, then I became agnostic.
I believed in something but I didn't go to a church, a temple
or so forth. I started reading about religions, and I wanted
to know – I wanted to experience. I became fascinated by
how a religion could make a race of people survive and keep
fighting, back over hundreds of years, and still maintain
dignity. What was the subtext, what was the foundation? And
the foundation was a religion. It is very, very traditional, and
– not that the other religions don't – it answers a lot of questions for me. And I think that's what we all have to do, find
it in our own way.

1976

Tony Bennett

Still going, still singing well at eighty-four, Tony Bennett is a
marvel. One critic said: 'The fact he's still out there doing it with
a voice that remains in astonishingly good nick, lends Bennett a
poignant and slightly miraculous aura. It's like going to Lord's
and finding Don Bradman still at the crease.' He remains one of
the few who can be talked about in the same sentence as Frank
Sinatra, and since Sinatra stopped making music, he has been
the torch illuminating the glory of the Great American Songbook.
Tony Bennett is a fascinating man. A bold civil rights campaigner
at a time when it could cost you your life, never mind a career,
he is also dedicated to the idea of providing young people with
the kind of musical education he was denied.

A talented painter, and as modest as he is gifted, he is an
admirable man.

Michael: Yours is an extraordinary life. You grew up in the
Depression, didn't you? How poor was it in the family?

Tony: Oh, it was very tough. We were given twelve pieces of coal a week to stay warm. We had to go to the police station to collect them, and those twelve pieces of coal meant the difference between freezing to death or the whole family staying warm enough.

Michael: And your mother worked?

Tony: She was a seamstress. My father died when I was ten, so she raised three children. She was magnificent, and of all things kept us very optimistic.

Michael: But you were also part of that remarkable generation who were shaped by a war. As a teenager, you went to Europe, you were an infantry man – a beetle crusher – and you saw action, didn't you?

Tony: Yeah, I saw the end of the war. I was a replacement for the Battle of the Bulge, and that was at the end of the war. It was horrific. It just made me a pacifist. After watching it, I would say it's the lowest form of human behaviour, fighting.

Michael: In the war as well, one incident shaped you for the rest of your life, and that was an episode of racism with a black friend of yours?

Tony: I was in an art school in New York City, and I had a great friend, Frank Smith. We had a vocal group in school, but we were all artists, all painters, and of all things I met him in Mannheim in Germany. It was Thanksgiving Day. He took me to his Baptist church and I went to mass. I was allowed one guest at the Truman Hotel in Mannheim, and I invited him to dinner. I got up into the lobby and a bigoted officer of the United States Army came up to me and took my stripes – I was a corporal, and he took a razor blade and took them off me, spat on them and threw them on the floor. He said, 'Pack up your gear, you're shipping out immediately.' I said, 'What are you talking about?' He said, 'Well, we don't like the kind of friends you have and we're going to send you to Graves Registration where you'll dig up bodies.' And it changed my life.

Michael: I bet it did too.

Tony: Changed my life. I've never understood racial prejudice ever since. It taught me that each human being is very, very important. No matter where it is in the world.

Michael: Is your friend, Mr Smith, still around? Do you talk to him?

Tony: He is, but it's too emotional. We can't even talk about it.

Michael: Even now?

Tony: Even now.

Michael: All those years.

Tony: We start talking on the phone and he starts tearing, and I start tearing.

Michael: When you got back and started singing as a career, we're now talking about the forties and early fifties, that was a time in America when, within your business, the great black artists suffered from racial segregation, didn't they?

Tony: Yeah. There was a lot of that.

Michael: You continued your campaign, and after the war you went on the Freedom Marches didn't you, with Martin Luther King?

Tony: Well, Harry Belafonte and I, we started out together, and he told me about the problem that was going down there in Selma, and I can't even explain it to the audience. I wouldn't do it, it was so horrific a situation. He said, 'You've got to do something.' And when he told me what they were doing to some of the African Americans there, I said, 'I'm going with you.' And as far as I was concerned, I was going back into the war, and it felt like that. Everybody was giving us very funny looks – I'm doing the march, and one night we entertained, to give the marchers relief, and they acquired sixteen coffins from a mortuary. That was our stage to perform on. It was very spooky.

Michael: Part of history, of course. It wasn't that long ago, was it, that these remarkable things happened that changed America?

Tony: Well, it's getting greater and greater every moment now.

Michael: You're last of that great era of American music, including the composers as well – you think of the Berlins, the Cole Porters and the great interpreters of the music, and you were part of that golden time. You must think you were lucky to have been born in that period?

Tony: I was, I love it. That's the renaissance to the United States. Very similar to the impressionist painters in France – Monet and Van Gogh. Well this was Cole Porter, George and Ira Gershwin, a renaissance period that will never be repeated.

2004 and 2006

Paul Anka

Paul Anka's journey from teenaged pop star to elder statesman of the music industry, surviving hanging out with the Rat Pack along the way, is one of the most eventful of them all. Throughout his career, his ability to write hit songs enabled him to surf the changing trends of the music industry. His most spectacular success came upon hearing a melody while living in France and thinking, if he could find a lyric, it might make a hit. The song he composed was 'My Way', which became Frank Sinatra's most requested song and a huge international hit, as well as being the choice of every maudlin drunk in any karaoke bar, anywhere in the world.

Back then, there was no drug problem. We could get all we wanted! Back then, you had chaperones with you, watching what you did. You were told what to sing, what your parameters were. So it was quite limited, although when I travelled, in some cases I was the only white kid on a bus with many black artists because of the nature of the business. It was nothing for me to see Frankie Lyman, sitting next to me, shooting up heroin. Of course, in life we all have to make choices and with everything that happened to me, I realised that I wanted to keep hold of it, this change of life. You just make choices and say, 'No, it's not for me.'

Being the youngest, I was on the periphery. I was there watching and keeping my mouth shut. But you'd see Marilyn Monroe – she would come to the parties – and there were a lot of politicians. You'd see JFK – they'd bring in a helicopter and, quietly, he'd be there. All the girls would be around, they were taking care of him real good! There was always a potpourri of people. At that time, Vegas was very stylish and when you went there, it was a who's who. It was run by the mob and there were just a few places. Today of course, it's like Disneyland for adults and you don't see that kind of environment any more. Back then, you'd see every actor – Humphrey Bogart, Marilyn Monroe, David Niven. You name it, they were there and it was an event.

The mob owned you only if you allowed them to. If you asked for a favour, like some did, they owned you. I was too young and yet they needed me because I was earning money, and the record companies and all of that were owned by them. If you didn't ask for a favour, they left you alone. Every night in Vegas, there were tons of them out there. Some of them weren't allowed to be there – if the spotlight left the stage, eight guys would jump under the table. But if you left them alone and were gracious, they left you alone and didn't touch you. Back then, their handshake was like gold. If you shook their hand on a deal, you had the play, you had the date.

When you hang out with Sinatra and Sammy Davis, it's booze, it's the girls, it's everything. The first time I met those guys, I got signed by the mob who ran Vegas and they took me to Sam's hotel, and I was the youngest kid to play Las Vegas. I walked into the steam room – that's where all the action was with the Rat Pack – you did the show and then they'd be in there. And I walked in and there was Frank

Sinatra, in the nude, singing, 'Little Things Mean a Lot'. I'm glad he's not alive now – there'd be a horse's head in my hotel tonight!

It was the cool time – it was frolic, it was style, and that's pretty much where I learnt to do what I do today as a performer and as a singer. If you want to be the best, you have to hang with the best, and I learnt a long time ago that good is the enemy of great, and hanging round with those guys you really learnt your craft.

I was living in a house down in France back in the sixties and I heard this French melody, and I heard something different. I got the rights, sat down, changed it at the piano, and put it in a drawer. About four months later, I was in Miami Beach playing and I got a call from Sinatra. He said, 'Hey kid,' because he called me 'The Kid'. We all had a name and a robe in the steam room. For instance, Sammy Davis was called 'Smoky the Bear'. So he said, 'Kid, I want to have dinner with you.' So we went to dinner and he said, 'I'm fed up and I want to get out of the business.' I was shocked. He said, 'I'm gonna do one more album and then I'm out of here.'

I was so moved by that. I'd not written him a song and he'd always teased me about writing for him. I went back to New York, sat down at one in the morning and started playing that melody, and I said, 'I'm going to approach it as if Sinatra were writing it' – metaphorically, now the end is near, the final curtain. I finished it at five in the morning and I called him in Vegas. He was at Caesar's Palace and I said, 'I've got something special for the album.' I flew out, played the demo, and he said, 'Kid, I like it.' Four months later, he called me from Los Angeles, put the phone up to the speaker and said, 'Listen to this, Kid,' and he played 'My Way' for the first time. And man, I knew my kids were going through school on that one!

2006 and 2007

George Michael

I think George Michael might have been the most forlorn pop star of them all. He was the one who never came to terms with adoration, success, riches. It seemed to me the more successful he was, the unhappier he became. Maybe, as he said in the interview: 'It's the things that are missing that make you, not the things you have.'

When he came on the show in 1998, I had just begun my second stint at the BBC. George Michael had just returned from America after he had been caught in an LA toilet and arrested for 'lewd conduct'. I wondered how we might most delicately approach the matter, which, if you believed the media, was the question everyone – but everyone – wanted answering. He gave me the perfect opportunity.

George: Before we start, I wanted to say that this is a great honour for me because I can remember being eight or nine years old and my mum would allow me to stay up beyond a certain time in the evening only to watch *Parkinson.* She thought it would be a bit of quality watching. So I'm very, very privileged to be here.

Michael: Well, that's very kind of you. It's good to have you.

George: And she probably wouldn't have been quite as thrilled that I had to take my willy out to get on here.

Michael: Let's talk about that incident, which led you to be here tonight. What happened?

George: I think it's fairly well documented by now. What happened was, I fell prey to one of these SWAT teams they have in America, and I think they probably still have them in parts of England. But basically, they're paid to nick guys who are looking for sex with one another, and the way they do this in the States, unfortunately, is actually to try and induce the crime and then, if they get a response, they nick the guys. Although the police reports suggested that I was a flasher – I may be screwed up but I'm not a flasher! –

what happened with me was I responded to something. And I responded to a very handsome, tall, good-looking American cop. They don't send Columbo in there to do that. So I responded to that and I can't be ashamed of the fact that it was there in front of me and I thought, 'Well, why not?' It was a stupid moment and obviously I've suffered for it.

Michael: Of course, the police say in their justification, they'd had complaints of lewd behaviour in that toilet.

George: All about me, of course.

Michael: I suppose a lot of people would ask the question why, as a public figure, as somebody recognised here and in America, you would take such an outrageous risk?

George: I suppose that's the whole point, isn't it?

Michael: Is it?

George: I think so, to some degree. I was not in the best state of mind, and it was a reckless thing to do, but ultimately you don't see it as a massive risk. If there's no one else around and there's someone standing there, waving their genitals at you, you don't think that they're an officer of the law! It's not your first presumption, so I fell for the trick. I fell for the trick, and it was very well done.

Michael: But nonetheless, you knew the risk you were taking, that's the point. And one wonders, it's been suggested that perhaps what you were doing is that you were begging to be arrested, so in fact coming out would be public.

George: Believe me, I wasn't begging to be arrested. And I have to say I've had the number-one album for the last four weeks, which I'm very glad of. If I was the bravest and most genius pop star in the world, maybe I would have done it deliberately, but probably not since the days of Wham! have I had a record that's done so well. So, yes, I can see from my own point of view, there would have been reasons that it probably would have been quite a good idea to do it that way, but believe me, I would rather have run up and down Oxford Street naked, saying, 'I'm gay, I'm gay,' than have it happen the way it did.

Michael: Let's go back. Your dad came over from Cyprus as an immigrant, a quid in his pocket, and worked hard and married your mum, built up a business. What sort of a background was it that you grew up in? Was it a very close family background?

George: Very close. I spent a lot more time around my mother, who was English and, in a strange way, kind of classless. She came from a very working-class background but she'd been sent to a convent school, because her mother was afraid she was going to be a tomboy. So that, firstly, put her straight off religion, and she spoke very well, almost with a middle-class accent. So I had this really weird thing that I spoke like someone who was relatively middle-class and yet my father was a first generation immigrant. And my mother was very British. I get my attitude to money from her – it was something to be afraid of, and it took a long time for me to get rid of that idea. And yet my father's attitude to money was you just grab it and move up.

Michael: Was to be rich and famous your ambition?

George: I realised about six months ago that at no point during my early life, even when I started to realise my ambitions, at no point did it ever occur to me that one of the by-products would be that I could buy whatever I wanted, or live in a big house, have a flashy car – all the things that are very pleasant. But it never occurred to me. I didn't want to be rich. I just wanted to be filthily famous.

Michael: Why was that? Did you think it would make you more attractive?

George: It was – like most singers – the feeling of not being listened to. It was lots of feelings of low self-worth, all the kind of screwed-up things that go together to make someone who becomes well known.

Michael: What was the low self-worth based on? It was about your looks wasn't it? About the way you were?

George: It was everything. I think my looks didn't help. I suppose I looked like a curly haired, fatter version of what I am now. But I don't know if it was really about that. I probably felt better about the way I looked when I was eighteen than I do now. But it was all kinds of things. It was more this desire to be recognised. People talk about them but I have never met a star who didn't come from the same insecurity. It's the things that are missing that make you a star, it's not the things you have.

Michael: Let's go back a bit, and talk about those Wham! days.

George: Must we?

Michael: Well, we must.

George: I have no problem talking about Wham! I have a problem watching Wham!, but I had a great time, I'm really glad the way it all turned out.

Michael: Was it fulfilling in the sense of you enjoying yourself? You were a kid – there was the glamour of it, the money, the birds.

George: There was the whole thing and I think we both gorged on it – not the money side of things, really. I was so afraid of money until probably the age of about thirty, that I really didn't live in any way according to the money I was earning. And actually Wham! wasn't making any money. For the longest time we were making no money. After our first *Top Of The Pops*, we went home on the bus. I remember the night before, we stayed in this little hotel off the Charing Cross Road because the mini record company we were on at the time was paying, and they wanted to make sure we got there in time for the recording. So they stuck us in this hotel that couldn't have been more than 80p a night and had polystyrene sheets and a child-sized bed. I was sitting with my feet over the end of it thinking, 'This isn't how it's supposed to be. If you're on *Top Of The Pops*, that means you're famous.'

But there you go. And those awful T-shirts with number ones that my mother and sister spent all night sewing on, poor things – apart from looking terrible, how annoying! How annoying must we have been to all those bands we were competing with, that we'd be tacky and cheesy enough to do that. But we thought it was funny.

It's just that everyone else thought we were completely
for real.

1998

Madonna

Any wannabe pop singer seeking a break on one of those TV
talent shows would be better rewarded by watching the one-
woman show with Madonna. Her way to the top is an unbeatable
demonstration of the maxim that success is achieved only by a
mixture of inspiration and perspiration. Her slog to stardom
defines what it takes to become a great star, and Madonna is
that. She is the most successful recording artist of her generation,
the benchmark for every other female singer – in short, a
phenomenon.

I didn't shave under my arms! I know, it's really gross. I had
this thing when I was in high school – obviously, it happened
way before I started making music – and I hated doing what
everybody else did. If the girls wore make-up, I didn't want
to wear make-up, and if the girls shaved, I didn't want to
shave. If girls did certain things to get boys' attention, then
I did the opposite. Of course, no one ever asked me out
because of this ridiculous behaviour.

I decided to form a 'Dead Mothers Club'. You could only
be in my club if your mother died, and I didn't know anyone
else whose mother had died, so I was the only one in my
club. It was kind of pathetic. I did feel isolated and lonely as
a child, and then again when I moved to New York, but I
don't feel sorry for myself. I think it was character building.

You're not actually going to believe this but I did nude
modelling. Shocking. It was artistic. It wasn't like page three
nude modelling. It was for art classes. I was a dancer at the
time, so modelling for all these different art schools gave me

freedom, because I would run in, get my kit off, as you say, and pose for a couple of hours in some fantastic ballet pose. Then run off and go to another class.

I'd gone to a trillion auditions for musical theatre on Broadway, because I finally figured out that being just a dancer wasn't going to get me anywhere in terms of paying the rent. So I decided to try musical theatre. It's a steady job where you get paid union rates. At the time, I didn't have any interest in being a singer. So I started going to auditions and I was being rejected again because I was too short. All the women in the chorus were gigantic, with long legs, and I was like a midget compared to them.

I finally went to this audition and danced every dance routine, and then they asked me to sing all these songs, and then they made me come back. They made me dance with this guy and sing another song, and it went on and on and on, and I thought, enough already, just hurry up and reject me. Then they didn't say anything, and said they'd call me.

That night this French guy called me, he was one of the producers of the show, and he said I didn't get the job. So I said, 'What are you calling me for then?' And he said, 'We want to make you a star. We think you're really special.' And I said, 'You do?' So they took me to Paris. They were French record producers and they put me in a studio with all these record producer guys, and they gave me all this money. They put me in a posh apartment and I had a car, a driver, and I freaked out because I went from having nothing to having everything.

I realised while I was there that I did want to be a singer, but I didn't want to be made into a singer. I didn't want to be part of a factory. I wanted to go back to New York and learn how to write music and play an instrument, without all these rich people behind me pulling my strings like a marionette. I wanted to earn it. So I made up this big fat lie. I said I really missed my friends back in New York and that I was going to visit them. So they said, 'Okay, see you in two weeks.' And I went back to New York and never came back. I'm very grateful to them because they made me realise that I wanted to be a singer, but I realised that I couldn't be given it. I had to earn it.

As time went on I became successful, and people started writing about me and photographing me, analysing me, criticising me and scrutinising me. I started thinking about my place in the world, and people's point of view about me, and I started thinking about pushing boundaries. I started reading what people wrote about me and one thing that really irritated me was that people didn't seem to put the idea of being sexual and being intelligent together. And I set out to defy the idea that those two couldn't exist together.

The reason I called my last show 'Reinvention' is because people have applied that word to me for so many years that I decided finally to take it and stick it over my head and put lights around it. But I was never consciously thinking about reinvention. For me, it's about growing and changing, and hoping and praying that my work reflected who I was at that moment. I always hoped that I was changing and growing. I call that evolution.

2005

Madonna: I'm sorry, is this too long this story?
Michael: No, no, no.
Madonna: If you start drooling on your tie!
Michael: That would be for different reasons Madonna!

Noel Gallagher

This was one of my favourite interviews. Engaging Noel Gallagher is a bit like lighting a firecracker. What fascinated me about him was the way he had survived a brutal, impoverished childhood and the prospect of life in a never-ending dole queue, to found, with brother Liam, Oasis, selling 70 million records worldwide. What I discovered was a young man with a pitiless contempt for those who might imagine the world owed them a living, and who found the golden shackles of fame and riches hard to bear.

Michael: What are relations like between you and Liam now?
Noel: They're all right. I find it fascinating that people find it fascinating, do you know what I mean? I haven't spoken to him for a few months, but not like I'm actively not speaking to him. It's just we live in each other's pockets while we're on the road, and I slip back into life when I get back home and so does Liam.
Michael: But most people think it's deeper than that, don't they? There are the well-publicised spats and all the quotes about not liking each other.
Noel: Well, he doesn't like me.
Michael: Why?
Noel: I don't know. You'd have to ask him next time he's on here.
Michael: You know why.
Noel: Because I'm better looking than him, obviously!
Michael: But has it always been like that? When you were kids growing up in Manchester was it like that?
Noel: He's five years younger than I am. When I was fifteen, he was ten, so the age gap was more prevalent then than it is now. I guess there is a lot of pressure being in a group, particularly a big group, and we kind of fall out on a regular basis, but it's not ever anything that's put the band in danger really. The only people who really suffer are the other people in the band, and there have been hundreds of them!
Michael: But do you wish you could define that brotherly love?
Noel: I can define it. Let's put it this way, if he was getting his head kicked in right now, I'd probably join in to save him. If I was getting mine, he'd probably join in to save me. I can't say any fairer than that.

Parky's People

Michael: No, you can't.

Noel: Other than that, you're making it something it's not. Do you have a brother or sister?

Michael: I don't and this interests me. I always wanted a brother or sister.

Noel: I always wanted a sister, an older sister, so I could cop off with her friends!

Michael: But you like women because your mum was your beacon in your life.

Noel: She brought us up, really.

Michael: Exactly. The friction with Liam you say maybe had something to do with the way you were brought up?

Noel: How can I put it? We don't like authority figures very much, me and Liam. And I guess everybody in the band kind of directs everything at me because I am, for want of a better word, seen as the leader. I think Liam rebels against that. And that creates friction between us, but growing up was different. We shared a bedroom and I always resented that because my older brother got his own bedroom. I had to share with Liam when he came along, and I've never really forgiven him for that!

Michael: And also there was violence in your family – your father was a violent man.

Noel: Yeah . . . probably not any more than any of my other mates' families on our street.

Michael: But that wouldn't be saying much, would it? You grew up in a very tough neighbourhood.

Noel: Yeah, but it was the seventies, and this was before the new-age man was the trendy thing to be. It was a violent time, the seventies.

Michael: It's not just not changing nappies, your dad used to beat you up.

Noel: Yeah, he did, yeah.

Michael: And you used to lie awake in bed at night, thinking is he going to come in and whack me?

Noel: Yeah.

Michael: And you developed a stammer because of that.

Noel: Yeah, how do you know all this?

Michael: People talk about sink estates and about youth and the problems they have, but you lived all that, and you lived it at a time when they weren't as concerned as maybe they are now. What fascinates me is how a kid who has no hope and no future grows up. What was it like?

Noel: I remember being young, and the worst part for me. I don't consider my upbringing to be worse than any other on my street, or any other guys my age who I used to knock around with. But it is kind of soul destroying, or it was in the eighties, when you're going to sign on with your dad and with your best mate and his dad. And you think, our dads haven't even got a job, so what hope is there for us? That in itself breeds frustration, but none of that has ever come out in my music. My music has always been pretty positive, and I've always been fascinated by life. I don't want to sound too weird about it, but every day I would wake up and it was great because something great might happen today. I wouldn't wake up in a negative mood any day, and I never do. But those were rough times when there was no work in Manchester, not only for your age but for your parents, too.

Michael: Yes, and drugs were around.

Noel: Oh yeah.

Michael: And you got stuck into them.

Noel: That's the difference between the middle classes and the working classes. The middle classes experiment with drugs and the working classes just get stuck in, man. Forget experimenting, let's just get them done.

Michael: So by the time you became a rock and roller, you were very well practised.

Noel: Well, that's the thing. You read all these stories about rock stars going into rehab and somebody must take them aside at some point and say, 'I think you're going off the rails. I think you might want to check in to the Priory or something.' We were off the rails to start with. We were off the rails before we got a record deal. We arrived in London hammered, out of it. So it's never been a problem for me and Liam. It fascinates me that out of all the people we hung out with, the only two who have never been in rehab are me and Liam. Ever.

Michael: And why have you resisted that? You are clean now, we should say that.

Noel: I don't like that term. I don't think I was ever dirty, seriously.

Michael: You're free of drugs, for what, eight years?

Noel: Eight and half, yeah. But you say that and you half expect a round of applause, but I don't think that there should be anything like that. Where we come from in Manchester, that was just the done thing. And I've never had a problem with it. The only thing that's bad about drugs is it makes you drink more and that eventually messes you up I think. But if there were gold medals for taking drugs for England, I'd have won a shit load. And I enjoyed it, but it got to a point where I'd done them all and that was it, and I thought, 'I can't be arsed any more.'

Michael: But there was a moment wasn't there?

Noel: How it's been portrayed in the past in the press is that I stood up at a party and said, 'And this will be my last line and after this there will be no more.' Well, I was at a party one night and I woke up in the morning and thought, 'I can't be bothered today,' and that turned into a week and that turned into a month and that turned into a year. And then I enjoyed not being out of it all the time, and as that state of mind took hold, I'd go out with the people I was surrounded with at the time and I'd start thinking, 'I don't really like you and your bird's an idiot, and what are you doing in my front room?' In the end, everybody kind of left the party if you like, and we were just left to get on with life.

Michael: Is it a struggle? Do you have to reorganise your life in a sense?

Noel: Not really.

Michael: There's no temptation there?

Noel: You've got to be strong-willed and vanity plays a big part in my life. My teeth were falling out and all sorts, and nobody wants to look like a weirdo. I don't want this to sound like 'my drugs hell' because it wasn't. I had some of the most monumental nights out ever, had some of the most monumental nights in, wrote some of the best songs, met some of the greatest people and went to some of the greatest parties, man! It just came to a point where I couldn't be bothered any more.

Michael: Have you ever thought of reconciling with your dad?

Noel: No. I don't have any bad feelings towards him for what happened because it's not shaped the psyche of who I am. I've never once sat down and thought, 'Right, I'll write a song about my childhood,' because who wants to listen to that nonsense anyway? It doesn't play any part in my make-up. I get asked all the time by journalists and they say, 'It must do, it must do.' And I say I could invent some kind of angst if you want, but it wouldn't be true. I don't dwell on that part of my life at all. It was just growing up and we didn't have any money. We didn't have enough carpet in our house – me mam'll hate me for saying that. Sorry, Mam. But when I look back on it, it was great because, not the thing with me dad, but the struggle of growing up makes you who you are.

Michael: It makes you self-sufficient.

Noel: Yeah.

Michael: So you didn't need the Priory!

Noel: No. Why would you pay somebody four grand an hour to tell you things that really you should already know about yourself? If any of you are watching, give me the money. I'll sort it out for you!

2006

Memories of Frank Sinatra

Bing Crosby

Sinatra and I were very good friends. I admired his work and I hoped to believe that he admired mine. We saw a lot of one another. He was on my radio show several times and I went on a couple of shows he had. He's a great singer. He creates a mood, which very few people are able to do. I don't think I create a mood when I sing. Nat Cole could do that. Sinatra does it in a memorable way. When he walks on with the top coat over his shoulders and the hat and he goes into 'Black Magic' or one of those kinds of things, he's created a mood right away and the audience is with him. And very few people can do that.

1972

Sammy Cahn

Michael: What is it like for you, as a lyric writer, when you listen to Sinatra singing one of your songs? What makes him different, what makes it better than when somebody else sings it?

Sammy: What makes it better is that he is singing my song. But I must tell you, singing a song for Sinatra is mere formality. Bing Crosby and Frank Sinatra have never turned on a song that Jimmy Van Heusen and I sang with them. They asked you to write a song and you write the song and they just listened to it. The first time I had to write a song, 'All the Way', was for a film called *The Joker's Wild*, based on the life story of the legendary comedian Joe E. Lewis. And so the day came for us to sing the song with Frank Sinatra and we were told to go to the Sands Hotel in Las

Vegas. When we got to the hotel, we were told that Sinatra would hear the song during the 'breakfast hour'. So five o'clock that afternoon, he came out of his bedroom suite looking like all the pictures of Dorian Gray. He saw me and he said, 'Listen, are you singing before breakfast?' I said, 'Frank, it's a draw. I'm going to have to look at you while I'm singing.' He said, 'Let me hear the song,' and we gave him the full treatment.

1975

Tony Bennett

Michael: Sinatra was a huge fan of yours. He did some nice things for you, didn't he?

Tony: A lot, yes. I was never part of the Rat Pack but we were very great friends. He had a magnificent sense of humour and a lot of people misunderstood him. One time he invited me to his birthday party, and here was the Rat Pack in the kitchen, laughing and having fun, and in the living room were Gregory Peck, Sidney Poitier and Sean Connery – all these great actors. And he put me in the playroom, where they played cards on a little cardboard table, and he sat me there by myself with an elderly gentleman. And as a young singer, I said, 'What's going on here?' First he invites me and then I'm not in on any of the fun. I turned around to this gentleman and said, 'Excuse me, my name is Tony Bennett.' He says, 'I'm Mr Giannini.' Well, that was the gentleman who invented the Bank of America. So he was always helping me out!

Michael: When did you first become aware of Sinatra, or him of you?

Tony: When I first started, I was very nervous. Perry Como gave me this summer replacement of his show on television, and the network gave me a bare stage with a band, and I was very frightened. I'd never met Sinatra but I was a big fan and I took a chance. I went to the Paramount

Theatre, where he was playing a reunion, and I asked if I could come up and see him. I had a couple of million-selling records, so he knew who I was. And he said, 'Well, what is it son?' And I said, 'I'm very nervous. I don't know if I could really perform properly because I'm so nervous.' And he was so wonderful to me, he said, 'Don't worry about that. The audience will sense that you're nervous and they'll help you out and support you.' It really relaxed me for the rest of my life. I analysed that – if they're nice enough to come in and get a nanny for their children and save up to come close to the stage, they're really friends. They're not an enemy. He really taught me, and he also said not to do a cheap song ever – do quality songs. And I took that advice and it worked.

2004

Buddy Rich

Buddy: Frank and I roomed together the first year he was in Tommy Dorsey's band, and we've done many tours. As a matter of fact, he sponsored my first band in 1946. I got out of the Marine Corps, and Frank gave me the money to organise my first band. And so we've been friends on and off for about thirty years or more. I'm a fan. When we appear with Frank, I sit in the audience after our perform-ance and watch him. I'm amazed. He's pure magic and I love him.

Michael: You've had one or two fist fights, have you?

Buddy: One or two in my life, yeah.

Michael: There were one or two legendary ones with Sinatra apparently.

Buddy: Yeah, we had one.

Michael: Did you? What happened?

Buddy: At the time, he was twenty-three and I was twenty-one. We were both striving to be the featured man in Tommy's band, and he made some remarks about the band's saxophone player, who was not qualified to take that kind of abuse. I stood up for him one night and about thirty seconds after my comment a big, glass water pitcher came flying across the room, and where I'd ducked, it smashed into about a thousand pieces. When I came up from bending down, I managed to catch him and hurt him and that was the end of that fight.

Michael: You severely chastised him did you?

Buddy: Severely, yeah.

1987

Paul Anka

Sinatra was not only the great performer, he knew how to communicate. He knew how to get the respect of all of us in that he was a great technician in the way he sang – the way he phrased, the versatility. You could sit at home, listen on the radio, and if you played Sinatra, in the first five seconds you were in a mood. That was the magic of this guy, and he made it very tough for anyone to stand in front of a band. They all came second because he was the master. He had a great sense of being a man's man, and there were not a lot of those guys around.

He was the most unusual guy you ever met. I mean, if he'd say you're going to dinner, you took your passport. You never knew where you'd wind up with this guy, or what kind of mood he'd be in, because he'd love to drink and he was not a good drinker. Unfortunately, when he'd had a few, if things went wrong, you said the wrong thing, there was chaos.

We were all together at the Sands, where we used to work, and Howard Hughes took the place over. Frank was a little pissed off because they wouldn't give him any more money, the reason being he'd never pay the markers. So we're sitting in the lounge and he got up after drinking. It's one in the morning and he got up on a blackjack table. He started saying, 'This place was sand when I built it and it'll be sand when . . .' and then he went on and on.

Well, they woke up Carl Cohen, who was one of the mob guys from Cleveland, and a dear man. I never heard this man raise his voice. He looked after me like a godfather. They woke him up and he drove over in his golf cart to the coffee shop from his cabana, which was on the property. And Jilly, who was Frank's right-hand man, said, 'Let's go. We've gotta take the old man over to see Carl because we've gotta get this worked out.'

So Jilly and I walked Frank, drunk, over to the coffee shop and up to Carl's table. Carl, in a very mild manner, said, 'Frank, we can't give you money any more. We don't own the place and you're not paying up the bills.' And with that Frank said, 'You fat, you da-da-da . . .' and pulled the tablecloth, and coffee went all over Carl. So Carl got up and he punched Frank right in the mouth, and his teeth, Frank's, all over the coffee shop. And that was that. We never went back to the Sands again!

2007

6 Leading Ladies

Lauren Bacall

It was the insolence of Lauren Bacall that made strong men weak. The hair, the come-hither eyes, the languid body all helped, but when she said to Bogey, 'If you want anything, just whistle. You know how to whistle don't you?' it was her cool impudence that, as one critic said, 'created a moment on screen when she became an instant addition to the fantasy lives of American males'. The three interviews I did with her spanned more than thirty years and, in that time, we had become friendly. Moreover, with the passing years, she lost none of her spark, nor that independence of spirit that makes her such an attractive and formidable personality.

Lauren: I started off so big at the age of nineteen, and was totally unequipped for it – no experience, talent completely undirected. I didn't really know what I was doing in a medium that was totally strange to me – and unprotected, because the man I was under contract to didn't think it was important to protect me, or any actor. So, from that point of view, it was start 'em overnight and then I dare you to live up to it. Well, I couldn't live up to it, so as fast as I went up, that's how fast I fell down, and spent the rest of my career just trying to get to some middle ground so I could function.

Michael: I know you don't like talking about Humphrey Bogart and there are very good reasons, which I respect, but could I just ask you a couple of questions?

Lauren: What was that 'but' you just threw in there?

Michael: You said you were unprotected in Hollywood, but in effect, you were protected – he was a great star.

Lauren: Oh, no question.

Michael: What did you learn from him about acting?

Lauren: Bogie always believed, as I do now, that you are not an actor if you don't act. You cannot just sit in your living room and say, 'Gee, I'm terrific folks but you'll never get to see it.' You have to try things. One must certainly aim for quality first because that is the most important thing, and work with the best people. He had great respect for the acting profession, which I do as well.

Michael: He represented this extraordinary sort of independent spirit, and he wouldn't take any nonsense.

Lauren: He was much more independent than I am. He was totally his own man. He knew exactly what he was about and followed that course, and fought anyone who tried to make him be less than he was, and would never compromise.

Michael: How difficult was it for you, afterwards, to live down the thing of just being Bogie's widow?

Lauren: Well, it's still going on, isn't it?

Michael: No, it's not. Not as far as I'm concerned. We'll move off the subject in a moment, but I just wondered how difficult it was, and still is, because you've got this cult thing about him.

Lauren: Well, I think that's wonderful. He deserved that. Anyone who's that extraordinary, that gifted an actor, in addition to being a gifted human being, really above and beyond what most people ever are in their lives, he rates every cult that there could possibly be from every generation. And he's timeless. I think this will go on forever, long after my life is over. But as far as my relationship with him is concerned, that was our own. I did say once, and I'll say it again, being a widow is not a profession, and that you live your life the best you can. When a certain section of your life is over, you deal with it as best you can. You have to press on and do something else for yourself, because you're the only one that's left. So I am entitled to a life of my own and I'm gonna have it, damn it – in spite of you, Michael Parkinson!

****

Michael: The famous 'look' in *To Have and Have Not*, was that contrived, or was it accidental?

Lauren: It was a result of my nerves, which if you look very closely you might see again! I used to shake so much that my head used to shake, and when a director says, 'Action,' there's dead silence on set. So all eyes are on you. And I was such a nervous wreck I discovered that one way to hold my head still was to hold it down, and then the back of my neck got so stiff that nothing would move. Then I'd look up, and that became 'the look'. But it was that combined with Howard Hawks' terrific eye, and shadows in the right place – it was a combination of what he saw and my panic.

Michael: But how much of what came over – that sultry, sexy, worldly look – was the real you at that time?

Lauren: None of it. What can you be, when you're nineteen years old and know nothing, and you have very limited acting and life experience? How sophisticated can you be, for heaven's sake? But if you have a deep voice and Howard Hawks directs you and lights you correctly, you can be anything.

Michael: An image was created from your very first film. How difficult was it for you to get rid of it, live up to?

Lauren: I've had that problem all my professional life. People have seen me in a certain way. Even including today, I am looked upon as a woman who's in total control and command of every situation, that I don't need anyone and I've got all the answers – just like all those parts I played. As we all know, no one's that sure of themselves, and if they are, I don't want to meet them. It's very tough to walk into any room privately and have someone decide what you're all about.

****

Michael: What is interesting is that the men you married, including Bogie, insisted you gave up your career.

Lauren: It wasn't a question of insistence. Bogie didn't tell me to give it up. He said, 'If you really want to focus on a career, I will do everything I can to help you but I will not marry you.' He'd been married to three actresses, three failures, and they put their careers first. And of course, I said, 'I won't put my career first.' He said, 'I want a wife. I love you and I want to marry you but I want you with me, no locations.' I promised him that I would never go on location away from him and I kept that promise and I'm damn glad I did. I wouldn't let him go to Africa without me! I continued to work but I worked when I was in California, at home.

Michael: And you weren't to know that the time you did spend together was to be a short time.

Lauren: Yes, very short, and thank God I made that decision. But it was never insistence and it was never like turning into the little woman. I'm too big to be the little woman!

****

Michael: What about predatory men? In your book, you tell of a meeting you had with a film star, Robert Montgomery.

Lauren: Well, what can I tell you? I had arrived in Hollywood, I was nineteen years old, and I was taken by my agent to this enormous party given by Elsa Maxwell. Every movie star on the face of the earth was there, all in their gowns. I was not glamorous. I was in a little gold-coloured silk dress that was buttoned all the way up, long sleeved, and low-heeled shoes and I was sitting in a corner, and I had always had a crush on Robert Montgomery. I loved him in movies, and I found that I was introduced to him. I was so young and thrilled but so nervous and we ended up walking in the same direction at one point, and he said, 'Would you give me your phone number?' And I thought, 'Oooh, he wants my phone number!' I was so naïve. Today would be a different thing! So I gave him my phone number and he said, 'Too easy!'

Michael: What a shit!

Lauren: Put it there pal! What a way to treat an innocent young girl.

Michael: I'd have taken you off to Barnsley immediately! What a fascinating life you have led.

****

Michael: Tell me, do you have any plans for future work at all?

Lauren: Work? No. My plan is to sleep for a year. My aim is to do nothing. I only beg for time. I just want the time to take a walk, to wake up when I want to, and go and have a drink when I want to, and to not live by the clock, which the theatre is a great deal.

Michael: That's a splendid ambition.

Lauren: It is. I may never fulfil it, though.

Michael: My favourite pipe dream, too, is to go to sleep for a year. Perhaps we'll do it together!

Lauren: You may all leave!

1972

Ingrid Bergman

When I tell people that I fell in love with movies when I saw *Casablanca*, that's not the entire truth. Fact is I fell in love with Ingrid Bergman and my only excuse – if I need one – is so did the rest of the world. Anthony Quinn said, 'I reckon there wasn't a man who came within a mile of her who didn't fall in love with her.' Her life was like a Hollywood movie – great fame, scandal, rejection, exile, triumphant return. I interviewed her twice. She was as beautiful and serene as I imagined but the bonus was to find a woman of effortless style and intelligence who, for all her relaxed approach to the telling of her life story, remained a beguiling mystery. But when I think of her, what I remember most vividly is that she had the most wonderful smile of them all.

There was great confusion during the shooting of *Casablanca*. We didn't have the script, it was written as we went along, and to tell you the truth, no one knew how to end it. So we went along until the bitter end. And it was very bitter because they said I should shoot it both ways – either I should go in the plane with the husband, played by Paul Henreid, or stay on the ground with Humphrey Bogart. It was very difficult to act out these love scenes because I didn't know which one of the two men I was in love with. But it doesn't show!

Humphrey Bogart was an excellent actor and he always played himself. As a matter of fact, I think he wore the same raincoat and hat in every movie. But he had that marvellous voice that you could hear right now. It was such an interesting and rough voice and, of course, he was also considered a tough man, but I think inside he was quite a loveable person.

I think he was as upset as everybody else about not having a script and not knowing exactly where we were going, and he used to stay very much by himself. In another interview, they asked me if I knew him, and I said, 'No, I don't know him. I kissed him but I don't know him!'

We have the Royal Theatre in Stockholm and that is a free school. I tested to get in there. We were about seventy-five youngsters and you came out on the stage in front of all the actors, teachers and the head of the theatre, and you read whatever you had to read. I had just begun when somebody said, 'That's enough, miss – out. You can go.' Of course, I thought I was so awfully bad that they didn't have the patience to listen through my test. I went out and I looked at the sea in front of the theatre and I was wondering if I should throw myself in the water and get it over with right away, because I wanted very badly to become an actress. However, I got a message to come back to the theatre and I was engaged. Later on I asked why they had done it and said it was very cruel of the jury to do that, and they said, 'Well, the minute you got in and the way you moved on the stage, we realised that you had it. We didn't want to waste any more time. You were in.'

I didn't have the patience to go through five years in the school and being engaged by the theatre. I went directly to the movies in Sweden. I worked for a couple of years and was then in a picture called *Intermezzo*, that you called *Escape to Happiness* in England. It was shown in a small arts theatre in New York. David Selznick had a lady reading books and looking for talent for him. The elevator boy in her office building was of Swedish descent and his parents had gone to see this Swedish movie, and he said to her, 'My parents were very much taken by the young Swedish actress and I think you're looking for talents. Why don't you go and see the movie?' She sent the movie to Mr Selznick and he asked me to come over to America and do a repeat. So I owe my career in America to the elevator boy!

I don't know where I got my determination and strength from. I was so young and I wanted so much to try my wings in Hollywood, but immediately I was considered too tall and they were going to do something with my face, knock out my teeth, put in other teeth, change my eyebrows to make then thinner and change my name. When I heard all that, I got terribly frightened. I said, 'I want to go back. I don't want to do all that, because it would be terrible if my first movie was a flop and I had to go back to Sweden with a changed face and a changed name. I wouldn't be able to pick up my career after that.' So I refused and refused and then they accepted my name and what I looked like.

I was so impressed with *Rome, Open City* because after ten years in Hollywood, it was so completely different. It was so realistic, and so true. It just struck me that it must be a wonderful man who was capable of putting that on the screen. So I wrote Roberto Rossellini a letter – a famous letter – and that's how we got together.

Well, I was a corruption for American womanhood, and I was a woman of evil. Now, of course, we look at things differently. I was shocked. I was very upset about it, and felt terribly guilty towards the people I had worked with and thought I had ruined the movies. *Joan of Arc* was being shown, and it was just the right publicity for *Joan of Arc*! I've been told that they loved me so much in America. I had played so many good girls – nuns and saints – and somehow I was put on a pedestal. I was used as a good example by the parents. There was nothing wrong, no gossip around me in my private life, and suddenly this happened. I had a child with a man before I was divorced and before he was divorced and we didn't do anything to prevent the birth of this baby. We wanted it, and that shocked the world.

I felt it was my private life, and people who judged and wrote and talked in the American Senate and wanted me forever excluded from American movies, and even prevented from putting my feet in America, they didn't know what they were talking about because they didn't know me. They didn't know what had happened, and the only judge I had was my own conscience.

I have many friends. People were very kind and wrote to me. Ernest Hemingway did. He was very upset about the whole scandal and he talked to the newspapers and talked to me. But most people were very afraid. People are often afraid of losing their career, and their name, and I know they went around and asked, 'What do you think about Ingrid Bergman's behaviour?' And people said, 'It's terrible. We really think she should never be allowed back,' and others said, 'No comment.' A little Swedish actress called Märta Torén said, 'I think it's all right. I admire her. I think she's courageous. I'm very proud to be Swedish and I like her.' Well, she almost got fired from the studio because she said that. So it wasn't easy for people to take my part.

I have a sense of humour, I think. It's thirty years ago and a lot of things have happened since then. I'm not bitter or resentful or full of vengeance. I'm not born with that. Now, of course, I have gone back to America and, twenty-three years later, another Senator very kindly asked for a pardon for what the other Senator had said. He said not only was I welcome in America but they were honoured to have my visits. So, if you live long enough, everything is fine again.

1973 and 1980

Shirley MacLaine

I interviewed Shirley MacLaine twice. She was a guest on the very first series of *Parkinson* in 1971, which was wiped by a BBC committee set up solely to save storage space at headquarters by deciding which programmes to get rid of. Ms MacLaine suffered the same fate as, among others, John Lennon and Orson Welles, which makes you wonder who the BBC committee believed was an artist of lasting cultural importance. The second interview, like the first, was an encounter with a funny, provocative and flirtatious woman. She gave the impression of enjoying the company of men, particularly when she sensed they could be both tempted and teased, like your interviewer.

Michael: You're very disconcerting, Shirley MacLaine, you know that.
Shirley: Yeah.
Michael: Deliberately so.
Shirley: No.
Michael: No, just you are normally provocative.
Shirley: Just a regular, middle-class girl. Mother was Canadian, Dad was a small-town, middle-class American WASP – White American Southern Protestant. He always wondered why I went around the world caring. He used to call me a 'missionary in a skirt', in a pejorative sense. The best way to conduct one's life was never to upset the apple-cart, to observe the status quo and not make any noise, because it upsets the neighbours.

Dame Judi Dench was once asked if there was any award left for her to win. She replied, 'There's still Cruft's.'

Richard Burton could read a gas bill and make it sound like poetry.

Peter O'Toole, star of *Lawrence of Arabia*, said, 'There's a thick vein of pure farce that runs through everything I do – even playing Hamlet.'

Richard Harris's philosophy was 'Life is a series of memories. What you can't remember, you didn't do.'

Ralph Richardson once said to a lighting cameraman, 'Don't come too close, you'll see through my talent.'

Sir Alec Guinness was an enigmatic man, who seemed possessed of his own means of camouflage. He starred with Grace Kelly in *The Swan*.

Sir John Gielgud: 'We all have a streak of exhibitionism in our nature and one is mixed in being ashamed of it and being delighted with it.'

Sir Ian McKellen in *King Lear*. He is that rarity, the great classical actor who is also box office, both on stage and in the movies.

Paul McCartney (*above*) first heard John Lennon (*below*) in a skiffle group at a Woolton village fete and thought he had something. Defending the eventual split up, John Lennon was quick to point out it was 'a lot for four big-heads like the Beatles to stay together for such a long time'.

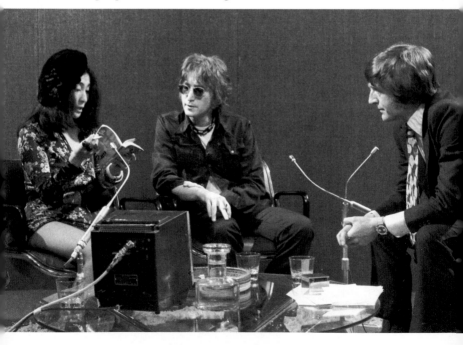

Of all the rock legends, Elton John was the one most able and willing to call it s it was.

As soon as you hear Tom Jones singing, you know he is Welsh

Sammy Davis Jr was a truly great entertainer – maybe the most remarkable of them all – but he was also a gutsy and resilient human being.

Madonna was determined to prove that being sexual and being intelligent could exist together.

Tony Bennett said Sinatra told him never to do a cheap song, and he took that advice and it worked.

It was the insolence of Lauren Bacall that made strong men weak.

Ingrid Bergman – seen here with Humphrey Bogart in *Casablanca* – was a woman of effortless style and intelligence who, for all her relaxed approach to the telling of her life story, remained a beguiling mystery.

Shirley MacLaine gave the impression of enjoying the company of men, particularly when she sensed they could be both tempted and teased, like your interviewer.

Michael: Well, you made a lot of noise, and upset a lot of people in your career. Have you always done this or is it something that came after you'd made it in Hollywood?

Shirley: I think I always did, because very early on, when I was really little, they told me always to be quiet. They inspire you to be radical and to be deviant when they want you to conform.

Michael: But it must have been very difficult for you when you were in Hollywood, because I think, of all societies, Hollywood is the most conformist, isn't it?

Shirley: Not really. I think that's a combination of things. Hollywood's looking for the individual who can break through and become a star, and sell their product as a result. After you become a star and sell their product, they want you to conform to making the money they want to make, but it's a mixture of art and industry.

Michael: Did you always want to be a film star? Was that your ambition as a kid?

Shirley: Oh, no. I never really cared about being famous or recognised. All I wanted to do was express myself. When you are in a conformist environment, you feel you have to bust your seams. It's another way of saying I wanted to express myself, whether it was in dancing, which is what I did originally, or in musical comedy. Then I got more specific with acting, and then it was in writing, and finally in political and social concern. It's all part of the same thing.

I come also from a background of rather abstract prejudice. I was born in the south, in a state that's on the Mason/Dixon line, the state of five presidents, so that's very politically and socially aware, but at the same time won't let black people in the living room. I was aware early in my life that something was wrong where that was concerned, and yet at the same time, I was stimulated to be culturally sophisticated, and the conflict bothered me.

Michael: Do you find that problem of being an artist in Hollywood all the more difficult because you're a woman, in the sense that Hollywood is run by men?

Shirley: Yeah. It is really interesting now, Michael, what's going on. The parts for women don't exist, you might have noticed. Robert Redford's playing all our parts. I started to figure that out the other day. I was walking on the beach in Marlborough, and I thought, 'What on earth is going on here?' Then I remembered that in the old days, meaning the forties and the fifties, when the Hays Office was the censorship board, you had Barbara Stanwyck, Joan Crawford and Katherine Hepburn playing women judges, women politicians, women mayors, women scientists. You were not allowed to play a love scene in the bedroom with a double bed. It had to be two twin beds, even if the couple was married, and regardless of what the scene was, one of the people had to have one foot on the floor.

Since they couldn't play any real good sexy love scenes, they had to resort to giving women these parts that were sensational in real life. The Hays Office was abolished in the name of more liberal sexual attitudes and the rating system came in. But men were running the studios, men were writing the scripts, and men were the directors – they put us back in the bedroom, and we haven't been judges or politicians or mayors since. We've been screwing in the bedroom!

Michael: Would you say that I was a male chauvinist pig? I'll tell you what, you've had great experience at doing this, how do you ascertain . . .

Shirley: You don't want me to answer that question?

Michael: I do, yes please. Off the top of your head.

Shirley: Off the top of my head, how about the bottom of my shoes? I think you're a great flirt. But that's important because a lot of male chauvinist pigs don't like to flirt, so I think the flirting part of it eases the pain of the fact that you are a male chauvinist pig.

1975

Raquel Welch

Raquel Welch was outrageously beautiful. There was a cartoon-like quality about her face and her figure, the exaggeratedly illustrated depiction of every young woman's aspiration and every man's dream. In the history of movies, Raquel Welch occupies a curious position in being one of the world's greatest sex symbols, yet emerging in the full spate of feminism. She was caught in the crossfire. She said, 'Being a sex symbol was like being a convict.' Moreover some critics concluded she was too beautiful to be taken seriously. Maybe that was a small price to pay for perfection.

Michael: When you were a young kid, did you always want to be a movie star?

Raquel: Well, not actually a movie star because I didn't think that that was real. I thought that was like Santa Claus and the Easter Bunny – just not real. But I did think that being an actress and being able to pretend all the time for a living would be a terrific idea, because we can't pretend in our real life enough, I don't think. We have to deal with the realities – over-population, war, the economy being depressed in some way, man's inhumanity to man, and the personal tragedies that we bring on ourselves, and it's just nice to be able to pretend.

I thought movies were all going to be Ginger Rogers and Fred Astaire and Betty Grable. I started out as a dancer, when I was about eight years old, and I thought that, if I ever got to be in films or on the stage, that's what I would like to do. But when I came along, that wasn't what was going on at all. People wanted to see realism and they didn't really take to the idea that glamour was a good thing. It was considered superficial, plastic and all of this, and perhaps it is in a way, but I think it also has something to offer.

Michael: I agree with you. Absolutely. You've got a lot to offer.

Raquel: Oh, ho, ho. I walked into that! Thank you!

Michael: No, but in the nicest possible way. Were you an attractive child, a good-looking kid?

Raquel: I don't really think I was. I had a hair parting in the middle and braids, and my dad always said that I should be very 'neat' in appearance. I wasn't allowed to wear ruffles or bright colours or have my hair in curls like a lot of girls at school. So I never really thought of myself as 'pretty pretty'. But, when I got a little bit older and the equipment arrived, well then I thought, 'Gee this is pretty terrific. Maybe I ought to try it out a little!' And I'd strut my stuff around, see how it all worked. And it worked pretty good!

Michael: When were you first aware of your sexuality? Of your ability to attract men?

Raquel: Well I never thought that was anything particular to me. I just thought boys like girls, and if you could get a good response from the opposite sex, that was a terrific thing. I soon found out that it didn't win a lot of friends in female circles and there was another side that said, 'How come you're doing such a show-off number all the time?' I thought, 'Well gee, I thought that was OK.' I thought it was all right to be proud to be a girl and all that. But I never really felt as though I'm it for the world or anything. I just thought it was nice to know that, if you're in the company of the opposite sex, there might be a few people who will respond to you, if you like them. The kind of security of knowing that you won't be a wallflower forever is nice.

Michael: I bet you can't tell me the last time you were a wallflower. What was your parents' reaction when you said you wanted to go to Hollywood?

Raquel: I didn't tell them as such. I really wanted to be a legitimate actress, because my father was pretty serious-minded and he felt I should study Shakespeare and all that. After he saw a picture of me in a bikini, he said, 'I told you, you should have studied Shakespeare.' And I said, 'Well, Dad, what can I do? This is the way it happened.' I didn't really plan it that way. But there was something about the reception, the success of what somebody noticed about the way I looked, that I did go along with. I just felt that somebody liked me for some reason, and I went along with it and didn't really analyse it. I think that people are all children underneath, and if they get compliments, or can find something they do well or somebody likes about them, then it's a natural thing to follow that.

Michael: There you were, you arrived in Hollywood with all the equipment, as you yourself said.

Raquel: With thousands and millions of other girls – and even the ones walking down the street were much, much better.

Michael: But was it a difficult thing there, to be treated seriously? I was thinking about the casting couch business in Hollywood. Did you get chased round the table?

Raquel: Well, I don't know. That's kind of an X-rated item.

Michael: Go on, tell the truth.

Raquel: Not really, no. There were a few times when people disappointed me a little bit, but no, it's not like *The Carpet Baggers*, which my mother had recently read and given to me. She said that's what Hollywood was all about, but it wasn't like that. There were a few wolves, but there are wolves in any nightclub, discotheque, restaurant. But it's not loaded with those types of people, no.

1972

Julie Andrews

Julie Andrews has been on stage all her life, and throughout her life she has demonstrated the style and ease in performance that is achieved only by a lifetime's practice. In a long, varied and distinguished career she won an Oscar, two Emmys, five Golden Globes and became Dame Julie – not bad for someone who made her debut in 1947 in vaudeville. She was a glorious Guinevere opposite Richard Burton in *Camelot* and the perfect Eliza Doolittle to Rex Harrison's Higgins in *My Fair Lady*, but when it came to the film, Hollywood turned her down. So she did *Mary Poppins* and *The Sound of Music* just to show what they missed.

Julie: With *The Sound of Music*, we were very aware it could be over-saccharin and sweet and we had to be careful – with religion and nuns and children and mountains, and all that sweetness going on, it was too much. So we all tried to play it down and make it as real as we could. I know there was a considerable amount of money spent on the film and hours put into it, but I don't suppose anybody had any idea how successful it was going to be.

Michael: That magnificent opening sequence, the huge shot over the mountains – it's a beautiful moment, I think.

Julie: And very cold. It was an amazing shot to be in the middle of. There was a helicopter coming in sideways. The cameraman was hanging out of the side of it, and how they ever do that, I don't know, because there was no door. We did many, many takes before they were satisfied. The helicopter would come towards me, closer and closer, then it would make a circle, go back and come through the trees again. I'd have to rush to the end of the field and start all over again, but every time it made the circle to go back, it would knock me flat from the down-draught. So I would do my lovely bit and then BAM! I'd pick myself up and I got so angry, because it just kept knocking me down.

Michael: You had three great stage hits in America and here, and yet never did the film versions. Twiggy did *The Boy Friend*, Vanessa Redgrave did *Camelot*, and Audrey Hepburn did *My Fair Lady*. You must have been very resentful about that?

Julie: I wasn't really resentful, because I understood why. The first one was *My Fair Lady*, and I understood why Audrey was chosen. I hadn't ever made a film before, and was a complete unknown as far as films were concerned. I was disappointed – I would have loved to have done it and was hoping I might be asked – but it's hard to be resentful when right around the corner Walt Disney happened to be waiting and asked me to do *Mary Poppins*.

Michael: You certainly got your revenge on the film industry with *Mary Poppins*, if one could put it that way. You got an Oscar for it.

Julie: Yes.

Michael: Why did that film work, do you think?

Julie: Well, I may be wrong, but it was the first really big musical in a long, long time. Also, it combined that fabulous thing of animation and live action and had incredible tricks and feats. Also, it had a joyousness, and Disney really did make magic. As a first film, it was a little staggering. When the penguins are dancing with Mary Poppins, of course there were no penguins. They were all drawn later and done as cartoons, but one had to play to them as if they were on that table.

Michael: What about the leading men that you played with? Do you have particular favourites?

Julie: Honestly, no. I think they've all been marvellous. Rex Harrison was fantastic. His timing was amazing. Sometimes I would be standing on stage with him, and because he would be so wonderful, my mouth would be open and I'd be learning, watching him do something, and the same with Richard Burton. He was brilliant. He had such control of the audience that he would say, 'I will make them cry in this speech,' or, 'Tonight, let me see if I can make them laugh in this speech,' and he would do it. There would be absolute silence where there would have been a laugh the night before.

Michael: Do you ever get the giggles on stage?

Julie: Oh, yes. Terribly. Sometimes Rex was very naughty. In *My Fair Lady* he would tease me, or do things deliberately to try to make me giggle. There was one classic evening. We were doing the famous scene at the end, where Eliza has run away from Professor Higgins and has gone to Mrs Higgins' house. Higgins comes storming in to talk to his mother, and Eliza gives a long lecture, saying the difference between a guttersnipe and a lady is how she's treated. That evening, I don't know what happened to Rex, he must have eaten beans before dinner, but he was extremely windy. That's putting it mildly. I was delivering my great speech, and suddenly across the orchestra pit there was this machine-gun volley – that's the only way it can be described.

There was utter silence, the orchestra was stunned, and at that precise moment Mrs Higgins was to say, 'Henry dear, please don't grind your teeth,' and I was absolutely gone. First of all I was so nervous I was going to giggle, that I was giggling anyway, and every other line I had to say in the scene had a double meaning. I would say things like, 'So you are a motorbus, all bounce, no consideration . . .' and this kind of thing. Finally, I could see the line coming closer and closer. All Higgins has to do in this scene is turn his back to the audience and listen to Eliza singing and carrying on, and I finally went up to him and sang, 'No my reverberating friend.' It took an extra ten minutes to finish the scene that night.

Michael: Poor Rex Harrison. Can I go back to the start of your career? You were sort of pre-destined to go on stage?

Julie: I don't know. My mother and stepfather were in show business, so I suppose it was fairly natural, growing up in that environment, that I would, too. My stepfather had a fine tenor voice and when I was about seven, decided that I should be taught to sing. Indeed, mine was a rather strong voice with a phenomenal range, but actually I think he taught me to sing more as an attempt to get close to me as a stepdaughter.

Michael: Really?

Julie: I think so. I know I wasn't very happy about the idea of learning to sing. I didn't like it. He was a very big man, physically, and I was always slightly in awe of him. He was always very sweet, but a little frightening at times, so singing was not the most pleasurable thing. But my parents made me stick to it and I had to practise for half an hour every day, and of course I'm very grateful now that they did.

Michael: What was it you objected to, though, in those days?

Julie: There is something very peculiar about singing. When you are singing, it is much a part of you – it's not like being a ballet dancer or a painter. A ballet dancer can look in the mirror and see a line. She can join a class, she can be among peers and there's a sense of competition. Singing is a very lonely, isolated business. You can't see it, you can only hear and feel, and I always used to feel tremendously vulnerable. I would find that, for no reason at all, I would burst into tears. It might have been my age, it might have been my mood that day, I don't know – but the fact that I was singing would sometimes get too much for me. So, I found singing lessons rather painful in a way.

Michael: Do you still get that when you sing?

Julie: Sad songs can twist me in knots. I can't play a Puccini opera without just dissolving. Now, I don't know if that's harking back to my youth, when I used to hear it, I don't know.

Michael: How difficult was it being a child star?

Julie: Well, it's only in retrospect it seems to have problems. At the time, you think you're tremendously special and you're made a great fuss of, and my mum was awfully good about trying to keep me as ordinary as possible under the circumstances. They weren't ordinary circumstances but she was very good, very strict with me. I'm sure to many I was a terrible brat. A lot of my problems came from facing audiences and wanting to be liked. Would they like me? Would I have enough to offer? Would I be compelling enough for them to sit still and listen, and could I get off with some grace?

Michael: And do you still feel that?

Julie: I think it's the reason I prefer film. Film-work is totally your own. Obviously, you're working with a crew, but you are very private. You don't have to perform for anyone other than the director, the camera and yourself, and I love that.

1974

Sharon Osbourne

I once went with Sharon Osbourne's dad to a club in Manchester. Don Arden was in the music business, an agent and promoter, and a man not to be messed with. Our way was blocked by a bouncer, determined not to let us in. Mr Arden opened his jacket and what he had tucked in his waistband was enough to make the bouncer change his mind. That said, I would still prefer to have his daughter, Sharon, in the same trench as me when the time comes.

Sharon Osbourne has lived a life beyond the imagination of any scriptwriter. It was that story, and her indomitable personality, that made her the perfect guest.

Sharon: As a child, I always had a problem with my weight, and it used to go up and down. It was like my addiction was food. And after I had my babies, I just kept putting it on, and I got to the stage when I thought I'm married, I've got kids, who cares what I look like. So there goes in another ten doughnuts.

Michael: And there are stories about you getting stuck in chairs . . .

Sharon: Oh yes. I was in New York at this very important meeting, and the whole office was very high-tech and minimalistic. Everything's little. The chair in the office was really small. I squeezed myself in and the meeting went on for a couple of hours, and I welded my bum to the seat. After the meeting, I go to get up and the bloody chair's stuck to me. One guy had to hold the back and a guy on each arm had to pull me out. So sad.

Michael: And you were in a high-powered job. What was the reaction that men, particularly, had to you?

Sharon: Oh, let me tell you something. When you're big, nobody holds the door open for you. When you're at the airport waiting for your case on the carousel, nobody wants to know. Nobody will help. And then when you become skinny and put your old boobies up a bit, it's like, 'I'll get your case for you.'

Michael: You had plastic surgery. It begs the question, if you lose half your body weight, it's got to go somewhere. What's left over, if you know what I mean?

Sharon: Oh, it was wicked. Especially the tummy. It used to hang like a little kangaroo. I used to have to lift it up to wash underneath, and I had National Geographic boobies. But let me tell you, they're not that way any more.

Michael: Your life has been dominated by two men – your dad and Ozzy, your husband. I knew your dad. I started working with Granada television in the sixties. I was a producer and we used to have a pop item on the show every night. Don Arden was then the most powerful man in the industry. Also the most frightening – he frightened me to death.

Sharon: And me.

Michael: Explain your relationship with him, because it seems to me an extraordinary story.

Sharon: When you're a child and you have someone who's so strong and powerful and successful as your father, you look up to him. I thought my father was right – whatever he said, his opinions, his actions, everything. He was my icon. And then, as I was getting older, I'd meet people at receptions and they'd say, 'Who are you?' I'd say, 'I'm Sharon Arden,' and they'd go the other way. It was because his reputation was so fierce, everybody was terrified of him. As I got older, I started to work for him. My father didn't exist on paper. Every company, every bank account, every loan was in my name, and then, when he started not paying the bills, they all came after me. And I still thought that was okay. And I used to think it was okay when the police came around looking for guns because he'd threatened someone with a gun and he'd be hiding. Everything in the house was knocked off.

He didn't have good moral fibre, but at the same time I loved him. It was an insane life. But when I married Ozzy, I wanted away. People thought that when I married Ozzy, my father was upset because I was marrying Ozzy. But he was upset because I was taking his cash cow away, who was Ozzy. He knew once we were married that was it, and we left.

Michael: It caused an extraordinary situation, didn't it? Didn't you, at one point, try to run him over in a car?

Sharon: Oh yes. Even though we'd parted from each other, the music industry is small and I used to get threats back and forth that he would make through people. One time, I was in Los Angeles and my babies were two, three and four, and he got somebody to call up the hotel and say, 'It's not safe for these kids to be here. I suggest you leave.' There were always threats coming through. It was a nightmare. I hadn't seen him for years and I was taking the kids for Sunday lunch. We were driving down the street and I saw him out the corner of my eye, and I'm thinking, 'I'm gonna kill him.' So I did a big U-turn and the kids are saying, 'Mum, what you doing?' I swung the car over, up on the pavement, and then my eldest daughter says to me, 'Mummy, why are you trying to kill Tony Curtis?' She thought it was Tony Curtis because he had all that grey hair.

Michael: Extraordinary. Are you reconciled with him in any way?

Sharon: Yes I am. Two years ago when I was going through chemotherapy, my brother called me and said that my dad was in a serious way. He had a bad heart and Alzheimer's, and my husband said to me go see him before he's totally wiped clean. I did, and now I take care of him.

Michael: What about this other extraordinary man in your life, Ozzy? Why did that survive? Because on the face of it, it's an extraordinary relationship.

Sharon: It's not really. You knew my father, so you know the sort of house I came from. When I met Ozzy, who was so truthful and just an honest person, I fell for him hook, line and sinker. He's a rock 'n' roller and did crazy things, but crazy was nothing compared to what was going on in my house.

Michael: But he tried to kill you.

Sharon: Oh yeah, but we forget about that now. It was just a little strangling. He was out of his bloody mind on drugs, but it was building – I could feel the tension in the house. We'd had fight after fight, and one night he came down and he was mixing everything in a pestle, and I'm thinking, 'Oh dear, I'm in for it tonight.' And I was. I called the police. I got him arrested.

Michael: Quite right.

Sharon: So he was put away for six months, not in jail but in rehab, and it changed everything, because when Ozzy was away getting his life together, I got my life together but in a different way. I turned the tables and said, 'I'm never ever going to be in this position again.' My whole life I'd done whatever my father wanted me to do and I took care of him. I took care of my husband, protected him, and then I was exhausted and I said no more.

Michael: The stories are extraordinarily amazing. Then to top it all, you got this very successful series, *The Osbournes*, and then you get cancer. In this remarkable life of yours, that must have been the most awful moment.

Sharon: It was the most embarrassing, because it can only be Sharon who gets it up the bum.

Michael: You damn well nearly died, didn't you?

Sharon: Yes, I did.

Michael: And you were working at the same time?

Sharon: Trying to. I lost all my hair, but I was wearing a wig for the show. And at the end of the day, the dog got my bloody wig. I was in bed, dying, and I took the wig off, put it on the bloody table and then the dogs are running around the house, chewing the wig.

Michael: We're laughing here, but I was going to ask you how you get through all this. I think the reason you get through it is you have a sense of humour about things, don't you? Is that what's pulled you through?

Sharon: I do, and my husband has a great sense of humour. He's the funniest guy you could ever meet, and the most honest and loving, and he pulled me through. When I was really sick, they told me I had a 33 per cent chance of making it, and I would just look in my husband's eyes and see the fear, and I would think, 'I've just got to fight. I cannot go, I've got to fight.' And that's what kept me going.

2004

Bette Midler

Bette Midler was no ordinary guest. She didn't just turn up for a show, she overwhelmed it. When I first interviewed her, she had yet to mature as the film star of *Beaches* and *The First Wives Club*. In 1979 she was a pineapple chunker turned Turkish-bath entertainer turned outrageous cabaret performer, singing songs about the clap. The *New York Times* described her as 'the entertainer who ignited a career by giving a good name to bad taste'. Interviewing her was like trying to bottle a whirlwind – exhilarating but ultimately impossible. An exhausting and enchanting woman, and unforgettable.

Michael: Your first big break, in a sense, was working in a Turkish bath in Manhattan. Now, that's extraordinary to somebody in England. We don't have singers in Turkish baths. How did you get the job?

Bette: Well, you have singers and you have Turkish baths, right? You sort of have to put them together. But it's a very special Turkish bath. This wasn't just your every day, run-of-the-mill Turkish bath. It was an all gay health club. I forgot to mention that.

Michael: All gay?

Bette: It was gay, gay, gay, and this was before there was any big gay thing in the States. They were all hiding and in the closet, as it were. And I was destitute. I didn't have any money. I'd quit this show I was doing and I was trying very hard to build my act and learn all the things you're supposed to learn as a performer. This teacher called me up and said, 'I have a man who has a gay health club and he has an idea. His idea is to put entertainment in this club and make it something more than a health club, make it a nightclub proposition, too.' And so I said, 'Oh yes, I'll take the job,' because I didn't care at that point. I was starving.

Michael: What sort of act did you do?

Bette: Well, it was more a mish-mash of possibilities. It wasn't the cogent noble work I'm offering these days. I tried everything. I wore everything I owned. I remember taking the pillow cases off my sofa and wrapping them around my head. I stole music from people, I stole arrangements, I stole clothes – literally. I would go into old friends' houses and look in their piano to see if they had anything I could use. And that's the kind of act that it was. But, fortunately, it was presented with enough élan, enough spirit and enough good nature that it went over, and besides it was bizarre to have this buxom blonde woman trying so hard to please these men who were totally naked.

Michael: I was going to ask you about that. Were they naked?

Bette: Well, they were naked, but they all, out of the generosity of their feelings for me, wore a little towel.

Michael: Out of deference.

Bette: Out of deference. See you speak English. I don't speak it so well.

Michael: And what did they do when you were singing?

Bette: They listened, of course! What did you think they were doing? On occasion they would . . . but I wouldn't pay any attention. I thought, well, if it makes them happy. Isn't it nice that I can inspire such romance and passion in people? Actually, they were very respectful to me, and as the days went on, and the weekends passed, it got to a point where it started getting very popular, and pretty soon they started letting women in, and after about six months it was no longer a gay club. Now it was a regular nightclub and people came and, of course, there were still the regular patrons, who were pissed off! They were furious! Now they didn't have any place to go, because of this gigantic success we had all had.

Michael: Was the idea to titillate?

Bette: Titillate? That sounds like your tits flew in a day too late! Just missed lunch or something like that!

Michael: Was the idea to titillate, in brackets provoke, or amuse?

Bette: No, actually, neither. Although one doesn't mind titillating every now and again. I think it's good.

Michael: It's very pleasant.

Bette: I think it's very pleasant. I like it when an audience sort of salivates. I do. I've changed a lot of people's lives, if I do say so myself.

Michael: You were born in Hawaii – can you do the hula-hula?

Bette: Of course I can do the hula-hula. Can you?

Michael: No.

Bette: Well my girls and I often do a number in the show – it's a truly tacky hula-hula. We know all kinds of tropical numbers. Tropical numbers are my life.

Michael: Really?

Bette: Oh yes, I know 'Fiesta in Rio' and 'I Had the Clap'. I know that one.

Michael: When you were in Hawaii, you once worked in a pineapple canning factory, wasn't it? What did you do?

Bette: I was a chief chunker. Are you trying to laugh, or are you trying not to laugh?

Michael: I'm trying to do a serious interview here. You're just destroying my act! What is it, a chief chunker?

Bette: I chunked pineapple.

Michael: You chunked the pineapple.

Bette: Yeah. They had your chipped and your chunked pineapple, and I was the chief chunker.

Michael: Is it very boring?

Bette: It was extremely boring. I used to come home smelling like a compote. Eventually, I smelt so much like a pineapple, they asked me to join a union. Don't you ever think of yourself as a small child and wonder how you grew up into this? Did you really grow up into what you thought you would?

Michael: I think that if you're making a living as a journalist and an interviewer, which is what I do, that you don't have that kind of fantasy life. You don't create something.

Bette: Oh, I thought you were in showbiz?

Michael: No.

Bette: They told me you were in show business. I didn't know you were a journalist, how dreary! Oh, that's unkind. I thought you were a song and dance man, like Bruce Forsyth. They play that cheesy intro music for you. I thought you were gonna do a buck and wing!

1979

Helen Mirren

It would be fair to say Helen Mirren and I are not bosom buddies. I use the word 'bosom' advisedly because Ms Mirren was always accusing me of having an obsession with hers. It is true that, on the two occasions we met, I raised the subject of her taking off her clothes in movies, but in both cases I could justifiably claim I did so, not because of any prurient obsession on my part, but in pursuit of a legitimate public interest in the pressures put upon attractive young actresses to take their kit off. That's my story and I'm sticking to it. Ms Mirren didn't buy it and our encounters varied between the antagonistic and the wearily wary. That said, I believe her to be one of the finest actresses of my time – with or without clothes.

1975

Michael: Do you get fed up with being branded in that way, of people saying, 'She's a sort of sex fiend?'

Helen: No. I think there must be some truth in it. People keep saying it.

Michael: I think they're right.

Helen: I hope they're not, but you are what you are, and you are what other people think you are, and you can't avoid that.

Michael: Do you think, you are, in quotes, 'a serious actress'?.

Helen: In quotes? What do you mean, 'in quotes'?

Michael: It's a kind of cliché. But do you find that what could be best described as your equipment, in fact injures you, perhaps, in that pursuit?

Helen: I'd like you to explain what you mean by 'my equipment' . . . in great detail.

Michael: Well, your physical attributes.

Helen: You mean my fingers?

Michael: No, I meant your . . .

Helen: Come on, spit it out.

Michael: Your figure.

Helen: My figure?

Michael: Mm.

Helen: What was the beginning of the question?

Michael: The question was, do you find that your figure, your physical attributes, which people always go on about, hinder you in your pursuit of the ambition of being a successful actress?

Helen: I'm a serious actress. Serious actresses can't have big bosoms, is that what you mean?

Michael: Well, I think that they might sort of detract from the performance, if you know what I mean.

Helen: Really? Oh, I can't think that can necessarily be true. What a crummy performance if people are obsessed with the size of your bosom or anything else. I would hope the performance and the play, and the living relationship between all the people on stage and all the people in the audience, overcome such boring questions, really.

Michael: Boring questions.

Helen: Pretty boring in the end, yes.

Michael: You came from a remarkably sober background, didn't you?

Helen: I hope my parents are listening to hear you say that. My parents were pretty sober, I suppose. I mean, they didn't drink.

Michael: So what kind of people were they?

Helen: I hate calling people anything. They're my parents, my beloved parents. I hope they're watching.

Michael: Well, I presume that they had jobs. People are different, they look different, they talk differently, they have different jobs. It's absurd to pretend that they're not.

Helen: Yes, but it's so dangerous to stick labels. If I was to say my parents were middle-class, everyone's got a different idea of what middle-class means.

Michael: Were they middle-class, in your view?

Helen: Well, I suppose so, yes.

Michael: And you went to a convent as well, didn't you?

Helen: Yeah, I went to a convent grammar school.

Michael: Did you enjoy that?

Helen: Not very much. I don't like schools. I was a teacher later on and I didn't enjoy that either. I don't find the school system at all conducive to education.

Michael: Did you find being at a convent in any sense repressive?

Helen: I find all schools repressive. I don't think the fact it was a convent made it any more repressive. There were a few silly rules, like not sitting down on the grass on a hot, sunny day, when all you wanted to do was sit down on the grass, and not undoing your top button, and not rolling up your sleeves, and wearing long, grey, woolly socks, but those are unimportant things. The much greater question of lack of liberty is what happens to people's minds in schools.

Michael: What happened to yours?

Helen: I don't know, I'm still finding out I suppose. I think you go on living with what happened to you in your early life, for the rest of your life.

Michael: Did you want to be an actress at that point, when you were at convent?

Helen: Yes, I did, very much so. I first discovered I wanted to be an actress when I was at primary school. I played the Virgin Mary. Why did they laugh?

Michael: I didn't laugh. I kept a straight face.

Helen: And I was really rather good. People said I was good anyway, and I got that terrific feeling of being good at something, I suppose, and other people recognising it. I remember very clearly that feeling.

2006

Michael: I have to tell you, I sat in that film thinking, what's the Queen doing with all those actors? It's an amazing portrayal. You look so much like her, too, it's quite extraordinary.

Helen: I do. You know, when I was younger and I used to play parts with a dark wig, people used to say I looked just like Princess Margaret. So obviously there is a genetic similarity there somewhere or other, although I hope when people look at me like this they don't think, 'God, she looks just like the Queen!'

Michael: But it is a wonderful performance. It's a very fine film, too. When you were approached to do this film, there must have been a misgiving, though.

Helen: Oh, more than a misgiving. I was terrified. I was more frightened of this than any other role I've undertaken – not because of the emotional demands of the role, but because it's a hot potato. You know that you're going to be under the most incredible scrutiny. There's going to be an enormous amount of press scrutiny. You don't know if you're going to get it right or not. So it was very, very nerve-racking, but it was a wonderful script. All of our work as actors comes from the script.

Michael: It was certainly, but then you had to get her right. It's not like inventing a part. This is somebody everybody knows, and everybody has an opinion about.

Helen: Yes, you've got to get the impersonation element as right as you can. But my attitude is I don't think it has to be perfect and I think that liberated me. I was doing a huge amount of research, watching tapes, reading books, and then I thought, 'I'll go and look at some portraits,' because every painter has their own vision of what they think the Queen is. So I looked at as many portraits as I could. And I thought, 'It's all right if you're not perfect because it's your portrait,' and I think of it as my portrait of the Queen.

Michael: Were there certain clues that made it easier when you found them? The voice, for instance.

Helen: Well it's interesting, her voice is very different. She has a voice for her speeches and then she has her own voice, and they really are quite different. It was very hard to get to the real voice because we hear it so infrequently. There were little bits of film here and there. But I found my heart went towards the young Queen, or at least the person before she became the Queen – the young girl.

Michael: So you watched tapes of that, did you?

Helen: I watched as much as I could, and there was one tiny bit of tape that I was very drawn to, and watched over and over again. And that was when she was about twelve, long before she knew that she was going to be Queen, and she was just a posh person. She's getting out of a big posh person's car and she's got on one of those little coats they used to wear with velvet collars and, I think, gloves and socks and shoes. They were dressed like children until the age of about sixteen or seventeen. And she's got this very grave, serious look on her face, a look of, 'I must do this right.' She's not smarmy and giggly and smirky, she's very serious, and she gets out of this big car, this little girl, and she puts out her hand, just beautifully, to meet the dignitary, who is much taller than she is, and I found that piece of film very moving – because I thought it revealed that sweet, responsible, dutiful, grave person that's kind of the little girl inside of the Queen. And that's the person I was always trying to reach for in my portrayal.

Michael: It's very moving that she's so resolute and so certain because that's what she's been brought up to be.

Helen: Yes, absolutely. And maybe she was right in the end. What I think about the Queen is that it's a point beyond ego and beyond vanity – you get to that place where you have no choice, and I don't think any of us can possibly comprehend what that must be like.

Michael: What would your late dad be thinking if he heard you say that now?

Helen: Interesting question. My dad was vehemently anti-monarchist, and my mum was, too. But really what they were was anti-class system, and obviously the monarchy is the apex of the structure that is the class system. They suffered under the class system, as basically working-class people in London before the war, during the war, after the war. But on the other hand, they had a direct understanding of the royal family because they are of the same generation.

Michael: Let's talk about the second important part that you're coming up with shortly, which is the return of Jane Tennyson in *Prime Suspect*. There was a quote in a couple of the newspapers where you said it was the first time that you didn't have to depend on the size of your breasts to get the part.

Helen: I'm glad you mentioned that Michael, because you can't resist can you! This is our problem. The first time we ever met he had to talk about my breasts, now it's full circle.

Michael: Now to be fair to me, they were hanging out.

Helen: Excuse me!

Michael: We took against each other didn't we.

Helen: I hated you.

Michael: Did you really? I didn't think much of you, either.

Helen: I thought you were a sexist person for mentioning my breasts, and also you wouldn't actually say the word 'breasts'.

Michael: I said 'your accoutrements' or something like that. It was all very, very silly . . . You objected to anything, because you just didn't like me at all. Mind you, have you changed?

Helen: I've changed, I've mellowed.

Michael: What an actress she is!

Oprah Winfrey

Oprah Winfrey strode down the stairs like she owned the joint. In America, she does. She is a one-woman media empire worth $2.4 billion, and an interviewer's dream, not simply because she knows better than most what is required, but because her life story is so compelling. It reads like some lurid novel – the abused child, raped aged nine, raised in poverty at a time of segregation, who became one of the world's most powerful media figures. You might wonder about the rise and rise of Oprah Winfrey and what it tells us about modern society and the power of celebrity, but what you cannot doubt, when you spend more than five minutes in her company, is her determination and ability to get exactly what she wants.

I remember as a child, I had gotten a terrible beating, and had to dress to go to Sunday school – that's the irony of it. I turned in the mirror to put on my little blouse and the welts on my back had swollen into little keloidal scars, and some of them were still bleeding. I put the blouse on, and remember getting whipped again because the blood came through the blouse. I hold no judgement or grievances or anger about it now. I did for a long time, but now I understand, as an adult – people do how they know, and when they know better, they do better.

I came from a time in our culture and history when people beat their children because they were beaten, and the parents before them were beaten, and that's how they knew how to handle children. I remember getting punished for the least offensive thing I could do – drop a glass while washing the dishes, speak out of turn. I was coming from the well one day, bringing water – because we had no indoor plumbing, no electricity – and I remember playing my fingers in the water and getting to the house and my grandmother saying, 'You were playing in that water. Put the bucket down,' and getting a whipping.

I grew up in an environment where there was a tin tub in the kitchen, and you would heat the water for the bath, and you would take your bath on Saturday night. Sometimes my grandmother, because this is all she knew, would save up the whippings until I was naked in the tub, and say, 'Remember Tuesday? Remember this, remember that.'

And I was sexually abused, beginning at nine. I was raped at nine. And all that has happened to me, I think has happened to make me a stronger, more vital woman, who can now share those stories in a way that, I hope, lifts somebody else up. 'Look at me. I made it, so can you.' That to me is the whole point of being famous.

You don't get out unless somebody helps you out. Nobody makes it alone. I had books. If you ask me, 'What is the feeling you had the most, the most overwhelming emotion you felt as a child?' I swear to you that it would be loneliness and a sense of abandonment. The only thing that held me together, I believe now, was books. I could read stories and know that there was another kind of life, that another kind of life existed. And I always believed. That is, I think, the secret, if I had one, of how I've become what I've become. I always believed that my life would get better.

I remember one day watching from the back screen porch,

through the screen door, and seeing my grandmother boiling the clothes, because that's how they would treat clothes – boil them and hang them on the line. And my grandmother said, 'You better stand there girl. You better stand there watch me, 'cause you got to learn how to do this.' I stood there because I didn't want a whipping, but I remember thinking, 'I don't have to watch this, 'cause I'm not going to be doing this.' I just knew, inside myself, that I was not going to be boiling clothes and hanging them on the line. I don't know how. We didn't even have television. I just knew in my spirit.

In 1970, I was in the Miss Fire Prevention contest, and this was the first year in Nashville, Tennessee, that they were going to integrate the contest. I was in there with all these other southern girls, a little radio contest for Miss Fire Prevention. All of us were lined up on the podium, and they'd asked the question: 'What do you choose to do with your life, when you're grown up?' And all the girls had taken up the best answers: 'I want to be a teacher, so that I can teach children,' or, 'I want to be a nurse, because I just love people, I love people, love people.' So nurse is gone, teacher's gone.

I had seen Barbara Walters that morning on television. So, I'm trying to come up with something I want to be. I hadn't thought about it till that moment. I said, 'I think I would want to be a journalist. I want to be a journalist because I believe that education and information is freedom, and if I can offer that to people in a way that helps them think about their lives, then I believe I will be able to lead a more productive life.' Won that contest! Now the funny thing is I had never thought about it before that moment. I'm standing there, trying to think, 'What do I want to be? What can I be?' And Barbara Walters popped into my head. After that, I went to this radio station that had sponsored the contest, to pick up my prize, which was a watch. And as I was in the radio station, somebody said, 'Would you like to hear your voice on tape? Can you read? Would you like to read some copy?' I read, and that's how it all started.

In my lifetime, I believe it has got better. The fact that I exist, the fact that I can be sitting here talking to you on this show about my life, means some things have certainly changed. A lot of things are still horrible for a great number of people, and racism exists every day. When I was a kid, I heard Jesse Jackson say in a speech, 'Excellence is the best deterrent to racism, the best deterrent to sexism,' and I took that on as my motto. I remember being sixteen in one of those boring high school auditorium programmes, going home and putting that on my mirror – 'Excellence is the best deterrent to racism. Be excellent.' I made it a vow within myself, 'Whatever I do, I'm going to be the best at it,' and I've done that with everything, except dieting.

1999

Jane Fonda

When I interviewed Henry Fonda in the seventies, he spoke movingly and with real pride about the talent of his daughter, Jane. He told me that when he saw her in *Klute* he thought it was one of the greatest performances he had seen and that he couldn't wait to talk to her, not as father to daughter, but as actor to actor. Thirty years later, I interviewed Jane Fonda about her auto-biography. In the book she had talked about her difficult life with her father, who never talked to her about her career and never gave her any indication of what he thought of her professionally. We showed her the clip of her father praising her, the first time she had seen it. She watched it with tears in her eyes. So did I.

Jane: You come down the stairs like Fred Astaire, it's quite wonderful.
Michael: Listen, when I had Fred Astaire on the show, I fell down the stairs, trying to walk like Fred Astaire! Now this book of yours, it's quite an extraordinary book.

Jane: Thank you.

Michael: To somebody like myself, who grew up watching your father and yourself, and forming opinions, as you do, from the silver screen, it's quite a shocking book in many ways.

Jane: How so?

Michael: Take your father as an example. To me, he epitomised on the screen that wonderful all-American hero – a lovely, gentle, charismatic man. Yet he comes across in your book as a kind of a cruel man – cruel to you, a bad father, cold, distant.

Jane: Cold rather than cruel. But you can also feel how much I loved him, right?

Michael: Of course. You spent all of your life trying to please him.

Jane: The disease to please.

Michael: Is that what it is?

Jane: Men understand it just as well as women. It happens when you're growing up – you feel, or are sometimes made to feel, that you're not good enough, that in order to be loved, you have to be perfect, and of course we're not meant to be perfect, right? God is perfect. We're meant to be complete. But you turn yourself into a pretzel to please. It happened with me. It was my father I was trying to please, and it doesn't stop when you grow up. It continued with the men I was with, all of whom I was sure were totally different from my father, but underneath, there was the same issue, which is that they didn't know, nor did I, how to be intimate. And that is universal.

Michael: What was the problem with your father, that he had lacked this intimacy with you, that he was distant, he was disapproving?

Jane: It's partly generational. How many of you saw *On Golden Pond*? The relationship in the movie, between me, Chelsea and Norman – my father, played by my father – was parallel to the real-life relationship.

Michael: But did he see the parallels?

Jane: I just assumed that he did, but he never told me he did.

Michael: So never in all the time that you knew him, did he ever give you the seal of approval, so to speak?

Jane: He did, on your programme.

Michael: Well he did in 1975. This is the point, and you didn't know about that, did you?

Jane: No.

Michael: He said that you were the most remarkable actress he had ever seen and that there was a moment in *Klute* when you did something and he said, 'I can't do that.' He never told you that?

Jane: No, no.

Michael: Isn't that strange, though, that he will tell me, but won't tell you?

Jane: Many of us know parents who are wonderful with strangers, especially after a few drinks, but in the living room or the bedroom with their intimates they don't know how to show up. They don't know how to love. And you can learn, but the generation of my father really didn't think that that was something . . . well, he didn't learn.

Michael: The other extraordinary thing is the way that your father, who cast this long shadow over your life, had this effect on your health, your bulimia for instance.

Jane: It's all part of 'I've got to be perfect to be loved.'

Michael: That's right. Your father didn't approve of the way you looked, so you didn't approve of the way you looked. You became bulimic.

Jane: And anorexic, for twenty-five years.

Michael: For twenty-five years and none of the people you were with knew about it.

Jane: Of course not. If you are an addict, which is what food addiction is, just like alcohol and drugs, you are always going to be attracted to people who are also addicts, because intuitively you can be quite sure they will never notice. They are too busy with their own addiction. Maybe the perfect man for me crossed my path at some point in my life, who was actually capable of intimacy, and you know what I would have done? Fled in terror. Addicts are attracted to addicts so that no one will call them on their issues. And when I got healthy . . . I'm alone. But I'm not alone, I'm here with you. I'm very happy and I have grandkids and children.

2006

Joanna Lumley

When I first met Joanna Lumley, she was plummy and yummy, the sort you wanted on your arm at Royal Ascot, the scrummy gal who could get out of an open-topped sports car with every hair in place and without showing her knickers. Beneath that façade was a tough and determined woman, Boadicea masquerading as a deb. Her fight on behalf of the Ghurkas was both inspiring and moving. Her emergence as an actor with a real comedic gift in *Ab Fab* was a revelation. Her greatest asset is that people admire her for who she really is as much as they laugh at Patsy Stone. She is a one-off, and still beautiful after all these years.

Michael: You have this reputation, don't you? Somebody compared you to an Enid Blyton heroine, sort of sugar and spice, and all the publicity stresses this convent-educated, goody-goody young lady. Now I'm interested to find out whether that's true or false.

Joanna: I didn't think they meant goody-goody. Convent is what they mean.

Michael: What do they mean by convent?

Joanna: Well I don't know, but there's this idea that convent girls are restricted, so when they leave school, they go completely mad. I think probably people have changed a lot, particularly children have changed a lot. But at school we were very childlike. When I was sixteen, I made a blood vow with my best friend that we wouldn't kiss men ever. We thought men were pretty revolting. We were climbing trees and I wore short socks, and it was jolly important to get into the lacrosse team.

Michael: Did you want to be an actress in those days?

Joanna: Yes. I wanted to be an actress when I was about seven, but I wanted to be an actress in a pink Cadillac. I'd seen an advertisement for cigarettes with two people leaning over a balcony in Manhattan and lights below, and she had a sleeveless dress. He was offering her a cigarette, and she was clearly a star. I thought, 'Oh I'd like to be like that.' I didn't think that I'd still be pushing my basket round the supermarket.

Michael: How did you set about being an actress?

Joanna: I did try to get into RADA, but I knew I had failed my audition. I walked off the stage, it was just awful and they sensibly said, 'We won't ever take you, ever.' I'd lost my nerve and didn't want to try anywhere else, because I knew they would all say the same thing. So I went and worked in a shop and became a model, which seemed to me a quick way of making money.

Michael: You've got a financial need beyond the normal actress to go on working haven't you? You have a child and are what's called a one-parent family?

Joanna: I am, and actually that was the best thing that ever happened to me. When I was a model, for reasons best known to the profession, I'd become quite popular. I worked every day with quite high fees in those days, four guineas an hour. I'd become quite rich and successful and there seemed to be no purpose in it. And when I had Jamie, there seemed to be a bottomless pit. I could continue chucking money into it forever and it would always disappear. And that's rather exciting. So you have to go on working. You can't say, 'I can't be bothered, I feel sick today.'

Michael: What are the problems, bringing up a child without a father?

Joanna: Most of them the difficulties of being one person as opposed to two people. So if you're late back from work, or the trains aren't running, whoever it is looking after him is in a panic and you're sitting on a train somewhere thinking, 'I don't know how to get back.' They're practical problems, not moral problems. And there are women all over the world, and men, who are single-parent families. It's quite possible to do it all. What you've got to do is do it properly.

Michael: Let's talk about the thing that actually made you, the starring role in *The Avengers*. How determined were you to get that part?

Joanna: Desperate.

Michael: Were you?

Joanna: Hadn't worked, you see. All I could see was that it would be a job that would go on for more than one week. Most jobs I had were in half-hour comedy series, which paid perhaps £120 or £250. That would be the only job for six months, and that's not enough money. So this one seemed to go stretching away into the future. I didn't think it would have a chance of surviving, because *The Avengers* had been long lost, and everyone was mourning the passing of Diana Rigg. I just wanted to get a job that would pay the rent, so I gripped them pretty tightly around the lapels and said, 'Just test me,' because they wouldn't see me for a long time. They wouldn't have me in the room, horrible.

Michael: Did you do all your own stunts?

Joanna: No. I couldn't ride a motorbike. They said, 'Can you ride a bike?' and I said, 'No.' They said, 'We'll give you quarter of an hour to learn,' and I said, 'Probably not quite enough time.' So I didn't do those, but I did quite a lot of strange ones. The most dangerous one was hanging underneath a helicopter. First, they said, 'Oh, you don't have to do this, Joanna. You can sit in the car.' So I went and sat in the back of the car, fell asleep, and they went tap, tap on the window and said, 'You're on now.' I said, 'I thought I wasn't doing this,' and they said, 'You are now.'

Now, the helicopter comes round and it has this little

ladder hanging underneath it. They said, 'It's just going to hover above you. All you've got to do is to step on the ladder. Be careful you don't step right on it – you'll pull the helicopter down and you don't want that.' No, I don't want that at all. They said, 'Just hang on tight, we're going to take you for a little two or three mile whiz around. We'll be hedge-hopping a bit, so watch out for your feet.' I hopped on, and I went around clinging on, and I thought, this is a bit cool. Got back and all the stuntmen were clapping, and I said, 'What's the problem?' They said, 'Nobody would do that.' I wasn't even insured.

Michael: You were a child of the Raj, weren't you?

Joanna: I was.

Michael: Growing up in India, it seems to me that it produces a remarkable child, a remarkable person – much more self-sufficient, with a different kind of approach to life from other people. It is discernible.

Joanna: Is it? I wonder how much of that is to do with the travelling, which was immense, because you never flew in those days. You always went via long boat journeys with lots of time on your own. You also had the great benefit of hearing different languages spoken, and understanding and hearing about different religions. You had a sense of a larger world.

Michael: Your dad was a military man, of course.

Joanna: Yes, he was. He was with the Ghurkas.

Michael: They were extraordinary soldiers, among the bravest there have ever been. You recently took up the cause of one Ghurka, a very brave man?

Joanna: Yes, Tul Bahadur Pun. Well, this was when my father was a Chindit – they were a specially selected group of highly trained men. They were sort of pre-SAS, Lord Wingate's men, and they were dropped behind enemy lines in Burma. It was a very bloody war, and most of them still won't talk about it. Most of them are gone now, but on one particular skirmish, fighting with the Japanese in these terrible jungle conditions, two VCs were awarded. One was to Michael Ormond, who died, and the other was to this tremendous Ghurka soldier, Tul Bahadur Pun. I knew his face and name ever since I was six. Daddy said, 'This is a great bloke, Tul Bahadur Pun.'

Wind the clock forward, maybe fifty or sixty years, and suddenly Tul Bahadur Pun VC, who is still alive and living in Nepal, became very frail and his condition became weaker and weaker, and he couldn't get the medical treatment that he needed in Nepal. He wondered whether he could come and be domiciled in this country and have the health care he needed, and our Government, for some unbelievable reason, said, 'He hasn't shown enough commitment to Britain,' or something. And he'd won a VC fighting alongside, and for, our Army. I don't know what more you can do. And so there was a great deal of banging and crashing, and suddenly they said, 'Oh sorry, what we meant was he can come in.' So he did.

1979 and 2007

Diana Rigg

I might as well come clean. The most desirable woman I ever met on *Parkinson* was Diana Rigg. For me, in *The Avengers* she was the first television sex symbol who both deserved and lived up to her reputation. When she came on the show for the first time, in 1972, she radiated a lustrous beauty. It was an added bonus that she was a joy to interview, being funny and frank as well as provocative and opinionated. She is now a Dame and a National Treasure without ever being in danger of becoming hoity toity. She is, of course, from Yorkshire, which helps.

Diana: I suppose now, I've got more money and more things, but the qualities that existed as a Yorkshire girl are still there.
Michael: What are the particular qualities, do you think, that that part of the country gives you?

Diana: It's the sense of reality more than anything else – the awareness that, even though you may be a success, there's that Yorkshire voice at the back of your mind saying, 'Aye, but nobbut just.' You've still got to keep working at it.

Michael: Coming from the background that you did, which I know very well, being from so very near you, it always struck me that, if I'd ever said that I wanted to go into the theatre, my dad would have thought he'd spawned a wrong 'un. Did you have something of this parental opposition to your ambitions to be an actress?

Diana: Not too much. Parents, they love you very much, and if they think you want to do something crazy, like being an actress, then they're behind you. But they always, in some sense, rationalise it, and I heard my mother's rationalisation only last week. She said, 'Well, of course, some time ago, one of your forebears was illegitimate,' and that seems to explain the fact that I became an actress.

****

Diana: I've taken my clothes off on stage.

Michael: Do you have to talk yourself into it?

Diana: Yes. I come from Yorkshire. Nobody takes their clothes off in Yorkshire except on a Friday night. So, Monday, Tuesday, Wednesday, Thursday, Saturday and Sunday, I had to talk myself into it. It was difficult.

Michael: How do you finally justify it in the end? Because it seems to me that, in the end, it was justifiable, because of the structure of the play.

Diana: Yes, it's a bit facile. Those are the very things that I said. However, because I was talking to the national newspapers at the time, and because they only had about three lines in which to quote me, I didn't see any point in talking about what I really thought was the issue, and that is that we all have breasts and we all have penises and we all have bodies in common, and that is not the most precious thing we possess. The most precious things we possess are our personalities and our spirits, and I think that from the

Victorian era onwards, too much emphasis has been placed on covering your body. I think to trust each other, and to love each other sufficiently to show our spirit, is infinitely more important.

Michael: On the question of nudity, can I ask you why you turned down the offer *Playboy* made you to pose nude?

Diana: It's not my reply, it's somebody else's, which I cared to quote at that time, which is, 'I don't want a navel stapled.' And also nipples always tend to be slightly purple in *Playboy*.

Michael: Well, some people might have purple nipples.

Diana: Yes, they might, but not everybody.

Michael: What about pictures of male nudity. Does the picture of a male nude turn you on particularly?

Diana: No. But nudes don't turn me on. I don't turn myself on nude, and I very much hope that I didn't turn other people on nude. In fact, when I was doing *Abelard and Heloise*, I think it was in the provinces, in Newcastle, I got a letter from a post-office worker – I know because it was written on a telegram form – and he said, 'I don't know why you bother. My girlfriend's tits are much larger than yours.' Well, although that was a bit of a put-down, it made my point.

****

Michael: You're a very independent person, aren't you? Where does that stem from, do you think?

Diana: I find independence can be a plus and a minus, and in terms of relationships, it can really detract, because whenever anything is remotely rocky, you withdraw into yourself very fast indeed and that may not be the answer. I figured out it probably started at the age of seven when I was sent away to school, and I don't wish remotely to give my mother a bad conscience about this – it was a necessity. But if you can imagine all the things that, as a child, you have taken to be permanent – your mother, your father, the house, the regimen, what you eat, the teasing, the intimacy, the loving and the knowing – all that is suddenly cut off completely, and you're put into a building, which is strange, with a lot of children, who are totally strange, and a discipline that is very strange to you because it is a discipline that exists for the good of the community as opposed to just yourself. That makes you survive as a sole entity. You have to learn to rely upon yourself.

Michael: What kind of a school was it?

Diana: Oh, it was posh. The first one I went to was Church of England, but the second one, when I was eleven, was Quaker. Moravian they call it. It's Czechoslovakian. In 1755 or something, they trekked from Moravia, because they were being harried, and there were settlements all over England, and they are basically Quaker. The men are on one side of the churchyard and the women are on the other. Never the twain shall meet.

Michael: Did it make you a rebellious person?

Diana: Yes. But then it's awfully difficult because everywhere you turn, there's no echo. Rebellion is self-destructive in lots of ways, and I rebelled constantly at school. It wasn't until I left school and didn't have to rebel any more, that I began to develop.

Michael: I read one very interesting thing about you, that at school you used to keep Smarties up your . . .

Diana: . . . knickers. Oh yes. Well, such was the school that kids nowadays just wouldn't understand it. We had sweets twice a week, and these sweets were sent to us by our mothers, fathers, aunts – whoever was around. They were put into sweetie jars and brought to the table on Saturday night after supper, just before prep. You were allowed to take two sweets out of this sweetie jar. Now, part of the uniform at the school was two pairs of knickers – you had white knicker linings, which you wore underneath and changed twice a week, and blue knickers, which you wore over your white knicker linings and changed once a week. A good way of stashing away sweets was, when the sweetie jars were brought to us, quickly unscrew them, spread the sweets out on the table, look as if you were choosing, but at the same time, scoop up a lot of very small ones, like Smarties, and shove them up between your knickers and your knicker lining, which actually made for a very sticky prep. You'd be sitting there writing, and a chocolate drip happened.

Michael: Did you know when you were at school that you wanted to be an actress?

Diana: Yes, I did, but it was a very unpopular decision. The headmistress, teachers and everyone considered it useless – what is an actress? She's useless. She's not a nurse, she's not even going to be a wife and mother, possibly at some time, but acting is the one career that can supplant that. She's not going to be a secretary. It's not even respectable. I was out on a limb, following something that was instinctive, without much encouragement. My parents did because they loved me, but they didn't understand what it involved.

****

Michael: You've got into hot water recently when you revealed in a newspaper article that you were in the habit of biting your baby's bum.

Diana: Yes.

Michael: First of all, why?

Diana: I can't resist.

Michael: Really?

Diana: My poor daughter. I say to her, 'Rachel, come here, I have to bite your bottom,' and she goes backwards and takes her knickers down and waits for this nutter to do what it has to do at the back. But the skin, the flesh, you just have to sink your teeth into it. And I've had letters from readers saying, 'Oh, how dare you, how dare you bring sex, filthy sex, into your relationship.' I don't care. But it's not only my child. I'll bite anybody else's.

Michael: Have you ever had your bum bitten?

Diana: Do you know, I don't think I did. I think that's what I missed. I don't think my mother or my father bit my baby bottom, but Rachel's chums, if there's a bare bottom going, it's got my teeth in it sooner or later.

Michael: Of course, your bottom gained some notoriety, did it not, some time ago when you did Tom Stoppard's play, *Jumpers*.

Diana: Yes. I had to bare my bottom. It wasn't just one of these cases where the director thought it would be good for the play. It was actually in the text, so I had to do it, and the only way I could do it was to make it up. Night after night I used to put three layers of dark Egyptian on my bum, because otherwise it just looked like a piece of old cod. Well, bottoms do, you know.

Michael: Have you got letters about it?

Diana: I got letters. I'd meet men years later who said, 'I fell in love with your bottom,' which is a testament to making up your bottom.

****

Michael: Do you have fun on the stage?

Diana: Oh yes. I believe in it.

Michael: What do you do?

Diana: Oh, naughtiness.

Michael: Like what?

Diana: Well, for the most part I just love doing it, but there are occasions when it becomes, you know . . . I was in *Macbeth*, which is a very difficult play. First of all, I've actually never seen a production that works totally, because of the witches and the drama of it all, and I discovered that Lady Macbeth was a great bore to do. At one point, the director had Denis Quilley sliding his hand down the front of my bodice and massaging a breast, and it was a matinée, and I muttered to him under my breath, 'Down a bit, left a bit, right a bit . . . golden shot.'

Michael: Throughout your career, you've been more or less universally acclaimed by the critics.

Diana: Yes, touch wood.

Michael: What was the worst thing that's been said about you?

Diana: I think every actor who's truly honest remembers their worst notice, because it actually carves itself on your soul. You live with it for weeks before you finally exorcise the pain of it, and this was a gentleman in New York, writing about the nude scene in *Abelard and Heloise*, and he said, 'Diana Rigg is built like the brick mausoleum with insufficient flying buttresses.' Live with that one. Doing a nude scene, what's more.

1972–80

Memories of Judy Garland

Blake Edwards

Michael: In your long career in the industry, you must have seen terrible things happen to child stars.

Blake: Well, I think Judy Garland is a classic example. I grew up with Mickey Rooney and that whole MGM younger crowd that was so important in those days, and if you examine Judy's career as a child star and then what eventually happened to her, it was very, very sad. She was a lovely, talented lady who, in my opinion, was really destroyed by the business, destroyed by the studio. Some pretty frightening things were happening at that time, and I know them to be true, to be factual. They aren't just stories.

Michael: What sorts of things?

Blake: Heavy pill-taking. They would put her on uppers to keep her going and on downers to get her to relax.

Michael: As a child?

Blake: Yeah, sure, and that can only lead to a really bad scene, and it did with Judy.

Michael: That's terrible, the way that they take a human being and just make the person a property, isn't it?

Blake: Just a commodity. You have it today, but not as it was in those days, that great big daddy running a major studio and treating his people like a bunch of bad little children.

1974

Jimmy Tarbuck

Michael: You worked with Judy Garland once, didn't you?
Jimmy: Yes.
Michael: Did you feel as sad working with her as I did when I watched her?
Jimmy: Well no, because I saw her magic. I saw her do a midnight matinée when she first introduced Liza Minnelli to the British public at the Palladium, and she was absolutely sensational. I was in the pantomime there, and she was at the Talk of the Town. She was ill and I stood in one night. I'd been on for about forty minutes and she walked on, brought the house down. She said, 'I'm sorry I'm late. You stay on the stage, little man,' and she did the act, and was magic.

Then they had a gala performance at the Palladium, live, and asked me to compère it. They'd got all the big names, and she insisted on them playing three minutes of all her hits – 'The Man who got Away', 'Swanney', 'Over the Rainbow'. Jack and the band start playing, and a man from the other side says, 'The cow's not going on.' The language was uproarious and I said, 'You're not going to get her on by swearing at the woman,' because she was a very frail figure by now.

I walked into the dressing room and said, 'Hiya, sweetheart. Look, I've introduced you, they're a fantastic audience. Do you want to take a stroll down with me and have a look? If you don't want to go on, don't bother. If you do, if you want me to come on with you or anything . . .' I'd got the Palladium's old stagehands stood there at the side, and as she's come out they all said, 'Nice to see you back, Miss Garland. Welcome back, Miss Garland,' because the woman was a great, great star, and you mustn't kick anyone in the guts when they're maybe not as great as they were. And she turned round as she walked on and said, 'You've got a lot of class, little man.' It was magic.

1976

7 Leading Men

Michael Caine

Sir Laurence Olivier once said – and we must never tire of quoting the classics – that Michael Caine was 'wonderful good company, ceaselessly funny and a brilliant actor'. He was also a wonderful guest on a talk show, with an unending supply of anecdote and opinion. He loves talking. He once said, 'I always give interviews. If the *Poultry Farmer's Weekly Gazette* rings me, I'm delighted to be asked my opinion.' I interviewed him many times – in fact, as often as possible – and found him an endlessly fascinating man. He takes acting seriously and is very accomplished, but he is the opposite of being a 'luvvy'. He sees himself as a jobbing actor, and if sometimes the film is a turkey, it doesn't curb his enthusiasm. As he once observed, 'They pay you for a bad movie like they do for a good one. I've bought one or two good houses from indifferent films.'

I play a lot of working-class people, which is what I love to do. I came into this business because I saw working-class people in English movies when I was young, and they were always played by guys from middle-class families. They were always saying, 'Yes, Guv, it's a fair cop and I'll come quietly, put the handcuffs on.' And they never, never knew how to fight. I became an actor to get my own type of person right. I thought, 'I can do that better than he's doing it.' There were just these guys poncing about, trying to be working class and grovelling. The working class never grovelled. They don't give a toss about anybody. The class thing in this country was much, much stronger when I was very young.

My father was a Billingsgate fish-market porter, and we lived in a prefab at the Elephant and Castle. He used to steal fish for us and always stole too much to put in our tiny fridge. One night, he brought home a lot of haddock. My brother and I slept in the same bedroom. My father was a stickler for health and always insisted that we sleep with the windows open for fresh air. So it was always freezing in the bedrooms, and he used to keep the fish in there, on the sideboard. This night he put some smoked haddock in there, and what I didn't know is that smoked haddock is covered in phosphorous. In the middle of the night I woke up and there was all this glowing at the end of the bed. I thought it was a ghost! It frightened the life out of me.

My father died of cancer in St Thomas's Hospital, and when he was dead and I was leaving the ward, the sister came and said, 'These are your father's belongings,' and she gave me whatever he had. He had one-and-elevenpence, which is about 9p. That's what he had, and he'd worked all his life, very, very hard, and that's what he had to show for a life. He didn't own the house, we lived in a prefab, for Christ's sake. We were bombed out and we lived in a prefab, and even the radio was Radio Rentals, which was half-a-crown a week. This radio was probably worth £10 and that's why the poor can't afford to be poor. Over the years, he'd probably paid somewhere near £100 for that radio, because he didn't have the money to buy it in the first place.

It made me determined to make something of myself, to try to get out of there. I read a lot. I was one of those very bolshie working-class people. I went to the library five days a week, learning, trying to find out what was going on and how to get away, using my imagination.

I don't know when I got a personality. I didn't have it for about twenty years – the first twenty years of my life I had no personality at all. I was a sort of shadow figure. We always have that period in our lives when we really don't know who we are and who we wanna be, and there comes a time when all of us, we all eventually invent ourselves and become what we've invented. I didn't invent myself because I became an actor. One day I called myself Michael Caine, and then I was someone else.

I was a National Service man, an infantry man – they tried to get rid of me! I was on patrol in Korea. It was like the

First World War – trenches on either side and no-man's-land in the middle, which each side tries to control at night, and then, if you're not lucky, you get sent out in the middle to control no-man's-land. I was not very good at that.

For me, it was rather like an initiation, like the Masai – they give you a short spear and say go and kill a lion to prove you're a man. Every man, I'm sure, wonders, if I was in a dangerous situation, would I burst into tears or would I run away? Would I be a coward and shame myself? And it's a very important thing to go through, as a young man. It happened to me accidentally in Korea when we were sent on reconnaissance – an officer, a corporal, another soldier and me. We got out there and could hear all the voices, and we knew we were surrounded. You literally pee yourself with fear. But we just sat there, all wondering what are we gonna do? And all four of us said, 'We'll die expensive!'

We decided that we'd charge. We knew we were gonna die. There must have been a hundred of them, and we charged. And we charged the wrong way! The four of us silly sods went charging through the rice paddies to surprise them, towards their lines. What we didn't know was they'd all gone round the back behind us to stop us getting back to our lines, and we just kept running and running, all night. When we got back, I realised what I'd done. I'd said, 'I'm gonna die dear, I'll die expensive,' and we were ready to kill as many of those sons of bitches as we could before we died. It was an extremely valuable experience because I knew then that in any situation in my life, you go against me, it's gonna be dear. You may win, but it's gonna cost you.

I was in South Africa, making *Zulu*. I'd never played a big part in a movie before, and I'd never been invited to rushes. I was just a small part, bit actor, and you always have a vision of yourself that's very good. So I went to see the rushes and this figure comes on, a weird looking figure with a strange voice, and I thought, 'What a berk.' Then I realised it's me and I threw up. The movie camera really gets into you. You think you're so great and then you look up to the big screen and it's, 'Oh my God.' I thought my career was over.

My first trip to Hollywood, Shirley MacLaine wanted me to play opposite her in a picture called *Gambit*. I was flown to Hollywood, and put in the Beverly Hills Hotel, and then nothing happened. I just sat there, no one rang and nothing happened. Then, I was in the lobby one day and I saw John Wayne. He landed a helicopter on the green outside and he'd come straight from the desert, covered in dust and dressed as Hondo. He came in and went to the desk, looked at me and he said, 'What's your name?' I said, 'Michael Caine.' He said, 'Are you in a movie called *Alfie*?' So I said, 'Yes.' He said, 'I think you're going to be a big star, kid, but remember one thing.' He said, 'talk low, talk slow and don't say too much.' And he said, 'Oh, another thing, never wear suede shoes.' I said, 'What?' He said, 'Never wear suede shoes.' So I said, 'Why not?' He said, 'Because you'll be in the goddamn toilet, you're taking a pee and there'll be a guy next to you and he'll look across, and this is what happened to me. The guy went, "John Wayne!" and he peed all over my shoes, my suede shoes, which, of course, were ruined.'

My philosophy is use the difficulty. I was rehearsing a play when I was a very young actor. I had to come on in this scene and was behind the flaps, waiting to open the door. There was an improvised scene between a husband and wife going on, and they got carried away and started throwing things. He threw a chair and it lodged in the doorway. I went to open the door and just got my head round and said, 'I'm sorry, sir, I can't get it.' He said, 'What do you mean?' 'There's a chair there.' He said to me, 'Use the difficulty.' I asked what he meant. He said, 'If it's a comedy, fall over it. If it's a drama, pick it up and smash it. Use the difficulty.' Now I took that in to my own life. Anything bad happens, you've gotta use the difficulty – how can we get out of this? There's never anything so bad that you cannot use that difficulty. If you can use it a quarter of one per cent to your advantage, you're ahead. You didn't let it get you down. Use the difficulty, that's my philosophy. Also, an added philosophy is avoid them if you can! At all costs!

1999–2006

Dustin Hoffman

If you read what people thought of working with Dustin Hoffman, you might have a sleepless night before interviewing him. Everyone agrees that the star of such films as *The Graduate*, *Tootsie*, *Midnight Cowboy*, *Rain Man* and *Kramer vs Kramer* is a compelling screen presence but not everyone is a fan of his creative process. Robert Mitchum said of Hoffman, 'I don't understand this method stuff.' Laurence Olivier asked him why he stayed up all night. Dustin looked really bad. He said in order to prepare for the scene in which he was supposed to have been up all night. Olivier said, 'Dear boy, why don't you just act the part?'

The writer Larry Gelbart said, 'Dustin Hoffman is the kind of officer who has to take the hill no matter how many bodies are left at the bottom. I told his wife [after *Tootsie*] I'd never work again for an Oscar winner who was shorter than his statue.'

The interview I did with Hoffman in 1975 was a battle, but eventually we reached the top of the hill together – more or less.

Michael: I read somewhere that you didn't like doing these interviews. Could that be right?

Dustin: That's correct, that's correct.

Michael: Why is that?

Dustin: It makes me tighten up in my throat, and it makes my heart beat . . .

Michael: Do you genuinely get nervous about going on television and being questioned?

Dustin: Yes.

Michael: Why is that?

Dustin: I fear that it's not going to work out very well.

Michael: So how come you wanted to be an actor? First of all you wanted to be a stage actor I presume, not a film star, or was your first fantasy to be a film star?

Dustin: Well, I didn't think about acting until I got into college, and my first fantasy was to be a sex-symbol film star.

Michael: That's as good a fantasy as any. But you became that later on, didn't you? So you got the ambition at college to be an actor, and then went to New York?

Dustin: Yes.

Michael: What was the first thing you did off-Broadway?

Dustin: I played a Nazi German hunchbacked homosexual with a bad limp, and that is the first truthful thing I've said on this show.

Michael: Did you play it well?

Dustin: Yes.

Michael: And what happened? Did you get . . .

Dustin: I got a lot of letters.

Michael: What, from homosexual Germans with limps?

Dustin: No doubt. It was only for three weeks. It was in a church. It was what we call off-off-off-off-Broadway and I got an agent out of that, and then he made sure I didn't work for a year, and then a year later I was in another play by the same author, and that started off my luck.

Michael: Because it was in this play you were seen by somebody and asked to go for *The Graduate*, is that what happened?

Dustin: No, no.

Michael: What did happen?

Dustin: The play after that.

Michael: It was a tremendous success, *The Graduate*. Why do you think it was such a huge success?

Dustin: They didn't think it would be. I think they thought it would get an art-house, small, cult kind of following, and as a matter of fact it got rather mixed reviews. It did not have lines outside the door like *Love Story* did, which came from a best-selling book, and no one seemed to know what was going to happen with it until about four weeks after it opened in one New York theatre and suddenly lines started. Apparently, it was word-of-mouth. I don't know the reason, if there is one. I think there were a lot of excellent things about the film – the music as much as anything, by Simon and Garfunkel. That will probably continue to go down as being one of the greatest music soundtracks to be used.

Michael: I think one other reason was that the character you play struck a chord in any man – that marvellous dithering, the moment of seduction. Was your own first sexual experience anything like that at all?

Dustin: When you say 'first sexual experience', what kind do you mean?

Michael: Any kind you care to talk about. The first time you ever made love to a woman? In the film, in the sequence, that was the first time you were going make love, right?

Dustin: Yes, well, I think it wasn't necessarily. Everyone seemed to think he was a virgin. I never thought of him as that when I did the film. I thought it was the first time he was making love to a woman who was old enough to be his mother, because she was his mother's friend, so I was always looking at it from that point of view. One of the things that Mike Nichols did, which I thought was wonderful, is we rehearsed it for three weeks, which you never do. And when the first day of shooting came, the entire cast could have gone on stage and performed *The Graduate* from beginning to end. We knew all the lines, and we had improvised all the way through and some of the best things in the film came out of improvisation. It was Nichols' point of view that you always must be as close to yourself in the most personal way to convey not only truth, but humour. Real humour perhaps is the purest truth when it works. In this scene, I'm just trying to get a room key. Now, I had never really done that in my life. As a matter of fact, I still haven't. I've never gone to a hotel. I usually just go behind a tree.

Michael: That's the answer to my question, but go on.

Dustin: When we were rehearsing, he said, 'You must find in your life, or think about, what is the most painful thing for you to do, with sexual connotations, in a public way,' because here he was in front of people at the desk. For some reason, and I've never understood, because I was always thought of as being rather dirty when I was in school, nevertheless I could never go to a chemist and order male prophylactics, as opposed to female prophylactics. And though I had not had a sexual experience, I thought I should be ready if and when it came. So I thought I should stock up, and I always would plan on a day when I'd feel brave and I'd say, 'This is the day I'm going to do it,' and I'd walk into the drug store and search out who was behind the counter. If it was a woman, I'd turn around and walk right back out. I wanted someone young but it was an older man, which was difficult. If it was someone somehow like a big brother image or someone close to my age, I thought I could do it, and I would go up and say, 'I'd like some Kleenex and some razor blades,' though I didn't shave. I'd get to that word and I couldn't do it, and I never in my life bought any prophylactics. So when we rehearsed this scene, he said, 'That's it,' and that hotel scene was really the pharmacy.

1975

Robert Redford

When Robert Redford was at his peak in Hollywood, the film critic Pauline Kael observed: 'A good script is a script to which Robert Redford has committed himself. A bad script is a script Robert Redford has turned down. A script that needs work is a script about which Robert Redford has yet to make up his mind.' He is one of the most successful actors of Hollywood's modern age. His partnership with Paul Newman in *Butch Cassidy* and *The Sting* was a flawless blend of charm and sex appeal, two great stars working in perfect harmony. Redford also won an Oscar for directing *Ordinary People* and founded the Sundance Film Festival. When he appeared on the show, he was stopped by a commissionaire as he went to enter the studio. 'But I'm Robert Redford,' he explained. 'They all say that,' said the doorman.

I wasn't a good student, which seemed like a good reason to drop out. I was not interested, I was not ready to be educated – at least in the formal, normal academic manner. I'd felt for some time, since I was very young, that I learned more from travel and experience than by sitting in a classroom, particularly in the school system I was raised in, which was very poor, in the State of California. It was a lower middle-class upbringing in an area that wasn't privileged at all, and so there was no real stimulation to my background and education. I spent most of my time looking out the windows, and doodling and sketching and cutting class, and things of that sort. So it was never really meant to be, me and the academic institutions. I was meant to leave it early or start later, so I left it early.

I was in a little town called Tours, just outside Paris, hitch-hiking to the south of France. It was so cold, and I had no way to get warm. I had no place to go. I had very little money and I was running back and forth in the street while waiting for a ride, and it didn't come. It was the middle of the night and the town had closed up. Finally, I just got tired of running and I started to get worried that I wasn't going to be able to get warm, and across the street was this mound of manure. And so I went over there and just planted myself in it and stayed there for a while until dawn came and I could go into a pastry shop. But needless to say, it was tough to get a piece of pastry! Going to Paris, getting out of California, getting out of the United States, I was beginning to feel like I was learning, which I never felt before.

I've always been interested in the West. I don't know why or how it started initially, unless it had to do with that feeling of wanting to get out of Los Angeles. I've always been attracted to, and comfortable with, the space. It was really just as simple as that. I like to ride, I like to climb, I like to be outdoors and *Butch Cassidy and the Sundance Kid* was a film that for me was very comfortable. The studio didn't want me for it, though, because I was not known. They were trying to have a star comparable to Paul Newman and I practically did it for nothing because I just felt comfortable playing that role. So I probably had more fun making that film than any other I've made.

Paul and I have done a couple of films together, and we played jokes on one another. He's obsessed with racing, and he would get so boring talking about racing that sometimes I just couldn't take it. And so, for his fiftieth birthday, I found an old wrecked 1964 Porsche that had been completely demolished, and had the thing wrapped up and delivered to his back door as a birthday present. We had homes that weren't so far from each other in Connecticut. Then I walked away from it and waited to hear, and he didn't say anything.

About three weeks later I came to my house and in the foyer was this huge package – I mean really huge. And I opened it, uncrated it and it was this gigantic block of metal, which had been melted down from an old wrecked car. And I thought OK. I liked that. I thought that was really good. So I didn't mention it to him. And I couldn't get it out of the house, either. So I just let it sit there for weeks on end. I would see him from time to time, we would see each other socially, our families would get together, and finally he couldn't take it any more. He said, 'Say, have you been to the house?' 'I've been to the house.' And he said, 'Anything different there?' I said, 'No, why? Oh, the basement was leaking.' And he said, 'Nothing else?' I said, 'No.' It drove him crazy.

So I got on to the people who had delivered the thing at some great cost – I think about $75 just to deliver it – and made arrangements to have this wrecking company come and take it out of the house. I had it melted down further and hired a sculptor to do a piece of garden sculpture and had it delivered back to his garden. As far as I know, that's where it still is. It may end up as a ring on somebody's finger.

Street reaction varies, from a freak-out to ignoring me totally, so that I have to tap somebody on the shoulder and say, 'Excuse me, do you know who I am?' I'll tell you the reaction I like the most, or the one that made me feel curiously the best – I guess it reminded me of my reactions when I was younger and set me straight. Pretty good friends set me straight and my kids set me straight, but this one really set me straight. I was in Beverly Hills, which is unreal enough as it is, and as I went to cross the street a car comes rolling by full of young teenagers. They spot me as I'm about to step off the kerb, and the car slows down. I thought, 'Oh, here it comes.' And they're screaming, clawing to roll the windows down. And finally they get the window down as the car rolls by and the guy yells out, 'Robert Redford!' And I said, 'Hey!' And he said, 'You are such an asshole!' OK, that was all right!

1980

Woody Allen

Maybe Woody Allen was the one who first kindled my ambition to host a talk show. I saw him on *The Eamonn Andrews Show* when he was known only as a stand-up comedian, and the idea of spending my working life sitting opposite such a funny and fascinating man seemed irresistible. When my chance came, I soon discovered that not everyone was as amusing and interesting as Woody Allen, particularly Woody Allen. By the time I did a one-guest show with Allen he had transformed his career by writing, appearing in and directing thirty or more movies, some of which deserve a place in the top 100 movies of all time. Moreover, the Jewish joker of the fifties had been replaced by someone wary of the media in the aftermath of a scandal involving Allen having an affair with Soon-Yi, the adopted daughter of his long-time girlfriend Mia Farrow. Allen later married Soon-Yi and began to work almost exclusively in Europe. I only mention this aspect of Allen's career because it became an issue when setting up the interview. He didn't want to talk about it. I felt it was a line of enquiry legitimised by the effect it had on his career. Read on.

Michael: What was it like, growing up with those parents of yours?

Woody: It was a little hectic because I was always the great disappointment in the family. In that kind of Jewish family they want their kid to be a doctor or a lawyer or a pharmacist and I went into show business. Show business to them is nothing – it's ephemeral. You can't put your finger on it, it's crazy. They think that I just never got into a secure field or anything. And so they were always disappointed and felt that I was not a good student. I was someone who played hooky from school and got into trouble, and went into show business, which, as I say, they didn't like. And all around me were model kids. All my friends became doctors and lawyers and psychiatrists and dentists, and I was a writer of jokes. What is that? What's a joke? They didn't understand that for second. And so they despised me. It took me years and years finally to get cooperative with them in a way that I think only Eugene O'Neill would have understood.

Michael: You once said that you thought seriously as a child, you contemplated being a criminal?

Woody: I did contemplate this, because it was one of the few interesting avenues open to me. And I used to get on and say that I failed. I couldn't do it because I couldn't make the height requirement. But the truth of the matter is that it was something that came up. I was an amateur magician when I was younger, and did many, many card tricks, and became very good at them. And from doing card tricks, I started to learn how to deal seconds and deal off the bottom, and false shuffle, and false cut, and I found that I could cheat other kids playing cards very, very easily, because I had a lot of skill. And no morality at all. Absolutely none. So I started playing cards, and I started winning money, and I saw that the road to riches could very easily be a life of crime. I thought to myself, 'Hey, I could probably rob banks or burglarise jewellery stores and be very clever about it.' I'm imaginative, I've got a sense of humour, I've got an original approach, maybe this could be an interesting career for me. And I thought about it for a while, and talked about certain con-man schemes with my friends, but by that time some of my jokes were already being accepted by radio and television, and I saw the light at the end of the tunnel and thought, 'Hey, I could probably make a living being a comic, a writer of comic material.' And I succeeded at that very rapidly. Fortunately, as soon as I started doing it, I started succeeding, and I started getting paid for it. So it saved me from a life of crime.

Michael: Of course, that was a long time ago, and now things have changed totally for you. You went into motion pictures and the rest, as they say, is history. If you were to be pushed into a corner, and asked about the movies that, in your view, were the three or four best movies you've done, what would they be?

Woody: What would *I* think?

Michael: Yes, your own view.

Woody: They probably won't coincide with other people's feelings. Some of the best movies I've done, from my point of view, would be *Purple Rose of Cairo*, *Zelig*, *Bullets over Broadway* and *Husbands and Wives*. And the reason I'd say that is because when I set out to write a film, I have a very grandiose conception in mind. I sit in my room at home, on my bed, and I write this thing, and I think, 'Oh, this is so great! Wait till people see this, they're going to think this is a major work of art!' And I'm very confident. And then, when I have actually to shoot the film and cast it, and make the real decisions that make the film, I always screw it up. So then I look at the film and think, 'My God, I had such a great idea in my bedroom, what did I do?' So those four films come very close to what I conceived in my bedroom. But my other films are so far off the mark. I had ideas that were so good and so powerful, and I wrecked them through carelessness and incompetence and stupidity and greed and gluttony, all these terrible things.

Michael: Could I ask you about the crisis you had recently in your life regarding your wife Soon-Yi and all the surrounding stories there were about that? Did that have an effect on your perception within America? Did it make you less popular? Did it have an effect on your work? Did it affect your mood?

Woody: No, it was an interesting thing. I had always been unpopular and when I was going through a public talk about my life – my private life – all it did, those people who had never liked me reconfirmed it. They said, 'I always knew he was a terrible little cockroach and this proves it.' Those people who liked me continued to like me. It was of no consequence that way. I was never popular and this didn't diminish my popularity or enhance it in any way. It was just a public airing of my private life, which is a terribly painful thing. Nobody likes that and me least of all because I'm such a private person. But you know, this is the down-side of celebrity.

Michael: Precisely.

Woody: Celebrity has a good side and a bad side. The bad side is your private life vanishes. You're always a victim of paparazzi, and journalists who want to write about every move in your private life. But there's a good side and the good side is that if I want to go to a restaurant and it's booked and I call up, they give me a table, and if I want to get tickets to a show or a basketball game, I get the tickets before somebody else. Or if I'm home on the weekend on a Sunday and I feel sick, I can call my doctor and he comes right over, whereas somebody else gets a Wednesday appointment. This is the upside. The bad side is that you have no private life.

Michael: But in your case it was particularly hurtful because the allegations being made against you were so extraordinary. A lot of people believed, probably still do, that you married your daughter.

Woody: I know, but that's illegal. You can't.

Michael: But you know what I'm saying, that was the public misconception.

Woody: Right, but that's crazy. If I went by that, I would be too crazy. You can't legally marry your daughter. Of course she's not my daughter, but yes, the public perception is often, you know – they get this from the tabloids. And this is what you have to resign yourself to as a celebrity, that your life is going to be banner-lined in tabloids in the most lurid way, and you never get used to it, but it's worth it to be able to get the tickets and the tables.

Michael: You must admit, in your case, that once you'd actually formed the association with Soon-Yi, you must have understood that you were going to be scrutinised in a rather particular way.

Woody: Yes, but I was always scrutinised and I never mind that. My life has always been a very open book. Even when I first started as a comedian, I always spoke freely about my life, about my marriage, my girlfriends, about getting thrown out of school, about my psychoanalysis. I felt I had nothing serious to hide and it was amusing to me, and I thought it would be amusing to other people.

Michael: The downside of it, as far as you're concerned, I imagine, would be the relationship you have with your children now – a legal requirement having been imposed upon you, by a judge, that you're not allowed to see them very much.

Woody: My relationship, yes, is a very . . . it's very sad. It was a very sad outcome. But I gave it my best shot. There's nothing really I could do about that.

Michael: Is it the case you can't see one of your children now, and the other one you can? Is that the sort of silly, topsy-turvy manner of it?

Woody: You know, why are you so interested? I feel that you have a morbid interest. Why?

Michael: I don't have a morbid interest in it at all. I think if I'm doing an interview with you about your life and times, I should mention an episode that has created an awful lot of public misconception.

Woody: But that's always going to be, I'm resigned to that.

Michael: I'm not going to pursue it to the point where you're going to be embarrassed by it. I wouldn't do that at all.

Woody: You promise?

Michael: I promise.

Woody: Why don't I trust him? I should, he's only being nice to me. OK, you can continue.

Michael: It was just that one final question.

Woody: Go ahead, you can still ask it.

Michael: The consequence of it, from your point of view, the worst one of all, has been the fact that it has disturbed your relationship with your children.

Woody: Yes, that has been very, very painful. And, as I say, I gave that my best shot. But there's nothing you can do, unless you're experienced at really being in the legal system. And in the United States – I don't know if it's true here – but the legal system, the matrimonial system, is so complex and so difficult, and so heavily weighted against fathers, that it's a very tough, uphill fight. And so it was a fight that I made, but could not win.

1999

Michael Crawford

If you want a demonstration of versatility, think of the gormless Frank Spencer in *Some Mothers Do 'ave 'em* and then conjure up the image of the Phantom in *Phantom of the Opera*. Any new visitor to our planet would take some convincing they were played by one and the same person. The real Michael Crawford is, on the face of it, much more like Frank Spencer and yet there was always the feeling of a lurking and significant sadness. He told his story on the show, the account of the father he worshipped as a hero turning out not to be his real dad. On stage, Michael Crawford has a reputation for being difficult and demanding. It is often the price you pay for being a perfectionist. As a friend and companion, he's a treat.

I'm sure I was the last person Andrew Lloyd-Webber actually thought of for the part. I think he was just about to offer it to his driver! And you talk about things happening and fate. I had worked with my singing teacher, Ian Adam, from the very first day of rehearsal for *Billy*. The sort of songs that I sang through the years, and used to develop my voice, were Scottish folk songs on to Italian arias, but that would be behind closed doors, in the studio where he taught. Nobody ever heard me sing this way – I'd never done anything with great passion and feeling in public. One day, I was rehearsing with Ian, and Andrew arrived with Sarah Brightman – they were married then. They were early for her lesson, so they waited in the kitchen downstairs while I was singing upstairs. Andrew heard me singing Handel's 'Care Selve'. I got to the end, said goodbye and left, and apparently Andrew came upstairs and asked, 'Who was that singing just now? Who was that?' Ian said, 'It was Michael Crawford,' and Andrew said, 'I think we may have found our Phantom.' And that's how it came about.

I think *Some Mothers* . . . got quite a hold, and it was an extraordinary period of my life. I think what we tried to bring into the stories were things that really did happen. When we did the birth, I had a pretty good contribution because thirty years ago when children were born, it wasn't really a very good idea that men were there. They didn't really welcome men into the delivery room. Somehow I wangled my way in there with Gabrielle, whom I was married to then. We were in the room waiting and she said, I think, 'Don't make me laugh – I think it's coming!' I said, 'That's all right, that's all right, I'm trained. I've read Dr Spock from beginning to end, three times backwards.' I said, 'Just wait there, wait there. You stay there, I'll go and get the nurse.'

And so I ran outside, went and got the nurse, brought her in and said, 'My wife's having a baby now.' She said, 'This is the right place to have it,' and she got the stretcher, the trolley, and I said, 'You get on there and I'll walk.' We went downstairs and along the corridor and I'm holding on to Gabrielle's foot. You don't know what you should do but you just know you want to be there to be supportive, but I'm holding her ankle. I'm being dragged along by the trolley going, 'That's OK, everything's all right.' And we get downstairs and they say, 'All right, just go and scrub up Mr Crawford.' And I said, 'No, no, no, it's fine, I washed before I came out. I'm ready.' He said, 'We all scrub up here.'

So I'm in there, and with all the tapes and the mask, and red whiskers coming through my beard, I looked like a wasp's backside. So I go into the delivery room finally and was told, 'Mr Crawford, stay there!' I said, 'But isn't it gonna happen down there?' He said, 'Yes, but get back to the other end of the bed!' So I was sent up the other end of the bed. He said, 'Hold your wife.' I said, 'Where?' He said, 'Just hold her hand, man!' So I held her hand. He said to speak to her. I said, 'Hi, how are you?' She said, 'I'm having a baby.' I said, 'Good, good! I know, I know! I'm really excited.' I said, 'And you relax 'cos I'm fine.' And the sweat's pouring down me. In the end, I'm on top of the bed screaming and shouting, 'I see, it's a boy! It's a boy! It's a boy!' The doctor said, 'It's a girl, Mr

Crawford, it's a girl!' I said, 'Well what's that?' He said, 'That's the umbilical cord!' This thing was getting longer and longer!

My mother was married to a young pilot officer in the Royal Air Force, during the war years, and it was, by all accounts from her, a beautiful marriage, an idyllic marriage. They lived on the Broads in Cambridgeshire, and they had a little red MG sports car – it was like out of a film. And they loved each other. I could never deny the love she had for this man. One could see it in their photographs and hear it in her voice in later years. I grew up with this man as my hero, as my father, and when I got to the age of about fifteen, sixteen, I went to see a war memorial because I wanted to see his name. I wanted something more tangible.

He was killed in the war. Life was so fragile then. He didn't come back from one mission. So I grew up with that, and then I went to see this memorial. When I got there – I took a friend from school – I found his name, and it had 'died 1939'. I was born in 1942. So I went back to school and sought out my maths master. He was a very reasonable man but under no circumstances could he identify that this could be my father. So at this age, I discovered he wasn't my father and I had, in fact, been born two and a half years later. My mother had met somebody else, had a brief relationship, and out of that I was born. But we were a working-class family, so no one could talk about it, no one could discuss that.

We lived with my nan, my mum's mum, in Sheerness, the Isle of Sheppey in Kent. My mum was sent away to Wiltshire to stay with my aunts and I was born there in 1942. My nan had thought out this great code. There were no telephones really, in those days, and the postal service was too slow, so they would send a telegram. And to save the whole village knowing – when you sent a telegram, the post mistress usually got it and then the whole village got it – the telegram would read 'parcel arrived safely' if it was a girl and 'parcel arrived safely tied with string' for a boy. And I had a piece of string, so I was a boy!

I can't explain families, the way we don't talk about some things. Some things aren't discussed. No matter how open our family was, with the Irish heritage, and we talk about anything, this was something that wasn't discussed, because there was a stigma attached to it and there was shame attached to it. And I'm stuttering and stammering my way through this story. It's still difficult to tell.

I just think if ever there was a man I wanted as a father, he's the one. I have his wings, and his service book, and the books he won at school. I have those things and that was sufficient for me. I've literally taken him as my father through my life. I haven't missed anything. I'm not sitting here feeling sorry for myself. That was a love relationship between my mother and Smudge. That was a great love affair. And I'm sure I would have been there sooner or later!

I lost my mum when I was twenty-one and so Nan and I kind of moved in together and we adopted each other for the rest of her life. It was terrific, and we had a good time. She would come and stay with me. When I was learning to do *Billy*, I had a mews flat with a little kitchen, and I was learning to tap dance, going from the fridge to the cooker, an area one fortieth the size of the Drury Lane stage. And I'm going step, shuffle, hop – and when I got really good, I opened the fridge door and performed to the Guinness bottles. Nan was sitting in the other room with a rosary just praying, 'Dear God, he's never going to be able to dance, this boy will never be able to dance!' And when we did open and I got half decent reviews, she said, 'I never, ever realised the power of prayer!'

She came to see the show at Drury Lane and at one point there's a whole fantasy sequence during which my parents come on and machine-gun me and I stand at the back of the stage and just shout, 'Oh, piss off the lot of you!' And I heard this voice from the Royal Box saying, 'Michael, I've never heard you use language like that! If your mother was alive today!' And with that, Nan was pulled back down into her seat!

1999

Will Smith

Will Smith is box office. His ability to 'open' films around the world caused *Time* magazine to place him in 'a category usually reserved for white guys named Tom'. Of all the stars I interviewed, he was one of the most agreeable. When we talked about how men can make themselves more desirable to women, he offered to show me how to dance. We went cheek to cheek. My wife said some men have all the luck.

Michael: You've got an Academy Award nomination for portraying a character I had a couple of run-ins with in my career, and that was Muhammad Ali. It was an extraordinary portrayal. In many ways, you must have imagined that it was an impossible job?

Will: Absolutely. Any aspect of that film is more than enough work for just one movie. It was a year and a half's physical training to learn how to box, and that would have been enough to have to learn, but then there was the concept of the sixties in the United States. I'm a child of rap music and the nineties. Essentially, we're reaping the benefits of what happened in the sixties, and I really couldn't understand that kind of segregation and that type of blatant racism, and then the dialect and trying to get the man's voice right – it was just very, very difficult.

Michael: You spent time with him of course?

Will: Yeah, we spent a lot of time together.

Michael: What kind of relationship did you have with him?

Will: He personally asked me to do the film and that was a shock and an honour, and I said to him, 'Why me?' And he said, 'Because you're the only person that's almost as pretty as me.'

Michael: And you watched the first showing of the film with him, didn't you?

Will: Oh yeah, I was sitting next to Ali and his whole family. And at one point he leans over to his wife while we're watching and says, 'Girl, why you ain't tell me I was so crazy?' So he was enjoying it, and after the film he told me he was honoured, and his family was very happy and it was emotional for them. So it was a year and a half of really hard work that paid off.

Michael: One of the things you got there, that not many of us do, was a privileged insight into the world of boxing.

Will: Absolutely.

Michael: And never mind the man himself, because we've got no idea how fit these guys are, have we?

Will: Boxers are in the best shape of any athletes, to be able to go ten, twelve, fifteen rounds with someone punching at you. I had an experience when I was boxing that guaranteed my life as an actor – the boxing world was gonna be free from Will Smith. Michael Bent played Sonny Liston in the movie and I was having a problem. I was scared so I was leaning back too much and my trainer was saying, 'Lean in, lean in. You gotta get your spine angle forward.' So just at the time I decided I was gonna get my spine angle forward, he decided he was gonna throw a heavy right hand. So I leaned in and I saw it coming.

I put my head down and the punch hit me square on the top of my head but it didn't fly my head back. It compressed my head into my shoulders. I felt an electrical shock and it went down the back of my spine and to both elbows, and I had an uncontrollable desire to find my car keys! I'm very certain that I do not want to be punched for a living.

Michael: There's another dimension to Muhammad Ali, and that's the political dimension. When all is said and done, there's a lot of stuff said about Ali but he was a very brave man. He took on all the government, for what he believed to be right. You must have faced that as well yourself, when you were growing up. You can't have been that removed from it?

Will: Oh, no. I've had experiences with racism, hearing a word from police and dealing with those situations, but being a child of the nineties, we have a thing called Internal Affairs. It's essentially the police who police the police. So to deal with that kind of thing, we'd go right to Internal Affairs and report the officer, and that wasn't an option in the sixties.

I talked to Geronimo ji-Jaga, who was formerly Geronimo Pratt of the Black Panthers, for the film. He said that the perspective then was that we were at war, a civil war going on in the United States, and that essentially sparked the idea in my mind of a war scenario. Ali viewed the situation with the American government in the same way he viewed being in the ring. It was a fight, he was being attacked and he had to win or die. That really gave me the insight into how he was dealing with these situations and approaching the government.

Michael: But politically did he make a difference?

Will: Oh, absolutely. You can always tell about someone's political power by the children – by how children of twelve and down are responding and reacting. And Ali was that guy, he was the guy the children wanted to be. They wanted to fight, they wanted to be able to stand up, they wanted to be able to make a difference. And for me, part of the bittersweet concept of playing the role was that I got to sit next to, and speak with, and define, and quantify greatness, knowing that life will probably never deal me the cards that would enable me to determine if I'm that great. Am I that much man? What would I have done? What would I do today?

2005

Kevin Spacey

An intriguing man, Kevin Spacey won a Best Actor Oscar for *American Beauty* and a Best Supporting Actor Oscar for *The Usual Suspects*. Yet his greatest achievement could be as artistic director of the Old Vic. He took the job in 2003, succeeding in reviving the fortunes of a classic London theatre made famous by Sir Laurence Olivier, Richard Burton, Sir John Gielgud and many others. It also gave Spacey the opportunity to demonstrate his versatility, when he played Richard II at the Old Vic and Lex Luthor in *Superman Returns* in Hollywood. He also invited Robert Altman to direct Arthur Miller's *Resurrection Blues* on stage as well as directing and starring in the biopic of Bobby Darin in *Beyond the Sea*. The musical gave him the chance to fulfil a lifelong ambition – performing in a series of concerts backed by a big band. He gives every impression of occupying that blissful state where the job is the hobby and the hobby the job.

I started out doing impressions. I just had an ear for it, so I did stand-up comedy, and in some unusual places. I played some of the famous venues in Los Angeles, which is where I grew up, but I also played bowling alleys, in midnight talent contests – you know what this is like? When you're doing your best material and all you can hear is the sound of bowling pins being knocked over, that's not going exactly as you'd hoped. But I found it great fun. It wasn't until I hosted *Saturday Night Live* that I really had a chance to do impressions in a public way.

I was fortunate that when I was growing up my parents used to come to England quite a lot. My father was in the war here. He was an army officer, a medic, and he spent a great deal of time here and also in Scotland. When I was around seven and eight years old, we would take trips here, and so from a very early age I began to have experiences here – going to the theatre a great deal. They really exposed us to a kind of British way of life. So for me, it's always been quite natural to come here.

I first came and did a play in 1986, Eugene O'Neill's *Long Day's Journey into Night*, and had the good fortune to play Jack Lemmon's son. For many, many months, I tried to get an audition for the play. I was just beginning in the theatre and

I couldn't get an audition – my agents couldn't get me in. I found out that Dr Jonathan Miller, who was directing the production, was going to be giving a series of lectures in New York at Alice Tully Hall, on the afterlife of plays. I got myself a pair of tickets and went along, very nervously. He gave this great, amazing, fantastic lecture, and the place was packed. And I just kept thinking through the show, how am I going to meet him? I don't want to go backstage and say, 'Hi, I'd like to be in your play.' I thought it's got to happen in the right way.

Sitting next to me was a rather elderly citizen, and she was asleep through most of the lecture, and looking around, I noticed sticking out of her handbag was an invitation to a cocktail reception in honour of Dr Jonathan Miller. I thought to myself, 'You know, she's tired.' So I pinched it, and then very quickly moved seats. I went to the cocktail reception and Dr Miller was sitting at a table with Kurt Vonegut on one side and Norman Mailer on the other, and Mr and Mrs Moneybags, and Mr and Mrs Filthy Rich, and I thought, 'Well, there's no way I can get over there.' But at one point, Kurt Vonegut got up and went to the men's room and didn't come back. So I bee-lined for this chair next to Dr Miller.

I sat down and just started chatting to him about how great his lecture was, and he gave me the great opening line, 'So what brought you to my lecture? I'm always very curious what brings young people to my lectures.' And I said, 'Well, oddly enough, Eugene O'Neill brought me.' And he said, 'Is he here? I've always wanted to meet him.' I told him the story of how I'd been trying for about eight months to get an audition, unsuccessfully. And he wrote down the hotel he was at and gave me his card and said, 'Get to me directly.' Two days later I had my first audition for the play and then about five months later I auditioned for the play with Jack Lemmon, because he had approval over who played his sons.

He was a big hero of mine. I'll never forget this audition.

We did about four scenes together and I wanted this part so badly I was just relentless with Jack. I toppled over his lines and I drove through his pauses and you could literally feel something started with us at that moment. At the end of the audition, he walked up to me, put his hand on my shoulder, and he said, 'You know what, I never thought I'd find the rotten kid, but you're it – Jesus Christ!'

I had actually met Jack Lemmon when I was quite a young theatre student. I went to a seminar and asked for his autograph, and asked some questions about what I should do if I was serious about being an actor. He gave me some great advice, and lo and behold there I was at twenty-six being able to work with my idol. I'm a sort of buff of the older movie stars. I grew up admiring Henry Fonda, Jimmy Stewart, Humphrey Bogart, Spencer Tracy – probably one of my favourite actors of all time – and was interested just to watch their trajectory, and how they learned about film. Almost every one of the actors I admired came out of the theatre. So I took that advice and that was really the lesson for me.

I think it was Katherine Hepburn who said that in her day there were a lot of people trying to become great actors and now there are a lot of people trying to become movie stars. If it happens along the way that you become successful in film, for me the great thrill is always to go back to the theatre. There's nothing like doing plays, and what it does to you and how it fulfils you – people who think it's the same thing every night don't understand. It's a little like sports to me. If you love playing tennis, or any game, every time you play it's a different game. The rules are the same, the lines are the same, but you're always working on a different part of your game, working on a different angle, coming at it a different way.

2002

Anthony Hopkins

Anthony Hopkins' account of auditioning for Laurence Olivier at the National Theatre records the beginning of a stage career that many prophesied would entail Hopkins becoming the natural successor to the great man. His portrayal of the odious Lambert Le Roux in *Pravda* remains one of the most memorable performances seen at the National Theatre. He followed it with an acclaimed King Lear and *Anthony and Cleopatra*. Then Hollywood called and off he went, like Burton before him, to become a hugely successful film star, forever being asked why he gave up stage acting. An indication that this is no ordinary actor is the fact that the man who played Hannibal Lecter is also the best impersonator of Tommy Cooper I have ever encountered.

I was raised on movies during the war years. My parents used to take me to the Plaza Cinema in Port Talbot, or the Odeon. We had five cinemas in a relatively small town and I used to go and see old Humphrey Bogart and James Cagney movies, and that's where lots of kids of my generation got their entertainment. And eventually, because I had nothing better to do, I became an actor.

I was stupid at school. I've used all kinds of excuses for myself by saying I was slow, I was a late developer – I was just thick. I was very antisocial, didn't have any friends. My father tried to persuade me to get out of the house and do something. I was about seventeen at the time and a real loner. I was just terrified of people. And he said, 'For goodness sake, join the YMCA or something.'

Our next-door neighbour, Jack Edwards, a grocer, took me up to the YMCA in Port Talbot and tried to teach me snooker. I gave it a go and got bored. He said, 'You're not really interested, are you?' I said, 'No,' and wandered down the corridor where an amateur dramatic group were meeting. I asked if I could join in, and they gave me a small part as a saint in an Easter play called *Emmanuel*. I had one line, and a sheet over my head, and that was about it. I felt so at home there. I thought, 'Well, this is better than working for a living. Maybe I ought to do it.' I come from the same town as Richard Burton, so I thought, 'He's a local boy made good. Maybe I'll have a go at it as well.'

I wanted instant stardom, but it took a long time. I remember meeting Richard Burton. He signed an autograph for me, and I was so impressed. He was home from Hollywood with his wife – not Elizabeth Taylor, his first wife, Sybil – and on his way to Cardiff Arms Park to see a big international between England and Wales. I was walking down the street afterwards, clutching my autograph, and he passed in the car. Sybil waved to me and I remember thinking, 'I've got to get out of here.' I don't mean out of Wales, but I thought, 'I've got to get out of my own situation. I want to become famous.'

And that's what I wanted. That was a long time ago, I was about fifteen at the time, and through some strange quirk of destiny – it's all luck – I found myself moving towards the acting business and went into the theatre. I was tremendously lucky. I've been very blessed. I'd spent two years in rep when I was called upon to go and audition at the National Theatre. I had literally twenty-four hours' notice, and I didn't have any really good audition pieces. The only one I knew was from *Othello* and I couldn't do that, I thought, because Laurence Olivier was already doing it at the Old Vic to great acclaim. But then I thought, 'Well, I don't have time to learn anything else.' I had two modern ones – a Chekov thing and something by Bernard Shaw. I couldn't believe that I was meeting Olivier. He looked a bit like Harry Worth to me – the glasses and slightly thin on top. With a three-piece suit on, he looked like a bank manager.

I'd asked one of the guys who'd just been in and came out very pale faced, 'What's he like?' He said, 'He's nothing like you think he is. He's very nice and all that.' So I was expecting to see this man in black, standing on the throne or something.

But I went in and he said, 'Hello dear boy, how are you? What are you going to do for us?' A group of people were sitting round the table, a couple of directors and casting directors, and he got out this silver pen. He said, 'What are you going to do for your first audition?' I said, 'I'll do a piece of Chekov, *Three Sisters*.' '*Three Sisters*, what else?' I said, 'Bernard Shaw, *Major Barbara*.' '*Major Barbara*. What are you going to do for the Shakespeare?' I said, '*Othello*.' '*Othello*? You've got a bloody nerve!' I said, 'It's the only one I know.' He said, 'Well, good for you!'

I did the first two pieces. I was so nervous I had my hands in my pockets in the first scene, just to try to relax myself. I was so frightened of the audition. I thought if in doubt, put your hands in your pockets, and as I made a gesture, a comb and some handkerchief came out. I managed to get through that and he said, 'Now, what are you going to do for dear old *Othello*?' I said, 'I'll do the bed chamber scene.' 'Good, off you go.' In those days, he used to smoke, and as I was about to start, he leaned over to one of the directors and said, 'Billy, do you have a cigarette?' He said, 'I'm terribly sorry, I need a cigarette. I'm so nervous in case you're better than me,' which was his charming way of relaxing me. I did the piece and it was all right, and he came up and said, 'Well done. I don't think I'll lose any sleep tonight, but I think you're awfully good.' He said, 'Would you like to join the company?' I said, 'Er, er, er, yes!' I worked under his direction there at the National and he gave me my first big break, and he was wonderful to work with.

My father was an amazing man. He was a baker and, I think, a frustrated actor. He was a great story teller, with one little proviso – he ended up running a pub and people flocked from all over Wales to come and see him. He was known as 'Dick the Ship'. We used to do a double act of Tommy Cooper behind the bar. He was a meat and potatoes man, very down to earth, and when I was working at the National Theatre he said, 'You don't want to hang around here, you know. You want to make money like Richard Burton.' I really had my eye on the main chance. I wanted to be in movies. I loved movies and I love doing them now. I'm afraid I'm not very good in the theatre, I get very rusty.

I like to drive, thousands of miles, wherever my instinct takes me. I'll take one direction and then end up in Texas. Not really – I take a map with me – but sometimes I change my mind and think, 'I'll go right,' and end up in Texas. I was there last year, and it was so flat, I thought, 'This is very boring,' so I turned left and went up to Washington. I have a wonderful time doing this. I remember going into a hotel in El Paso, a Holiday Inn under a freeway, on a miserable, rainy night. The woman behind the desk had curlers in and a scarf on over them. I said, 'Could I have a room?' She said, 'Oh my God. Hannibal Lecter!' So I have a lot of fun meeting a lot of people. It's a way of relaxing. So I bit her on the neck.

1988 and 1998

Tom Cruise

The best description of being Tom Cruise was supplied by his ex-wife Nicole Kidman. In talking about their time together, she recollected a sightseeing trip in Rome, when the two of them waited until the city slept and the paparazzi had gone home, and then 'broke into' the Colosseum. It was, she said, the only way they could be tourists without an armed guard. His embrace of Scientology makes him a controversial figure with the tabloids. The fans don't seem to care, nor should they. He is still box office, still a superstar, his film releases treated more like events than movies.

Tom: I love movies. That was the thing. I'd cut grass and deliver newspapers so I could save my money and go to the movies. I never thought I'd one day be acting in them and have that opportunity, ever.

Michael: So it was just a dream.

Tom: It was a just a dream. I'd actually saved about $900 and I was gonna go to France and ride a bicycle through the country, and I decided, 'You know what, I'm gonna go to New York and I'm gonna try.' I went to fifteen different schools and actors hate hearing this, but at my first film audition, I got the role.

Michael: It's interesting, too, that you had a problem with dyslexia when you were a child. How bad was that?

Tom: It was fascinating. They wanted to put me on medication when I was young and my mother said, 'No.' Unfortunately, now in the United States, they can ask you not to go to school unless you are medicated. I was fortunate that I didn't have that. I did everything I could and then, when I became a Scientologist, I found a study technology that L. Ron Hubbard developed. I started applying that and realised that it's just a label, dyslexia. It's the same for Attention Deficit Disorder, ADD – there's no science behind these things whatsoever.

Michael: And they are curable?

Tom: Yeah, absolutely.

Michael: So, just how bad was the dyslexia?

Tom: I was a functional illiterate, and there are different levels of that. I remember for *Top Gun* I wanted to learn to fly an aeroplane for research, and it's very difficult. I would just sit there and listen. A lot of times I wouldn't say anything. I would just try to listen and pick things up. Now I'm a commercially rated instrument pilot. I fly P51s and I run three companies. I've worked very hard and I help families – educate them on the horrific aspects of psychiatry and these diagnoses, and putting children on these horrible psychiatric drugs. Medically, it's harder getting kids off these drugs. We actually have an easier time getting people off heroin than methadone or these psychiatric drugs, and I've worked very diligently to educate people about this, because it leads to drug abuse, or significant complications.

Michael: The other thing that's interesting about your life is that you were brought up by your mum. Your parents divorced, so you were living with your mum and your three sisters . . .

Tom: And mum worked three jobs, too. We all worked.

Michael: She was plainly a remarkable woman, from what you read about her. She had three jobs, and brought up four very decent and nice children. That's an extraordinary achievement, isn't it?

Tom: Yeah. She really taught me how important it is, not what you get out of life but what you give to life, in terms of helping people.

Michael: But what was it like being . . .

Tom: The only guy?

Michael: The only guy.

Tom: It was great. I have to tell you – amazing women, each very distinctly different and beautiful. But you know that they're gonna get all the hot water. You learn to do things very quickly. When the door knocks, you're out. But we're really close because we travelled around a lot and I always felt very protective of my sisters and they of me. The girl-friends I brought home were scrutinised to an intolerable degree.

Michael: I read that they actually used to make you go through kissing practice with them.

Tom: Not them.

Michael: No. Their friends.

Tom: Leanne. Her friends were at that age when they wanted to practise for their boyfriends. So that school bell rang and I would sprint home when I knew her friends were gonna be there. They'd take me into the bathroom and practise, teach me how to French kiss. And, you've gotta breathe when you're kissing. The first time I was kissing, I thought, 'I'm gonna pass out,' because I was holding my breath. So, sisters have friends. It's a good thing.

Michael: Can I talk about your relationship with your father? Your mother comes across as this very large figure in your life, and your father's a bit more shadowy. He's kind of in the background. Is that how it was?

Tom: That's how it was. My mother was there. She was the strength, the guide. I'm not saying that he was a bad person but she was the one who helped us.

Michael: And when they divorced, you didn't see your dad?

Tom: No. I saw him right before he passed away in Kentucky. It was tragic for him because he looked at what he'd missed out on. I believe people are basically good and that you see what they do to themselves. He finally had that realisation, as a father, as a man, what he created for his life – it was tragic and I felt for him very much. He was my father, and I loved him. Most definitely.

2004

8 Raconteurs

Henry Kissinger

Tony Blair

Kenneth Williams

Alistair Cooke

Malcolm Muggeridge

John Mortimer

Peter Ustinov

Stephen Fry

Roald Dahl

Clive James

Jonathan Miller

Henry Kissinger

This was the only interview I did without an audience. Henry Kissinger's security men insisted on a closed studio. I walked on in silence to the presence of a semi-circle of bodyguards who stood facing the non-existent audience. It was bizarre. My producer, John Fisher, decided to have some fun with the music for Kissinger's walk down the stairs. He chose 'I Wonder Who's Kissing Her Now'. Geddit? The good doctor didn't.

Born in Germany, he was the immigrant who became President Nixon's security advisor and recipient of the Nobel Peace Prize – a ponderous presence of lugubrious manner, yet revealing the odd twinkle when we talked about sex and power. We spoke before Richard Nixon died, in 1994.

I remember going to school, when somebody came into the classroom and said Hitler had been appointed chancellor. The lifestyle of my family changed completely. We were ostracised after that. With all the ground troops on the streets, it was my first experience of totalitarianism. What it meant, for example, is that I had to go to a Jewish school and that my father lost his position. He had been teaching. Many of the friends of our family would no longer associate with us, so that brought it on rather dramatically.

It was my first experience of the tenuousness of modern society and how rapidly things can disintegrate and how rather elemental forces can break forward. I had an uncle who was immediately sent to a concentration camp where he stayed for two years. All of these things show you that modern civilised life has its limits, and one has an obligation to fight for freedom, or at any rate to try to vindicate it.

I was fifteen when I came to the United States, so for a year I went to high school. I went to night school – first to high school and then to college – and I was planning a sort of professional career, probably as an accountant.

I think I had an understanding of what America represents to the world that native-born Americans cannot fully have, and that maybe you in Britain can have from your memories of the Second World War, better than people who have never suffered setbacks, who have never had to look potential disaster in the face. I have therefore always had to believe that America, with all its failings, represented a hope for free people in most countries of the world. And I could never go along with those who saw in every American mistake, every American failing, a justification to assault the fundamentals of American society.

Nelson Rockefeller invited me to join a group of scholars who acted as advisors to him in 1954 to 1955. I think I had just finished my PhD and I'd had no exposure to the world of affairs at all. He was a man of great intuition, enormous courage. He was not verbally as precise or as articulate as some other American statesmen, but he had an artistic intuition. He could understand the essence of a problem even when he couldn't articulate it very well. And he showed tremendous courage in seeking to achieve what his insights had taught him. So over the years we became very close friends. He had something I liked – very good human insight – and I had something perhaps he liked, which was a more formal, theoretical mind.

I had absolutely no use for Nixon before he became president. My disdain was only matched by my ignorance of him. I'd met him once at a cocktail party and he was, and is, painfully shy with strangers, and I wasn't socially super at that time, so we had the most stilted conversation that you can imagine for three minutes, and we gratefully parted from each other. That was the last I saw of him until after he was elected president of the United States.

His appointment secretary invited me to call on him at the Hotel Pierre in New York, which was his transition headquarters in the United States – there's a three-month period between election and the time the new president takes over.

I'd no idea what he wanted. One of Nixon's characteristics is that he's so afraid of being rebuffed that, when he has a proposition to make that he doesn't know will be accepted, he puts it forward in such an elliptical way that sometimes the recipient doesn't know he's made a proposition, which happened to me. I left him and I didn't know he had offered me a job.

Two days later, his associate called me up and said, 'Are you going to take the job?' I said I didn't know I'd been offered a job. So he said, 'You'd better come down here. He's messed it up again.' And so I came and saw him, and this time I knew I was offered a job. But I had so many doubts about Nixon that I had the unusual bad taste of telling the president – or president elect – that all of my friends had thought so ill of him and that I couldn't perform my duties adequately unless I had the support of my friends, that I wanted a week to consult them. And that was, after all, the second or third most important job in the country, to be security advisor to the president. I must say it was, in retrospect, colossal impudence to do this. But he told me to take a week and I actually spent three days talking to friends until I got to Rockefeller. Rockefeller said I had a moral duty to take that job, that if anything went wrong in our foreign policy when I had been offered an opportunity to help and had refused, I could never forgive myself, and he would never forgive me. So after three days I called up Nixon and said that I didn't need a week.

As a professor, my image of Nixon was very condescending. All of the people I knew thought that Nixon was morally inadequate and electorally really below par, but I think he knew a great deal about foreign policy. He made very important decisions in foreign policy with great courage. He and I were never personally close. We had a professional relationship, but no one can take this away from him – he's a man of enormous complexity.

Here is a man who, all his life, had wanted three things –

conspicuous success in foreign policy, a spectacular electoral success, and recognition as deserved president of the United States. He achieved all of these three things within a three-month period, and he lost them all within a two-month period thereafter. So that has some of the elements of a great tragedy. He's not a natural politician. He has a very strange combination of characteristics, a man who really doesn't like people, who's a politician. To be sure, he had himself to blame for most of what happened. He made terrible mistakes, but they didn't make it any less painful. That was a very tough period for him, and certainly he behaved there in a way that men under stress tend to behave.

I honestly believed that it was possible to negotiate a settlement, and I accepted – as it turned out, wrongly – the belief of almost all American intellectuals that it was possible to achieve a compromise with the North Vietnamese. Well, after some period of negotiation with them it became clear to me that was unlikely to be the case, but still, our responsibility had been established by then and our problem was to extricate ourselves in a manner that did not undermine either the self-confidence of America or the faith of those who had relied on us, or the confidence of our allies.

We couldn't pull out immediately. When you have 550,000 Americans engaged, plus 80,000 others whom you got involved, you cannot turn off such an enterprise like you switch television channels. Secondly, Richard Nixon had been an anti-communist all his life. His constituency was on the hard side, not on the soft side. He could not possibly begin by doing the things that those who had gotten us in had not even considered. What we did do was withdraw about 150,000 to 200,000 Americans each year that we were in office. Our aim was to do that without calamity, while attempting to negotiate a settlement. Could it have been done a little faster? Who knows. It took De Gaulle four years to get out of Algeria.

When I started out, strange as this may seem, I had never conducted a negotiation in my life, I'd never held a press conference in my life, I'd never run large organisations. So I was really going into a void. At that time, it also seemed that we might face a major calamity in Indochina, with hundreds of thousands of American troops really begging for passage, or negotiating about a passage home. We had no contact with China, no serious negotiations with the Soviet Union. Now at least we have seen that one can reverse these situations. And the fundamental strengths of the industrial democracies are there. Now I think I have a sense of what can be done. I have pessimistic predictions about the near-term future but I'm quite optimistic about the middle and long-term future.

I really have no plan. I think when you've been at the centre of events, you become quite fatalistic. You see what you cannot affect. It could happen that a contention of events makes it possible for me again to play a role. But if that contention of events doesn't occur, I've had more of an opportunity than is given to almost any human being to make a contribution, and I think I've been fortunate that I've had this chance.

1979

Michael: You have the reputation of being what's called in America a swinger. Now what is – a gentle smile plays round your lips when I say that!

Henry: Because once you have the reputation, you don't have to fulfil it any more.

Michael: Once you've been given the accolade! But was it justified?

Henry: Yes. I used to say then that once you have the reputation, even if you bore a young lady to death, she'll think it's her fault, not yours. So, it was to some extent justified. I wasn't married at the time and when one is in a powerful position, it opens many horizons, but I didn't take it seriously.

Michael: Is power really an aphrodisiac, do you think?

Henry: I think it is to some extent, yes.

Michael: You could vouch for that, could you?
Henry: I would, based on limited experience.
Michael: You're very diplomatic, Dr Kissinger.

Tony Blair

When I interviewed Tony Blair, he was affable, likeable and on his way out. It was a good time for him to reflect on a remarkable political career, particularly on the subjects of power and responsibility.

From an early age, when I saw *All Quiet on the Western Front*, I have been fascinated by war, by those who fight them and those who told them so to do. I have known brave soldiers who survived a war physically intact and yet were crippled psychologically, reliving horrors even in their slumber. I have always wondered if the generals who dictated events, and the politicians who gave them the power to wage war, were similarly damned. So when I asked Tony Blair what responsibilities he felt for sending our troops to Iraq and for those who died, I didn't know what to expect. His answer was encapsulated after the interview in the headline in the *Guardian*: '"God will judge me" PM tells Parkinson'.

Michael: Let's talk about the musical career of Tony Blair.
Tony: This will be a brief conversation!
Michael: No, no, you were very committed at one point to being either an entrepreneur or a rock singer in the manner of your great hero, Mick Jagger.
Tony: Well I had hair down to here at the time, so one of the problems with my kids, if I ever get angry with them, is they produce the photograph and say, 'Whatever else we've done, we have never looked like that!' But I was very keen on it. I loved it, but to be honest, the talent was somewhat missing, not that it mattered a great deal in those days.

Michael: But the story about your band at university – you fronted a band called Ugly Rumour.

Tony: A-ha.

Michael: And the story of your debut performance, if it's right, would put anybody off, wouldn't it?

Tony: We had a drummer who was great but enthusiastic and he kind of modelled himself on Keith Moon from the Who. So we went on stage and went into the opening number and he started really battering the drum kit and the whole thing fell to bits! It didn't make much difference actually, to be absolutely honest, I just carried on singing, which was worse I think! But it was great. I think everybody, when they're young, should go through that time of joining a band and going on stage.

Michael: Of course, allied to that is the acting you did at school, where you were called the best actor of your generation. It does raise this interesting question doesn't it? The obvious point is the link between actors and politicians. Many people have remarked upon it. Do you see a link? Do you see that degree of performing you did as a kid is exactly the same as you are doing now?

Tony: If you are doing prime minister's questions, or making a big speech at a conference, there's an element of it, when I suppose you are putting on a show, a performance, and I think some of the same things apply. I was just saying to Kevin [Spacey] before we came on, how nervous do you get before you are about to go on stage and perform. And I think some of that same thing is there. There's no point in going into politics unless you want to be in the public eye and in that sense it's a stage. It's more than that, obviously, but yes.

Michael: But what about, to take an example of someone you know well, Bill Clinton. He's always struck me as being like an actor. He has that presence. When he walks on, people look at him, they're grabbed by his presence. You've witnessed this at first hand?

Tony: He's the best politician as a politician I've ever come across. The one thing in politics you would never want to do is fight an election against Bill Clinton. He's a really, really good guy and was very helpful to me when I first came in and got the job. Always giving good bits of advice.

When I had literally just started, we went to a summit – I'd better not say the country because it wouldn't be very diplomatic – but we went to this summit and sometimes what happens is they get the local people, who do all the fashion and the rest of it, to try to get the leaders to wear something at the summit so it can be photographed and so on. Anyway, I went to my hotel room just before the summit dinner and there were three shirts laid out on the bed, ranging from ghastly through to unbelievably hideous!

So I thought I'd put on the least worse – I put on the ghastly. I go into the summit and they're all milling around, then in comes Bill Clinton and he's wearing the unbelievably hideous one. So I go up to him and I say, 'Bill, that looks awful!' And he says, 'Yep!' And I say, 'Why?' And he says, 'Tony, let me tell you something, when the folks back home in America see this, they're going to say, "Look at our Mr President. Someone has made him wear that shirt to be nice to all those people out there." But when the folks back home in Britain see you in that shirt, they might just think you chose it!'

Michael: There was, at that time, a general mood of euphoria wasn't there? You had made Labour electable again. You had got in, it was a new beginning.

Tony: And people used to like me then!

Michael: Was there a sense you were carried away by that euphoric moment?

Tony: Do you know something? No, because all the way through I was thinking, this is all very well, but at some point the job really begins. A famous American politician once said, 'You campaign in poetry but you govern in prose.' And you know, I remember the very first day after the election when there was this sort of euphoria, but you go in to Downing Street and behind the famous front door there's a very long corridor down to the cabinet room at the end. The tradition is that when the new prime minister comes in, all the staff line up on either side of the corridor and basically clap you in. Now, we hadn't been in Downing Street for eighteen years, so everyone in there was used to the other lot. So, as I was going down, some of them, for very natural reasons, were crying! By the time I got to the end of the line, I really felt a bit of a heel about the whole thing!

But you go into the cabinet room and there is the cabinet secretary, who sits you down, and I'll never forget his first words to me, 'Well, Prime Minister, what do you want to do then?' And suddenly you're thinking, 'Yes, it's now begun.' And the whole sense of that moment . . . the euphoria drains away pretty quickly and in comes the reality of knowing that you've got to start taking decisions.

Michael: Has there ever been a point in your entire nine years that you've felt, 'I wish I'd not walked through that door'?

Tony: No.

Michael: There hasn't been?

Tony: No. There's been some really difficult moments and really tough decisions.

Michael: What are the toughest ones?

Tony: The tough decisions are any relating to conflict or war. And look, the job is a privilege. That's the first thing to say. And the second thing to say is it's voluntary, so if you ever complain about it, go and do something else. But the point about it is, it's a decision-making job and so you are always making decisions. Every day you will make four or five, and maybe one or two of those are really important, and the trouble about decisions is usually there are two points of view. So pretty quickly you realise the best you can hope for is to please some of the people some of the time and certainly not all of the people all of the time. But that decision making makes it tough and it's a responsibility, but on the other hand, as I say, it's a privilege as well.

Michael: You mention there that the prime minister, the commander in chief, has the ultimate say about the nation going to war, and that's the most serious decision you can take in any event. You've been called a liar and a warmonger and all that sort of thing. What's your feeling, your attitude, when you read that? And when you read of casualties and people blame you for those casualties, that's a terrible, awful thing to live with, and I wondered how you coped with it?

Tony: Well it is, but it's even more difficult for the people out on the front line doing the job.

Michael: Of course.

Tony: And that's what you have to remember.

Michael: And you sent them there.

Tony: Yep. And that decision has to be taken and has to be lived with, and in the end there is a judgement that, well, I think if you have faith about these things, then you realise that judgement is made by other people. And also by . . .

Michael: Sorry, what do you mean by that?

Tony: I mean by other people, and if you believe in God, it's made by God as well. And that judgement in the end has to be . . . when you are faced with a decision like that, and some of those decisions have been very, very difficult, as I say, most of all because there are people's lives – this is not just a matter of a policy here for a thing there – but their lives and in some cases their death. The only way you can take a decision like that is to try to do the right thing according to your conscience. And for the rest of it, as I say, you leave to the judgement that history will make.

Michael: So you pray to God when you make a decision like that?

Tony: Well, I don't want to go into sermons, but of course you struggle with your own conscience about it because people's lives are affected, and it's one of these situations that very few people ever find themselves in, but in the end you do what you think is the right thing. And sometimes, of course, these things are brutally controversial and a lot of people passionately disagree, as they did over Iraq, beyond any doubt at all. But in the end, I think if you do the job, you've got to be prepared to take the decisions of the job and in the end you've got to live with those decisions and live with your own conscience in them.

2006

Kenneth Williams

I think Kenneth Williams was the unhappiest man I ever met. Even when making people laugh there was a sadness about him, a sense in which the funny voices and the outrageous anecdotes were false trails, directing you away from a troubled soul. His diaries are an account of a man battling manic depression and of a homosexual living at a time when to be so was to risk a cruel law as well as the condemnation of a society more censorious then than now. Moreover, he was the serious actor who ended up in the *Carry On* films. He was someone who wanted to talk about intellectual matters to an audience who preferred him going on about his piles.

For all he gave the appearance of being a fastidious man, he was at heart a vulgarian. He loved the double entendre, the smutty innuendo, the jokes about tits and bums. His ultimate contradiction – and sadness – was that of being a man who knew how to make everyone happy except himself.

I went into the Army under the most inauspicious circumstances. I was sent to Carlisle to do my training with a lot of Geordies and I couldn't understand half of what they were saying. They couldn't understand me, either. I didn't enjoy any of it and ran about with the dixies of tea, generally not behaving like a soldier at all. When I eventually arrived in Singapore, I applied for a posting to entertain because I thought I'm not very good at soldiering. I had an audition in front of the colonels, majors and staff officers in the

Victoria Theatre in Singapore, the same place they tried the Japanese generals for war crimes. They were trying us for the same really, and I went up and did impersonations.

They said, 'No, no. Get off. Dreadful.' I kept hearing this word 'RTU'. A corporal got me on the wings and said, 'RTU!' I said, 'What's all this RTU?' Everything in the Army was initials and they said, 'Return to unit,' so they didn't want me there. I said, 'I can't go back,' because I'd left with me kitbag, saying goodbye to all the blokes, and they all said, 'Goodbye, Willy, all the best,' and I said, 'I'm going to be a star.' I was convinced I was going to be a great star and I thought, I can't go back, so I went into the stores and sat with these colonels and cried. 'Oh no, I can't go back. Couldn't I do something? Couldn't I do anything to stay?' And they said, 'Well, what else can you do?' I said, 'Well, I was a draughtsman.' And they said, 'Could you draw posters?' and really the kind of cartography I was doing had nothing to do with posters, but I went out on a limb and said, 'Yes.' So I drew the posters for them, and that's how I got into the entertainment unit.

My family was working-class, poverty-stricken. We were brought up in one room off the Caledonian Road and it was just awful. Euphemistically, I would describe it as a slum. My father was a van boy on the LMS. He used to call the company 'hell of a mess' and that's why I always remember it. My mother took in washing. She told a marvellous story about how she had to wheel her washing to a hotel in Piccadilly. She had a little trolley and she said, 'I'll never forget the day the wheel come off, the axle broke, and it broke near Eros.' Under Eros in them days were those women that sold flowers, with their lovely hats on. One of them said, 'Don't worry, girl,' and she pulled a great steel hatpin out of her enormous hat, and stuck it through the axle for my mother and she was able to take her laundry on. That always stuck in my memory.

I suppose as a child, when the children at school were better dressed than I was, I occasionally felt twinges of envy about it. I did say as much to my father on one occasion, and he said that we're instructed by the bible not to covet our neighbours' goods and told me it was wrong to think like that, so I proceeded to adjust my thinking. What my father told me during my lifetime was very important to me. He gave me a lot of maxims to live by.

First of all I was an apprentice draughtsman. That was interrupted by the Army, which involved a personal choice I wasn't very happy about. I'd been brought up in the Christian faith, and the idea of holding guns and killing people was abhorrent to me, quite apart from the fact that I'm not really born for that kind of thing. I don't look good with a gun. Some people can hold them, trying to look tough, and it really isn't my *forte*. You have to accept it's just part of one's limitations.

I went to my father again and said, 'I don't want to join the Army,' and he said, 'Look, this country's facing a tyrant.' He said Hitler was an evil man and the situation had become such in Europe that the only thing to do was to fight, and I believed what he said was true, because I thought him in a better position than I to judge. I was only eighteen and he was considerably wiser and had been through another war, which he thought was for good reasons at that time, but he certainly thought this was an even better reason. So I joined the Army and spent three years of my life there, which of course was an awful thing for me to do. Not only did I not believe in killing, and I was being put into a machine that would do exactly that, but it also infringed my freedom and involved a way of life I'd never faced. I'd never undressed in public and I didn't like it. I did not like taking my clothes off in front of a lot of people, and in barrack rooms I had to. So I used to arrange the shirt to cover the dick, and then they checked. They'd shout at you and say, 'Go on, show us your willy,' and accused you of a lack of manhood because you didn't show it. So eventually I got exhibitionistic and started going, 'Yeah!'

I was in weekly rep initially, in Swansea, and there were marvellous people there to play with. Richard Burton was playing Konstantin in *The Seagull* and I was understudying that role, but never bothered to learn it because I thought, 'Well, he's as strong as an ox, he'll never be off.' One day I came in and the stagedoor people said, 'You better get up there and get that costume on, he's off.' 'You're joking. Off? What do you mean, off?' I flew up the stairs to his dressing room and he was lying there, green, and apparently he'd eaten something and wound up with food poisoning, and I said, 'You're going on, aren't you, you're not really ill?' and he said, 'No, I can't. You have to go on.'

'What do you mean, I'll have to go on?' I said. 'You're the understudy, you can do it.' I said, 'No, I never learnt it.' And he said, 'Are you joking?' I said, 'No, I'm not. I thought you were strong, I thought you'd always go on. I don't know a line. I'll tell you what I'll do, you go on and I'll give you my salary.' He said, 'How much do you get?' and I said seven quid. 'Wouldn't cover my expenses.' That's what he said, because he was a film star. So he eventually agreed, because I did plead with him on bended knees. All I'd done in the play was to be the cook who had to say, 'Think no evil of us,' and I used to do that every night. I used to vary it – 'Think no EVIL of us. THINK no evil of us.'

Alec Guinness helped me out marvellously. I was doing a brothel sequence, and I was supposed to come in and say, 'Ooh, what a night I've had,' and I'd forgotten that in the dressing room, I'd unzipped my flies – the trousers were terribly tight so I unzipped them and I used to sit reading my book and go straight on, and I forgot to do 'em up. I came on and he kept covering me, saying, 'It's very interesting to see you,' and Joan Plowright was immediately behind him and I thought, 'Well, this is a bit much, isn't it? I'm not even getting a look in.' When he came into the wings, I said, 'You co-fronted me all the time,' and he said, 'It was your flies.' 'Oh,' I said. 'Oh dear, yes. Didn't realise that,' and did them up again. He said, 'Always remember before you go on the stage, blow your nose and check your flies.' I thought that was marvellous advice, I've never forgotten that.

The dressing room, especially when everyone's gone, you imagine to be completely private. I remember once, I was in my dressing room and a knock came at the door. I said, 'Oh, who is it?' and a voice said, 'Noel,' and I thought it was the stage manager and I said, 'Piss off,' or something like that. Instead, the door opened and Noel Coward came in, and I was sitting on a chamber pot. I had warm water in it with which I was washing myself and I shot up. In shooting up, I upset the pot and the water went all over the place. He said, 'What on earth are you doing?' and I said, 'I was washing myself because I was told by the surgeon after my operation that I should never use toilet paper ever, but always completely wash it, you see.' And he said, 'Oh, my dear, I do understand. Every word of my book, *Present Indicative*, I discussed that very operation myself. It's a dreadful operation, piles.' And I said, 'No, no, no, I didn't have that. My operation was for papile. I had papile, you see.' And he said, 'Papile? My dear, it's an island in the South Seas.' And that's right, it is. I got it all wrong.

I think a lot of humour is the channelling of a private misery. After all, I've gone through terrible experiences, which leave you feeling awful, and you relate them to somebody and they fall about laughing. Like when I had my nose done, the doctor said, 'I'll have to bore through because your passage is blocked and you've got no air coming in,' and he bored right through. The pain! 'We're going to give you this local anesthetic,' but they are boring right through and it's murder, and when I said to people, 'I had me passage blocked and they had to bore right through,' they just fell about and said, 'Oh, what a joker.' It's not funny at the time, is it?

I think all artists desperately need reassurance from the outside about their own worth. They haven't got it within. It's a sort of paradox, that though they may appear to be people of power and strength, in actual fact the reverse is true. They're the most vulnerable people. An idol at the time, Sir Godfrey Tearle, was giving a marvellous performance at the Haymarket, and I was in his dressing room, full of awe. I was a very young actor and very green, and couldn't even find words to say how marvellous I thought his performance was. He said to me, 'I've been terribly downcast because this woman brought her little boy to see it, he was ten, and he said my trousers were too high and the socks were showing!' And that worried him, this little boy!

Edith Evans had this extraordinary ability to rise above any kind of adversity. I remember after *Gentle Jack*, there was terrible booing and shouting, and she said to me as the curtain fell, 'Well, I heard one bravo,' and I said, 'No, that was "Go 'ome!" ' She said to me, 'Did they give you any notes?' and I said, 'Yes, I got a couple of notes. Did they give you any?' and she said, 'Well, they actually said Hardy Amies has designed very regal costumes, you should look equally regal in them. Should you think that's justified?' and I said, 'No, I think any criticism of your deportment is tantamount to impertinence,' and she said, 'Yes, mm. You're a very pleasant young man, and there's no reason why the right girl shouldn't come along.'

Then we got into a taxi and got back to the hotel where we were staying and it was 11 o'clock at night, so everyone else had gone. We sat in the corner of this empty room and an old fart who was the night porter and waiter came in and said to Dame Edith, 'Your partner in crime's had her grub.' Her partner in crime was her advisor on spiritual matters – she was a Christian Scientist – who was accompanying her on this tour.

She would not take any medicines but believed the spiritual faith would resolve any kind of illness, and he said, 'Your partner in crime's had her grub, she couldn't wait about till half-past eleven when you were starting, but she said you might wanna drop of wine. Do you fancy a drop?' and she said, 'Oh yes, a half bottle of Beaujolais would not come amiss.' And he said, 'I thought you'd fancy that. I've got a drop in the sideboard for you,' and he bent over to get it and then broke wind with alarming velocity. It really rang out appallingly, and she said to me, 'This place has gone off terribly.'

1972–82

Alistair Cooke

Alistair Cooke kept an eye on America for near on seventy years. There has never been, nor likely ever will be, a more conscientious observer of the special relationship than Mr Cooke. He was a hero to succeeding generations of journalists, particularly those of us who operated in the drab era of the 1950s, when his 'Letters from America', as well as his writing for the *Guardian*, betokened a lifestyle far removed from a Britain of smog and ration books. The difference between Cooke and a Fleet Street hack of the time was that between a Cadillac and a Ford Popular. I came to know him when he was in his seventies, but still vigorous and still capable of talking the leg off an iron pot, as the Aussies have it.

I always felt Alistair believed an interviewer was unnecessary except to turn the page of his script. All he needed was a prompt and off he would go on an unstoppable monologue, which would encompass anecdotes about presidents, boxers, film stars, writers, philosophers and intellectuals as well as gangsters and their molls.

He might not have been a good audience, but he was one of the best one-man shows I've ever heard.

My father was an art metal designer and my mother was a very strict Wesleyan. She had chronic bronchitis, and in the beginning of the First World War she was told by a doctor that the only cure for this was to go to one of two places – Egypt or Blackpool. On the whole, it seemed more convenient to go to Blackpool. My father was drafted into the Airplane Design Factory, and he got lost – he appeared every two months on leave. Then the Americans came into the war. Blackpool was twenty miles of sand and the entire American army, it seemed to me as a boy, came and trained there. Everybody had to take some in, and we took in seven Americans.

I think that really decided my life. Little boys of eight are very impressionable. We had four officers and three men, and we didn't know the difference. That was an interesting thing to me, because of the whole class business in England in those days. There was a plumber, an economist, a university professor, there was probably some Bostonian family, but they all seemed alike to us, except they were fascinating, exotic and terribly pale. I now realise we must have had more southerners than anything. My father, who'd never been to America, explained to me they were pale because of the skyscrapers – they kept the sun off their faces. And I took this as gospel. They were absolutely charming. And the thing that strikes me whenever I've been here and go back to America is the vitality. It's the fact that it's affirmant, and people are talking about the problems of today, not about the past.

I went to Cambridge, and one of the most interesting things about college years – and college is a world of its own – is that there are at least twenty-five young men who are going to be the greatest poet, and most are never heard from again. But there was one whom I met on the second day. I was walking out of the college along a walled corridor called the Chimney, and this little roly poly man, very black-haired with a strange accent, came up to me and said, 'Do you play chess?' And I said, 'Yes I do.' My father taught me to play chess and I got to the point where I beat him, which happens to all boys. So, of course, I thought he was a great chess player. We went to the university chess club, sat down and arranged the pieces and the first thing he said was, 'Do you play classical or romantic?' I said, 'I play chess.' And of course, he beat me in about five moves. His name was Jacob Bronowski.

I absolutely hated America for about five months, because it was alien, because it was strange, because I suffered from the delusion, which is absolutely universal among Englishmen, that Americans are Englishmen gone wrong and they're always judging it by that standard. I was lucky to do the best thing, which was not to be a visitor or tourist, but I went to a university and made friends. And they, in the nicest way, put me right. People are always making false analogies – the tourist arrives, as our crew did, for instance, stay in eighty-seven motels and say, 'This is nothing like home in Berkshire, is it?' Well of course it isn't. There was an Englishman who wrote a book called *Americans in Glass Houses*. It was a kind of satire on the English condescending attitude to America, and he made the greatest analogy that has ever been made. He said, 'America has many virtues, but it was to be admitted that practically every old Etonian knows more Latin than the average West Virginia miner.' And I think we all do that, we do not make the correct comparison.

G.K. Chesterton said that the world is divided into two types – those who believe that if a thing is worth doing, it's worth doing well; and then those more fortunate people who believe that if a thing's worth doing, it's worth doing badly. I'm a perfectionist. I'm too vain, I suppose, to do things badly. I want to do them well. The first thing I did well was caricaturing, and I earned my first money by doing caricatures of famous authors for the Bodley Head. But the thing I love doing most, for the radio, is writing for talking. The greatest compliment anybody's ever paid to me is to say, 'How can you do it for thirteen and a half minutes, not knowing what to say?' thinking there's no script.

My first talk was done on 5 October, 1934. In the early days, they used to be sent to London on these great sixteen-inch disks, which were very clumsy. When taping came in, they

'There is something very peculiar about singing,' according to Julie Andrews, seen here in *My Fair Lady* with Rex Harrison. 'Singing is a very lonely, isolated business.'

Sharon Osbourne has lived a life beyond the imagination of any scriptwriter.

Above: Raquel Welch: 'When I got a little bit older and the equipment arrived, well then I thought, "Gee, this is pretty terrific. Maybe I ought to try it out a little."'

Above: Interviewing Bette Midler was like trying to bottle a whirlwind – exhilarating but ultimately impossibl(

oanna Lumley – seen here in her
vengers guise – is Boudicca
nasquerading as a deb.

I might as well come clean. The most
desirable woman I ever met on *Parkinson*
was Diana Rigg.

always give interviews.
f the *Poultry Farmer's
Veekly Gazette* rings me,
m delighted to be
sked my opinion,' says
Iichael Caine.

eft: I believe Helen
Iirren to be one of the
nest actresses of my
me.

Dustin Hoffman is a compelling screen presence, but not everyone is a fan of his creative process.

Robert Redford's partnership with Paul Newman in *Butch Cassidy* and *The Sting* was flawless blend of charm and sex appeal, two great stars working in perfect harmony

Will Smith offered to show me how to dance. We went cheek to cheek. My wife said some men have all the luck.

Anthony Hopkins, the man who played Hannibal Lecter, is also the best Tommy Cooper impersonator I've encountered.

Henry Kissinger: 'I had absolutely no use for Nixon before he became president. My disdain was only matched by my ignorance of him.'

'"God will judge me," PM tells Parkinson' was the *Guardian* headl‌ after I interviewed Tony Blair.

'I'm rather a ham barrister,' John Mortimer (*left*) confessed. 'I orate, which is what Rumpole does.' Rumpole (also known as Leo McKern) looks non-committal.

Alistair Cooke kept an eye on America for near on seventy years

eter Ustinov relished being interviewed
nd once he told me why. 'It's only when
'm asked a question I find out what I
eally think about something.'

Roald Dahl's life could not have been
more extraordinary had it been written
by the man himself.

ir David Attenborough is, quite simply,
he greatest broadcaster of my time.

Lord Carnarvon, Porchie to his friends,
was everybody's idea of the slightly
barmy English aristocrat.

W.H. Auden was the only person I met
with dust in his wrinkles.

Dame Edith Evans would say, 'Off stage you
may pass me by, but on stage, look at me.'

My favourite interview was with Jacob
Bronowski because it went exactly the way
I had planned it, and because, for seventy
five minutes or more, a great man gave a
masterclass in the art of communication.

Commissioner Catherine Bramwell-
Booth was a remarkable and
inspirational woman.

asked me if I wanted to do it live and I said no, because as far as I'm concerned, my whole idea of radio is talking to one person in a room, not to the Albert Hall. So they agreed that we would tape them ahead of time. It led to trouble in time, but I record them on Wednesday, they're flown over Thursday, examined carefully by Customs for contraband, and then played Friday night, Sunday morning, and then they go around the world. And that's the problem, sometimes there's a week's interval. I've had excruciating experiences because of this interval. The worst was during the days before the Nixon abdication. Things seemed to be coming to a head, and now all the historians will say it was inevitable, but I was in San Francisco and had just taken a bet with a friend of mine that Nixon would not abdicate, he'd brazen it out. I did that talk on Sunday because, being in San Francisco, the tape had to go to New York, then to London, and I got up to the point of knowing that the minority leader and two other very conservative republicans were the people chosen to go to him and say you have to go. But they hadn't decided, and Nixon had no intention of resigning yet. So I went right up to that moment in the talk, saying the time had come when not the liberals, not the press but his own right-wing buddies would have to go to him and maybe say, 'You have to go,' and I thought, now what do I say to finish it? So I put, 'And the rest you know.' So by the time it came out, he'd gone. And the rest, they did know. But that was the scariest sentence I ever wrote.

The worst year I've spent in America was 1968. I call it the 'black year'. There'd been riots everywhere and then the assassination of Martin Luther King. I was at the funeral. And then the election campaign was just riots, and I happened to be in the hotel pantry when Bobby Kennedy was killed, and then there were the conventions and on to Chicago where the police went berserk. It was a dreadful time.

I'd been writing, unappreciatively shall we say, about Vietnam. This was way back in 1965 and I was summoned to the White House. There was a gentleman named Lyndon B. Johnson, I say for the younger members of the class present, who was president at that time, and he was enormous, larger than life, the most intimidating man I've ever met and in some ways very attractive. But he came at you like a rogue elephant, and if he decided to blow his nose, he took out a handkerchief the size of a tablecloth. Everything he did, he embraced you and you couldn't breathe. And he said, 'Now what's this you've been writing?' and he let you talk, and then he started to talk, and meanwhile he had a console with lights flashing and he was talking to Sweden and Hanoi, no doubt. Then eventually he said, 'Well, look.' He called in some minion and said, 'Close the lines down. I'm spending a little time now with President Cooke,' which really threw me. Then he said, 'Now you're a president, and I've told you some of the problems,' and there were a thousand problems, and then he started to ask questions. He was Socrates B. Johnson. It was absolutely terrifying because you realised, if you don't have the responsibility, how little you knew. He kept this up for over an hour. What you find yourself saying is, 'Well, of course, I can see, and yet on the other hand . . .' Absolutely great. I staggered out ten pounds lighter, and it took weeks to recover before I started writing unappreciatively again about this.

I've known about seven presidents since I've been in America, from Roosevelt on. Roosevelt was the most impressive. I've often thought about this. When people have asked what was the best time to be in America, I say during the New Deal. It was also the worst time. There were thirty million unemployed. One family in three or four had nothing coming in. Dreadful time. But he lifted the country up by its boot straps with the New Deal, and the whole place took fire. We had coward leaders in Britain. They knew Hitler was coming up and they were afraid. There was a dreadful feeling in Britain in the thirties, but there, suddenly Roosevelt was tremendous. But I've often thought maybe it wasn't the New Deal, maybe it wasn't America of the 1930s that I found so impressive – it was my own youth. That happens very often, I think.

Two years before Hitler came to power, I was at Cambridge and we put on three plays in Munich – *Julius Caesar*, which every German probably knew backwards, Bernard Shaw's *Arms and the Man*, which they also knew, and for some idiot young reason we did *Young Woodley*. We received a dead silence from the audience for that. We brought along a great friend of mine who was a wonderful musician, and he also spoke German. One day we were sitting in a beer garden, and I kept calling to the waiter and nothing happened. And I said, 'What's the matter with these people? They're supposed to be courteous, hospitable.' And he said, 'They don't like my face.' I said, 'What does that mean?' And that really was a baptism of fire for me politically. He said, 'Well, this Hitler has an idea that he will eradicate the Jews if he comes to power.' And I'd never heard anything like it, coming from Manchester or whatever.

Shortly, we heard a rustling sound, not quite a cheer, over the trees, and I asked the waiter what it was, and he said, 'Oh, it's the Thursday afternoon speech at the Brown House,' which was Hitler's headquarters. So we went there, and they used to close the staff offices and get these malevolent women and pimply men to come out to listen, because he didn't get a big crowd. There must have been sixty people there, and a nurse – this impressed me – and a little van. He came out, stood on a box and made a speech. It was scary. Not because he was screaming – he didn't scream. He was a marvellous actor. I've always felt that about Roosevelt, Lloyd George, Hitler – the most impressive orators I've ever heard. You thought, my God, what's going to happen? The bomb's going to drop. And three or four women fainted, and in comes the nurse, and hence the van. Apparently, at all rallies he had a nurse and a sort of ambulance. This was his effect on people. He was absolutely magnetic. And that made me understand a good deal later, how he could take over.

There was a time I felt, in the late thirties and the middle forties, when all the stories about the London coffee houses and the great wits were outshone by the table at Romanoff's on Thursday afternoons, where you had Perlman, Herman Mankiewicz and Robert Benchley, and they were the best that's ever been that I know.

Mankiewicz was a funny man, but melancholy, and rather sour. He had a running feud with a Hollywood producer, Hornblower, who suffered from the enormous disadvantage of having gone to an eastern prep school at the time when every Hollywood producer had gone into a glove factory. They thought he was hoity-toity, which he wasn't, but he was an enormous fusspot about wine, always had five glasses and would taste it and say, 'Well, I think it's a little virginal.' Mankiewicz had no use for this, and used to hit the bottle quite a bit. He came to a dinner party at Hornblower's once and by the time he got to the table he was fairly stoned, but got through the meal, and then they served the sweet. It was a baked Alaska, and the sight of this flaming thing was too much. Mankiewicz threw up, and everybody sort of said, 'Oh, you were saying?' and turned to their neighbour and left him there. He slid under the table and as he did, he looked up to Hornblower and said, 'Well Arthur, you've to admit, at least the white wine came up with the fish.'

1972 and 1980

Malcolm Muggeridge

Malcolm Muggeridge was one of the great commentators of the twentieth century. He wrote with flawless style and lacerating humour. The *New York Times* said he 'delighted in outraging the Establishment and impaling the pompous on the lance of his lethally keen wit'. On television, he was a formidable interviewer as well as an entertaining and enlightening commentator. His posh, highly articulated delivery of an opinion kept impressionists happy for a long time, and his disdain of a fool was marvellous to behold. In the sixties he chaired a television debate on the subject of whether or not we should play sport against South Africa. A supporter of 'building bridges' with the apartheid regime was in full flow, and the longer he went on, the more Malcolm's face creased into a look of utter disdain, until, nose averted as if to avoid a bad smell, Muggeridge said, 'My dear sir, do shut up – you are such a twerp.' A splendid warrior to have on your side. He died in 1990 aged eighty-seven.

Michael: Reading your autobiography, one of the things that struck me is that you never seemed to have an ambition like most children to be a train driver or footballer, or anything like that.

Malcolm: I didn't. It's an awful confession to make, but the only thing I ever was interested in is words – the use of words, written words, spoken words, just words. I never thought any achievement in life was of any significance by comparison. I never wanted to be a great general or millionaire, or a great lover. I decided the most marvellous thing would be to use words.

Michael: Can I ask you about your ambition, or lack of it, to be a great lover. Did you have any girlfriends when you . . .

Malcolm: Oh, yes. I was very keen on girls. But in my time it was much less exhausting. We still accepted the idea that to make passes at girls was bad manners, and that if you did, you might either catch some nameless disease or get her in the family way, both highly dishonourable things. We were enormously protected in this matter.

Michael: That's hardly desirous, I would imagine?

Malcolm: Looking back, I sometimes think it wasn't too bad an idea.

Michael: Why?

Malcolm: I think the very early indulgence in sex deprives the young of this romantic period when they have quite illusory views of girls, which is delightful, and perhaps a necessary part of life. To put it simply, when I went to Cambridge as a youth in 1920, I would think the great majority of undergraduates had never slept with a female.

Michael: Had you?

Malcolm: No, I hadn't.

Michael: You were a virgin until you were married?

Malcolm: No, I wasn't, but there was this very good period between becoming adolescent and beginning to seduce women, and that gap was a very valuable period in life, full of extremely pleasant things.

Michael: A lot of people might say that many married in those days to explore sex for the first time, and finding it not quite what they thought, there was a rather high incidence of unhappy marriage and divorce.

Malcolm: But my dear man, would you say that today there are fewer unhappy marriages?

Michael: I would say there are unhappy marriages but for different reasons.

Malcolm: That may be, because I think that's the whole point. This naïve idea that, if people are sexually experienced, they are more likely to be happily married, is just as much an illusion as imagining, as Hindus do, that if their two horoscopes match, they're going to be happily married. The truth is that it is very difficult for two people to live together through their life, and not just because of sex. That's just one item in it.

Michael: Your view of morality today, of sex and the lot, is it fair to say that it's the viewpoint of a sated old lecher?

Malcolm: No, it's not. You would find that it's not a view that came upon me in old age, and rather that was part of the experience of living. It's very well put by someone who is not greatly regarded today, but I regard him as one of the greatest men who ever lived – St Paul. He said, 'To be carnally minded is death, but to be spiritually minded is life and peace.' That has really been at the core of Christian morality for two thousand years. It doesn't appeal much to people today, but for what it's worth, that saying has seemed to me to be more and more true.

Michael: On to another period, and the sort of colossal mistake you made in early life when you decided to seek Utopia in Russia.

Malcolm: The point is that it goes back to my childhood. My father and his friends were early socialists, and believed that if they captured the government, they knew exactly how to make a perfect human society. They could make men brotherly, cooperative, gentle – all the things we want them to be. I thought this was absolutely true. Then you had a couple of Labour governments and those governments didn't produce this result, so there was some fallacy in it. At the same time, when I went to Manchester to work on the *Guardian,* which was a liberal newspaper in those days, it held up this idea that through government and power you could make a humane society. At the same time, of course, the Depression was happening. Towns such as Burnley had 60 per cent or 70 per cent unemployed. The whole place was at a standstill.

With Russia, the thing to do was to go there, identify yourself with that, let your children grow up in that, write about that, so the world may know the salvation ahead. That's the mood I went in and, of course, as soon as one was there, as a journalist, one realised that men in power are very different from men seeking power. It was a dramatic realisation that man cannot save himself through power. All the flower of intelligence of the Western world gravitated to Moscow, and I suddenly realised they were a collection of buffoons.

Michael: When you look back over all the things you've done, which was the most absurd?

Malcolm: It's a hard question, because when human beings are being most serious, they're most absurd, and the two most ridiculous activities are war and sex. Those are the times when everybody's most serious. When I was editor of *Punch,* I tried to find a definition of humour, and the only one I could hit on was that humour is an expression of the preposterous disparity between human aspiration and human achievement. In the war, I was in the Intelligence Service, which, contrary to its name, was one of the most stupid activities possible to imagine. It was full of hilarity, but the particular situation I remember was in a place called Lorenzo Marques, a Portuguese colony in Mozambique. It was the only piece of neutral territory in that part of Africa, and therefore there was a German consul general called Wertz, an Italian consul general called Campini, and myself, who was a bogus vice-consul, and we were the three operators of intelligence. We all lived in the same hotel, all bribed the same local policemen, and this little image of a great war in this rather ludicrous place and ludicrous situation, struck me as almost the funniest thing that ever happened.

Michael: Did you ever find it difficult to take yourself seriously?

Malcolm: Well, I don't take myself seriously. I don't think any man should take himself seriously.

Michael: Should we take you seriously?

Malcolm: No. Because no man is great enough to be truly serious, and a man who ultimately takes himself seriously is mad. But not to take oneself seriously doesn't mean not to be serious. It's a different thing. I would like to believe that I am deeply serious about life, which I think is a marvellous thing, but to take oneself seriously would be to believe that such a stupid, fallible, self-indulgent, inconsistent, ludicrous figure as one is, is to be taken seriously.

Michael: How do you entertain the thought of death?

Malcolm: I look forward to it keenly.

Michael: Really?

Malcolm: Yes. I'm longing for it, not because I don't like the world – I love the world and my fellows – but I think the thing making life wonderful is that it comes to an end. If someone were to invent something that would enable one to go on living forever, I should regard that as peculiarly disgusting. In *Gulliver's Travels*, in the third journey to the island of Laputa, there are people who live forever, and they are the most melancholy people. They sit with their heads in their hands, envying all the others who die, because dying is a great, joyous thing. It means you've lived and it's come to an end – the drama, the exile, scene five, curtain. It's a wonderful moment because you know the drama on which the curtains come down is a drama related to a much larger one.

1972

John Mortimer

The barrister who created *Rumpole of the Bailey* once described himself as 'the best playwright who ever defended a murderer at the Old Bailey'.

He was a relentlessly optimistic man and a passionate opponent of do-gooders who would set themselves up as our moral guardians. He was the best of company – even when stricken with illness and in a wheelchair, he still transmitted a zest for living and a love of the 'handmaidens' who cared for him.

Unlike most great talkers, he was also an exceptional interviewer. The interviews he did for the *Sunday Times* are an inspiration for anyone seeking guidance in the craft of persuading strangers to confide in you. He worked, without sign of decline, until his death in 2009 aged eighty-five.

My father was a divorce barrister, and he was like Rumpole in a way. He always quoted poetry to me, and was rude to solicitors, which barristers aren't meant to be. But he specialised in divorce, so I grew up in a very 'divorce' atmosphere.

My father used to come home when I was a child and sit on the end of the bed, and instead of *Goldilocks and the Three*

Bears I used to get *The Duchess and the Three Co-respondents*. He used to come in and say, 'Today, we managed to prove adultery with evidence of inclination and opportunity.' So I said, 'Wonderful, Dad.' Then he used to say, 'A great part of the evidence was footprints upside down on the dashboard of an Austin Seven parked in Hampstead Gardens.' He told me that divorce was never dull because it was always connected with sex, and then I went into it.

My father was a very dramatic old barrister, and he was blind. He went blind when I was about seventeen, which made absolutely no difference to him. He used to fix witnesses with his glittering eye and say, 'Remember the whole thing?' And then he became deaf, and then he couldn't stand up any more, and by that time he was absolutely irresistible. When he was sitting down and couldn't see or hear, no judge could possibly refuse him anything. So I'm looking forward to that.

My first job was as an assistant director in a government propaganda film unit during the war, because the man who ran it had seen my Punch and Judy show when I was about eight, and was so impressed by it that when we fought Hitler he thought I was just the man to work on propaganda films about the war.

My job was to say, 'Quiet please,' at the start of every shot, and I was so nervous I used to say it very, very quietly so nobody took any notice, and they all went on hammering and so on. Finally, I said it very loudly and they all went on strike, so they moved me from that to be the scriptwriter. We did propaganda films about how to put your old toast rack up for salvage, and lots of films about the RAF bombers rising into the sky to the music of Vaughan Williams, and always hitting their targets – which later we found out wasn't strictly accurate.

My father told me that if I was a writer, I'd stay at home all day and my wife would leave me, because it's dreadful to have a writer stumped for words hanging about the house. And he offered me the law, like girls who want to go for the stage are offered secretarial courses – you know, something to fall back on. So he offered me that to fall back on, and I've been falling back on it ever since.

I did divorce cases and divorced people like shelling peas, because they got divorced after the war, and then divorce suddenly became easier and then they all got divorced. Old people who had been living happily together for about fifty years suddenly got divorced and remarried, and left each other rather soon afterwards. I married a lady who had four children, so I had to support all those, and I just divorced people night and day.

It was a very strange area. We had things like matrimonial offences in those days. So you had to investigate who flung the fish slice at someone in 1932. It was a very painful piece of litigation. And, of course, you learnt all sorts of things about writing. You learnt that there were two languages in courts. Half of my clients, after the judge had passed judgement, didn't know what had happened to them, whether they'd been condemned to death or awarded enormous damages. Often you had to explain to them that they were still married, which made them even more confused.

I took to crime once I became a QC, because the heart had rather gone out of divorce. Your own beliefs, in a way, don't enter into what you do in court. But I am profoundly opposed to censorship in any form. I don't think anybody has the right to decide what I read, or what I think, or what I write. And one of the risks that you take, if you believe in that, is that there will be pornography. Personally, I find it an acceptable risk. I don't think it's particularly harmful, but that doesn't mean to say that I necessarily welcome pornography. I just think it's a part of what you've got to have if you believe in free speech.

I always defend and never prosecute. I would find it, I think, distasteful to use my skill at cross-examining people or appealing to juries in order to put someone in prison. I think the present institutions, with three or four people crowded in with their own chamber pots for very long periods of time, are inhuman, totally useless, do nothing at all but solidify the criminal classes into their patterns and are ineffective altogether. I think that there is a very small proportion of people who have to be immunised from society. I suppose the Kray brothers, or big gangsters of that sort who live by murder, should be immunised from society in some sort of way, under some sort of condition. But a great many of the people, I should think 75 per cent, even more, who are in prison needn't be there, and they're there because of their inadequacies and because of their environments and all sorts of reasons.

There are all sorts of different criminals. The criminals I like to defend are those who blunder into crime out of mistake, out of inadequacy, out of stupidity – those are who most murderers are. Murder really is usually either an extension of a Saturday night punch-up or a domestic disagreement, and those people are not really criminals in that sense. Now, there are professional criminals for whom prison is part of their whole way of life. It's totally ineffective to stop them being there, it does them no good, it does society no good, but nobody takes any time to think of any alternative.

I don't believe in original sin. My clients – I don't honestly think that that is the right way of describing them – I've found them to be usually people who are stupid, live in environments that they can't cope with, or else are brought up in environments where crime is the normal behaviour. Just as for me, whose father was a barrister, so I want to succeed in the law, I think there is a whole part of society in which crime is the acceptable way of getting on. And that's what you've got to change.

I'm rather a ham barrister. I rather orate, which Rumpole does. I catch myself saying the most terribly hammy things in court. I remember once in the Uxbridge Magistrates' Court I was defending a lady pop star for passing rather curious cigarettes through London Airport, and she was there in the dark in a black dress, tearful and dramatic, and I was standing defending her. And I came to my pre-oration and I actually heard myself say to the magistrates, 'Give her justice,' I said, 'which is what she's waited and prayed for all these weeks, but let that be justice tempered with that mercy which is the hallmark of the Uxbridge and Hillingdon District Magistrate.' So I thought to myself, 'How corny can I possibly get?' She was triumphantly acquitted and drove off, and the whole magistrates' court was in tears.

1979

Peter Ustinov

Peter Ustinov relished being interviewed and once he told me why. 'It's only when I'm asked a question I find out what I really think about something,' he said. When you saw him lumbering towards you, slightly pin-toed, he gave the impression of being eager to engage. There was no settling-down period for Peter. First question, no matter what, he would fix you with an amused look that said, 'That wasn't a bad start, but don't worry, here comes a brilliant answer.' He had, of course, all the gifts required by the raconteur. He possessed a faultless memory, a vivid use of language, an unfailing sense of humour and an enviable capability as a mimic. He also had a clear memory of past conversations, which enabled him to avoid repeating an anecdote, even though the interviewer had forgotten and asked him the same question. I once enquired about a particular incident on the set of *Quo Vadis*. 'You asked me that five years ago,' he said. He was the perfect guest. Moreover, he provided one of the great musical moments of the show when he and Dudley Moore performed an impromptu duet as opera singer and accompanist. I interviewed him seven times, most of them one-guest shows, without ever sensing I had come anywhere near to giving but a sketchy outline of a remarkable life, or exhausting the talents of this truly remarkable man. That said, he was a genuine conversationalist as opposed to a man with a limitless reservoir of prepared monologues. He once told me that the way to be a good conversationalist was to listen as well as talk.

Michael: You mentioned earlier this thing about being a lonely child – not necessarily unhappy, but isolated from other children, and one wonders how you managed to cope with prep school. Was it difficult? Did you adopt any camouflage?

Peter: I automatically gravitated towards making people laugh at me because I noticed at school, also in the Army later on, that I got out of trouble by being so hopeless that it amused people. Every unit and every school has the butt for unmalicious jokes, and I became that, which was sad in a way, because I was rather good at one or two things that I was never allowed to do because I was too odd. They didn't fit. I would have loved to play tennis properly earlier on. As it was, I could nearly always beat people in the school team at Westminster, but was never allowed to play because they didn't take it seriously. Now at the end of my road, I've been asked semi-officially to be a linesman at Wimbledon, but I said I'm not old enough, I can still see the ball.

Michael: Westminster, of course, is a public school. Did you have any choice of going to public school?

Peter: Oh no, I had a choice – between Westminster and St Paul's. I found a school report in my mother's things after she died, which said, 'He shows great originality, which must be curbed at all costs.' I realised also when I went to Westminster that British schools of that sort, at the time, were geared towards producing diplomats, lawyers, solicitors, publicity executives – people who exploit one aspect of the truth, sometimes at the expense of others. When I arrived at Westminster, I was told by a master that I was talking in the debate that night, and that I was proposing the motion that the death sentence should be maintained as a deterrent. I said, 'But I'm opposed to the death sentence, Sir.' 'Ustinov, I don't think you heard what I said. You're proposing the motion.' I said, 'I don't understand, Sir.' 'You will.' And I spoke against the death sentence, but because I was speaking for it I got some laughs. We won – the wrong side – so I began to understand the way those things were weighted.

Yes, I was given the choice by my parents, who could afford neither, of Westminster where they wore top hats and looked like Fred Astaire, or else St Paul's where they had boaters and looked like Harold Lloyd. I thought, at the age of thirteen, if I'm going to look ridiculous, I might as well look completely ridiculous and put on a top hat. I was a boarder most of the time, but when I was a day boy, I had to cross the virtual slum that existed in those days between the Cromwell Road and Earls Court underground station, dressed in a top hat, tail coat and hard collar and carrying a furled umbrella. The school prospectus said the umbrella distinguished us from City of London bank messengers, who didn't have umbrellas but who were nearly all eighty. And, of course, my real education took place there.

Michael: It did?

Peter: Yes, I received all sorts of tomatoes and heavens above, so that no dramatic critic has worried me since those days.

Michael: Was there any such thing as sex education at a school like that?

Peter: No. There was none at all, and I was left totally in the dark. But things were perhaps a little more evolved else-where. My old friend, Sir Clifford Norton, told me what it was like in Rugby, round about 1910, when the headmaster decided that the time had come for certain boys to be instructed in these delicate matters, and said, 'Are we all here? Is Armstrong here? Oh yes, there you are, you're so small. Come forward, Armstrong. Bailey, shut the door, is your brother? Your brother, yes, that's right. Right, shut the door. Are you all here? Very well. Now, look here. If you touch it, it will fall off. Right, return to your dormitories,' and they left equipped for life. But I never learnt that even.

Michael: You didn't? Nothing at all? You had to find out by trial and error?

Peter: I was given one of those Russian toys, that rather bulky lady that you unscrew and inside there's a smaller one, then you unscrew her and I vaguely thought that when people were pregnant, they had another fully dressed woman inside, but that's the nearest I got in my guesswork. And when I finally discovered, I had a moment of absolute panic. I wonder if that's a common thing, but I don't think many people find out as late as I did. I was just not terribly inquisitive, I suppose. I thought some thunderclap would reveal everything to me. I never believed in the stork or anything like that. I knew that was nonsense, but I had nothing to put in its place. I had terrible claustrophobia.

Michael: Claustrophobia?

Peter: How on earth did I breathe? There must be some arrangement by which one can breathe. Because if you're inside your mother . . .

Michael: You moved on from Westminster to drama school. How did you get in?

Peter: My mother saw in advance that I'd never pass these exams, that I was making myself ill preparing for them, and she sent me to the drama school where a gentleman called Monsieur St Denis, a very imperious Frenchman with a pipe, said, 'At sixteen he is too young,' and my mother had the sense to say, 'He has eyes very much like yours, you know.' 'He has good eyes, all right, we will take him.' She did that fiddle very well and I went into the drama school. I was interested in it because it was my first co-educational school. I was close to girls for the first time. It was really thrilling and exciting. It's especially thrilling when you know nothing at all.

It was an advanced drama school and we were supposed to be animals for one term in order to stretch our imaginations, and all the ambitious girls decided one South

African girl was ill because she played a springbok. She lost about two stone during the year, leaping from rock to rock. I knew better. I was a salamander and just lay on a rock for one term.

Michael: Let's turn to another aspect of your life, to the war years. Your father was working for the German Embassy, in the press office, at the time?

Peter: Yes, he was a press attaché in 1935. He left with the help of Lord Vansittert, and they put notices for if you wished to become British in a Welsh-language paper in Carmarthan, which frustrated even the ingenuity of the Gestapo.

Michael: It certainly would. With the position your father had and the intimate knowledge that you had of what was going on, did you have any forewarning at all that war was imminent?

Peter: Well, we had one extraordinary incident. My father was worse than a rich man. He was a rich man without money, and he said to me in 1934 that the time had come for me to have pocket money, and I was now going to receive a shilling a week. I was delighted with the initiative but disappointed by the amount, as well I might have been, because it was the first and last shilling I ever saw. So in 1938 I came back from my drama school to find him rather agitated. We lived then on the fourth floor of 34 Redcliffe Gardens, in London, and he said, 'Why are you so late? I want you to go to the movies.' He'd never offered me that before, and I said, 'Well, if you want me to go to the movies, I need some money.' 'But you've had your money,' he said, remembering the shilling. And I said, 'Well, no,' and he gave me sixpence rather grudgingly and I said, 'It costs more than that.' 'Since when? You don't have to go in the expensive seats, you know.' I said, 'It costs ninepence since about two years,' and he called my mother and gave me ninepence. It was so uncharacteristic for him, who was always saying, 'You spend your time at the movies, you don't study enough.'

I didn't understand it but off I went. I understood that he was agitated. Some old men were climbing the stairs laboriously. They looked like a lot of elephants trying to find somewhere to die. I stood flush with the wall as they passed, about nine old men, and I went to my movie and came back home. There was a bar of light under the door, and an asphyxiating smell of cigar smoke. I went to bed and never mentioned it again until the middle of the war. I said to my father, 'What was that evening, now that I think of it,' and he said, 'Well, I had left the German Embassy three years before, and all the contacts I'd made for them had been dissolved by Ribbentrop, who behaved like such an idiot while ambassador. Now, in 1938, I got a call from a phone box from the German military attaché, General Geyr von Schweppenburg. He said, "Look here, as an ex-officer of the German Army, I'm appealing to you. We're in such bad odour with the British, we have no contact any more. We simply must get the British to stand firm at Munich, because it's the last chance we have of stopping Hitler, and if you can arrange a meeting between members of the British General Staff and members of the German General Staff, our generals will take leave all at the same time, go to various European capitals and come to England incognito by commercial airliner." ' This was the meeting.

Michael: In your house?

Peter: Yes, and the British decided that they couldn't risk it, it may be a trap, and so we all started preparing for Dunkirk.

Michael: Of course, you'd had previous knowledge of the Nazi Party in Germany.

Peter: Oh, I'd been there. I saw the Reichstag burning. I was there visiting my grandmother. Since everybody around her was very old, they tried to find me young friends, and they found me, unfortunately, the son of a neighbour, who was a screaming Nazi, and another neighbour's son who was inseparable from the Nazi boy, and who was Jewish. We went for a walk in the Gruenewald, which was a lovely park near Berlin, at that time full of the rustle of leaves, and suddenly you'd hear a shout and a stick would come into view, chased by an Alsatian dog. They were all being trained. Everything was belligerent at the time, and in this sylvan setting, with nothing but the songs of Nazi youths marching through and singing in unison, suddenly these boys revealed themselves to be much more sinister than I thought. The German boy said to the Jewish boy, 'We must end our friendship because of geopolitical reasons,' something he'd heard from his father, and the Jewish boy concurred, and they suddenly started a most repellent ceremony of trying to blend their blood for the last time in a kind of Wagnerian farewell. Since I didn't trust them at all – they had a rusted penknife for this work, and there was no evidence they knew the difference between veins and arteries in any case – I ran a much faster mile than Bannister ever managed. I still shudder as I think of it now, this kind of awful complicity, a sort of vaguely homosexual feel to the whole thing and yet mixed with history in a horrible gruel.

Michael: Did that experience, though, make you a more willing soldier when the time came for you to go and fight the Hun?

Peter: Oh, a willing soldier, no. In spite of my claustrophobia, which I told you about earlier on, when I was actually called up, I was asked by the officer at the centre, 'What arm would you like to serve in if it were possible?' and I said the tank corps. 'Oh, really?' He became terribly excited. 'Why?' And I said, 'because I would like to go into battle sitting down.' I was called into the infantry two days later.

Michael: Going back to the time that you made your break into Hollywood, it was a film called *Quo Vadis*, wasn't it?

Peter: Yes.

Michael: And that was directed by Mervyn LeRoy. First of all, how did you get that job? What made them think of you as Nero?

Peter: It was John Huston who did, and he did the test with me as Nero. I overdid it enormously and he said, 'Do some more, do some more,' and I couldn't do any more. I thought I was going way overboard but it was what they wanted, and apparently I was very restrained as an actor in those days. There was a delay of a year while they changed every-thing, and eventually Mervyn LeRoy came on the scene and cabled me saying that he liked my test very much but he thought I might be a little young for the part, and I cabled back saying, 'If you go on delaying any longer, I'll be too old for the part,' because Nero died at the age of thirty-one, I think. And they sent back a treasured telegram saying, 'Historical research has proved you correct. The part is yours.'

Michael: Did you get any sort of assistance from Mr LeRoy?

Peter: Well, I was very much nearer my dramatic student days then, and very serious about certain things, and so I wanted to find out from my new director what he thought of the part I was about to play. I saw him for the first time twenty-four hours before we shot, and he was on a huge stage, standing smiling with his cigar, and I said, 'How do you think I ought to play Nero?' He said, 'Nero? Son-of-a-bitch!' I said, 'Yes, I agree.' We agreed so far, I said, and then he thought and he said, 'You know what he did to his mother?' with decent concern, as though there was something that could still be done about it. I said, 'Yes, I do know. That was very reprehensible.' 'Yeah, son-of-a-bitch.' Then he began to tap dance, and he said, 'I used to be a hoofer.' I thought for a terrible moment he wanted me to tap dance in the part of Nero, but he didn't. He considered what I'd said and he said, 'The way I see it, Nero's a guy that plays with himself nights.' That's the only instruction I got and I thought it was pretty foolish, but in retrospect I think he's absolutely right. In point of fact, it's the briefest, the crispest kind of instruction I've ever had from a director.

Michael: What about some of the other people you've worked with? You've worked with just about every great name in the business. Did you work with Sir Alec Guinness at all?

Peter: Yes. We worked on a film called *The Comedians*, and we'd worked on the radio once. I'm tremendously devoted to him. I think he's a marvellous character. This is a story he told himself, and I really have no right to use it, except that I watched his show with you, and I don't remember him telling it himself, which I thought was a shame because he's a bewitching kind of demure man. He suddenly had an irresistible desire to play Hitler, which defies everybody, because you couldn't find two people more different, quite frankly. And it got to such a pitch that I believe when he heard that Dustin Hoffman had the part, he became desperate. He said, 'Hitler's mine,' very unlike him, and he went to the extent of going to a famous firm of theatrical costumiers where he found a Hitler outfit to fit him. He went to a photographer's somewhere in Bayswater and had pictures taken in a fairly isolated street – there was Alec Guinness standing on the sidewalk and nobody took any notice. People passed with prams, people hesitated, they didn't stop, and it was extraordinary that this passed un-noticed by everybody except one policeman, who wandered up to him and said, 'Excuse me, Sir, is that your car over there, on the double yellow lines? Well, actually, Sir, that is a no-parking area. I'm only going to warn you on this occasion. I'm not giving you a ticket as I have no desire to spend the rest of my life in a concentration camp.'

1978 and 1980

Stephen Fry

Stephen loves cricket and that being the case the greatest compliment I can pay him is that when I think of guests who could be termed 'all-rounders', he is Garfield Sobers. He has the lot – wit, intellect, a vault of anecdote, a remarkable memory, a talent to amuse. Indeed, it's easier to think of him as many people rather than an individual. The writer Douglas Adams said, 'There's more than one of him. I think there's a cupboard full of Stephen Frys.' His other gift, often unremarked, is that he is a great listener. Some guests see little requirement for a supporting cast. I remember Alistair Cooke, upon being told he was appearing with another guest, saying, 'But I don't require company when I'm being interviewed.' Stephen, on the other hand, not only listens to what people have to say but has the greater gift of making them feel as if they are more interesting than he is. It's not a ploy, nor a demonstration of false modesty, more an example of Peter Ustinov's dictum that to be a great conversationalist you must first learn how to be a great listener.

My entire schooldays were made a living hell by trying to avoid sport. I loathed it. I thought the others were mud-spattered barbarians who had some ghastly key to puberty and growing hairs in unlikely places, and I was weak and thin. I was just hopeless and wasn't bulging in the right places at all, and felt absolutely ghastly. Every morning I'd wake up with a sort of hot lead leaking into my stomach with fear, knowing that it was a games day and I was going to have to devote more energy than you would ever devote on a rugby field to getting out of sport. I just hated it, absolutely despised it. Fortunately, I had some devil in me that managed to take the offensive. I wouldn't allow myself to be a weed, so if it was cricket, I would lie on the field with a limp-bound copy of the *Rubaiyat of Omar Khayyam* and say, 'Wait a minute, girls, I'm just coming to the last verse. I can't possibly catch balls at the moment.' It was very hard and I'd get bullied, but I'd say, 'No, no, no, don't beat me up. I'll just get an erection.' I'd recommend that to anybody out there who's been threatened by bullies. That is a very good ploy, it worked every time.

When I was seventeen, I tried to take my life. I've been diagnosed with what the doctors called cyclothymia, which the Americans rather splendidly call 'bipolar lite', which is not the worst kind of bipolarity by any means. I can't complain. I'm not on any medication, as some are. I went to see the great Carrie Fisher and did an interview with her. I've known her for many years and she's mostly a bouncy, manic person, and it just so happened she was in a very down phase. The point about calling it 'bipolar' is that there's the manic polar, when your mood is very elevated, you're immensely energetic, you can go for days without sleep and you feel like you're king of the world; and then the other pole is the black depression. We caught Carrie when she was like that. She was almost physically transformed and it was so sad. You realise this is a terrible illness. But it's also a spectrum because most people will say, 'Well I have up days and down days.'

I spoke to a Hollywood producer, and he said, 'Contrary to rumours, you don't have to be gay, you don't have to be Jewish, to get on in Hollywood, but by God you've got to be manic depressive.' And it's certainly true that an enormous number of Hollywood people are. I don't know why, whether it's cause or effect – whether it turns you into a manic depressive or whether, to be serious for a moment, manic depressives are attracted to creative jobs and jobs, indeed, where you don't have to work nine to five. It's almost impossible to do that if you are seriously bipolar.

Mental health is an incredibly important issue, and, of course, to persuade the BBC to do a programme that had the word 'depression' in the title was something, because they just think, 'Oh God, what a turn-off,' but people watched. There isn't anybody watching here in the audience or at home who doesn't know somebody for whom mental stability is an issue. It has been for me for most of my life, and I'm not embarrassed or ashamed about it any more than I am about the fact that I occasionally get asthma.

I saw a wonderful man who served on the Royal Yacht Britannia for many years and had a very senior naval position. And he developed the most appalling conditions, pretty serious psychosis and terrible depression, and he was hospitalised. His depression got so bad that he went out and threw himself in front of a lorry. Amazing that he survived but his legs were smashed to pieces, bones sticking out. I said to him, 'The pain must have been unbelievable.' And he said, 'That's why I tried to kill myself.' I said, 'No the pain of your legs.' And he said, 'The pain of my legs was nothing compared to the pain inside.' That gives you some idea of what depression can be. But the extraordinary thing is that when faced with the question, 'You've got a button and if you press it, you can take away your bipolarity and you would never have had it. Do you want to press the button?' only two of about thirty people said they would.

Do you know how Churchill would often sort out his black dog? His black dog was what he called his depression. He would sit for a while in the company of a pig and talk. Someone once asked him, 'Why a pig?' And he said, 'Well, cats look down on you, dogs look up at you, but a pig regards you as an equal.'

To some extent, I'm rather glad to have been able to talk a little about my own struggles with mental health, which always sounds dreadful, but also to address what is a serious matter of stigma. It's much easier for me, rather as it was twenty years ago for me to talk about being gay in a profession where being gay is pretty easy – not everybody feels comfortable about coming out. In the same way, it's much easier for me to talk about the fact that I have days when I'm peculiarly manic and odd and go on spending sprees and am sort of weird and uncontrollable.

When I first started in television, way back in Granadaland, the director who used to work on *Coronation Street* took Hugh Laurie aside and said, 'Is Stephen on drugs?' And Hugh said, 'No, that's just how he is.' I can talk about it like this to some extent because I don't feel I'm going to get fired, and people are not going to look at me too oddly. But there are hundreds of thousands of people whose lives are really blighted by the fact that their mood swings are so great. And they feel that if they are diagnosed, and tell someone they're bipolar and on medication, they may lose their job and have a lifetime of people looking at them oddly.

Like you, I love cricket, and the MCC is such a good way of going to see it. There are some weird creatures under the stands of the Marylebone Cricket Club. I was there a couple of years ago and a friend, who was club president at the time, introduced me with great relish to Field Marshal Bramall, who said, 'I've got a bone to pick with you, young man.' It turned out that in my first novel I had written a character called Colonel Bramall. When you think up character names, you don't know where they come from. I was convinced I'd made it up. Unfortunately, the subject of the fictional Colonel Bramall in *The Liar* was some of the work of the Household Brigade near Buckingham Palace. In the fifties and sixties, if you were a young, adventurous, amorous man, and were not after girls and wanted a bit of sport, it was said that you could find a guardsman in the bushes of St James's Park for five shillings. So I wrote about this kind of thing and mentioned this Colonel Bramall, and so when I met Field Marshal Bramall, he'd read the book and was staring at me with wild eyes. I thought he was going to get me to peel potatoes for four years or something awful – do my buttons up and break my sword over his knee.

But he warmed up, was very sweet and told me a story that I thought was just such a fantastic contrast to politics today. He said Churchill was woken up one Sunday morning when he was prime minister in the fifties by a private secretary, who was rather worried, and said, 'I'm afraid there's some bad news, Prime Minister.' 'We've lost Somalia? What is it?' He said, 'No, no, it's one of our backbench MPs. One of our squires from the shires was arrested last night in St James's Park with a guardsman, and sadly it's in the *News of the World*, the early edition. I'm afraid there's going to be a bit of a stink about it.' Churchill said, 'Last night?' He said, 'Yes, yes, Prime Minister.' 'It was very cold last night, wasn't it?' and the secretary said, 'Yes. In fact, I believe it was the coldest February night for seventeen years.' And there was a slight pause and Churchill said, 'Makes you proud to be British.'

I was lucky enough to know Sir Martin Gilliat, the Queen Mother's private secretary, and he told me once, 'This was some years ago now but I noticed Queen Elizabeth,' as they all used to call the Queen Mother, 'Queen Elizabeth's television was a little on the blink. I said to her, "Ma'am, I think our television needs looking at." She said, "You're quite right. I'll go down to lunch, you get on to those nice people at Harrods and see if we can have a new television." '

So he made the phone call and by the time she had toddled up and sat down in her chair, there was this brand new television and he said, 'Ma'am, I think you'll be as excited as I am. As you see, it's a very big screen. Now you see that little grey box next to your gin and Dubonnet? If you want to change the channel, instead of getting up to press a button, you press one for BBC1, two for BBC2 and three for ITV,' and she looked at it and said, 'Oh, how clever, but I still think it's easier to ring!' Marvellous.

1999–2007

Roald Dahl

Roald Dahl's life could not have been more extraordinary had it been written by the man himself. He was the fighter pilot and spy who married one of Hollywood's most desirable women, became one of the world's most successful writers quite by chance, and, when his son was seriously injured, helped devise a medical procedure that saved his life, which is still used today. Similarly, when his wife Patricia Neal suffered a series of strokes, he nursed her back to health. She credited him with her recovery. He will always be remembered for his children's stories, including *James and the Giant Peach* and *Charlie and the Chocolate Factory*, which appeal to succeeding generations of young people. He was a courtly man who carried with him an air of intrigue and mystery. Fascinating.

To be quite honest, I had no thought of writing at all right up to the age of about twenty. I was wounded in the war and sent to Washington. It was early days, and I was sitting in my rather grand office in the British Embassy, wondering what to do, and there was a knock on the door. I said, 'Come in,' and a tiny little man came in, wearing thick glasses, and said, 'Excuse me, are you busy?' and I said, 'Not in the least.' I thought he was going to ask for a job, and he said, 'My name's Forester, C.S. Forester,' and I said, 'Get on, you can't be.' He was one of my heroes, one of the great writers of that time, *Captain Hornblower*. He said, 'Now you've been in the war. America's only just coming in. You've been in action. I'll take you out to lunch. Tell me your most exciting exploit, I'll write it up in the *Saturday Evening Post* and we'll get the British a bit of publicity.'

I said, 'Well, I don't have any wildly exciting stories. I haven't done half the things that other fighter pilots have done.' He said, 'It's all right, come on.' We went out to lunch and I remember we had roast duck, and he was trying to take notes and eat this bloody duck at the same time and he couldn't do it. I said, 'Why don't I scribble it down for you this evening in a rough way, and you can put it right when I send it to you?' and he said, 'Oh, that will be super, will you do that?' So we finished our duck and I kept looking at him. He wasn't very exciting – writers aren't very exciting, as you can tell – no sparks were flying out of his head or anything. We finished the meal and I went home that evening and I wrote this thing out and sent it to him. I got a letter back about a week later saying, 'I asked for notes, not a finished story. I didn't touch it, the *Saturday Evening Post* bought it at once for $1000, the agent takes 10 per cent, so here's my cheque for $900.' And I thought, 'My God, it can't be as easy as all that.' It was.

****

I like writing short stories. First of all, you finish it quicker than you finish a novel. I'm a lazy sort of chap, and I'm absolutely terrified with every sentence and every paragraph I write, that the reader is going to shut the book and say, 'I can't get on with that book,' and throw it away. Now a novelist can't do that because a novelist has got to spread himself, and take a lot of time to describe scenery and the sunlight coming through the pine trees, and I couldn't do that because I'd be frightened of losing the reader.

Someone once said to Stravinsky, 'Maestro, where do you get your great ideas? While shaving in the bath? Or while strolling in the woods in the evening sunlight with the long shadows?' And he said, 'At the piano,' which has a lot of truth in it. It may be true for Stravinsky, three-quarters true for a writer, and the other quarter is the spark for the plot. That is going to have to come into your head, and then you rattle it around and buzz it about. It has to come from something, somewhere, or something you hear. You can't just think of it. Something sparks, and then you sit down and try to make a plot out of it.

****

If it's possible to make something out of tragedy, you try to do that, but sometimes you can't. When my son Theo was a baby, his nurse pushed his pram into a taxi in New York and he got severe head injuries and developed hydrocephalus. This happens when there's too much cerebral spinal fluid in the ventricles and you get pressure in there, and the old brain suffers damage unless you're very swift to relieve the pressure. This was sixteen years ago and they did have a shunt – a tube – with a valve in it where you could drain the fluid out, but they weren't very competent. They were much better than nothing but he had to keep going back and having new operations.

The shunts kept blocking and I said, 'Bugger this, we must be able to make a better shunt than this.' So I thought of a lovely man I knew who was an inventor – I had been flying model airplanes with him a couple of years ago. What I'd admired so much about him was that instead of buying these tiny model airplane engines, he made them all himself and turned them in his workshop. So I went along to him and said, 'Stanley, how about you doing this?' He's an eccentric fellow with nothing much to do, and he said, 'Yes, all right.' I was only the catalyst and medical liaison. We went and watched operations at Great Ormond Street, and had the enormous advantage that the head of neurosurgery there, Kenneth Till, was a tremendous cooperator in this. He told me exactly what was wanted and I told Stanley, and Stanley slaved over this thing. He produced this splendid little valve, which has got to be open at a certain pressure. It's very complex, and this was taken up and is still used in Great Ormond Street on children.

1980

Clive James

I had little reason to like Clive James before I met him. During his time as television critic on the *Observer*, he took a dislike to the talk shows of the time, and once suggested that dear Russell Harty and I might seek alternative employ doing something more useful like invading Russia. He won me over with his first volume of autobiography *Unreliable Memoirs*, which caused me to be restrained by the cabin crew on a flight to Australia when I suffered uncontrollable and hysterical bouts of laughter brought about by reading his book. Moreover, when Mr James himself became a practitioner of the talk show, he found it wasn't as easy as it seemed. Whatever his shortcomings as a talk-show host, he was indisputably a marvellous guest. The conflict in Clive's career has always been finding the balance between the glitter and rewards of television and his talent as a critic, novelist and poet, which places him in a different milieu, where a career in television is regarded disdainfully and thought of as a kind of betrayal. Indeed, anyone witnessing Mr James's hilarious demonstration of how to dance the tango, which took place in the Green Room after a show, would have found it impossible to believe that such a wonderful comic could also be taken seriously in literary circles. It was the performance of a naturally funny man whose greatest gift of all the many he possesses is in making people laugh.

My family was rich in personality, and not in any other way. I grew up in a low-income area of Sydney, but that is different from low-income in Britain. The standard of living is high. If you aren't doing well, you're still doing quite well. Everyone had steak three times a day and I swear I had meat for breakfast every day of my life. Cold meat from the fridge, surrounded by white fat – that was the way we lived.

All the loos were outside. In fact, you were doing well if you had a loo at all. They were non-sewered – in other words, every week a man came to take away the full pan and bring an empty one. He was the 'dunny man' and he arrived on the dunny-cart, which came down the street clank, bonk, clank, bonk, and you drew your blinds and didn't look because it was accepted – not discussed – how the pan was changed every week. It happened by magic.

I won't go into detail but it's hot in Sydney, right? It's a very grim scene. He'd put down the empty pan, and run back down the side of the house with the full pan on his shoulder, and he never missed his footing. Every Christmas you acknowledged the dunny man's presence by leaving a bottle of beer in the dunny, and by the time he got to us at Christmas, he must have been sampling the beer, because I heard him come down the side of the drive dong, clank, bonk, change the pan, 'Whee . . .' as he put the full pan on his shoulder and then came running back up the side. I'd left my bicycle lying out and on the way down he must have hurdled over it, but on the way back he forgot. So I heard this terrific noise, which sounded exactly like a man who's carrying a full dunny pan on his shoulder, tripping over a twenty-six-inch inch frame bicycle, and then there was the even more sinister sound of the lid springing off. I looked at my mother and she had her hands over her eyes. She wasn't acknowledging his existence. I went out, took a look down the side of the house, and there he was. The stunning thing was that none of it had missed him. He was a very disappointed man.

Australia is a very toxic country. In the whole of Britain there's nothing to attack you except about three adders, all of which have licence plates and contracts with BBC television, and I think one kind of poison ivy. Apart from that, nothing can hurt you. Australia is crawling with things that want to bite and sting you – two or three different kinds of lethal spider, about half a dozen kinds of lethal snake. About the worst snake is the taipan. They live in the sugarcane in Queensland and will attack a man riding a horse. It will kill the man, and the horse, in a few seconds. Gangs of taipans have been known to steal cars and cruise up and down the Pacific Highway. The black snake is dangerous, the brown snake is dangerous, and then you get to the spiders. There are two different kinds of extremely important lethal spiders, the funnel-web and the trapdoor. The funnel-web digs a hole in the ground, lines it with silk and emerges from this tunnel at high velocity, revealing itself to be a ping-pong ball in a fox-fur coat. It can leap an incredible distance, sink its mandibles into you and you've had it. The trapdoor is the same only it puts a little trapdoor on top of the hole so you can't see it. It's like an American guided missile.

There's an even worse spider – the redback – small, fragile-looking, with a little red stripe on its back, a lot like a German single-seater fighter from the First World War. It wouldn't be worthy of remark, but it's got one very bad habit, and this brings us back to an earlier theme – it hides under the lavatory seat. If you're creeping down to the outside loo in the dead of night, you're thinking all the time, 'Is there a redback under that seat? And if it bites me, where am I going to put the tourniquet?' Or, 'Who's going to suck out the poison?' You can become obsessed with these things, and obviously I still am. I still lift up the dunny seat, and give it a casual glance.

Sex was very funny in Australia in the fifties. There wasn't any. It wasn't available, so you thought about it all day and night. We thought about nothing else and everything we did was geared to this one forbidden activity. And there was no way of actually doing anything about it, but you thought and talked about women all the time. The funny thing is you didn't talk to a woman while she was there, because that wasn't done. Every Saturday, they'd have the church social – the only reason you went to church was so you could go to the social, which took place in the church hall. The music struck up and all the men went up to one end of the hall, all the women to the other, and that's the way it stayed for three hours and then we went home.

The biggest change in Australia was when the first immigrants arrived from Europe and the men went and talked to the women. Some of them got beaten up for it. The Australian men would be up one end drinking beer and they'd say, 'Let's go up and beat up that . . .' and take the new Australian outside and beat him up because he'd been talking to women. There was no language for addressing women, so it was a kind of miracle when you got to meet one.

About two years ago I went back for one month and I found it quite an unsettling experience. In fact, I cowered in my room. I resented everybody for having got on so well without me, because Australia's come on a long way in the last eighteen years. It's a very self-confident nation, which it wasn't in my time. But eighteen years is too long to be away from anywhere and then go back, because the ageing process, which has happened to you day by day and you've learned to live with, has happened to all the people you used to know. It's like coming back from space, from a trip round the universe. I found that quite startling. I was reminded, for the first time, of my mortality.

1980 and 1981

Jonathan Miller

Jonathan Miller appeared on the show nine times, which didn't come anywhere near accommodating the many people he is. However, I did manage to interview the doctor who became a comedian, the neuropsychologist who directed opera, the film critic and documentary film maker who, late in life, became a sculptor. I thought his greatest gift was as a teacher, the one you always hoped as a pupil you might find to inspire and inform you, but rarely did. My favourite Miller was the humorist, who was one of the funniest men I ever encountered. As you read his account of trying to cope with a stammer, or witnessing an orgy in New York, you will understand my enthusiasm.

Generally speaking, we have not made the most of Jonathan Miller. Critical bickering from people with not an ounce of his talent, particularly in the rarefied world of opera, has sometimes driven him to work in a more agreeable, appreciative environment abroad. Sometimes we are careless with the greatly gifted, seeming incapable of accommodating and celebrating their genius. This neglect is the one subject Jonathan Miller finds it difficult to be funny about. One of my very favourite guests and a most endearing man.

I can't play sport of any sort. I brought notes to school whenever I could to avoid sport, usually claiming it was on account of flat feet, and I used to avoid a lot of boxing this way, although there was one contest in the middle of the year that no one could avoid. It was a sort of giant Darwinian struggle in which every single person in the school was forced to contest with everyone else, or rather they were paired off with people at the beginning of the year, and then out of this huge, bloody contest, one victor would emerge.

I would always look down the lists at the beginning of the year and find myself paired with the same man, H.C.V. Jones, and would pass him in the corridors, hoping I would somehow ingratiate myself so he wouldn't hit me too hard, or offer to lay down in the first round. I tried to negotiate all sorts of settlements, but he was very keen on boxing and wanted to see it right the way through to its sporting conclusion, but it always ended the same way – I would do a lot of very elaborate footwork, which I thought was rather evasive, but he eventually tracked me down and simply held out his hand. I always noticed in boxing that as soon as you were hit on the nose, there was this very strange smell of aluminium. When the aluminium smell came I'd try to lie down and avoid the rest of the contest.

I had a stammer as a child, but it got troublesome, as it does now, only when I'm anxious or ill-at-ease. It always got troublesome on trains or on buses, having to ask for my fare. The awful thing about stammering is that you never quite know which consonants are going to be the fatal ones. You think you've got it all taped – avoid 't's and 'd's today – and then suddenly you find you're tripping up over an 'm'. I remember having a very bad time with initial 'm's and I would make the sound tube trains make when they're waiting – 'Mmmm.' Once, I was travelling to Marble Arch and I could see the conductor coming down the corridor and I knew I would have to say 'Mmmmm . . .' and as often happens with stammering, a fantastic act of creation took place. I said, 'One to the arch that is made of marble, please.'

I used to be given extra fare money by my parents for the days I'd find that the only station I could possibly say was somewhere like Wembley Park, and I'd need the money to cover these gigantic journeys out into Hertfordshire. At school, I had a friend who also had a stammer, and there were terrible moments in roll calls when I would stammer over my name but I could say his, and vice-versa, so we would simply swap identities for the purpose of the roll call. We'd have to say, 'He, he, he's Miller, Sir.' 'And he's so-and-so.'

I began to imitate animals and trains when I was about eight or nine, and on wet days at prep school I was brought out to the front to entertain rather disgruntled children with sounds of trains leaving Euston Station. Gradually, I became addicted to Danny Kaye. He seemed to represent all that was glamorous about America. At that time, shortly after the war, America seemed to be an El Dorado. It was partly because one saw all sorts of wonderful American soldiers on trains, and half of my childhood was spent following my father around, who was a military psychiatrist, from one hospital to another.

Wherever one travelled during the war, the whole place was filled with the military on the move. There were piles of sleeping soldiers propped up against one another with kitbags and helmets, and occasionally there were these very glamorous American soldiers who somehow looked much better than ours. Ours were all dressed in itching blotting paper and looked like something out of the First World War, and suddenly these paragons of glamour used to appear, wearing those rather marvellous clay-coloured trousers and dark olive jackets, giving one chewing gum and speaking like people spoke on films. They somehow seemed to be charmed creatures, whereas all of ours seemed to be cannon fodder, at least to a child.

Medicine seemed glamorous in a very peculiar sort of way. It was partly because of my father – not that he ever really encouraged me to become a doctor – but he would seduce me in the direction of medicine by dropping objects in my path, like a brass microscope, and I started getting interested in it. I suppose it was connected also with reading H.G. Wells, and the sense of the solemn mahogany and teak-benched world of South Kensington laboratories, and controversies between Victorian *savants* about the origins of some fossil's skull. There was something about my father's consulting room that was very attractive. It was the place where he went and had a mysterious other life, which we couldn't penetrate, and he seemed to be mysteriously renewed whenever one visited him. He was some other person, much more dignified and serious, and wasn't just simply boring Dad.

When I first started doing medicine, it still had its roots in nineteenth-century dignity. It wasn't so electronic and ultra-scientific, and a lot of my models of medicine were drawn from Victorian physicians and neurologists. The idea was still to observe patients rather than prodding them and interfering with electronic and bio-chemical investigations. It's the biographical aspect of medicine that I found interesting, or at least that curious boundary where man as a bag of enzymes meets man who has a biography, that strange frontier where man, the mechanism, and man, the person, meet.

As so often happens with these things, they're accidents. You think you've decided what you're going to do, you make a small choice and find it's committed you to a large change of life. While I was practising medicine, I was asked to do a revue at the Edinburgh Festival and to combine with three other chaps – Peter Cook, Dudley Moore and Alan Bennett. The four of us came together and did the show with a view to doing it for a week or so. That was *Beyond the Fringe*, and gradually it became more successful, and that put in train another series of choices, and you look back after five years and find you've made a much larger decision than you knew you were making at the time.

I certainly wasn't intending to go into show business. During the run of the show, I deluded myself into thinking I was still going back into medicine, but gradually all sorts of other interests began to develop, and I suppose the leisure and money the show made for us allowed me to exploit all those other interests, which might otherwise have remained dormant.

Directing is like medicine. What I liked about medicine, and what I like about directing, is this very delicate relationship you have between a group of people working towards some end on the basis of analysing and reproducing human behaviour. Since you spend a lot of time while training as a doctor watching what human beings do, and trying to diagnose them as a result, that sort of skill pays enormous dividends when you try to reproduce what people naturally do.

When I went to America, I got invited to all sorts of showbiz parties in New York. There, showbiz is mixed up with everything else. If you were successful in a show, you got to meet everyone – politicians, presidents, whatever. Fame was totally transferable in America. If you had made it, then you met the other people who had made it. It was all one great big sort of élite party where everyone who thought they had made it met all the other people who thought they'd made it, and it was a sort of monstrous self-congratulation in a penthouse.

There were occasional, rather more disreputable, parties set up for entirely sexual purposes. I was once invited to one and sat rather anxiously on the edge of a bed in total darkness while all sorts of grunting went on. What was so wonderful about it was the way in which decorum was preserved in the middle of chaos because, while there were these sort of heaving things, one could see occasionally against the slatted blinds, a decorous man in a white coat was walking around with a silver tray, offering whisky to people who were otherwise engaged. It was all very odd. It started off a perfectly normal evening, and then, rather like a Cinderella scene, at midnight, suddenly, the werewolves took over. Everyone was talking and chatting quite normally and then suddenly the light went out. There was total silence for about five minutes and then faint rasps and noises and giggles, and I sat on the edge of the bed, hoping that I would be seriously interfered with, but nothing happened at all.

There was a rather famous man, whose name I won't mention, but when the lights came on, I discovered this man, with one leg, having it off with someone, and his artificial leg was standing alone in the middle of the room. I don't know why he wasn't more embarrassed by the artificial leg than the misconduct he was using his other leg and limbs for. I said, 'Don't mind about me, carry on. Hope the leg gets better, or reattaches itself at least!'

Embarrassment is an extremely interesting thing. If we do something that might discredit us in the eyes of others, we will always broadcast something from our repertoire of apologetic behaviour, to redesign what might have been an offensive image of ourselves. Why is it that people in the street who trip ostentatiously go back three paces and inspect the pavement? It's in order to show the fault is in the pavement and not myself. Why is it that when people hail taxis and fail, they stroke their heads? It's somehow to adjust the opinion of others – 'I'm not a failed taxi hailer, I'm an accomplished hair smoother!' We put up an enormous range of non-verbal behaviour the purpose of which is to adjust adverse opinions.

I think in some ways I would like best of all, but don't think I ever shall, to go back to medicine and be a neurologist. I always feel a sense of remorse at not having done that. When you make these small steps away from something, you find when you look back, you've gone a long way off your original aim, and I think that my sense of what is good and true is associated more with medicine than anything else. It's not that I look down on the theatre. I think it's a marvellous and admirable thing, but I was so deeply imbued with medical ideals at such an early stage that I do regard going away from medicine as a sort of treason, and that's unfortunate.

1972–2007

9 Wisdom

Sir David Attenborough

To spend time interviewing David Attenborough was not a job but a privilege. He was, and is, the greatest broadcaster of my time. No one comes near. His documentary output over the past forty years or more is his everlasting legacy. If we and future generations ever wonder about life on the planet we occupy, then his programmes not only provide the answers but do so by adhering to the Reithian principle that the broadcaster's duty is to 'inform and entertain'. In that sense, Attenborough's work reminds us how far television has strayed from that basic mandate, and how cheap and shoddy it appears when compared to his example. I can think of no broadcaster in the English-speaking world who has ever come near to equalling Sir David's achievements, or possessed his ability to explain and enthuse about the world we live in. Now in his eighties, he still works, still sets the standard and the rest of us labour in his shadow.

We've now surveyed every major group of animals that live on land. It's down to about forty hours, and if you put it on DVDs and put it on the shelf, you can say, well, it's superficial and brief and so on, but that's what the natural world looked like at the end of the twentieth century. I'd be quite happy with that.

What is fascinating about animals is to realise that a centipede, a spider, a frog, a bat, a whale are all faced with the same problems – how to find a mate, how to find food, how to raise the kids. We all have those problems, and what is marvellous about natural history is you see there are an infinite number of different ways of solving those problems. That's what makes natural history fascinating to me.

It's extraordinarily romantic. The most romantic thing I remember as a child, aged seven, was hitting a rock, seeing it fall open and finding a perfectly preserved shell – beautiful, glistening, shiny – of a kind I'd never seen before in my life.

The chap I was with said, 'That shell is a hundred and fifty million years old and your eyes are the first ever to fall upon it.' Now, that's romance, isn't it?

I was in publishing as a junior editorial assistant, dreaming up books about this, that and the other, but they took such an awful long time to come out. You'd think of an idea and it'd be eighteen months before it happened, and I thought, 'There must be a quicker way of doing this.' I saw an advertisement in *The Times* for a job in the BBC. It was in radio, and I applied for that job, which I didn't get, and then a letter arrived, saying would I consider coming to television? This was in 1952 and television was very small. A lot of people didn't bother to go into television.

The enormous thing was that it was live, that's the huge difference – not just talk shows, every show, with all the players live, hardly any film, and of course the equipment was incredibly committed. So appearing on television was very difficult, and we producers wanted to drill people to get them to perform and allow for the cameras to go down. They tended to get a bit staid, a bit pinched. I remember one of the first jobs I had. Somebody had got the great idea that what you really wanted were 'natural jewels' on television – people who'd just come along and they weren't rehearsed, and nobody told them what to do. They would just tell the stories. And as the most junior man around, I was put in charge of 'natural jewels'.

I looked around and found a rat-catcher who was full of the most marvellous stories about catching rats. He was a 'natural jewel' if ever I've seen one. The only thing wrong with his rat stories was that they all ended in the most appalling way – the poor rat was cut in two with a sabre or smashed to pulp with the back of a spade and so on, but they were very good stories otherwise. So I said, 'Look, would you come on and be a natural jewel?' and he said he would, and I said, 'The thing is, we won't rehearse you. Just come on and tell your stories, but when you come to the end, if you could just make it appear that the rat, as it were, went to sleep or passed away, because we are a nation of animal lovers and people wouldn't like to hear of them being smashed to pulp.'

Ten minutes before the programme was due to start up at Alexandra Palace, he turned up and had two large wire cages full of solid rat. I said, 'Good Lord, what have you got those for?' He said, 'Well, they want to see what I catch.' So he took them up to the studio and we put him in. We were just about to go and I said, 'Now remember, Bill, no cruelty, just you know, nice going to sleep,' and he said, 'Righto, don't worry.'

So I went up to the gallery and cued the music, and fade up camera one, and Bill came on the screen and he said, 'Now I am a rat-catcher and I'd like to show you what it is I catch,' and he produced the cage with this appalling thing, a rat. Then he produced the other one and he said, 'This one is *rattus rattus norwigicus*, and this one is *rattus rattus rattus*, a sewer rat, and he's the one I'd like to show you first,' and, to my horror, he got hold of the cage, lifted the lid and closed his hand around this massive rat. He got hold of the biggest rat I have ever seen by the tail, whipped it out, slammed the lid shut and started spinning him around, and while he was doing it, something went in his mind. He looked at the rat and he said, 'I don't want you to suppose that I am in any way maltreating him, but unless I get him slightly dizzy, the bastard will bite me.'

The technology these days . . . oh, I had a nasty time, the other year. We were trying to record a scene with some Indian rhinoceroses, and the idea was – this was in Nepal – we'd be on the backs of elephants. The cameraman and sound recordist would be on one, and I would be on the other. Then we were going to find a rhino, and they would take a shot of me saying, no doubt in a bit of a whisper, 'There's a rhinoceros.' Well, we were on a rather skittish female elephant, and we went for three days and didn't see any rhinoceroses at all, and on the fourth day we caught sight of one. When we caught sight of it, the elephant was so alarmed, she started bucking, so the mahout tapped her on the head and said, 'Settle down.' The cameraman said, 'Right, away you go,' and I suddenly realised that this radio mic transmitter, which I'd put underneath where I was sitting, had gone. It had fallen off.

I said to the director, 'Microphone's gone! You can't hear what I said,' and he said, 'Well, find it.' I said, 'It's dropped off, it's down in that grass somewhere.' 'Well, find it.' I said, 'I can't find it. It's a little thing. How am I to find it with a rhinoceros standing over there?' And the recordist said, 'Well, you've got the transmitter on it. It'll make a noise. Get off and call to it and I'll tell you when you're getting warmer and when you're getting colder.' So the elephant sits down and I slide off. The rhino's about thirty yards away and I'm saying, 'Hello, hello!' and the recordist is saying, 'Warmer, warmer,' and finally we got it. So I said, 'I've got it, I've got it.' He said, 'Well, don't get back up, do it now,' so I had to do this thing. It's lunatic. However, it was all right. So technology, you know . . .

Fifty years ago I don't think anybody thought there was a crisis. Really far-seeing people, including Peter Scott, started to campaign, and the World Wide Fund for Nature, as it's called now, was set up, but people thought, oh they're just cranks, they like butterflies, let them do their stuff. And then after about ten years, naturalists began to realise that not only are these animals important in themselves, they actually have an even bigger importance because they're like bits of litmus paper – they're an indication of what's going wrong with whole ecosystems. And that went on for about another ten to fifteen years, but within the last ten years we've realised that this is a global problem, and it affects not just tigers, not just butterflies, not just gorillas, but the whole of humanity itself, because if the planet becomes unhealthy, we suffer as well.

1975–2007

Lord Carnarvon — a portrait of an English aristocrat

Henry George Alfred Marius Victor Francis Herbert or 'Porchie', which he preferred, was everybody's idea of the slightly barmy English aristocrat. He didn't wait to be invited on the show, he demanded it. He wrote to me from his London club, informing me he had written his autobiography and was available on the following dates.

He was the most marvellous guest, a relic from a disappearing England, a character beyond the imagining of Ben Travers or even P.G. Wodehouse.

Porchie's father, the 5th Earl, was responsible for the unveiling of Tutankhamen's tomb and died shortly thereafter, prompting the legend of the curse. Whatever power the jinx possessed, it had no effect on the 6th Earl, who continued on a blissful journey through life until he died aged eighty-nine.

Michael: What should I call you? Should I be terribly formal and refer to you as Lord Carnarvon throughout the interview?

Lord Carnarvon: I wish you'd call me Porchie, it's much nicer.

Michael: Porchie?

Lord Carnarvon: Yes, everybody does. It's my second title. My son is called Lord Porchester and when he succeeds me, his eldest son will be Lord Porchester, and so on. It's a courtesy title.

Michael: I see. Your father called you Porchie, didn't he?

Lord Carnarvon: No, he called me Porchester. He was a very tough guy. Of course, things were different in those days. You know, little boys should be seen and not heard. That was the theme of the whole thing.

Michael: We're now talking about the Edwardian era, aren't we?

Lord Carnarvon: I was born in 1898, and I used to get an awful lot of stick from my parents, which was normal, the ordinary thing. One only saw him rather rarely.

Michael: And you were kept away from the adults?

Lord Carnarvon: Oh very much! One was kept away from one's family. We used the red stairs – the back stairs – and were occasionally brought down after lunch, especially if there was a big party, and my father would look at his watch and say, 'Well children, that's right, now go for a nice long walk.' That was the form.

Michael: So you never grew up in a kind of loving relationship?

Lord Carnarvon: Nothing cosy or loving about it, no. I once went to the length of hiding behind a bush with a stiletto I'd found somewhere in the house, because my father had beaten me with a homemade birch rod. And beaten me good and proper – bare bum and so on. And I was tied up to a bed post.

Michael: Really?

Lord Carnarvon: Oh rather! My tutor had to rub in ointment and he said to me, 'My friend, I think you'll be eating your meals for the next few days standing up.' How right he was!

Michael: You started off that story by saying you took a stiletto?

Lord Carnarvon: Well, I did because at one moment I had thoughts of being very clever, hiding behind a bush – I was only about knee high to a duck – leaping upon my father, who was athletic and six foot, and stabbing him. I thought I'll get my own back, I'll be happy.

Michael: You actually lived in terror of him, did you?

Lord Carnarvon: I really did, yes. A very sad thing really. One wishes one hadn't now, because in later life, when I got older, I found he was awfully nice in his own way.

Michael: Tell me about your mother and father's relationship. Your father got a dowry for marrying your mother, didn't he?

Lord Carnarvon: He fixed that all right! Very cunning he was

– because he had a lot of debts. He owed about a quarter of a million or more. So he went to Alfred Rothschild, who he knew would love his daughter to marry my father. She was absolutely a lovely little thing – small, petite, divine. And Alfred was very anxious for this to come off. So my father went and said, 'Look here, I shall expect you, my dear friend, to make provision both for your daughter and also for me. After all, you want us to be happy, don't you?' 'Oh yes,' he said. My father said, 'I should think if you'd pay my debts off – oh, £200,000 or £300,000 – just to put the record straight, and after that, say, we have a quarter of a million each, so that if I predecease her or she predeceases me, it'll always be kept like that and everything will be hunky dory.' He took a deep breath and said, 'Well, that'll be fine.' After which, everything went smoothly. And when I married my beloved wife, my father said to me, 'You must be a bloody fool. If you're going to marry an American, marry a rich one!' I said, 'I adore her, she's an angel.' 'She may be,' he said, 'love in a cottage is not funny.'

Michael: You've come from one of Britain's top aristocratic families – did you mix much with royalty when you were a child?

Lord Carnarvon: Yes, in a way I did. I went to a children's party at Buckingham Palace, one of those afternoon garden parties on the lawn. There was an enormous paper tiger full of toys, and great big markers that said 'no children to go beyond this'. But, being a greedy little devil and wanting to try and get the best toys when the old tiger went up and dropped them out of his belly, I thought, well I'll be in a good position, so . . . and with everybody watching, I popped out as the blooming toys fell down. Like an idiot, I'd got on a little bum-shaver Eton jacket and a top hat – very first time I'd ever worn it. I turn round and run, and what do I do? Catch the king, Edward VII, bang in his tummy, knock him arse over tit, the dear man. And what happens? Picked up by courtiers, everybody saying, 'You little beast, what are you doing!' And me, absolutely terrified. Whereupon darling Princess Mary, who was sweet, came up and said, 'Come on, I'm going to take you and give you an ice.' Oh, I thought, well that's heaven.

So away we went to have an ice, and what do you think I do? In my nervousness and trying to help her, I upset the whole of a raspberry ice right down her beautiful white dress, whereupon her governess called me every name she laid her hands on, punctuated with a good kick. By that time, I was absolutely mortified!

Michael: Now, you used to come down near where I live, Maidenhead way, didn't you?

Lord Carnarvon: Yes. Well, I'll tell you. There was a darling girl. She was called Mae, and I met her at Lingfield Races. So I happened to fall madly in love with this girl. Remember I'm at Sandhurst at the time. She was dreamy. I suppose after about a month, we became what they now call – I'm old-fashioned, I used to be taught, very rightly, kiss and never tell – but now in the permissive society they say lovers. So at Sandhurst we were allowed one Saturday off. You marched off to the tune of "The British Grenadiers', saluted smartly and you had from 12 noon till 8 p.m. the following night. Luckily for me, she lived in Thorn Road, Maidenhead. I parked the car in a hayfield and she said to me, 'What would you like for lunch, darling?' I said, 'Cold salmon, lovely glass of Moselle and preferably raspberries and cream.' It was July. She said, 'Angel, you shall have it all.' 'Thank you, darling love,' I said. 'Wonderful!' What happens? After a snack, off we pop and go to bed. At 4.30 p.m. I'm fast asleep, she wakes me up, shaking me and says, 'Oh! Get dressed like lightning. Your clothes are in the bathroom. My husband's outside and he's frantic. He can't make out why he can't get in. Could you beat it?'

So, what do I do? Throw on my clothes and I hear all this sort of thing: 'Darling, I've got a ghastly headache. I feel so awful. I'm coming in a minute, don't make such a fuss,' and I'm throwing my clothes on, brown belt this way, shoes not done up, and she says, 'It's only about twenty feet into the geraniums.' Imagine my feelings at that time. Into the geraniums I go, roll over like a shot rabbit, run across a tennis court, rusty wire, fight my way through, up on to the Great Western Railway, where four plate-layers and a ganger with picks say, 'You're a ruddy Hun, you're an escaped prisoner, we know what kind of a bastard you are. And you come from the prisoner of war camp at Bray?' 'Never, it's a lie,' I said. 'I'm gentleman cadet Lord Porchester.' Disc, identity, everything, and in the end I convinced them, and then – I'll never forget this – the foreman looked at me and said, 'Little Lord Fauntleroy, if you don't mind me calling you that, was it worth it?'

Michael: Your father's chief link to fame was that he discovered the tomb of Tutankhamen.

Lord Carnarvon: Yes, that's a wonderful story, and of course was his finest hour. When you say he discovered it, what happened was this. In 1902, he went out to Egypt. He had a weak chest and was told he must go to a sunny clime. Lord Cromer, who was our minister at the embassy there, said to him, 'My dear friend, if you're coming out here regularly, you'll get frightfully bored unless you do something to keep you occupied. You can't play golf on this lousy golf course every day and do nothing else.' So my father said, 'What am I to do?' So he said, 'Take up Egyptology and, what's more, I've the very fellow for you. His name's Howard Carter, he was a civil servant, £300 a year. He quarrelled with his boss, said he's not going to apologise and I think he's quite right, but I've got to support his boss. He's going to be fired, and he'll be free tomorrow. Offer him £400 and he'll work for you and you'll love every moment of it.' That's how it started. Carter went and bought scarabs in the bazaar. In those days, we employed four or five hundred fellows, but there was a foreman and there was this, that and the other. Fairly expensive. And remember, they dug the whole time. They dug from 1902 to 1914 without stopping. Somewhere in the Valley of the Kings was the missing tomb. Carter knew that. Question – how to find it? Like looking for a needle in a haystack. Then World War I comes. Digging stops, whole thing comes to end and my father's very fed up with this rather dreary war, and with the whole thing. When the war ended, he said to Carter unless you find this ruddy tomb – and pretty damn quick – no more money, no more digging, whole thing caput.

'Oh,' said Carter, 'for heaven's sake, my dear friend, don't do that. We're very nearly arriving at the moment when we're going to find it.' My father said, 'I've heard that for a long while. Get on, find it.' Anyway, we come to 1921, he gets a cable: 'Found tomb, come out.' Oh, seventh heaven. Papa, who immediately did go out with my sister, took a quick look, but the poor man, in the Winter Palace Hotel in Luxor, shaving, cut a mosquito bite off his chin. Off he goes thinking nothing of it to the tomb, gets infected, comes back in the evening and my sister said, 'Better take your temperature.' He said, 'I'm shivering, I feel awful.' Right, bed, asprin, usual things, you know. In the morning he gets up again, perfectly all right, ostensibly. Back he goes to the tomb. Comes back in the evening, temperature 102. Aha! My sister wraps him up, pops him on the train, takes him down to Cairo. Everything is done to keep him comfortable. There were one or two good doctors in Cairo but his own doctor, Marcus Johnson, was in London. So the doctor gets in an aeroplane, jolly brave fellow, and my mother equally brave, if not braver, and they flew as quick as they could to my father's bedside. By the time the doctor got there, my father was really very, very ill. Next thing, gets pneumonia. By that time, I've arrived in Egypt. Off we go, puff, puff, puff as quickly as we could, cross the desert, and my father was dying by inches, so they tell me. We get there, he's absolutely delirious.

When he died, at 2 a.m. on 5 April 1923, I was in my room and, being an old soldier, I'd put an electric torch by my bedside. At five minutes to two, a nurse comes and taps on the door, and says, 'Lord Carnarvon, come at once, your father's just drawn his last breath, your mother is closing his eyes. She wants you to hold his hand and say a prayer while it's still warm.' At which moment I leap out of bed, throw on a dressing gown, pick up the torch, walk along the passage and every blooming light in Cairo went out for five minutes! Why? Nobody knows to this day. It was said by all the papers the following morning, it was the way in which Tutankhamen revenged himself for the infidel having disturbed his eternal rest. That's what was said. Hence the story of the curse.

Michael: You also involved yourself, it may be peripherally, in some affairs of state, from time to time. You played a rather significant part in the abdication crisis, didn't you, in a Turkish bath of all places?

Lord Carnarvon: Yes. I was devoted to the Duke of Windsor. He was one of my very best friends, and although towards the end of his life he may have done one or two rather foolish things, such as fiddling about with Hitler and that sort of thing, on balance, look what he did for this country. He was a wonderful emissary, he was so gay, debonair. He was beloved everywhere he went. That was when we had an empire. He happened, in my opinion, to be very badly advised, because he was told that if he made a morganatic marriage, that would be acceptable to the British people. I told him never will the British people stand for a twice-divorced lady being the Queen of England. Never. So there you are, he did it. I did my absolute utmost at the very last minute, at the request of Prince George, who said to me on behalf of all the family, 'Will you go round to the hammam, see David,' – they used to call him David. 'Do everything you can to the last hour, the very last moment, to stop this ghastly marriage.' So I did go round there. We were both stark naked in the hot room, sitting there, sweating like blazes, and I said to him, 'Sir, with deep respect, it's an awful thing to think that you should give up your birthright for a mess of pottage.' 'How dare you call Wallis a mess of pottage?' he said. He had a great sense of humour.

1976 and 1977

W.H. Auden

Whenever people ask what Auden was like I say: 'He was the only person I met who had dust in his wrinkles.' I don't think I imagined it although my sight may have been somewhat distorted by the cigarette smoke that encircled his head like cloud round a mountain peak. He was a great example of how, in the early days of the talk show, we could accommodate Auden and Max Wall, Enoch Powell and Tommy Cooper, Jacob Bronowski and Bing Crosby. What is more, millions would tune in. He was a great poet and I treasure his observation that the poet's one political duty is to protect the purity of the language.

It was one afternoon in March 1922, I was walking across field at school with a friend of mine, who later turned into a painter, Robert Medley, and he said, 'Do you ever write poetry?' and I said, 'No, I've never thought of it.' And he said, 'Why don't you?' At that moment I knew that's what I was going to do.

Looking back, of course, I can analyse certain things. I'd had this very elaborate imaginary world I lived in connected with lead mines and a certain kind of landscape, but this suggestion of writing poetry came as quite a surprise to me. When I started to write, my earliest influence probably was Hardy, then later Frost and Edward Thomas. As a child, the things I liked were poetry and sick jokes. I loved cautionary tales. I adored *Ruthless Rhymes for Heartless Homes*. I still love them, too. I can remember the last line of the first poem I wrote, which is set by Blea Tarn in the Lake District. It ran:

'And in the quiet of thy waters let them stay.' I can't remember who 'they' were.

A poet, pardon me, a citizen, has one political duty, which is to try, and by one's own example, to protect the purity of the language. I'm a passionate formalist on hedonistic grounds. After all, everyone knows if you play a game, you can't play it without rules. You can make the rules what you like, but your whole fun and freedom comes from working within them. Why should poetry be any different? There are a few poets, such as D.H. Lawrence, who, you feel, had to write in free verse, but I think they're the exception, not the rule.

In order to write, at any given moment I have two things on my mind. One is a certain subject I'm interested in, and the other is a series of formal questions connected with language. It may be metre, it may be diction, what-have-you, and all right, the subject looks the right form, the form looks the right subject. When these things come together, then you're able to write. What one secretly hopes from readers is that they'll say, 'My God, I knew that all the time but I never realised it before.' That's the ideal reaction, and then you know you've said something that's true.

By all means, let a writer, a poet, if he feels like it, write what we now call an 'engagé poem', but he must not imagine that by doing so he will change the course of history. He might also remember that the chief benefactor from it will be himself. I know this from certain things I wrote – a number of things about Hitler, which I don't take back for a moment. But who benefited from it? Me, because it gave me a certain kind of literary interpretation and people have felt the same as I did. Nothing I wrote postponed the war for five seconds or prevented one Jew being gassed.

I think if you ask what is the function of not only literature but of all the arts, I would say firstly what Dr Johnson said: 'The aim of writing is to enable readers a little better to enjoy life or a little better to endure it.' And then the art's our chief means of communication with the dead. Homer is dead but we can still read *The Iliad* with relevance, and I personally think, without communication with the dead, a fully human life's not possible.

I think there have been exceptions, we have to think about the societies we know, but I would normally say that in the case of social political evils, only two things are effective. One is political action and the other is absolutely straight journalistic reportage of the facts. You must know what they are.

Now, in countries such as Russia it may be slightly different because they've never had a free press. Therefore a writer may say something that people can't hear from any other source, and the fact that he risks his liberty, and perhaps his life, to say it gives him a moral authority that writers from the West can't possibly have.

For my generation, which was too young for the First World War to be real – all right, my father was in it but it was quite unreal to me – when we were undergraduates we just thought we were back before 1914. After all, England hadn't had inflation or a civil war. It's only when I got to Germany I realised the foundations were shaking, and this was very important.

On the whole, when one makes a move, one often doesn't realise till later why. If you ask me why I did it now, I would say that British cultural life as I knew it was a family life, one knew everybody. I love my family but I don't want to live with them. And I agree with Somerset Maugham when he said, 'In order to understand your own country, you have to have lived in at least two others.'

I'm much more conscious of my sensibility being British than I ever was when I lived here. I mean, if you live in a country – I think it's only fair that I decided to become an American. I wouldn't say I feel American. I can call myself a New Yorker, which is a rather special brand of character. I think of myself as a New Yorker.

A writer is a maker, not a man of action, though in a sense everything he writes is a mutation of his birth and experiences. Nothing you could learn about his experiences will tell you why particular things are what they're like. I think that an author's private life concerns simply himself and his family and his friends. It only becomes interesting, as a rule, in the case of people who are really bad hats. I mean, Wagner's life would be fascinating to read, even if he hadn't written anything, because he was such a monster.

1972

Edith Evans

Dame Edith was the greatest actress of her time, and even those who might dispute that claim are bound to admit that she behaved as though she was, which is not to say she was vainglorious. Indeed, as a religious person, she knew the meaning of humility. She would say, 'Off stage you may pass me by, but on stage look at me.' I adored her. She was marvellous company. I lunched with her a couple of times at her home in Kent. You knew it was time to go when she closed her eyes and fell asleep after the pudding. She said she was born intoxicated and her spirit made her appear immortal. Bryan Forbes, who directed her in *The Whisperers,* her best film role, and became her biographer and friend, said that when he told his daughter Dame Edith had died, she said, 'That's not possible. She's not the type.'

That's one of the lies I live, you see. People always think I'm a Lady. I had very strict parents, and they did their best to bring me up as a well-bred woman, and so perhaps some of it has rubbed off. And I'm passionately fond of good workmanship. When I was sixteen or so, I used to save up to have my clothes tailor-made because I liked good workmanship.

My father was a minor civil servant, and my mother, at one time of her life, was a cook. Of course, a cook in those days was a very special person. You had to be very good at it.

A lot of educated women were cooks, but she had an idea that this raving mad thing she'd produced was going to be an actress. I'd no idea. I was apprenticed to millinery. I'd got my indentures, my two years, and I loved it because I loved all the beautiful materials and colours.

I didn't have to try to go on the stage. I was put on the stage. It never occurred to me to be an actor. I thought I should just marry the boyfriend I married much later, and we should have an ordinary life. When I was alone, I would 'be' people, but I had no ambition to do with the theatre. Dear William Pearl, the great old master, saw me do something for a friend – I had a friend who did performances – and he asked me to do something for him. It was such a long time ago, I can't remember much about it, but George Moore, the author, saw me, and said I ought to be in the theatre. He said, 'I shan't give you your first job, you go on turf and get the spots.' But he did give me my first job and I started right in the West End of London. And it was marvellous because I was with first-class people who all spoke beautiful English, and I've always been mad about words.

The audience, they're darlings if you love them. When they're naughty, sometimes I have to scold them. I don't say anything but I just press a little. I say to them inside myself, 'Now darlings, listen. I know what's coming and you don't and it's going to be nice, so listen and you'll have a lovely time.' It's like your mother, when you're tiny she says, 'You're laughing a lot this morning, you'll be crying tonight.'

I always spend a little time at the side. I never rush on because I want to listen to what their temperament is so I can come in and either quieten them down or ginger them up. I like to take care of them, I want them to enjoy themselves, and I think I've trained myself to make them enjoy themselves. You can't leave them just to flip about and do what they want to.

I've never been what was called a pretty girl. You see, the extraordinary thing is that I've got a face that paints well. The make-ups can always make me. If I've got to play a beautiful woman, I can be beautiful. If you feel beautiful inside, and you've got a face that takes the paint well, you can suggest beauty. Any woman can do it if she takes a little bit of trouble and has a lovely feeling inside. I once said something, which I think is rather nice. I said, 'Beautiful was a primitive passport.' It's rather good isn't it? If you're a beautiful woman, it doesn't matter where you are. You're in, aren't you?

I'm like Ivor Novello. He says he was born intoxicated. I was born intoxicated. My mother tells a story that is rather sweet. When I was very tiny, we used to live in Ebury Buildings and we had a lodger. He sounds a charming man. She used to have his meal ready but I would be saying, 'Turn, turn!' for my skipping rope. So the poor man ate his lunch with one hand and turned it for me with the other. Even then I got the boys to do what I wanted.

I believe in glamour. I think glamour is part of any public person, especially acting people. You shouldn't have scrubby clothes and hair and a mingy car. I saved up and bought a Rolls and I tell you, it's a beauty. I feel nice when it drives up, and you feel, oh, *somebody* when getting out. You know what I mean?

I would have liked a family. I must say, I don't think if I'd had children I would have been able to act, because I feel so strongly. When my husband died, it did nearly send me crackers, and I remember thinking, 'If this was a child, I couldn't take it. I could not take it.' My mother was a very free woman with strong feelings and I've had strong feelings all my life.

If I could petition God personally, I should say, 'Would you please give me a lot more courage? Mental and physical courage.' I do things sometimes but I'm very frightened and I would like to do them with courage.

It's funny that thing about wanting to be noticed. I don't like it, you know, except when I want to be noticed. If somebody raises their hat when I get out of the car, I bow in return, but I don't like being looked at, because I'm not acting, you see. When I'm acting to be looked at, look at me! I should hate it if you didn't!

1972–5

Dame Edith: When they gave me the DBE, I thought they've got to write it down. They can't throw me away. I don't want to be thrown away.

Michael: Oh, you won't be thrown away. Your achievements in the theatre will last forever, and the things you did on film.

Dame Edith: I won't be remembered forever. I don't mind that.

Michael: But you'd like to be remembered forever?

Dame Edith: No, I don't know. I don't suppose I'd care for myself very much if I knew her well. I know a lot about her inside, which I don't like.

Michael: Really? What don't you like?

Dame Edith: Oh, I don't like the way I feel aversion to people and things. Terribly strong sometimes – I have to be really fierce with myself. I was like it as a girl.

Michael: Really?

Dame Edith: Yes. If the wrong boy came near me, I couldn't bear it. Wouldn't let him touch me!

Michael: And you still have that?

Dame Edith: Yes. I still have it.

Michael: You don't have that with me, do you?

Dame Edith: No, I've got the other feeling with you!

1974

Ben Travers

Ben Travers was a playwright specialising in farces, such as *Thark* and *Rookery Nook*. He was eighty-nine when he first came on the show; ninety when he made a comeback in the West End with *The Bed Before Yesterday* starring Joan Plowright and Helen Mirren.

He was an exhilarating man, ripe with age but in no way enfeebled. He showed me his daily exercise, which involved lying on his back and lifting his legs until his toes touched the floor above his head. I tried it and it took me a year to recover from a strained back. I still get a twinge. No one I interviewed conjured up a lost time like Ben Travers. Here was a man who tried to shoot down the first Zeppelin to raid London, who piloted the experiment with the first parachute and who saw W.G. Grace score a century. Most important of all, he recalled everything with the eye of the humorist.

It was 1886 when I was born, so I don't suppose there's been a century, or near century, in recent history when more has happened – two wars and all the enormous, amazing scientific improvements and inventions. It's marvellous.

Before the first war, in the height of the Edwardian period, that was marvellous. The West End of London, with the old hansom cabs, was a great place. The beautiful Empire was at one end of Leicester Square. It was a magnificent old music hall with an inscription right across the front – The Cosmopolitan Club of the World. And that, indeed, is what it was. Anybody home on leave from India or the East, or anywhere, made a beeline for the Empire, in full evening dress, of course, and there was the chap who was the chucker-out, with the marvellous uniform and top hat. He had a wonderful job, with a perk – he was the chap who selected and admitted a certain number of the ladies of the town to promenade in the promenade. They were very streamlined prostitutes, with a very disdainful air, walking down the promenade, which ran behind the dress circle.

And then opposite, or rather at right-angles to it, was the Alhambra, another vast music hall. But really the feature of the whole thing was across the road, and that was at the corner of the square itself – the gentlemen's lavatory. In

Edwardian days, it was a magnificent thing, decorated with marble stairs, marble walls, and all these sort of pedestals, compartments for gentlemen, all beautifully spotless and shining. Above each of them was a plate-glass tank containing water for the flush, and believe it or not, in each of these tanks were goldfish.

Even in those days the water was operated automatically, so that every now and then there was a *whoosh*, and these wretched goldfish were all milling about, on their faces expressions of great apprehension and anger and antagonism. Just at the critical moment as this awful struggle for life was going on – *whoosh* – they were swimming away as though absolutely nothing had happened. And there's an analogy there. I've often thought of that. In our lives – our social life, our domestic life, our public life, our international life, our sports life, every aspect of life – how like we all are to those poor goldfish.

In the First World War, in the first Zeppelin raid over London – that was the last day of May 1915 – I was detailed to go up in a plane and chase the Zeppelin when it came. They knew it was coming, they had some sort of spy information or something. I was in the Naval Air Services and Mr Winston Churchill, the First Lord of the Admiralty in those days, came down and inspected us. I was sent up as a gunner. Now, this Zeppelin came over at about 10,000 feet, dropped a bomb or two and went off again, and an hour after it had gone, it was halfway back to the North Sea. We were ordered to go up and chase it and shoot it down.

I was given a rifle to shoot it down with, and we had a ceiling of 4,000 feet. The Zeppelin was at 10,000 feet. London had the most sketchy and really inadequate defences in those days. We crashed and my pal was killed. I got concussion, and then later I was detailed to test a parachute. They never had any parachutes in the First War, but they did test one or two. They strapped it underneath the undercarriage of the plane and in order to get something like a man's weight, they went to Hamleys and got the biggest teddy bear they could find. They told me to go up and I went up to a thousand feet and pulled a plug, which released the thing, and it fell beautifully, and worked. All these inventors were trying to bring out the patents for this thing, and they were standing round. Wonderful. They took it, strapped it together again, put it back in the undercarriage, and up I went again. Down it went and it fell about twenty feet below my machine but the parachute wouldn't release from the undercarriage, so there I was, flying around with a twelve-stone teddy bear swinging underneath. It was a perilous moment. I had to dodge the tops of the sheds, then let the teddy bear hit the ground and it pulled off my undercarriage. They were very primitive days.

Cricket has been a passion all my life. When I was a little boy, I saw W.G. Grace make a hundred. When the old man had finished playing for Gloucestershire, he didn't want to pack up altogether and he founded a thing called London County, which used to play at the Crystal Palace. I lived at Bromley in Kent, and used to go over to Crystal Palace when I was a boy of about ten or eleven. I saw the old man batting there once against Surrey. He made a hundred.

The funny thing was, they always had this legend about W.G. Grace refusing to get out. The score was in the 20s in this innings and he hit a ball to a Surrey pro, Brockwell. He caught the ball, threw it up, but the old man – no way. He claimed he'd hit it on to the ground before Brockwell got it. And he went for Brockwell, brandishing his bat, and poor Brockwell didn't know what to do. He appealed to the umpire. The umpire was utterly intimidated by this old man and gave him not out. Very good thing he did, otherwise I'd never have seen W.G. make a hundred.

Farce is, I think, a very underestimated thing. I always try and concentrate on somebody getting into the most frightful bit of trouble. And, of course, that's what the audience laughs at, and it's a very healthy thing we do. Farce produces laughter, or seems to, and very often succeeds, and laughter, apart from religion, is man's most precious possession.

Often it can come out of sorrow and distress. I lived all the middle part of my life very happily in a place on the Bristol Channel, Burnham-on-Sea. In the old days, Burnham had the ambition to become a popular seaside resort, but something always went wrong. One day a chap died there, a resident, very sad of course, and he left a written request to be buried at sea. This was very optimistic on his part because at Burnham, the tide goes out a couple of miles and there's two miles of just eternal mud. However, he was in luck when he died because the tide was exceptionally high. In the boat was a single boatman, a couple of chaps from the undertaker's place, the vicar and the coffin, so off they went.

They started to row out to a reasonable distance, but unfortunately the sea was not only exceptionally high, it was also exceptionally rough, and the vicar wasn't a very good sailor. He rather began to feel the effects of this. It got worse and worse, and he thought it was about time to start, so he began, 'We brought nothing into this life . . . and it is certain we can take . . .' By this time, the two undertaker's chaps – two mutes – didn't look so hot themselves, so they thought it was time to put an end to this. Each of them grabbed one end of the coffin and deposited the deceased into the Bristol Channel. The damn fools had forgotten to punch a hole in the coffin, so it was floating off . . . I doubt if the vicar made evensong that night. Michael, what is the basis of that funny story? Death.

I was always very impetuous and that sort of thing, and made decisions in a hurry. When you grow old, you grow mellow and you're more considerate about things. You think things over. But also you have memories. How often have you said, or heard it said, 'If you look back at it, it's really rather funny.'

Age is a great healer. You forgive any sort of misunderstandings. And also there are the youngsters, you see. One's children have grown up and you have grandchildren. When you're old, you begin to think not so much of yourself, you begin to think of your family and friends. Oh yes, it's a great boon to be old.

1975 and 1978

John Betjeman

To walk a while with John Betjeman was to realise you had spent most of your life with your eyes shut. We once perambulated down Fleet Street, constantly stopping to look at the rooftops of buildings. 'People don't look up, you know,' said the then Poet Laureate. 'If they did, they would discover the meaning of serendipity.' He was an endearing man, a beguiling blend of *savant* and jester. There was also a rage in him, an anger sometimes daringly explained. Think of what he wrote about Slough. I always thought he did for the Art Deco period in England what L.S. Lowry did for the north country at the same time. Like Lowry, he didn't so much depict it as give you a real sense of what it must have been like actually living in England through those times. He made several appearances on the show, including one when he came to discuss his poems being set to music. By the way, he told me his favourite lyricist was Cole Porter.

Michael: How musical are you?

John: Can't sing a note in tune. I know about rhythm, I think, and the sound of words. I'm not really musical. I was always told by my parents I wasn't musical because I couldn't sing in tune.

Michael: Was there any music in your family at all?

John: Oh, I had forebears who were musical. There was an old thing called Gilbert Betjeman who was a great friend of Grieg and was something to do with Covent Garden – I think he was first violin – and he introduced Wagner to

Glasgow. When the music started, the audience began to laugh, so Gilbert Betjeman tapped his baton on the whatever-it-is and said, 'Are you going to listen to this music or are you not, because if you don't, I shall go home and enjoy a whisky toddy.'

Michael: And they stayed?

John: They did, yes.

Michael: Tell me about writing poetry. As you get older, is it easier or harder to write poetry?

John: Harder and slower. A very kind question.

Michael: Why is it a kind question?

John: Because it doesn't get easier. I find I only think of something in the morning when I wake up. A line occurs, then if I've got a pencil near, I write it down. Then I look at it at breakfast and it's awful, and I hope for the best and that it will gradually be added to during the day. Walking about is, I find, the best way of writing poetry.

Michael: Was it ever easy for you?

John: Yes. I longed to do it all the time, and I felt every time I didn't write a poem when I had a bit of spare time, I was wasting my time.

Michael: Really? And the words literally flowed in those days?

John: Yes, and nothing made time rush by quicker than sitting down with a poem in mind and writing it out. Part of the pleasure is writing it on the page and seeing how it looks, and then reciting it again and again. Then trying it out on a friend whom you can trust, and then you can tell whether they like it or not. If they cough, you know it's a bore and it won't work. I had a very kind publisher whom I knew at Oxford. I think everything is done by graft, and if I hadn't known this man, I would never have been printed, I don't expect.

Michael: When did you last write a poem?

John: About three days ago I was trying to do one on Peterborough Cathedral, an unregarded, beautiful building, which has got in it a chapel called St Sprite. I imagine that's the Holy Spirit, and it's such a nice name for a chapel

I thought I'd try and do a thing about the Sprite in Peterborough Cathedral. I got the first words out and I've now lost them.

Michael: You've lost them? Mislaid them?

John: Mislaid them.

Michael: Can't you remember them?

John: No.

Michael: So what are you going to do?

John: Hope I'll find them again.

Michael: You, of course, were many things before you were a poet, Sir John. You had some remarkable jobs. You were once a copywriter for Shell, weren't you?

John: Yes indeed. I didn't like it very much. I started there as a journalist, as you did, and it teaches one to write things simply and not like government department forms.

Michael: It's a very good training in economy, isn't it?

John: Yes.

Michael: Which of all the jobs you did on your way to becoming a poet did you enjoy the most, in the sense that it inspired most poetry for you later on?

John: Undoubtedly being a schoolmaster, because it was being a single act on the stage and having to keep everybody interested, whatever their boredom was. You had to entertain and instruct. And boys are very decent to talk to, young boys, when they're sitting in a class. You can feel when they're bored, and you can feel when they respond. And I think it's a splendid training, being a schoolmaster.

Michael: But what you explained to me is standard training for a performer rather than a poet.

John: I see that now. I always admired music hall above everything, because the music-hall artiste has to establish himself in the first few seconds, otherwise he's a flop.

Michael: You've also written an awful lot – and beautifully, it's the most evocative of your poems – about your childhood. What kind of a childhood was it?

John: Comfortable. I had kind parents who, on the whole, let me alone. But they sometimes left me with nannies who weren't all that jolly and were rather alarming, but I've always found I liked my own company better than anyone else's, except the children next door in Highgate. They were marvellous.

Michael: We're talking now, of course, about an Edwardian upbringing?

John: I'm seventy-one, yes.

Michael: How strict was that upbringing?

John: Oh, getting to school in time, running up Westfield feeling sick with breakfast inside one, coming home, not wondering what mood my father would be in or my mother, and then often having to eat things I didn't like at all. Can you remember that? Hating fish, I remember, and finding it very chewy.

Michael: But the theory was that you ate what was put in front of you – you weren't allowed to pick and choose?

John: Oh yes, finish it up. The most awful idea, wasn't it?

Michael: I came across a line of yours that interested me, about your childhood, which I'd like to talk to you about. You used to go shooting?

John: Yes, with my father.

Michael: And the line is, 'How many times must I explain the way a boy should hold a gun,' that's your father talking to you. 'I recollect my father's pain of such a milksop as a son.'

John: That's right. He wanted me to be an open-air boy, with nice greased hair and a happy smile, and very keen on sport. I was no good at any of it.

Michael: Did you try hard to fulfil his ambition in those respects?

John: Not very. Shooting I couldn't bear. I didn't like killing the things, and then I was always missing and wounding the unfortunate bird or rabbit. It was horrible.

Michael: Yes. What about the sort of moralistic attitudes prevalent in those days, because in Edwardian times things were proper, weren't they?

John: Oh yes, and I didn't know anything about sex. I don't think I found out about it until I went to my public school. I used to be told vague things about plants and didn't know what they were talking about. And then I thought there was something very wicked when I found out about it. I thought if there was a sin again the Holy Ghost, then it was sex.

Michael: And what about that? Did you have crushes?

John: Oh Lord yes, endless crushes. The purest love of one's life is before one's had any sex, and when one doesn't know what it is, this passion. I'd do anything for the person I loved. It didn't matter whether it was girl or boy. The first people I noticed were girls and it moved on – I don't believe that one's indifferent to either sex.

Michael: But you went more strongly towards the girls?

John: I did, yes, on the whole.

Michael: When you had these crushes, did it move you to write poetry?

John: Yes. Deeper feelings than I've ever felt. I never felt so sick with love as when I was in my teens, and indeed at the age of about seven, I think, was the first love I felt.

Michael: Really?

John: The most beautiful girl with gold hair, called Peggy Purey-Cust. She lived in West Hill, Highgate. She had blue eyes and a slightly turned-up nose, and a sort of down over her cheeks, so that ever since then, people I've loved have had to look slightly like Peggy Purey-Cust.

Michael: And everyone you've met like that, you've fallen in love with and written a poem about?

John: Generally, yes.

1977

Catherine Bramwell-Booth

One day a man from the Salvation Army rang. He said Commissioner Bramwell-Booth, granddaughter of the founder of the Salvation Army, had just won Speaker of the Year award at the age of ninety-six. We were intrigued enough to send a researcher, who reported back that the Commissioner was a remarkable and inspirational woman. She wasn't wrong. In fact, no one could have anticipated the impact she had as she sat, serene in her poke bonnet, and captivated the nation with her eloquence and, most of all, sense of humour.

Her gentle rebuke of the host for his clumsy use of the language of the betting shop is a moment of great comedy created by a woman with a wonderful sense of timing as well as mischief.

At the end of the interview she said she wanted to live to be a hundred. In fact, she was a hundred and four when she died. I treasure her memory.

Michael: Tell me, what is the earliest memory that you have of childhood? How far back can you go?

Catherine: I can go back quite easily to when I was three. Perhaps a little more. I remember I'd gone to dinner with my grandmother, and my Aunt Emma was there, and after dinner she knelt down in front of me and said, 'Oh Cath darling, such a lovely thing has happened. God sent you a new baby sister and Mama wants me to take you to see her.' Well, 'My heart,' I thought, 'a new sister, a baby.' I was thrilled and I don't remember going, but we walked – it was very easy – and then it didn't strike me as peculiar that my mother was in bed and by her side was this beautiful cradle, muslin and pink, and I was lifted up and I burst into a howl of misery. I'd never seen anything so dreadful in my life. It was like a red beetroot covered with hair and I had to be taken in to my mother's arms to be comforted. I think that's almost my earliest memory.

We were so happy. I never remember quarrelling. Mind, plenty of disagreements, plenty of arguments. We argued in the nursery and we've argued ever since – my sister and I have been arguing about this or that in connection with this show. But we don't quarrel, I've never quarrelled.

Michael: Commissioner, you didn't go to school did you?

Catherine: No.

Michael: Why was that?

Catherine: I don't really know. I don't think obligatory schooling was in when I was quite young. At any rate, my mother educated me, and my father had a hand in it. And I wouldn't change what they did for me for Oxford and Cambridge rolled together.

Michael: You wouldn't?

Catherine: No, because they brought me into touch with life, they opened so many avenues – the love of reading, the love of beauty, the love of music. Every door was opened to us.

Michael: Let's now look back on the stock that you came from. What do you remember of your grandfather?

Catherine: My father was very different from my grandfather. He was like his mother – but he was devoted to his father, and to please my father was the highest joy you could aim for at, at home. And to please my father we had to be in touch with my grandfather as much as possible when he was at home. Of course, he spent his life travelling.

Michael: Yes, but when you met him as a young girl, do you remember any of the advice he gave you?

Catherine: Oh yes, some of it. Do you want me to?

Michael: Please.

Catherine: I do remember one occasion, he was very interested in what we did in the little corps, you might call it – a little church, the group to which we belonged. If he was at home, it was important to tell him how it had been on Sunday. 'Well, how did you get on?' and 'Was there anyone at the penitent form?' and 'Did you do anything?' and I said that day, 'Yes, Grandpa.' I can see the room and him and myself. 'I sang a solo.' 'Oh,' he said, 'How did you get on?' I said, 'Well, I did my best.' And then he suddenly seemed to be angry with me, roared at me. And he could shout.

But we had to learn to shout in the army, and he had a splendid voice when he got on to the platform and held himself up and shouted. Well, he shouted at me that day and I was all in a shiver, and he said, 'Your best? What's the good of that, Catherine? You'll never be any good to me in the army if that's all you can do.' Well, I felt dreadful. I should have liked to burst out crying. I was that kind of child.

Michael: Were you?

Catherine: Very shy and very easily overcome, but I thought it would let the others down if I did, so I did nothing, and then he suddenly stopped and changed. 'Did you see, dear child, when we believe in God and God helps us, we can do better than our best,' and then he opened up that idea of God being within reach and understanding how we felt.

Michael: Commissioner, you said recently, in a speech, that you hope to live as long as Moses?

Catherine: No, that's quite wrong.

Michael: Oh, I see. I stand corrected. What did you say?

Catherine: I said there's no hope – it's no use hoping to live. But, you see, this was for the Age Research, how to make age more comfortable and so on, and I think it's a jolly good thing if they could. But I said I should like to go through, to finish my old age as Moses did, when it says in the Bible that 'his eyes were not dim'. Well I've got to wear spectacles, so my eyes are dim, and his natural strength, that's what attracted me, was not abated. Think how wonderful it would be to be ninety and still as strong and vigorous as you were at nineteen.

Michael: Yes, but he was a hundred and twenty, wasn't he? So they say.

Catherine: Yes, a hundred and twenty. And I should think being a hundred's about equal to it today.

Michael: Commissioner, I must tell you, my money's on you.

Catherine: What does that mean?

Michael: What it means . . .

Catherine: I hope you're not a betting man!

Michael: No, it was a betting phrase . . .

Catherine: What did it mean?

Michael: What I meant to say was that if I were a betting man, which I'm not, and there was a book made, if there was a bet going . . .

Catherine: A book?

Michael: All I'm trying to say, Commissioner, in my own clumsy way, is that I would imagine that you would reach a hundred, actually, the way you are.

Catherine: Well, I should like to.

Michael: And I would like you to, you're a very remarkable woman.

Catherine: Oh no, don't say that. If you'd known me when I was younger, you wouldn't have thought that – shy. My life has been in contradiction to my nature. My darling father gave me very good advice. I think I'd been an officer for about twelve months, and I was home on furlough, and he said, 'Cath, darling, remember this. It doesn't matter how much your knees tremble, so long as the people don't notice it.'

1979

Jacob Bronowski

If I could save one interview from the thousands I have done, it would be the one-man show with Professor Jacob Bronowski in 1974. He was a scientist who visited Nagasaki to assess the effect of the dropping of the atomic bomb. What he saw there and at Hiroshima caused him to change his direction of scientific study to biology. What he witnessed haunted him and eventually led to *The Ascent of Man* for the BBC, regarded by some as one of the greatest documentary series of all time. This is my favourite interview because it went exactly the way I had planned it and because, for seventy-five minutes or more, a great man gave a masterclass in the art of communication.

I was in Germany as a child. The war broke out in 1914 when I was six. It came to an end in 1918 when I was ten. I was very patriotic as a German, but in fact I was a Russian by nationality, so I was an enemy alien. My parents were enemy aliens. We were not very well treated by the Germans, but I think it just made me at home in the world. I've always lived in countries that I haven't been born in. I was born in Lodz and the last time I was in Lodz was in 1913, that's sixty years ago.

I have lived, you have lived, most people here watching us, have lived through the two great catastrophes of the twentieth century – the coming to power of Hitler in 1933 and the dropping of the atomic bombs in 1945. These are the two most ghastly events that have overtaken the human race, I think, in the last hundred years. Those two events made a deep impression on me, because in 1933 I was still a pure mathematician, much devoted to the idea of doing mathematics. I had never done a broadcast, I had never done a public lecture, I had never spoken to any group other than a class of students in rather professional terms.

I was convinced in 1933 that, if the German people had known my fellow scientists, had known the people I loved and admired, such as Einstein, Max Born, Niels Bohr and a hundred others, had known them as I knew them with their wonderful warm humanity, they could never have been deceived by a cold, brutal, monomaniac like Hitler, and learnt to hate them as if they were vermin. And I was convinced at that moment that those of us who could had a duty to show not only that science was wonderful, but that science was human, that scientists had some right to say that they were doing the most human things in the world, the most natural things, and that we must stop being professionals and become people.

But then, of course, I was even more shocked to find in 1945 that we had invented a means of re-establishing a distance between the technician and his victim, by making these terrible bombs – a man sits in a plane, or nowadays he sits in an underground silo, and he presses a button that says, 'Hey presto!' and he goes on munching his sandwich out of his brown paper bag while in Nagasaki 40,000 people and in Hiroshima 80,000 people die in less than a second. So my life has been much shaped by the fact that I have thought that my first moral duty was to make people warm and real about science and make science about people. Those are the two objectives I've had. Now I've been speaking to you about making humanity understand what part science had to play. Then we come to the responsibility of the science. What should have been done in 1945? What should have been done between 1933 and 1945?

I don't claim to have any answer about this. No one has. Einstein said at the end of his life, 'If I had known the Germans were nowhere near making a bomb, I wouldn't have lifted a finger.' Well, of course. If the sky fell, we would all catch lots. If we all knew what God knows, then we would all act much more sensibly, but on the knowledge that we had in 1933, I am convinced that when 1939 came, we had to make bombs. That wasn't wrong. But with the knowledge we had, I'm equally convinced that in 1945 it was a crime to drop the bombs merely because we'd made them.

I'm enormously optimistic about the human race, because I think that the human race learns by making mistakes. It was a terrible mistake to kill 120,000 people in Hiroshima and Nagasaki, but by comparison with the mistakes that we have no doubt avoided as a result of having to use those bombs, I suspect that we may well have prevented the use of one or two hydrogen bombs, which people have tended to use in the last few months. I'm optimistic about the human race because I know nothing else but democracy, which does what I believe must be done, that is gives me the chance to persuade, and gives others the chance to be persuaded, or to refuse to be persuaded.

In my opinion, all the physics in the world has in the end,

at this moment, added up to this – that we are beginning to understand more about the process of life. We're beginning to understand first of all what makes animals work, and then why human beings are so special, and that's what *The Ascent of Man* is about.

I wasn't very keen to go to Auschwitz. I wasn't very keen to go because many of my relatives from Poland had died in Auschwitz. However, the point of the series was that it wasn't an entertainment, it was about life the way it is, the way it has been. I went through these terrible wooden and iron gates that say 'Arbeit Macht Frei' at the top, 'Work makes free', to these unhappy people who went there to their deaths. And I looked at the gas ovens. I was particularly keen to see bunkers twelve and eleven where people were beaten and shot for breach of regulations, because I felt that you must see it all. But it turned out that the things that were far more moving were ones that I couldn't have imagined at all.

The Germans are terribly methodical, so there would be whole areas that contained nothing but old spectacles. It's all been very carefully collected. They weren't the slightest use but the Germans weren't going to throw them away. There were areas that were entirely full of human hair. There was a terrible area, which was entirely full of wooden legs and crutches and artificial limbs, and the most pathetic area of all, an area that was just full of little tin chamber pots. The children who had come to the camp had brought them with them and the Germans collected them. Well, by this time I was in a pretty low frame of mind, and the most awful thing was that there were pictures in the corridors, of prisoners. They were just the ordinary picture – front, face, number on the bottom – but many of them were pictures of quite young people, children, and to see these pictures of people taken as if they were criminals with the tears streaming down their faces, was just unbearable.

We then drove over to the pond. We had arranged that I was just going to say a piece to close that programme, which would arise out of what I'd see in the morning. So I walked up and down for five minutes, making up my mind what I was going to say, and then we did it – one take and we'd go home. We had made up our minds that it was a piece that you couldn't possibly do twice. You just had to say what came into your mind, and the thing that came into my mind, absolutely out of the blue, was the phrase from Oliver Cromwell that I quote: 'I beseech you in the bowels of Christ, think it possible you may be mistaken.'

My life has been happy because, although I have suffered many conflicts of loyalty of which I spoke to you earlier, I've never had any uncertainty about the meaning of the word 'good', the meaning of the word 'true', the meaning of the word 'beautiful', and the meaning of words such as 'original' and 'new'. I've always had a tremendous pride in being a human being and being born in the twentieth century. I'm terribly sad that thirty years from now I shall be dead, not because anybody will miss me but because I will miss them, because so many more marvellous things will be known.

Now, should you listen to me? Yes, you should. Not because you have to believe any single thing that I say, but because you have to be pleased that there are people who have led happy and complete lives, who feel that they can speak out of a full heart and a full mind all in the same breath.

1973 and 1974

The Evolution of Talk

Erin Reimer

It's been done by sportsmen, spry singers, even the odd politician. Now a staple on our screens across the multi-channel spectrum, you could be forgiven for thinking the talk show was a deliberate creation. Yet, like most programmes in the formative years of the box, its design lies somewhere between experiment and accident.

The talk show for some time was a uniquely American phenomenon, its roots lying squarely in variety. American comedian Jerry Lester became the first late-night talk-show host in 1950, at a time when radio was the most influential tool in the land. He was spotted on an NBC programme, and impressed so much that the network bosses granted him his own slot with a more or less blank slate, and thus began *Broadway Open House*. Filmed in a theatre, it featured music, celebrity guests and variety acts. At the time, there was no particular intention to carve out a niche among the viewing public, but the show garnered a regular following.

Shortly after, Steve Allen, a comedian and musician, became the first host of NBC's *Tonight* – the legendary programme that gave rise to Johnny Carson and Jay Leno. He introduced gimmicks along with conversations, occasionally propelling himself into vats of jelly and initiating the strong vein of comedy that has pervaded American talk shows for over half a century.

During Allen's short tenure on *Tonight*, NBC truly realised the potential of late-night talk – it was relatively cheap to produce, certainly helped network enthusiasm and, operating five nights a week, presented ample opportunity to raise revenue through adverts. Bill Carter, chronicling the late-night industry in his book, *The Late Shift*, rightly described the bourgeoning show as 'the champion cash cow in the network pasture'.

While these men laid the foundation, it was Jack Paar who became the first real star of the genre when he succeeded Allen in 1957, and paved the way for lofty contract demands that were to become a defining element of the talk-show culture in America. He infamously quit on air in 1960 after the network censored what was a relatively tame joke, essentially a play on words between 'water closet' and the Wesleyan Church. Too close to the bone at the time, the joke was pulled, and he was furious. He walked off the set mid-programme and didn't return.

Demonstrating the power the talk-show host had acquired, he was quickly offered a much more lucrative contract by NBC, and returned a month later, opening with the line, 'As I was saying . . .' Despite this power broking, the damage was already done for Paar, and he didn't stick around for too much longer. In 1962, the King was crowned in the form of Johnny Carson, and he fronted *Tonight* for the next thirty years.

Sitting behind his trademark desk, Carson set the benchmark, and his style has been replicated ever since, from Letterman to Leno and beyond. His opening monologue became the linchpin of the programme, and set the public agenda. Attracting up to forty million viewers at its peak, the show and its presenter became intrinsic to the fortunes of the host network. Bill Carter in *The Late Shift* notes that, grossing more than $100 million a year, *Tonight* became responsible for fifteen to twenty per cent of NBC's profits.

With that kind of leverage, it's hardly surprising that Carson managed to tip the traditional scales of power. The network needed him far more than the reverse. When he walked out on NBC for several weeks in 1967 over a contract dispute, he returned to a $1 million per year pay packet. By the eighties, he had become the country's highest paid TV performer, drawing a $5 million salary from *Tonight* alone.

Carson's success spawned a sprawling array of new contenders, trying varying styles. The format has expanded and splintered into wildly successful, and sometimes outrageous, adaptations. Through her daytime programme, Oprah Winfrey became one of the most powerful and richest women of the twentieth century. Following another path, installing real people in the hotseat to mull over their dirty laundry, Jerry Springer became a global phenomenon and spawned Jeremy Kyle's show.

Since Carson's abdication, David Letterman and Jay Leno, who took up the *Tonight* post, have come to typify the modern era of American talk shows. Letterman, a former stand-up comic, founded *The Late Show with David Letterman* on CBS in 1982 and introduced his own variant – a more ironic tone with a tendency to flip the cameras on the show itself, placing backstage antics centre stage.

If power is money, American talk-show hosts hold an unprecedented position. In 2009, *Forbes* magazine listed David Letterman's annual earnings at $45 million and Jay Leno's at $32 million, giving the latter eighty times the salary of President Obama. When comparing the powerbase of differing entertainers, *Forbes* in fact rates Letterman as having greater sway than Obama, as far as 'personalities' are concerned.

There's a good reason for this perception. In recent years, it has been seen as impossible for presidential candidates to woo the public without engaging in the culture of talk shows. Bill Clinton was dubbed a 'talk-show president' because of his penchant for appearing on them and his resultant behaviour as a wily celebrity. His original candidacy was given a serious lift after he whipped out his saxophone and gave a rendition of 'Summertime' on one late-night vehicle. Barack Obama cemented perceptions of his celebrity candidacy with his cool ease in appearing with David Letterman.

So how did the talk show transfer to the UK? There's no doubt that seeing the enormous power of Johnny Carson's show created quite a stir within the bowels of the BBC, and the hunt was on in the early sixties for the best man to fit the bill.

Bill Cotton, heading up the corporation's Light Entertainment Department, was particularly keen to introduce this format to the British public. ITV jumped the gun with Eamonn Andrews trialling the US style in 1964, while the BBC's first major experiment was *Dee Time* in 1967. The popular DJ Simon Dee embodied the swinging sixties with his Beatles hair-do and womanising image, but the show didn't last. In 1969, he left the BBC and signed for more money at ITV. That experiment failed, he was quickly denounced as a has-been and spent the rest of his working life identified more with the fickle nature of celebrity than those few years spent at the top.

In the meantime, David Frost's satirical and topical *That Was The Week That Was* became a British television landmark. The show didn't attempt to emulate its US counterpart, but looked at how parameters might be broken. It injected audience participation, diversified from showbiz guests, and took on a sometimes campaigning tone. With *The Frost Report* he pioneered his adversarial style, most famously while questioning Dr Emil Savundra about the collapse of his car insurance company, in front of some of his victims. It became 'trial by television', and Frost became one of the most entrepreneurial faces ever to appear on British TV.

Parkinson was created under Bill Cotton in 1971, chiefly in the quest for a local Carson. In its maiden series, there was even an opening monologue and a cartoonist offering a satirical spin on the week's news. But with an instinctive journalistic approach, Michael Parkinson quickly dropped the peripherals in favour of simple conversation. However, the lack of complication in its structure and the success in eliciting candid responses from glittering stars had one drawback for others – it made talk shows look easy despite this being far from the truth.

In the four decades following the initial success of *Parkinson*, the talk show became the darling of commissioners, and since then the central role has been offered to everyone from comedians and sports people to singers and even former prime ministers. Some, notably Jonathan Ross and Paul O'Grady, have enjoyed tremendous popularity and longevity, while others have been less fortunate. Along with these two, Russell Harty, Harold Wilson, Clive James, Michael Aspel, Terry Wogan, Dame Edna, Clive Anderson, Joan Rivers, Steve Wright, Gabby Roslin, Jack Docherty, Frank Skinner, Mariella Frostrup, Ian Wright, Sarah Ferguson, Patrick Kielty, Graham Norton, Sharon Osbourne, Davina McCall, Charlotte Church, Russell Brand, Pamela Connelly, Al Murray, Katie Price and Peter Andre, Lily Allen, Suggs, Alan Carr, Justin Lee Collins and Piers Morgan have all had a stab with varying degrees of success. As hosting duties became more disparate, the brilliant parodies *Mrs Merton* and *The Kumars at No. 42* formed an identikit for the pitfalls of the ill-executed programme.

Reviewing the long list of hopefuls – some much more successful than others – it's easy to spot the tendency to take someone who is 'of the moment' and give them a talk show, disregarding the dilemma that someone who is good at conversation is not always adept at leading it. Hence the sometime disasters that spring from this strategy.

So why does it work for some people and not others? While some hosts – Dame Edna and Joan Rivers, to name but two – set out to discomfort their unsuspecting guests to riotous success, in some respects the talk show is a recipe for chaos. You can prepare the beast within an inch of its life, but since the virtue lies in its unpredictability and that frisson between guest and host, it opens the floor for both the best and the worst. The handling of such can become the mark of success, or spell the beginnings of failure.

American talk-show host Dick Cavett holds the prize for the absolute worst luck. Interviewing seventy-three-year-old nutrition expert J.I. Rodale, the septuagenarian announced that he was 'so healthy that I expect to live on and on', and then proceeded to have a heart attack and die on the spot. With the programme taped ahead of schedule, the interview was never broadcast, but Cavett was left to explain the unfortunate event in the following show.

Away from the tragic, there's nothing the audience likes to see more than a 'car crash': an irate guest or an on-set calamity, producing no other result than humiliating the host. Almost everyone who has taken a stab at the genre has had their Emu moments. Russell Harty looked at one stage under threat of being clobbered by formidable Bond girl Grace Jones in 1981, when she objected to him turning his back to her, while Clive Anderson could be little else but a spectator when the Bee Gees stormed out mid-interview.

Plenty of on-screen fiascos have been the fault of over-indulgence in the green room. Many British viewers witnessed the unhappy sight of George Best slurring his way through an appearance with Terry Wogan, while the lewd antics of an intoxicated Oliver Reed caused Channel 4's *After Dark* to be pulled mid-broadcast.

So where does the future lie for talk shows in the UK? Despite the multiple failures exhibited by those with little experience in moderating conversations, channels on both sides of the Atlantic seem addicted, and keep rolling with the idea. There's no doubt it is one of the cheapest ways to produce prime-time entertainment. All that's needed are a studio, a host and guests, who usually appear unpaid. Little editing or other technological interventions are required, which would drive up the cost of programmes, so the talk show is not difficult to assemble, but it has been chronically difficult to execute in a winning way.

Bernard Timberg in his analysis of the genre, *Television Talk*, hit the nail on the head in saying, 'While it must appear to be spontaneous, it must be highly structured,' and some may well fall down by not adhering carefully enough to the latter without taking away the illusion of spontaneity.

In looking at the evolution of the talk show, the *Independent* pointed to the 'slow eradication of the aura of celebrity' to account for its largely limited success in the UK. One of the great advantages of *Parkinson* is that, especially in the early years, celebrities were more likely to be enigmas. Today, with many opening their doors to reality TV cameras in order to rebuild careers, and the overwhelming saturation of the minutiae of celebrity lives, perhaps the mystery has been snuffed out.

Nevertheless, this is not to say that the flame has burnt out in the art of good conversation, which is essentially what wins or loses the audience. More likely the problem lies in finding someone who is good at it, and convincing modern programme commissioners that that is the whole point.

Erin Reimer is a producer for Sir Michael Parkinson's company, Parkinson Productions, and was associate producer of Parkinson *for ITV.*

Parkinson Guests

19/06/1971	Ray Bellisario; Arthur Ashe; Terry Thomas
26/06/1971	Pierre Salinger; Shelley Winters
03/06/1971	Art Buchwald; Peter Finch; Polly Toynbee
10/07/1971	Peter Ustinov
17/07/1971	John Lennon; Yoko Ono; George Melly; Humphrey Lyttleton; Benny Goodman
24/07/1971	George Best; Michael Caine
31/07/1971	Rod Steiger; Kenneth Tynan; Denis Norden
07/08/1971	Orson Welles
14/08/1971	Robert Shaw; Ringo Starr; Spike Milligan
21/08/1971	Trevor Howard; Freddie Trueman; Harold Pinter
28/08/1971	Jimmy Saville; Claire Rayner
04/09/1971	Shirley MacLaine; Dowager Queen of Sarawak
10/10/1971	Dirk Bogarde; George Axelrod; Nina
17/10/1971	Muhammad Ali
24/10/1971	Robert Morley; Chief Red Fox; Arthur Mullard; Marian Montgomery
31/10/1971	Rt Hon Lord George-Brown; Peter Fonda; Jacques Loussier
07/11/1971	Henry Higgins; Jackie Stewart; Don McCullin; Blaster Bates
14/11/1971	John Arlott; Jacques Tati; Mel Calman; Marian Montgomery
21/11/1971	Joanne Woodward; James Cameron; Kay Garner; Barbara Kay; Lynn Cornell; Ralph McTell
28/11/1971	Sarah Miles; Gwyn Thomas; the Peddlers
05/12/1971	Sir Ralph Richardson; Frankie Howerd
12/12/1971	Charlton Heston
19/12/1971	Stephane Grappelli; Yehudi Menuhin; Chan Canasta
03/06/1972	Peter Ustinov; Jackie Charlton; Jimmy Reid; Blossom Dearie
10/06/1972	Fanny Cradock; A.J.P. Taylor; Bernard Manning; the Tony Mansell Singers
17/06/1972	Yul Brynner
24/06/1972	Peter O'Toole
01/07/1972	Tony Curtis; Patrick Moore; Vivien Neves
08/07/1972	Jonathan Miller; Jackie Stewart
15/07/1972	Andy Williams; Benny Green; Johnny Mercer
22/07/1972	Shirley Temple Black
29/07/1972	Ben Lyon; Vincent Price; Danny Blanchflower
05/08/1972	James Mason; Fenella Fielding; Albert Modley
12/08/1972	Dame Edith Evans; Deborah Kerr; Annie Ross
19/08/1972	Robert Mitchum; Harry Pitch
23/09/1972	Malcolm Muggeridge
30/09/1972	Chris Finnegan; Derek Nimmo; Victor Borge; Ralph McTell
07/10/1972	Sir John Gielgud, W.H. Auden; Cleo Laine; John Dankworth; John Taylor

14/10/1972	David Niven
21/10/1972	Kenneth Allsop; Lauren Bacall; Tom Paxton; Danny Thompson
28/10/1972	The Goons: Harry Secombe, Peter Sellers and Spike Milligan; Ray Ellington; Alf Costa; Jay Neill
04/11/1972	Gore Vidal; Diana Rigg; Douglas Fairbanks Jnr; Mickey Newbury; Tommy Reilly
11/11/1972	Eric Morecambe; Ernie Wise; Raquel Welch; Janet Webb
18/11/1972	Jonathan Miller; Alan Bennett; Peter Cook; Dudley Moore
25/11/1972	Jack Lemmon
02/12/1972	Patrick Campbell; Frank Muir; Kenneth Williams; the Peddlers
09/12/1972	Michel Legrand; Petula Clark; George Melly
16/12/1972	Alistair Cooke; Peter Ustinov
23/12/1972	Bing Crosby; Don Hunt
06/01/1973	Thor Heyerdahl; Jacques Tati; Blossom Dearie
13/01/1973	Harold Evans; Juliette Greco; Spike Milligan
20/01/1973	Georgia Brown; Clive Jenkins; Sir Geraint Evans
27/01/1973	Jimmy Edwards; Eric Sykes; Ernest Borgnine; Shusha
03/02/1973	Richard Harris
10/02/1973	Sir Robert Helpmann; Claire Bloom; Eartha Kitt
17/02/1973	George Best; Sir John Betjeman; Maggie Smith; Kenneth Williams
24/02/1973	Duke Ellington
03/03/1973	Oliver Reed; Lady Isobel Barnett; Mickey Spillane; Sherri Spillane; Jacques Loussier Trio
10/03/1973	Kenneth Williams; Jimmy Reid; Dr Rhodes Boyson
17/03/1973	James Stewart
24/03/1973	Robin Day; Rt Hon Jeremy Thorpe MP; Robert Vaughan; Marian Montgomery
08/09/1973	Donald Sutherland; Elliott Gould; Al Capp
15/09/1973	Johnny Speight; Jack Dempsey; Georges Carpentier; Lord Shinwell
22/09/1973	Joel Grey; Ingrid Bergman
29/09/1973	Emlyn Williams
06/10/1973	Vic Feather; Mike Yarwood; Artur Rubinstein
13/10/1973	Michel Legrand; Lord Arran; Max Wall; Mike Yarwood
14/10/1973	Anthony Quinn
20/10/1973	Brian Clough; Marcel Marceau; the Peddlers
27/10/1973	Beryl Reid; Buddy Rich
03/11/1973	Sir Matt Busby; James Coburn; Dr Jacob Bronowski
10/11/1973	Johnny Morris; Jackie Stewart; Helen Stewart; Miquel Brown
17/11/1973	Orson Welles
24/11/1973	Eric Morecambe; Ernie Wise; Glenda Jackson; Marjorie Wallace
01/12/1973	Michael Crawford; Liberace
08/12/1973	Oscar Peterson; Orsted Pedersen; Phil Silvers
15/12/1973	Andy Williams; the Ken Thorne Orchestra
18/01/1974	Jack Benny
25/01/1974	Muhammad Ali; Joe Frazier; Dick Cavett
01/02/1974	John Wayne

08/02/1974	Dr. Jacob Bronowski
09/02/1974	Andrew Cruickshank; David Frost; Alan Price
16/02/1974	Robert Morley
23/02/1974	Ted Moult; Jack Warner; Labi Siffre
02/03/1974	Edith Evans; Lord Soper; Pete Morgan
31/08/1974	Edna O'Brien; Hughie Green; Charles Aznavour
07/09/1974	Sammy Cahn; Ethel Merman; Roger Moore
14/09/1974	Michael Caine; Helen Hayes; Soraya
21/09/1974	Dave Allen; Dee Brown; Otto Preminger
28/09/1974	Lyall Watson; Telly Savalas; Gina Lollobrigida
05/10/1974	Julie Andrews; Blake Edwards
12/10/1974	Harry Secombe; Harold Robbins; Anita Loos
19/10/1974	Henry Cooper; Lawrence Durrell; Terry Thomas
26/10/1974	Glynis Johns; Nanette Newman; Bryan Forbes; Dame Flora MacLeod
02/11/1974	Patrick Moore; Oscar Peterson; Ronnie Barker
09/11/1974	Peter Sellers
16/11/1974	Nettie Bainbridge; Eva Von Rueber-Staier; Twiggy; Les Dawson
23/11/1974	Richard Burton
07/12/1974	Muhammad Ali
14/12/1974	Dickie Henderson; Henry Mancini; Louis Mordish
21/12/1974	Dr Magnus Pyke; Andy Williams
04/01/1975	Leslie Thomas; Charles Aznavour; Pat Phoenix
11/01/1975	Rachel Roberts; Helene Hayman; Dame Alicia Markova
18/01/1975	Barbara Kelly; Emlyn Williams; Stephane Grappelli
25/01/1975	Sammy Cahn; Richard Leonard
01/02/1975	Monty Modlyn; Jimmy Logan; Annie Ross
08/02/1975	Helen Mirren; Mai Zetterling; Lord Boothby
15/02/1975	Billy Connolly; Humphrey Lyttelton
22/02/1975	Sheila Hancock; David Hemmings; the King's Singers
01/03/1975	Larry Adler; Tessie O'Shea
08/03/1975	Dustin Hoffman
30/08/1975	Bing and Harry Crosby
06/09/1975	Lord Hailsham; Valerie Perrine; Lieutenant Colonel G. Styles
13/09/1975	Dame Margot Fonteyn; Shirley MacLaine
20/09/1975	David Niven
27/09/1975	Lee Remick; Jonathan Miller
04/10/1975	Gene Kelly
11/10/1975	Cleo Laine; John Dankworth; Billy Connolly
18/10/1975	Bette Davis; Ron Moody; Ronnie Cass
25/10/1975	Graham Hill; Eric Sykes; Michael Winner
01/11/1975	Henry Fonda
08/11/1975	Pete Murray; Frederick Forsyth; Blossom Dearie
15/11/1975	Rt Hon Edward Heath; Dame Edith Evans
22/11/1975	Mort Sahl; George Best; Barney Kessel
29/11/1975	Marti Caine; Sandy Powell; Ben Travers

06/12/1975	Bernard Braden; Harry Lorayne
13/12/1975	Arthur Askey; James Hunt; Paul Simon
20/12/1975	David Attenborough; Andre Previn
25/12/1975	Bob Hope
03/01/1976	Rene Cutforth; Robert Morley
10/01/1976	Walter Matthau; George Burns
17/01/1976	Michel Legrand; Jack Jones; Tony Hawes
31/01/1976	Diana Rigg; Malcolm Muggeridge
07/02/1976	Michael Caine; Elton John
14/02/1976	Fred and Ava Astaire
21/02/1976	Yehudi Menuhin; Stephane Grappelli; Peter Cook
04/09/1976	Jimmy Tarbuck; Ben Travers; John Snow
11/09/1976	Joyce Grenfell; William Blezard; Gwyn Thomas
18/09/1976	Roger Vadim; Twiggy; Spike Milligan
25/09/1976	Dudley Moore; Kenneth Tynan; Harvey Smith
02/10/1976	Sammy Davis Jnr
09/10/1976	Phyllis Diller; Wilfrid Hyde-White; Vincent Price
16/10/1976	Michael Crawford; William Rushton; Pam Ayres
23/10/1976	Glenda Jackson; Desmond Morris
30/10/1976	Les Dawson; the 6th Earl of Carnarvon; Tom Paxton
06/11/1976	George Burns
13/11/1976	Jimmy Hill; Max Bygraves
20/11/1976	Sacha Distel; Juliette Greco
27/11/1976	Billy Connolly; Anna Raeburn; Rod Hull and Emu; Frank Evans
04/12/1976	Michael Bentine; Gerald Durrell
11/12/1976	Rudolf Nureyev; John Curry
25/12/1976	Fred Kaps; Ricky Jay; Richiardi Jr
01/01/1977	David Bellamy; Dr Magnus Pyke; Patrick Moore; Rowland Emett
08/01/1977	Sir John Mills; Anthony Hopkins; George Melly; John Chilton's Feetwarmers
15/01/1977	Esther Rantzen; Magnus Magnusson; Bernard Manning
22/01/1977	Sir Harold Wilson; Mike Yarwood
29/01/1977	Jonathan Miller
05/02/1977	John Arlott; Julian Bream; Peter Ustinov
12/02/1977	Michael Aspel; Katie Boyle; Max Wall; Ralph McTell
19/02/1977	Oscar Peterson; Peter Cook; Danny Blanchflower
07/04/1977	Alex Haley
03/09/1977	James Stewart; Geoffrey Boycott; Elkie Brooks
10/09/1977	Alfred Marks; Rita Hunter; David Essex;
17/09/1977	Ronnie Scott; Arthur Schwartz; Robert Powell
24/09/1977	Woody Herman; Spike Milligan
01/10/1977	Cliff Richard; Robert Morley; Leslie Caron
08/10/1977	Dr Desmond Morris; Diana Dors; Kenneth Williams
22/10/1977	Paul Daniels; Barbara Dickson; Sir Huw Wheldon
29/10/1977	Little and Large; Cleo Laine; John Dankworth; John Williams
05/11/1977	Sir John Betjeman; Gracie Fields

12/11/1977	Penelope Keith; the Earl of Carnarvon; Jimmy Tarbuck
19/11/1977	Alistair Cooke; Alan King
26/11/1977	Perry Como; Nick Perito
03/12/1977	George Melly; Roger McGough; Marty Feldman
10/12/1977	Marvin Hamlisch
18/12/1977	Sir Alec Guinness
02/01/1978	Borra the Legendary 'King of the Pickpockets'; Billy Connolly
07/01/1978	Peter Ustinov; Dudley Moore
14/01/1978	Erin Pizzey; Edna O'Brien; Claire Bloom
21/01/1978	Elizabeth Craig; Ben Travers; Lord Shinwell
28/01/1978	Russell Harty; Zandra Rhodes; Larry Grayson
04/02/1978	Joe Gormley; Cliff Morgan; Max Boyce
11/02/1978	Tony Curtis; Stanley Holloway; Don MacLean
18/02/1978	Petula Clark; Leslie Bricusse; Anthony Newley
21/03/1978	Bruce Forsyth
02/09/1978	Brian Johnston; Frankie Howerd; Manhattan Transfer
09/09/1978	Derek Nimmo; Alan Jay Lerner; Jessie Matthews
16/09/1978	John Conteh; Peter Cook; Dudley Moore
23/09/1978	Sheila Hocken; Peter Alliss; Johnny Mathis; Frank Zottoli
30/09/1978	Shelley Winters; Sir Robert Mark; Anthony Burgess
07/10/1978	Kenneth More; Barry Manilow; Geoff Boycott
14/10/1978	Bricktop; Tim Rice; Andrew Lloyd Webber; Julian Lloyd Webber; Robert Morley
21/10/1978	Sammy Davis Jr; Buddy Rich
28/10/1978	Jonathan Miller; Roald Dahl
04/11/1978	Roy Hudd; Chesney Allen; Rod Steiger
11/11/1978	Stanley Holloway
18/11/1978	Rolf Harris; Jim Henson; Frank Oz; Kermit The Frog; Mr Fozzie Bear; Miss Piggy; Messrs Waldorf & Statler
25/11/1978	Sir Ralph Richardson; Barry Sheene
02/12/1978	Gloria Swanson; Olivia Newton John; Barry Humphries (as Dame Edna Everage); Elton John
09/12/1978	Mickey Rooney
25/12/1978	Arthur Askey; Pat Kirkwood; Charlie Cairoli & Company; Les Dawson; Roy Barraclough
06/01/1979	Dolly Parton; Oscar Peterson; Cyril Fletcher
13/01/1979	Ray Reardon; Britt Ekland; Edward Fox
20/01/1979	Catherine Bramwell-Booth; Richard Stilgoe; Spike Milligan
27/01/1979	Billy Connolly; Jimmy Reid; Lauren Bacall
03/02/1979	Dick Emery; Kirk Douglas; the Pointer Sisters
10/02/1979	Arthur Marshall; Annie Ross; Val Doonican
17/02/1979	Michael Bentine; Wynford Vaughan-Thomas; Sir Edmund Hillary
22/09/1979	Tommy Steele
26/09/1979	Tony Benn; Stewart Grainger; Dorian Williams
29/09/1979	Carol Channing; Terry Wogan; Douglas Bing
03/10/1979	Posy Simmons; Malcolm Muggeridge; Quentin Crisp

06/10/1979	Lawrie McMenemy; Desmond Morris; Kenny Everett
10/10/1979	Tony Jacklin; Reverend Don Lewis; Anthony Hopkins
13/10/1979	Kevin Keegan; Lorraine Chase; Kenneth Williams
17/10/1979	Warren Mitchell; Billy Connolly
20/10/1979	Rex Harrison
24/10/1979	Benny Green; Henry Cooper; Frankie Vaughan
27/10/1979	Andre Previn; Harry Mortimer; the Black Dyke Mills Band
31/10/1979	John Mortimer; Bernard Levin
03/11/1979	Lord Snowdon; Dame Margot Fonteyn; Barbara Cartland
07/11/1979	Tammy Wynette; Olga James; Bernard Manning
10/11/1979	Julian Pettifer; Dr Christian Barnard; Luciano Pavarotti
14/11/1979	Walter McCorrisken; Norman Mailer; Andy Williams
17/11/1979	Bette Midler
21/11/1979	Dr Henry Kissinger
24/11/1979	The Muppets
28/11/1979	Catherine Bramwell-Booth
08/12/1979	Joanna Lumley; David Bellamy; Frank Muir
12/12/1979	Max Boyce; James Burke; William Shatner
15/12/1979	Faith Brown; Tom Conti; Ben Travers
19/12/1979	Reginald Bosanquet; Pamela Stephenson; Jimmy Tarbuck
22/12/1979	Ronnie Ross; James Galway; Laurie Lee
25/12/1979	Catherine Bramwell-Booth; Peter Cook; Dame Edna Everage; Tommy Cooper
29/12/1979	Martin St James; Brian Inglis
05/01/1980	Alistair Cooke
09/01/1980	Twiggy; Percy Edwards; Larry Adler; Max Wall; Janet Suzman; Dr Jonathan Miller
16/01/1980	Cliff Michelmore; Dame Freya Stark; 'Sky'
19/01/1980	Jeannie Little; Peter Murray; Alfred Marks; Rupert Holmes
23/01/1980	Dudley Moore; Norman St John-Stevas; Dr Robert Runcie
26/01/1980	Lynda Carter; Elaine Stritch; Mike Yarwood
30/01/1980	Alan Alda; Rene Cutforth; Jimmy Saville; Terry McDonald
02/02/1980	Peter Ustinov; Placido Domingo; the King's Singers
06/02/1980	Michael Bentine; Magnus Magnusson; Oscar Peterson
09/02/1980	Mike Harding; Gerald Durrell; Dennis Waterman
16/02/1980	Joan Collins; Leslie Thomas; Jon Pertwee
20/02/1980	Isla St Clair; Shirley Williams; Dr A. L. Rowse
23/02/1980	Angela Rippon; Raymond Burr
27/02/1980	Norman Collier; John Arlott; Emlyn Williams
01/03/1980	Buddy Rich; James Blades; James Mason
05/03/1980	Ron Pickering; Wayne Sleep; the Chinese Magic Acrobats
08/03/1980	Dick Evans; Oliver Reed; the Chieftains
12/03/1980	Robert Redford; Billy Graham
15/03/1980	Ken Dodd; the Diddymen
19/03/1980	Barbara Woodhouse; Diana Rigg; Dirk Bogarde
26/03/1980	Clive James; Steve Martin

20/09/1980	Denis Healey; Sian Phillips; Lee Marvin
24/09/1980	Lee Trevino; Dickie Henderson; Olivia Newton John; Bob Hope
27/09/1980	Billy Connolly; Barbara Woodhouse; Angie Dickinson; the Barron Knights
01/10/1980	Dudley Moore; Willie Carson; Barry Sheene; Michael York
04/10/1980	Kenneth Williams; Tom Lehrer; Robin Ray
08/10/1980	Katie Boyle; George Shearing; Jack Fingleton
11/10/1980	Maureen Lipman; Val Doonican
15/10/1980	Michael Bentine; Sir Peter Scott; Graham Chapman; Alan Price
18/10/1980	Lilli Palmer; Itzhak Perlman; Larry Adler
22/10/1980	Dr Jonathan Miller; John Cleese
25/10/1980	Adam Faith; Trevor Howard; Lynda Carter
29/10/1980	Robert Morley; Sheridan Morley
01/11/1980	Telly Savalas; General Sir John Hackett; Ingrid Bergman
05/11/1980	James Coburn; Prof. Eric Laithwaite; Spike Milligan
08/11/1980	Jonathan King; Douglas Fairbanks Jnr; Jimmy Tarbuck
12/11/1980	Brian Clough; Lynn Seymour; Warren Mitchell
15/11/1980	Lionel Jeffries; Arthur Marshall; Lillian Gish; Roger Moore; Al Read; Wall Street Crash
22/11/1980	Danny La Rue; Basil D'Oliveira; Charles Aznavour
26/11/1980	Mary O'Hara; Robert Kee; Barry Manilow
29/11/1980	Paul Daniels; William Rushton; Englebert Humperdinck
03/12/1980	Bryan Forbes; Trevor Nunn; Frankie Howard; the Roches
06/12/1980	Sammy Cahn; Placido Domingo; Cliff Richard
10/12/1980	David Kossof; Jim Davidson; Tessie O'Shea
13/12/1980	Rt Hon Enoch Powell; Sir Ralph Richardson
17/12/1980	Robin Cousins; Bob Geldof; Kenny Everett
25/12/1980	Penelope Keith; James Galway; Ben Vereen
01/01/1981	James Cagney; Pat O'Brien
07/01/1981	Lord George-Brown; George Melly; Malcolm Muggeridge
10/01/1981	Clive James; Suzi Quatro; Donald Sinden; Ben Vereen
14/01/1981	Harry Secombe; Cliff Morgan; Wynford Vaughan-Thomas
17/01/1981	Muhammad Ali; Freddie Starr
21/01/1981	Omar Sharif; Prof. J.K. Galbraith; Bette Midler
24/01/1981	Des O'Connor; Sarah Miles; Rowan Atkinson
28/01/1981	Robert De Niro; David Jacobs; Sir Peter Parker
31/01/1981	Brian Glover; Brian Johnston; Tommy Trinder
04/02/1981	Ron Pickering; Clare Francis; Denis Compton; Earl Okin
07/02/1981	James Brown; Mike Carter; Peter Cavanagh; Hudson Peter
11/02/1981	Lord Carrington; Stewart Granger; Cantabile
14/02/1981	Max Wall
18/02/1981	Goldie; Lt John Blashford Snell; Thora Hird; Harry Stoneham Five
21/02/1981	Marvin Hamlisch; Gemma Craven; Bruce Forsyth
25/02/1981	Kim Novak; Julian Pettifer; A.J.P. Taylor; Rose Murphy; Major Holley
28/02/1981	Harry Stoneham
04/03/1981	David Shepherd; Don McCullin; Ian Wallace

07/03/1981	Richard Stilgoe; Shelley Winters; Pete Townshend
11/03/1981	Marti Caine; Michael Medved; Fyfe Robertson
14/03/1981	John Huston; Mary Martin; Petula Clark
18/03/1981	Phil Drabble; Kiri Te Kanawa; Lord Bernard Miles
21/03/1981	Andrew Lloyd Webber; Michael Medwin; Lily Tomlin
03/10/1981	David Niven
07/10/1981	Mel Brooks; Pamela Stephenson; Dr A.L. Rowse
10/10/1981	Jimmy Young; Terry Wogan; Andy Williams
14/10/1981	Ronnie Barker; Meryl Streep; Chris Bonington
17/10/1981	Sir Douglas Bader; Windsor Davies; Dame Vera Lynn; Kenneth Williams
21/10/1981	Lord Patrick Litchfield; George Shearing; Hayley Mills; Nell Dunn
24/10/1981	Sir Harry Secombe; Andrew Sachs; Mel Tormé
28/10/1981	Eamonn Andrews; Marian McPartland; Danny Blanchflower; Desmond Morris
31/10/1981	Dave Allen; Toyah Willcox; Peter Skellern
04/11/1981	Michael Winner; Mike Harding; Bernard Levin
07/11/1981	Arthur Scargill; Diana Dors; Ian Dury
11/11/1981	Joanna Lumley; John Romer
14/11/1981	Diana Ross; Helen Reddy; Andrew Sachs; Cannon & Ball
18/11/1981	John Arlott
21/11/1981	Billy Connolly; Jeremy Lloyd; Glen Campbell; Dr Christiaan Barnard; Anouk Aimée; Jacques Cousteau
28/11/1981	Celeste Holm; Billy Eckstein; Roy Castle; James Casey; Eli Woods
02/12/1981	Michael Foot; Spike Milligan
05/12/1981	Barry Took; Twiggy; Ken Dodd
09/12/1981	Peter Bull; Gerald Durrell; Issac Sterne
12/12/1981	Jimmy Tarbuck; Tim Rice; Ringo Starr; Barbara Bach
16/12/1981	Tito Gobbi; Susan Hampshire; Bob Monkhouse
19/12/1981	Felicity Kendal; Elaine Paige; William Conrad; the Bee Gees
02/01/1982	Pam Ayres; Jack Jones; Sammy Cahn
06/01/1982	Lulu; Walter McCorrisken; Arthur Marshall
09/01/1982	Jaqueline Bissett; Henry Mancini; Placido Domingo
13/01/1982	Chad Varah; Alec McGowen; George Shearing; Mel Tormé; Brian Torff
16/01/1982	Barbara Castle; Cleo Laine; Les Dawson
20/01/1982	Alfred Marks; Isobel Buchanan; Kyung Wha Chung
23/01/1982	Leslie Caron; David Bellamy; Mike Yarwood; Elkie Brooks
27/01/1982	Mel Smith; Kenneth Griffith; Christopher Reeve
30/01/1982	Barry Humphries; Dame Edna Everage; Sir Les Patterson
03/02/1982	Lorraine Chase; Bill Wyman; Frank Delaney
06/02/1982	Larry Adler; Anthony Andrews; Joan Collins
10/02/1982	Jonathan Miller; Eric Idle; Chris Brasher
13/02/1982	Ben Vereen
17/02/1982	Tippi Hedren; Julian Pettifer; James Stewart; Blossom Dearie
20/02/1982	Roy Hudd; Christopher Timothy; Chesney Allen

24/02/1982	Rudolf Nureyev; Tony Bennett; Bluebell Emmett Rowland; Kelly Monteith; Stanley Unwin
06/03/1982	The Buddy Rich Orchestra; Kenny Everett; Roy Castle; Sammy Davis Jr
10/03/1982	Alan Whicker
13/03/1982	Michael Palin; Jimmy Savile; Donald Sinden; Andrew Lloyd Webber; Marti Webb
17/03/1982	Anthony Burgess; Peter Cook
20/03/1982	Peter Ustinov; Derek Nimmo; George Melly; John Chilton
24/03/1982	Alistair Cooke
27/03/1982	Julian Bream; Michael Caine; Jim Davidson; Chas & Dave
31/03/1982	Ronnie Corbett; Florence Desmond
03/04/1982	Jimmy Tarbuck; Billy Connolly; Spike Milligan; Kenneth Williams; Mary Parkinson; Marion Montgomery; Laurie Holloway; Sammy Cahn; Harry Stoneham
28/03/1987	Jack Lemmon; Walter Matthau
04/04/1987	Billy Connolly
11/04/1987	Buddy Rich
18/04/1987	Elton John
25/04/1987	Ian Botham
02/05/1987	Tom Jones
09/05/1987	Spike Milligan
16/05/1987	Jack Lemmon; Walter Matthau
28/05/1988	Boy George
04/06/1988	Adam Faith
11/06/1988	Robbie Coltrane
18/06/1988	Terence Stamp
02/07/1988	Cliff Richard
09/07/1988	Anthony Hopkins
16/07/1988	Phil Collins
23/07/1988	Richard Harris
09/01/1998	Paul Merton; Barry Manilow; Sir Anthony Hopkins
16/01/1998	Michael Palin; Stephen Tompkinson; Sir Elton John
23/01/1998	Billy Connolly; David Attenborough
30/01/1998	Gary Lineker; Patricia Routledge; Morgan Freeman
06/02/1998	Phil Collins; John Prescott
13/02/1998	Rory Bremner; Ewan McGregor; Robbie Williams
20/02/1998	Liam Neeson; Lily Savage; Cilla Black
27/02/1998	Dame Kiri Te Kanawa; Jacques Villeneuve; Dame Edna Everage
06/03/1998	Bryan Adams; Jeremy Clarkson; Joan Collins; William Hague
13/03/1998	Bob Hoskins; Pauline Quirke; Brian Conley
05/12/1998	George Michael
21/12/1998	Ewan McGregor; Robbie Williams
08/01/1999	Geri Halliwell; Dawn French; Carol Vorderman
15/01/1999	Robert Lindsay; Stephen Fry; Lee Evans
22/01/1999	Caroline Aherne; Prince Naseem; Gary Barlow

29/01/1999	Alan Davies; Mo Mowlam; Warren Beatty
05/02/1999	Michael Caine; Harry Enfield
12/02/1999	Jim Davidson; Thora Hird
19/02/1999	Oprah Winfrey
26/02/1999	Diana Rigg; Eddie Izzard; Robbie Coltrane
05/03/1999	Lenny Henry; Rolf Harris
19/03/1999	Jack Dee; Barbara Windsor; Simon Callow
26/03/1999	Neil Morrissey; Joanna Lumley; Sir Ian McKellen; Marion Montgomery
02/04/1999	Woody Allen
03/12/1999	Paul McCartney
10/12/1999	Michael Crawford
17/12/1999	Billy Connolly; Sting
21/01/2000	Mel Smith; Ralph Fiennes; Mick Hucknall
28/01/2000	Paul Merton; Clarissa Dickson-Wright; Victoria Beckham
04/02/2000	Alexei Sayle; Martin Kemp; David Blunkett
11/02/2000	Clive James; Sanjeev Bhaskar; Filippa Giordano; Richard Briers
18/02/2000	Alistair McGowan; Richard E. Grant; Lesley Garrett
25/02/2000	Griff Rhys Jones; Minnie Driver; Stacey Kent
03/03/2000	Rory Bremner; Lulu; Vanessa Feltz
10/03/2000	Jimmy Tarbuck; Harry Connick Jr; Kate Winslet
17/03/2000	Kenneth Branagh; Bob Monkhouse; Esther Williams
24/03/2000	Victoria Wood
31/03/2000	Ronan Keating; Cindy Crawford; Alan Titchmarsh
07/04/2000	Stephen Fry; Max Hastings; Elaine Paige
08/09/2000	Dawn French and Jennifer Saunders; Mike Reid; Tom Jones; Heather Small
15/09/2000	Ben Elton; Andrew Lloyd Webber; Hannah Waddingham; David Ginola
22/09/2000	Frankie Dettori; Julie Walters; Mark Knopfler
29/09/2000	Robson Green; Hugh Laurie; Chris Moon
06/10/2000	Patrick Kielty; Sir Nigel Hawthorne; Jane Horrocks; Steve Redgrave; Heather Small
13/10/2000	Meera Syal; Tom Courtney; Barry White
21/10/2000	Ian Botham; Richard Attenborough; Richard Wilson; K. D. Lang
28/10/2000	David Beckham; Rory Bremner; Sacha Distel
04/11/2000	Terry Wogan; Betty Boothroyd; Harry Enfield
12/11/2000	Sir Elton John; Ronan Keating; Kiki Dee; Robbie Williams
17/02/2001	Tracey Ullman; Denise Lewis; Dolly Parton
24/02/2001	Kirk Douglas; Goldie Hawn; Clive James; Sade
03/03/2001	Ardal O'Hanlon; Esther Rantzen; Amanda Donohoe; Lionel Richie
10/03/2001	John Cleese
17/03/2001	Kevin Costner; Lee Evans; Martin Clunes; Texas
24/03/2001	The Bee Gees; Sir John Mills
31/03/2001	Rod Stewart; Maureen Lipman; Tamzin Outhwaite
07/04/2001	Hugh Grant; Amanda Burton; Robbie Williams

13/04/2001	Alistair McGowan; Ulrika Jonsson; John Hurt; the Corrs
21/04/2001	David Jason; Jack Dee; Ronan Keating
22/09/2001	David and Victoria Beckham; George Best; Sir Elton John
29/09/2001	Bob Geldof; Victoria Wood; Ann Widdecombe MP
06/10/2001	Jim Davidson; Jamie Oliver; Elle Macpherson; the Beautiful South
13/10/2001	Ewan McGregor; Nicole Kidman; Anne Robinson; Andrea Bocelli
20/10/2001	Billy Connolly; Pamela Stephenson; Ricky Tomlinson; David Gray
27/10/2001	Larry Hagman; Gabrielle; Stephen Fry; Cher
03/11/2001	Sting
17/11/2001	Robbie Coltrane; Samuel L. Jackson; Ben Elton; Diana Krall
24/11/2001	Martine McCutcheon; Jennifer Lopez; Terry Wogan; the Corrs
01/12/2001	Cilla Black; Liza Tarbuck; Michael Crawford
24/12/2001	Robbie Williams; Lenny Henry; Dame Edna Everage; Geri Halliwell; Charlotte Church
23/02/2002	Russell Crowe; Kylie Minogue; Cate Blanchett
02/03/2002	Mel Gibson
05/03/2002	Jason Barlow; Dominic Littlewood; Karen Parkinson
09/03/2002	Dame Judi Dench; Kevin Spacey; Rory Bremner; the Lighthouse Family
23/03/2002	Celine Dion; Ian Hislop; Nigel Havers
06/04/2002	Jon Culshaw; Sue Johnston; Eamonn Holmes
13/04/2002	Michael Ball; Sheryl Crow; Sanjeev Bhaskar; Ali G; Jools Holland and his Rhythm and Blues Orchestra
20/04/2002	Jeff Bridges; Tony Bennett; James Nesbitt
27/04/2002	Chris Tarrant; Timothy Spall; Rob Brydon; Raul Malo; Bryan Ferry
04/05/2002	Martin Clunes; Jimmy Tarbuck; Michelle Collins; Travis; Enrique Iglesias
18/05/2002	Ben Elton; Charlotte Uhlenbroek; Barry Manilow
21/09/2002	Tom Hanks; David Bowie
28/09/2002	Michael Palin; Kate Adie; Ricky Gervais; Norah Jones
05/10/2002	Stephen Fry; Robin Williams; James Taylor
12/10/2002	Gillian Anderson; Paul O'Grady; Paul Whitehouse; Madness
19/10/2002	Bob Monkhouse; Peter Kay; Lulu; Ronan Keating; Shania Twain
26/10/2002	David Attenborough; Nigella Lawson; Eddie Izzard; David Gray; Chris Rea
09/11/2002	Steve Coogan; Jeremy Paxman; Elaine Stritch; Diana Krall
16/11/2002	Halle Berry; Natalie Cole; Rod Stewart; Pierce Brosnan
23/11/2002	Charlotte Church; Michael Aspel; Lionel Richie
30/11/2002	Sir Michael Caine
24/12/2002	Tom Jones; Dame Edna Everage; Alistair McGowan; Martine McCutcheon
22/02/2003	George Clooney; Heather Mills; Dawn French; Simply Red
01/03/2003	Jamie Oliver; Jack Dee; Damian Lewis; Jools Holland and his Orchestra; Beverley Knight; Lisa Stansfield
08/03/2003	Lenny Henry; Donny Osmond
15/03/2003	Robbie Coltrane; Ardal O'Hanlon; Anne Robinson; Dionne Warwick

29/03/2003	Rowan Atkinson; Pierce Brosnan; Rory Bremner; David Gray
05/04/2003	Neil Morrissey; Jeremy Clarkson; Denise Van Outen
12/04/2003	Paul Merton; Jerome Flynn; Sir Ian McKellen; Gloria Gaynor
19/04/2003	Martin Clunes; Sanjeev Bhaskar; David Dickinson; Badly Drawn Boy
26/04/2003	Matthew Perry; Hugh Jackman; Des O'Connor; Heather Small
03/05/2003	Amanda Holden; Hugh Laurie; Ronnie Corbett; Shirley Bassey
20/09/2003	Helen Mirren; Cilla Black; Jo Brand; Annie Lennox
27/09/2003	Ewan McGregor; Stephen Fry; Ronni Ancona; Dido
04/10/2003	Sir Sean Connery; Ricky Tomlinson; Boris Johnson MP; Michael Bublé
11/10/2003	Clint Eastwood; Jennifer Saunders; Ben Elton; Sheryl Crow
18/10/2003	Sir Michael Caine; Billy Connolly; Pamela Stephenson
25/10/2003	Meg Ryan; Shane Richie; Trinny Woodall and Susannah Constantine; Jamie Cullum
01/11/2003	Emma Thompson; Rod Stewart; Michael Palin; Luciano Pavarotti; Rod Stewart
15/11/2003	Dame Judi Dench; Peter Kay; Charlotte Uhlenbroek; Will Young; Clare Teal
22/11/2003	Sarah, Duchess of York; Gwyneth Paltrow; Eddie Izzard; Sting
29/11/2003	Victoria Beckham; Clive James; David Bowie
21/02/2004	Sir Ian McKellen; Johnny Vegas; Rhona Cameron; Alicia Keys
28/02/2004	Robson Green; Lily Savage; Paul O'Grady; Kylie Minogue; Peter Cincotti
06/03/2004	Patrick Stewart; Lionel Richie; Harry Connick Jr
13/03/2004	George Michael; Jon Culshaw; Bill Nighy
27/03/2004	Ross Kemp; Alastair Campbell; Jimmy Carr; Norah Jones
03/04/2004	Nigel Harman; Rory Bremner; John McCarthy; Joss Stone; the Pet Shop Boys
10/04/2004	Jonny Wilkinson; Michael Portillo; Jeremy Clarkson; Diana Krall
17/04/2004	Anne Robinson; James Nesbitt; Mick Hucknall; Travis
24/04/2004	Gordon Ramsay; Laurence Llewelyn-Bowen; Davina McCall; Ronan Keating; Leann Rimes; Sarah McLachlan
08/05/2004	Bruce Forsyth; Patrick Kielty; Boris Becker; the Corrs; Jamie Cullum
04/09/2004	Tom Cruise; Billy Connolly; Kelly Holmes
11/09/2004	Denzel Washington; Naomi Campbell; Simon Cowell
18/09/2004	Lenny Henry; Matthew Pinsent; Frank Skinner
25/09/2004	Ant & Dec; Dame Julie Andrews; Michael Palin
02/10/2004	Ricky Gervais; Joanna Lumley; Kevin Kline
09/10/2004	Joan Rivers; Jamie Oliver; Sir Cliff Richard
16/10/2004	Jeremy Clarkson; Eddie Izzard; Donny Osmond
23/10/2004	Paul O'Grady; Nigella Lawson; Lauren Bacall
30/10/2004	Sharon Osbourne; Dame Judi Dench; Dame Edna Everage
06/11/2004	Kevin Spacey; Renee Zellweger; Mel Brooks
25/12/2004	Joe Pasquale; Barbara Windsor; Lily Savage
12/02/2005	Bruce Willis; Bob Geldof

19/02/2005	Samuel L. Jackson; Dara O'Briain; Twiggy
26/02/2005	Julie Walters; Will Smith
05/03/2005	Jerry Springer; Patsy Kensit; Ray Winstone
12/03/2005	Peter Kay; Nicholas Lyndhurst; Sandra Bullock
19/03/2005	Jamie Oliver; Billie Piper; Ewan McGregor
26/03/2005	Goldie Hawn; John Sergeant; John Travolta
02/04/2005	Stephen Fry; Martin Clunes; Sharon and Ozzy Osbourne
09/04/2005	Meera Syal; Olivia Newton-John; Lauren Bacall
08/10/2005	Antonio Banderas; Ricky Gervais; Robert Lindsay
15/10/2005	Matt Lucas and David Walliams; Gloria Hunniford; Will Young
22/10/2005	Chris Tarrant; Susan Sarandon; David Attenborough
29/10/2005	Gordon Ramsay; Ben Elton; Rod Stewart
05/11/2005	Charlotte Church; Trinny Woodall and Susannah Constantine; Bradley Walsh
12/11/2005	Madonna
19/11/2005	Chris Evans; Ian Hislop; Dawn French
26/11/2005	Thierry Henry; Sarah Lancashire; Matthew Kelly; Stevie Wonder
10/12/2005	Michael Flatley; Robbie Williams; Peter O'Toole
17/12/2005	Dave Spikey; Rachel Weisz; Paul McCartney
24/12/2005	Joan Rivers; Martine McCutcheon; Cilla Black
04/03/2006	Tony Blair; Kevin Spacey
11/03/2006	Dara O'Briain; Kathy Burke; Tim Rice and Andrew Lloyd Webber
18/03/2006	Sharon Stone; Bette Midler; Stephen Fry
25/03/2006	Jane Fonda; Jo Brand; Daniel Day-Lewis
01/04/2006	Noel Edmonds; Thandie Newton; Timothy Spall
08/04/2006	David Jason; Paul Anka; Ardal O'Hanlon
15/04/2006	Melvyn Bragg; Martin Freeman; Kathleen Turner
22/04/2006	Jamie Foxx; Alan Alda; George Michael
16/09/2006	Elton John; Bernie Taupin; Matt Lucas and David Walliams
23/09/2006	Dame Helen Mirren; Trinny Woodall and Susannah Constantine; Dame Edna Everage
30/09/2006	Liza Minnelli; Sharon Osbourne; Lionel Richie
07/10/2006	Shane Richie; Sheila Hancock; Jeremy Paxman
21/10/2006	Eric Idle; Joan Bakewell; Ray Winstone
26/10/2006	Kate Winslet; Justin Timberlake; Jude Law
02/11/2006	Sir Michael Caine; Tony Bennett
09/11/2006	Peter Kay; Sir Ian McKellen; Take That
16/11/2006	Wendy Richards; Patrick Kielty; Michael Palin
25/11/2006	Noel Gallagher; Dustin Hoffman; Rod Stewart
02/12/2006	Daniel Craig; Ben Elton; Robin Williams
09/12/2006	Rory Bremner; John McEnroe; Cameron Diaz
23/12/2006	Lenny Henry; Dame Judi Dench; Katherine Jenkins
05/05/2007	David Tennant; Amanda Holden; Michael Bublé; David Mitchell
12/05/2007	Patrick Stewart; Ian Hislop; Gene Wilder
19/05/2007	George Michael; Stephen Fry; Joan Rivers
02/06/2007	Dara O'Briain; David Dimbleby; Russell Watson

09/06/2007	Orlando Bloom; James Nesbitt; Keith Allen
16/06/2007	Piers Morgan; Sanjeev Bhaskar; David Attenborough
23/06/2007	Dr Jonathan Miller; Meera Syal; Ken Dodd
15/09/2007	Michael Palin; Dame Diana Rigg; Sir David Frost
22/09/2007	Jennifer Lopez; James McAvoy; Billie Piper
29/09/2007	Colin Firth; Al Murray; Harry Connick Jr
13/10/2007	Ricky Hatton; Paul Anka; Michael Winner
20/10/2007	Sophie Dahl; Joan Rivers; Sharon Osbourne
27/10/2007	Joanna Lumley; Lord Richard Attenborough; Sir Bobby Charlton
03/10/2007	Daniel Radcliffe; Dawn French and Jennifer Saunders; Ray Winstone
09/11/2007	Lewis Hamilton; Rory Bremner; David Cameron; Sir Ian McKellen
17/11/2007	Kenneth Branagh; Paul Merton; Ewan McGregor
24/11/2007	Rod Stewart; Michael Bublé
15/12/2007	Billy Connolly; Sir Michael Caine; Sir David Attenborough; David Beckham; Peter Kay; Dame Judi Dench; Dame Edna Everage